Business in Context

David Needle

Van Nostrand Reinhold (International)

VNR
International

First published in 1989 by
Van Nostland Reinhold (International) Co. Ltd
11 New Fetter Lane, London EC4P 4EE

Typeset in Times 10 on 11½ pt by
Best-set Typesetter Ltd, Hong Kong
Printed in Great Britain by
Richard Clay Ltd, Bungay, Suffolk

ISBN 0 278 00005 3

British Library Cataloguing in Publication Data

Needle, David
 Business in context.
 1. Business studies
 I. Title   II. Series
 658

 ISBN 0–278–00005–3

To Doris and Jack Simpson

Series foreword

This book is part of the Business in Context series. The books in this series are written by lecturers all with several years experience of teaching on undergraduate business studies programmmes. For a number of years we have been conscious that many of the books we were recommending to our students never catered specifically for business studies courses. Although there are some good books covering the different disciplines found in the business studies curriculum, very few of these texts are aimed specifically at the business studies student. Many of the best management texts assume a level of managerial experience and the worst take a simplistic and pre-scriptive view of business life. The interdisciplinary nature of business studies often means presenting students with a range of books dealing with various specialist topics, which can prove both daunting and expensive.

It is certainly not our intention to offer up our individual texts as a panacea. Indeed, our policy throughout this series is that books are well referenced and the student is guided to further reading on every topic area. However, we do feel that our books provide a focus for the student attempting to seek some meaning in the range of subjects currently offered on business studies programmes.

Business studies has attracted a growing band of students for a number of years and is currently one to the most popular undergraduate courses. Whilst many books have emerged to feed a hungry BTEC market, the undergraduate business studies student has been sadly neglected. One of the causes of that neglect has undoubtedly been the difficulty of many, academics and members of the business community alike, to define business studies, beyond a list of loosely connected subject headings. With this series we hope to make good some of those missing connections.

With the exception of the text, Business in Context, which takes the series title as its theme, all our texts take the approach of a particular dis-cipline traditionally associated with business studies and taught across a wide range of business studies programmes. The first books in our series examine business from the pespectives of economics, behavioural science, law, mathematics and accounting. However, whereas in traditional texts it is the subject itself that is the focus, our texts make business the focus. All the texts are based upon the same specific model of business illustrated in the Figure. We have called our model Business in Context and the text of the same name is an expansion and explanation of that model.

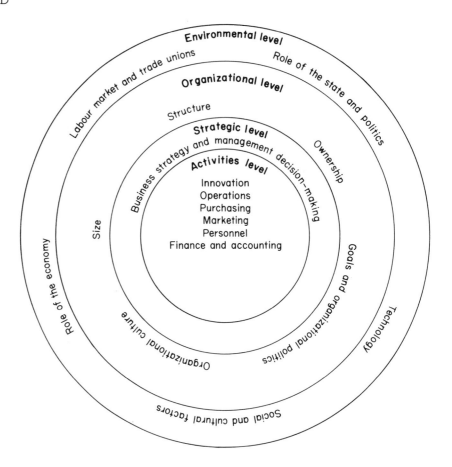

The model comprises four distinct levels. At the core are found the activities which make up what we know as business and include innovation, operations and production, purchasing, marketing, personnel and finance and accounting. We see these activities operating irrespective of the type of business involved, and are found in both the manufacturing and service industry as well as in the public and private sectors. The second level of our model is concerned with strategy and management decision–making. It is here that decisions are made which influence the direction of the business activities at our core. The third level of our model is concerned with organizational factors within which business activities and management decisions take place. The organizational issues we examine are structure, size, goals and organizational politics, patterns of ownership, and organizational culture. Clear links can be forged between this and other levels of our model, especially between structure and strategy, goals and management decision–making, and how all aspects both contribute to and are influenced by the organizational culture. The fourth level concerns itself with the environment in which businesses operate. The issues here involve social and cultural factors, the role of the state and politics, the role of the economy, and issues relating to both technology and labour. An important feature of this fourth level of our model is that such elements not only operate as opportunities and constraints for business, but also that they are shaped by the three other levels of our model.

This brief description of the Business in Context model illustrates the key features of our series. We see business as dynamic. It is constantly being shaped by and in turn shaping those managerial, organizational, and environmental contexts within which it operates. Influences go backwards and forwards across the various levels. Moreover, the aspects identified within each level are in constant interaction with one another. Thus the role of the economy cannot be understood without reference to the role of the state; size and structure are inextricably linked; innovation is inseparable from issues of operations, marketing and finance. The understanding of how this model works is what business studies is all about, and forms the basis for our series.

In proposing this model we are proposing a framework for analysis, and we hope that it will encourage readers to add to and refine the model and so broaden our understanding of business. Each writer in this series has been encouraged to present a personal interpretation of the model. In this way we hope to build up a more complete picture of business initially through the eyes of an economist, a behavioural scientist, a lawyer, a mathematician and an accountant.

Our series therefore aims for a more integrated and realistic approach to business than has hitherto been the case. The issues are complex but the authors' treatments are not. Each book in this series is built around the Business in Context model, and each displays a number of common features that mark out this series. Firstly we aim to present our ideas in a way that students will find easy to understand and we relate those ideas wherever possible to real business situations. Secondly we hope to stimulate further study both by referencing our material and pointing students towards further reading at the end of each chapter. Thirdly we use the notion of 'key concepts' to highlight the most significant aspects of the subject presented in each chapter. Fourthly we use case studies to illustrate our material and stimulate further discussion. Fifthly we present at the end of each chapter a series of questions, exercises, and discussion topics. To sum up, we feel it most important that each book will stimulate thought and further study, and assist the student in developing powers of analysis, a critical awareness and ultimately a point of view about business issues.

We have already indicated that the series has been devised with the undergraduate business studies student uppermost in our minds. We also maintain that these books are of value wherever there is a need to understand business issues and may therefore be used across a range of different courses covering BTEC Higher, and some professional and masters courses.

David Needle and Eugene McKenna
January 1989

Contents

Acknowledgements

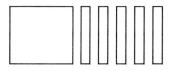

There are many who deserve my thanks for helping me write this book. The students and staff at The Polytechnic of East London* have assisted me in developing many of the ideas and gathering much of the material. In particular I would thank Alan Neale, Eugene McKenna, Terry Godwin and Colin Madill for their helpful comments on individual chapters.

Geoff Hardern at Trent Polytechnic has been most helpful in his review of the first draft, and many of his suggestions have been incorporated in the final version.

Stephen Wellings of Van Nostrand deserves a special thanks for his support of the project throughout, his editorial advice, and above all for his faith in this book when it was not there.

I would like to apologise to my family and friends for all the insults they have suffered for asking me when the book would be finished, for it could not have been completed without their support.

The greatest debt is owed to my wife Jacquie for her love, support, inspiration, and fund of valuable ideas that have gone into this book.

*formerly North East London Polytechnic

Preface

The origins for this book lie in a course I taught for a number of years to undergraduate business studies students. That course was called 'Business and its Environment' and it attempted to introduce students with little prior notion of business to the major business activities. An important theme of the course was the inter–related nature, both of the activities themselves, and of their dealings with the strategic, organizational and environmental contexts in which they operated. A second important theme was the identification of what were considered at the time of be key issues in business, such as the interest in small firms and in Japanese management. These two themes are the basis of 'Business in Context'.

The Course was always a challenge to teach, but almost impossible to support with reading material sympathetic to its aims. Students were faced with daunting reading lists, and I was faced with a growing criticism from students over the lack of a textbook. This book is an attempt to stifle those criticisms and happily coincided with the plans of Van Nostrand Reinhold to broaden their activities in the business and management field. Like many authorship ventures the book has been slow to arrive, and confirmed my deepest suspicions as to why the writers of textbooks often hunt in pairs.

In teaching the aforementioned course I developed a model to show the complex workings of business. With a few refinements the model forms the basis of the Business in Context series and is the main linking factor in that series of related texts. This book, the first in the series, presents a detailed examination of the workings of that model, stressing the inter–relationship between business activities and the various contexts in which they operate.

Whilst the origins of this book relate to a specific course, the growth of business studies as a discipline, or group of integrated disciplines (a debate I shall not prolong), means that ever more students are in need of a book which at least attempts to introduce them to the complexities of their chosen subject. I strongly maintain that this book is suitable for any course where an understanding of the integrated nature of business activities is required, and particularly where students need to develop perspectives on key business issues. Most undergraduate business studies programmes contain such courses, and this is the main market at which this book is aimed. It is also suitable for some BTEC, postgraduate, and professional programmes.

As we state in the series editors' foreward, business is treated through-out the series in its widest possible context, and this book is no exception, including as it does illustrations drawn from a variety of contexts, including polytechnics. One of the interesting features of the 1980s is the convergence of all types of organization towards similar methods of operation, either by choice or through the pressure of external influences. Certainly, whatever our perspective, many educational establishments are currently display-ing the kinds of strategies we normally associate with more traditional businesses.

As with any book which takes the broad sweep that this one does, there is bound to be a great deal of selectivity. This is true of the material in general but particularly true of the various illustrations I have used. The main criterion for their inclusion is that they interested me. Many are attributed to their rightful source, but many are the product of years discussing business issues with students, friends and colleagues. It is an author's privilege to claim for himself the ideas of others. I acknowledge all those sources here. The only reason for their inclusion is that they should stimulate the reader's own thoughts to develop new perspectives on business issues.

David Needle
January 1989

The concept of Business in Context

The major theme of this book, and of the series of which it forms a part, is that businesses are complex. They cannot be understood by reference to their activities alone. These activities, which include innovation, production and operations, marketing, personnel, finance and accounting and so on, take place in a series of contexts. It is our contention that they can only be understood fully when those contexts within which they operate are also understood. In this first chapter we will explain what we mean by business and identify the relevant contexts. It also our contention that the relationship between business activities and these contexts is dynamic. In the foreword we introduced a model of business around which this and other books in the series are based. We present the model once again in Figure 1.1 and use it to illustrate the elements of this dynamic relationship. The workings of the model are explained by two case studies. The first concerns changes that have occurred in the shipping industry over the last twenty-five years, while the second focuses more specifically on a single organization, News International, and the events surrounding a major dispute with its workforce in 1985. We introduce briefly two theoretical approaches to the analysis of business organizations; the systems and contingency approaches. These are often used as the starting point for our analysis throughout this book, and reference will be made to them in other chapters. We will conclude this first chapter by outlining the layout of this book.

Businesses and their contexts

The popular image of a typical business firm is invariably that of a manufacturing industry, and probably large scale mass production at that. In this text we hope to present a broader view of business. Businesses operate in all kinds of areas, including manufacturing industry, but also embrace such activities as retailing, banking and other financial services, transport and so on. The publishers of this book are engaged in a business activity, involving the production, marketing and selling of books to generate income both to make profit and finance future operations. Businesses also vary considerably in terms of size. Indeed, in recent years the focus has shifted away from large–scale operations and small businesses have become popular with governments and academics alike and, accordingly, will be acknowledged in this text.

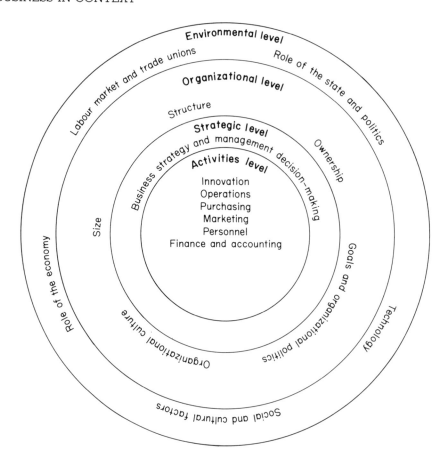

Figure 1.1 The Business in Context model.

The image that businesses are exclusively profit–oriented will also be challenged. Business systems and methods operate in all kinds of organization. Many institutions of higher education operate with budgets in excess of £25 million, and represent fairly complex organizations in which all the activities normally associated with business may be identified. For example, there are few colleges who do not market their courses, or from time to time experience the kind of industrial relations problems normally associated with manufacturing industry. Hospitals too are large complex organizations experiencing the type of management problems found in businesses anywhere. In any case, the distinction between profit and non–profit organizations has become increasingly blurred. All universities and polytechnics are actively engaged in income–generation through selling their services to business firms. The growth of medical provision outside the National Health Service has seen the growth of profit–oriented private hospitals which compete in the market place for customers and advertise their wares.

As we can see from Figure 1.1 we have identified a number of business activities. In this book we deal with them under five main groups; innovation, production, marketing, personnel and finance and accounting.

A business is the organized effort of individuals to produce and provide goods and services to meet the needs of society. We view business as a broad concept, incorporating profit–making concerns such as manufacturing firms and banks, and non–profit–making concerns such as schools and hospitals.

KEY CONCEPT 1.1

BUSINESS

We identify a number of major business activities.

The innovation function is concerned with the development of new business ideas, in terms of products, processes, and methods of marketing, organization and management (Chapter 5).

The production function comprises those activities concerned with the creation of goods and services through the bringing together and mixing of a number of resource inputs, including materials, labour, finance, and plans (Chapter 6).

The marketing function deals with all those activities which relate directly to the consumer. These involve researching the market and using that information in the development of the product, pricing, promoting, and ensuring that the product eventually reaches the consumer (Chapter 7).

The personnel function is concerned with the planning, acquisition, development, utilization and reward of an organization's human resources. An important part of the role is the management of conflict through those activities associated with industrial relations (Chapter 8).

The finance and accounting function deals with the raising and management of funds, and the production of information to facilitate these two processes (Chapter 9).

KEY CONCEPT 1.2

BUSINESS ACTIVITIES

Each of these groups is sufficiently broad to cover a number of related functions. For instance, it is acknowledged that purchasing is an important business activity, but it is dealt with under the heading of production for the purposes of this text. The production function itself is regarded in the widest operational context and as such is present in all forms of business organization. There are two points to consider when examining business activities. Firstly, they interact with one another, so that operational decisions influencing the quantity and quality of the goods produced and the services provided will have significant implications for the other functional areas. Secondly, as we have already indicated, these activities do not exist in a vacuum, but are shaped by and in turn shape the contexts within which they operate.

In our Business in Context model we have identified three types of context; strategic, organizational, and environmental. We will deal briefly with each of these in turn.

At the strategic level we are concerned with those management decisions, and the influences on those decisions, which determine the direction of business activities. Strategic decisions will influence such factors as the

KEY CONCEPT 1.3	Interaction is a process which involves a two-way influence. It occurs when two elements are able to exert influences which bring about changes in each other. The process of interaction is central to the workings of the Business in Context, model and is illustrated throughout this book, as in the interaction of businesses and the economy in Chapter 2.
INTERACTION	

product range, the amount spent on advertising, the recognition of trade unions and so on. Strategies are often a question of reconciling opportunities and constraints which exist within both the organization and the environment in which it operates. The managing director of a small firm with a potentially profitable innovation often faces a strategic dilemma. Its organizational size means that expanding production capacity is impossible, and its credit standing is such that it may be unable to raise sufficient development capital. The availability of finance is, in any case, a function of the economic and political climate. Alternatives might be to sell the idea for development by a larger firm or simply accept a merger with the larger organization; both of which may be personally unacceptable to the owner of the small business. In this way, strategic issues are inseparable from the organization and environment in which they operate, and can in fact alter those two other contexts. It is widely accepted that the structure of a firm is often a product of its strategy (Chandler, 1962). The overseas investment strategies of large multinational corporations have been seen to have considerable influence on the economic and political affairs of other nations, especially those in the Third World.

At the organizational level we are concerned with such issues as size, ownership, goals and structure. Many such issues are inter-related. The public ownership of business firms may well mean the pursuit of social as well as business goals, and publicly-owned firms invariably have bureaucratic structures. This is partly a function of organizational culture, and partly a function of the large scale of most public sector operations. All firms as they increase in size tend to adopt more formalized structures. Such organizational factors can place limitations on the nature of business activities; formalized structures can inhibit certain types of product and process development; the existing size can be a restriction on expansion, as we saw in our illustration of strategic issues. In more general terms these organizational factors combine with management strategy to create distinctive organizational cultures.

We have identified five factors which operate at the environmental level; the economy, the state, labour, technology and culture. Some of these factors are deliberately broad. The state includes discussion of government, legal and political issues; labour takes into account both the workings of the labour market and the activities of trade unions; culture includes both social factors related to business as well as those issues which differentiate businesses in different countries. As with the other factors in our model there is considerable interaction between these various environ-

A strategy comprises a set of objectives and methods of achieving those objectives. A strategy is usually formulated by top management and is based on a mixture of careful analysis of the environment and the organization (Key concepts 1.5 and 1.7), the personal preferences of the managers involved, and a process of negotiation with other interested parties such as shareholders and trade unions (Chapter 4).

KEY CONCEPT 1.4

STRATEGY

An organization refers to the way in which people are grouped and the way in which they operate to carry out the activities of the business. We define the key elements of the organization as the goals of the business and the way they are formulated, ownership and control, size, structure and organizational culture (Chapter 3).

KEY CONCEPT 1.5

ORGANIZATION

An organizational culture is a key feature of business, in that it is the distinguishing feature which marks one organization from another. It is the sum product of all the influences which exert themselves upon an organization, incorporating internal, external and historical factors. More recently the concept has been used to imply a common philosophy which runs through the organization and influences its activities in a positive way (Chapter 3).

KEY CONCEPT 1.6

ORGANIZATIONAL CULTURE

mental factors. The membership and power of trade unions is a function of the level of economic activity and the restrictions imposed by the law, which in turn reflects the policy of governments. The composition of the labour market reflects changes in technology, and the mobility of labour within different countries varies with the social and cultural traditions of those countries. Technological innovations are often motivated both by declining economic fortunes and by direct state intervention. Similarly we can cite illustrations of the interaction between the environment and our other contexts. The technological complexity of the product market in which the firm operates will largely determine the extent of its research and development activity, and hence its strategies and structure. In traditional manufacturing industry, a strong trade union presence will determine the size, shape, policies and activities of the personnel department. Goals, size, structure and activities all tend to change as the economic environment changes.

The interplay which typifies the relationship between business activities and the contexts in which they operate will be a constant theme in this book. We will attempt to show that many of the relationships are two-way. The economic environment referred to above not only shapes businesses, but is in turn a product of business activity. Changes in technology are

KEY CONCEPT 1.7 **ENVIRONMENT**	The environment includes all those elements which exist outside the organization and which interact with it. These interactions occur on three levels: at the local level, as with competition among firms offering the same product in the same market; at the national level, as with the influence of government policy; and at the international level, as through the operation of multinational companies or the interchange of business ideas from different countries. We define the key elements of the environment as the economy, the state, technology, labour and cultural factors relating to specific societies or nations.

products of innovation activity at the level of the firm. We are thus able to build up a model of business as a constant interplay of interactions and influences.

We are able to illustrate the workings of the model by reference to two cases, the first concerning the worldwide shipping industry and the second focussing on a single, albeit large firm in the newspaper industry. In both cases we will explain the events and central issues, following this with an analysis of each case using our Business in Context model as a framework.

The shipping industry

The shipping industry referred to in this case is that industry concerned largely with the transport of goods by sea, and not to be confused with shipbuilding. The information for the case is taken largely from a study of the shipping industry, titled *Innovating to Compete* (Walton, 1987). Walton examines eight countries; Denmark, Holland, Japan, Norway, Sweden, United Kingdom, USA and West Germany. The choice of the eight nations is significant in that they represent the world's traditional merchant fleets and accounted for 74% of the entire world tonnage in shipping prior to the second world war. Since the war the powerful position of these shipping nations has been challenged by a variety of factors. By 1973 their collective tonnage had fallen to 43% and by 1983 to 26%. The case study identifies those factors and examines the strategic responses of the shipping companies concerned. It should be remembered that while merchant fleets are invariably linked to nation states, shipping is operated as a business and shipping companies are privately owned.

In Walton's study, two phases were be identified, the first 1963–73, and the second 1973–83.

Period 1: 1963–73

For the eight nations listed above, this period was one of economic prosperity. The demand for shipping exceeded supply, and that demand was increasing throughout this period at a rate of 7% a year. It was also a period in which unemployment was extremely low and the shipping

industry faced intense competition for its labour from land-based industries. The lure of seafaring had declined with the prospect of long periods
away from home and the increasing development of functional ports in
unglamorous locations away from the main centres of urban life. Furthermore, time spent in port had been sacrificed to the fast turn-around of
vessels to save cost and maximize operational time. Combined with these
factors was a growing resistance to the quasi-military regime of the merchant navy, especially in the face of attractive job opportunities elsewhere.
Labour shortage became the norm in the shipping industry of all these
nations. Under such conditions the bargaining power of trade unions is
substantially strengthened, as was the case in the majority companies cover-
ed by the study. Wage rates were increased to attract and keep labour, with
a corresponding increase in costs. Nevertheless demand for shipping was
still high and the industry remained relatively healthy with increased costs
being born by the customer through increased freight charges.

Period 2: 1973–83

1973 was a watershed for the shipping industry in the eight nations. The
problems caused by the high costs of labour were superseded by very high
interest rates and a dramatic increase in the cost of fuel. Unfortunately as
far as these developed countries were concerned, price competition within
the industry had increased through the activity of two types of new entrant.

Firstly, there had been the fast growth of shipping operating under 'flags
of convenience'. Such shipping is associated with such countries as Liberia
and Panama, where the cost of registering and insuring ships is much lower
than in traditional shipping nations. The advantage to the shipowner is not
just in terms of registration and insurance. The regulations which cover
shipping operations and shipboard practices tend to be far less restrictive,
and labour tends to be cheaper too. A country like Liberia has actively
marketed this service and sees it as an important source of foreign investment. Under such a mechanism, overheads and labour costs are kept to a
minimum, and shipping operating under a 'flag of convenience' is able to
enter the market place offering an attractive price to the customer. It is
hardly suprising that the eight nations saw a defection of shipowners from
their fleets to such 'flags of convenience'. The bulk transport of the world's
oil supply quickly became the prerogative of the Liberian tanker fleet,
heavily underwritten and supported by the major multinational oil corporations.

Secondly, certain governments, particularly those of the Soviet bloc
nations and those of developing countries, see their own shipping industry
as a means of achieving highly prized international recognition. The industry becomes both metaphorically and literally a flag carrier for its
sponsoring nation. Government–backed shipping from such countries has,
like the 'flags of convenience' reduced the price and widened the choice for
the customer.

The problems facing the eight nations were therefore intensified and by
1983 the entire industry was suffering from problems of overcapacity. This
became particularly acute as the decade from 1973, unlike its predecessor,
marked a decline in the demand for shipping.

The strategic options of shipping companies in the established nations

We can see that a combination of rising labour costs, rising fuel costs, high interest rates, cheap competition and overcapacity had seriously weakened the competitive position of the eight developed nations in Walton's study. Those firms still operating were faced with a number of options in order to maintain their competitive position. The strategic options and the problems associated with them may be identified as follows.

☐ Some firms found that the move towards much larger vessels enabled them to achieve economies of scale and compete on price. Such an option was not available to all due to the very high investment costs needed for this type of strategy.

☐ Some governments decided to assist their own shipping industry by setting up subsidies and by granting generous tax allowances. Protectionist strategies and trade agreements have been used to safeguard the position of national fleets. Such agreements might include the provision that all coastal traffic should use national carriers, or that the exchange of imports and exports must be accompanied by a corresponding exchange of shipping services. Whilst some governments were committed to such policies, others showed a complete uninterest and, in some cases, ideological opposition to state intervention.

☐ A popular strategy involved product specialization. Some companies decided that they could not compete with developing nations and 'flags of convenience' in the transport of bulk cargoes or in the oil tanker trade. Instead, they opted for those cargoes requiring specialist facilities and handling, such as liquid gases and other dangerous chemicals; or they chose to operate with highly mixed loads in relatively small batches. However, overspecialization can be threatened by the lack of demand, and the cost of transporting loads in small batches raises its own logistics problems.

☐ A classic response to the problems of labour shortages and increased labour costs was process innovation. Containerization has been a popular option in many cases; cargoes come ready packed in large containers, reducing the need for dock and shipboard handling. Inevitably, containerization was supported by the development of the 'roll on–roll off' process, where the containers are driven directly on ship and unloaded by container lorry, obviating the need for cargo handling at all. Such developments have been matched by the automation of shipboard engineering, control and monitoring processes and changes in telecommunications rendering traditional methods of ship–to–shore communication redundant. In all cases such innovations reduced the need for labour or enabled formerly specialized tasks to be be substituted by those with a lower skill requirement. However, such changes carry high investment costs and often meet employee resistance to change, more especially union opposition to both reduced manning levels and more flexible work practices.

☐ In shipping, as with all industries, technical innovations invariably offer the possibility of organizational changes to underline the advantages of the former. In particular, automation and changes in telecommunications introduced the possibility of flexible manning, and hence even greater labour savings. Some companies went even further and attempted to introduce permanent crews operating as a team and ensuring continuity of labour, a radical innovation in an industry built on a history of casual hiring. The move towards teamwork was a deliberate attempt to improve the quality of working life and was accompanied, in some cases, by the creation of less hierarchical organizational structures. These new structures offered more opportunity for delegated authority and participation. Some companies saw such moves as inevitable to match conditions in shore–based industries and to change the merchant navy's image of authoritarian man–management systems to attract labour. Bringing about such changes is not without its difficulties. The very structures that are identified for change are likely to provide the biggest obstacle. The shipping industry is typified by highly bureaucratic structures and shipboard relations steeped in naval tradition, where ship captains are highly resistant to participative forms of management.

The options are not mutually exclusive and some shipping companies had pursued all five options in an attempt to maintain their competitive position. Far from being mutually exclusive, some of the options were dependent upon the support of others for maximum effectiveness. The major point of Walton's study is that competitiveness can only be achieved when technical innovations are accompanied by organizational innovations. Our point in using this case is that it serves as a useful illustration of our model of business. It is to this aspect we now turn.

The shipping industry in a business context

Environmental aspects

Economic factors have had a significant impact on the shipping industry during the period of the study and illustrates, among other things the interplay of selling price, wage costs, and competition. With a buoyant demand the industry could combat labour market shortages by higher wages offset against increased freight charges. With increased competition together with falling demand other strategies became imperative for business survival.

The *state*, through the activity of national governments has had a major impact on the fortunes of individual shipping companies. This occurs in a number of different ways. One key variable would seem to be a nation's economic structure; support for the shipping industry assumes a greater importance when shipbuilding and oil interests are at stake. The governments of developing countries and those of the Soviet bloc have seen shipping as a matter of national prestige and have supported it accordingly. The response to increased competition by the eight industrial nations has tended to vary with differing levels of state intervention. Denmark, Holland, Japan and the USA have received most government backing and protection, and it is these four nations that have been most successful in preserving their tonnage. Nation states have also laid down regulations governing the activity of shipping in the interests of those employed and the environment. Sometimes such regulations have stood in the way of organizational changes, especially those involving reductions in manning levels. Conversely it is the very lack of such restrictions that has made 'flags of convenience' attractive to some shipowners.

The *technological* aspects of this case centre around process innovations aimed at reducing manning levels and costs. Some of these innovations, such as containerization and 'roll on–roll off' are direct responses to shipping industry problems. Others such as automated control systems and communication systems are the adaptations of state–of–the–art technology for use by the shipping industry.

Labour issues represent a key element in this case. The difficulty in attracting labour to the shipping industry in the period 1963–73 was a major incentive for technical and organizational innovation. The case also illustrates the links between economic conditions, labour market forces and trade union power.

In terms of *culture*, the study compares the different responses of eight nation states to the same problem. These differences do not always follow the expected pattern. For instance, the USA not known for its state intervention has taken several steps to protect its merchant fleet, with a subsequent increase in its share of world shipping. A major cultural difference that does occur is that which marks out those nations in the developing world and the Soviet bloc from the eight industrially developed nations of the study. An interesting feature of the case from a cultural point of view occurs not at the national but at the industrial and organizational levels and will be dealt with in the next section.

Organizational aspects

The organizational aspects of this case are dominated by issues relating to *structure*. Environmental influences, especially those concerned with competition, new technology and the labour market, together with the individual company's strategic response, have resulted in changes in the organization structure of many shipping firms. The major changes have been the breakdown of a traditional hierarchical naval structure with its emphasis on formalization, specialization, and authoritarian management style. In its place have emerged much more flexible structures with an elimination of class barriers between officers and ratings, much greater job flexibility and delegation of authority. The case therefore shows the inter–related and interactive nature of environmental and organizational aspects.

Overall the changes identified above represent a major attempt to change the *organizational culture* of individual shipping companies as part of a strategic response to a weakened competitive position.

The case also shows how *goals* differ between shipping companies in different nations. The eight nations appear to be linked by the superordinate goal of survival, whilst the state sponsorship of shipping in the Soviet bloc identifies political as well as business goals. While the survival and competition goals of the shipping companies may find broad agreement, the means through which such goals may be achieved does not. Unions may oppose manning reductions and flexible work practices; some management may resent a shift away from authoritarian naval traditions; national governments, trade unions, and many seamen may object to the migration of shipowners to 'flags of convenience'. The last illustration of goal conflict also raises the issue of *ownership* versus control. Owners faced with problems of profitability may seek solutions that are unpopular to other interested parties.

Size is an important variable in the shipping industry. The sheer scope of operations and the investment costs of fitting out a large ocean–going vessel tend to favour the large company. This relationship has been further underlined by the costs of containerization, automatic control systems and the like. Additionally a fair proportion of shipping trade is associated with large multinational corporations like the oil companies. There are however niches in the industry for the smaller operator, such as tramp steamer operations where goods are transported on an irregular basis up and down the same stretch of coastline.

Strategic aspects

In our presentation of this case we have isolated from Walton's study a number of strategic responses employed by shipping companies to maintain their market position during a period of change from 1963 to 1983. The case is a good illustration of the role of strategy in our model of business.

Firstly we can see how strategic options were formulated in response to environmental conditions. In this way shipping companies are adapting to the environment in which they find themselves and conforming to a classic contingency response. However, an important theme of this book is that the relationship between the business environment and business strategy is not just a case of the environment determining strategy. Here we can see that some firms responded to rising costs by transferring the registration of their ships to 'flags of convenience'. The strategy of some shipping companies thus became an additional competitive factor to which other firms had to respond; a case of strategy changing the business environment. In the same way, decisions to change to container cargoes would affect the interplay between shipping, port and other transport industries.

Secondly the case illustrates the inter–relationship between strategic and organizational aspects, especially structure. We have already noted Walton's main conclusion concerning the interplay between technical and organizational innovations. This is not simply a case of structure following strategy, but structure being an integral part of that strategy.

Functional aspects

The case illustrates the interplay between the functional areas of our model and the environmental, organizational and strategic aspects identified above.

The *production* function in many of the companies had undergone quite radical changes in both the nature of the product (e.g., containers, specialist chemicals), and the nature of the operating process (e.g., roll on-roll off, automated engineering control systems). Moreover, changes in the organization structure had significant impact on the way work was organized (e.g., flexible manning). Many of these changes are the direct result of product and process *innovation*.

In terms of *marketing*, increased price competition from 'flags of convenience' and other nations has forced many shipping firms in the eight countries to seek new, more specialized markets to replace those, like the oil tanker trade, which are no longer profitable for them. There is a clear interplay between marketing and production through product innovation. The development of containerization, for example, has particular implications for distribution.

Changing *personnel* policies are a key feature of the case. These include flexible work allocation, a more participative management style and an attempt to eliminate casual hiring practices. A focus on personnel issues reveals how not all elements of the business model fit neatly together. Changes which reduce the need for labour are likely to meet with trade union opposition; calls for workforce participation may be strongly resisted by some management, especially in an industry like shipping, influenced by traditional practices.

Accounting decisions lay behind most if not all of the strategic options pursued by the shipping companies in this case. The industry in these eight nations was in slump and profit margins had dwindled. The case reveals that not all the options would be cost–effective for all companies, and a divestment of assets may be the only viable solution.

News International and Wapping

For almost a year every Saturday evening, the residents of a fashionable warehouse conversion on the edges of London's docklands were denied free access to their property. The residents' access was blocked by mass picketing resulting from an industrial dispute between News International and its former Fleet Street employees over the printing of newspapers at the company's newly commissioned Wapping plant. In this section we will examine the background to the dispute and the events from December 1985 to February 1987. Although what has become known as the Wapping dispute focusses on the events of that period, the seeds of that dispute were laid much earlier. As with the shipping industry we will see how this case illustrates our model of business.

News International is a company controlled by Rupert Murdoch, Australian by birth but with recently acquired American citizenship, and with considerable newspaper holdings in Australia and the USA. The British company controls three daily newspapers, *The Times*, *Today* and the *Sun*; and two Sunday newspapers, the *Sunday Times*, and the *News of the World*. The *Sun*, the *Sunday Times* and the *News of the World* are the best selling newspapers of their type in Britain, and *The Times* is arguably the nation's most famous daily paper.

In 1978 land was purchased in Wapping with a view to building a large printing works using the latest technology in newspaper production, and construction began within two years. At that time News International owned just the *Sun* and the *News of the World*, and the plant was part of plan to increase both the output and the size of both newspapers. In 1981, the company purchased both *The Times* and the *Sunday Times*, in the face of accusations that News International would be operating a monopoly against the public interest. Once again there was a desire to increase both the production runs and the size of both newly–acquired newspapers. In all cases the size of the newspapers and the quantity of production were restricted by the size of the existing plants around the Fleet Street area of central London, and what management saw as uneconomic manning levels imposed by the trade unions. The issues of new technology and trade union control over work practices lay at the heart of most major national newspaper disputes. No national paper was immune and in 1985 alone 95.6 million copies were lost to industrial disputes of one type or another.

A little background

The major technological innovations were direct input and photocomposition. This means that the printing operation could in effect be carried out by journalists or typists, eliminating the need for traditional printworking through a method referred to as 'cold–type' printing. Computer keyboards and VDUs are used to input material to be stored on a central computer, which also contains programmes for page composition. The computer prints off its stories and advertisements on photographic paper, which are then pasted up to form the eventual pages of the newspaper. These are photographed, and a negative is produced. The negative is converted into a flexible polymer plate to be clipped to the existing presses for the printing to commence.

Under this method around three thousand lines a minute could be typeset compared to seven lines per minute using the conventional technique, with the added advantage that stories and whole pages could be changed and mistakes corrected quickly and cheaply. Such methods had been used by American newspapers since the early 1960s. In Britain however, the introduction of new technology had been slow. There was a strong adherence to the traditional process of using linotype, a method involving the creation of the type from molten lead, sometimes known as the 'hot metal' process. This method is labour intensive and is often performed by compositors using equipment some fifty years old. The new generation of printing presses are much cheaper and can therefore be scrapped when further technical improvements are made. Even where photocomposition had been introduced, the process was not used to its full potential as, under management–union agreements, keyboard operations were still being performed by print workers and not journalists or typists.

The printing industry is one of the most traditional of the craft industries and has a long history. The print unions have been vigilant in maintaining control over the apprenticeship system, entry to the profession, and over the way the job is done. These are traditional craft controls aided by the rigid enforcement of a union closed shop. Such controls were greatest in Fleet Street were job entry was reserved only for existing members of a recognized trade union (a pre–entry closed shop). The two major unions are the National Graphical Association (NGA), covering the printers themselves and the Society of Graphical and Allied Trades (SOGAT '82), covering despatch, distribution and clerical workers.

In this way the union controlled work allocation and above all, manning levels for each job. Frequent management complaints concerned over-manning and the inability to implement changes that would invariably be accompanied by uneconomic manning requirements. There was consider-able resistance to the introduction of new technology, as this would effec-tively reduce the craft control of the job and make it accessible to those not trained as printers.

Despite management's frequent complaints, the situation was largely of their own making. Concessions to trade union control of manning levels had been made due to the highly competitive nature of the national newspaper industry, the highly perishable nature of the product, and the need for maximum flexibility, especially when dealing with late changes in news items. Competition was not just for readers, but for advertisers. Lost production could never be regained and lost distribution could not be sold at a later date. These factors also gave the trade unions considerable strength in wage negotiation, and Fleet Street workers were able to achieve higher rates than those earned by other print workers.

It was partly competition which led to Fleet Street management adopting a new approach to the introduction of new technology. The relative cheap-ness of cold type over hot metal reduced one of the major barriers to entry to newspaper production. The initial challenges came in the provinces with the growth of the 'free newspaper' industry. These are essentially cheaply produced local papers where advertising takes precedence over news items. The income from advertising is such that the newspapers can be distributed free to all householders in a given area. This sharpened com-petition in the local paper market. The response among some existing local papers was to force through the introduction of new technology. The *Nottingham Evening Post*, in the face of union opposition from the NGA simply replaced the print workers.

The real focus was in 1983 with the case of the Messenger group of free local newspapers in south Lancashire, and its proprieter Eddie Shah. In expanding his distribution and introducing direct input printing, he over-came bitter opposition from the NGA. He was backed in his quest by new laws redefining industrial disputes and imposing greater restrictions on picketing, drawn up by a government intent on curbing the power of the unions. The NGA were fined by the courts and Shah achieved all his objectives. He built upon his success with the local newspaper industry and launched a new national daily paper *Today* using new technology and non–traditional workers in a labour force one tenth the normal size for such a newspaper. At the same time plans were announced for the launch of other new daily and Sunday national papers. Although Shah's ownership of *Today* was brief and unprofitable (he sold the paper to Lonrho, who in turn sold it to News International), the relationship between Fleet Street management and the print unions had changed irrevocably. At the same time, Express newspapers announced plans to reduce its workforce by 30%.

Competition came not just from within the industry but through the coverage and the expansion of the television news services. The advent of breakfast television posed an even greater threat to an already declining total newspaper readership. The newspaper industry needed new technology to provide a better quality product with clearer newsprint and sharper pictures and an ability to respond quickly to changing news stories.

Events at Wapping

Before Murdoch's acquisition *The Times* had attempted to force the new technology issue, but an eleven month shutdown in 1978 altered very little, and the NGA retained exclusive control over typesetting operations. The completion of the plant at Wapping and the expense involved in interest payments alone gave new urgency to some form of agreement with the print unions. However, negotiations to move the production of the *Sun* and *News of the World* broke down in early 1984. The unions had refused to give way on the issue of manning levels and demarcation. Murdoch was clearly frustrated by the failure to reach agreement and undoubtedly spurred by Shah's action against the NGA, ensured that Wapping was protected against the action of pickets. During the dispute the building was popularly known as 'Fortress Wapping'. Plans were laid to treat Wapping as a greenfield site for the production of a new London evening paper staffed with non–Fleet Street people. At the time the unions saw this as a diversion to mask the true intention of transferring production of all four newspapers to Wapping.

Whatever the intention, Murdoch was determined to introduce total management control over manning levels and achieve total labour flexibility. News International terminated all its existing collective agreements with the unions with the aim of replacing them with a legally binding contract and a no–strike clause, the elimination of the closed shop, and binding arbitration in the case of a dispute. The penalty for breaking the agreement would be instant dismissal for individuals and the right to sue the union for unlimited amounts. Such a strategy was calculated to confront the unions on the issue of job control, and not suprisingly was rejected by NGA and SOGAT '82. The two unions insisted that any move to Wapping should be accompanied by no redundancies and the maintenance of existing work practices. As a result Murdoch declared that negotiations were over and gave his printworkers six months notice and no option of jobs at Wapping.

One union, the Electrical, Electronic, Telecommunication and Plumbing Union (EETPU) was prepared to negotiate on the basis of the new proposals, much against the advice of the trade union movement's central body, the TUC. For some time the electricians' union had been keen to expand its membership in new areas, and viewed its members as key workers in all workplaces increasingly operating under the demands of new technology. One of those areas was printing, and the union had even gone so far as to provide training for its members in newspaper production.

Electricians were recruited by News International, initially to commission the new presses. However, by the end of January 1986 the Wapping plant was producing the four newspaper titles amid much secrecy, using electricians recruited from outside London and transported daily by an organized bus network. This led to considerable recriminations within the trade union movement and calls to expel the EETPU from the TUC. They were eventually expelled at the 1988 TUC Conference. The move had also affected the journalists on all papers. Many moved to Wapping for increased salaries but several refused to work under the new arrangements. For their part the print unions held a secret ballot which showed that most were in favour of strike action. Picket lines were set up outside Wapping and SOGAT attempted to prevent the distribution of the newspapers with the help of the transport workers union (TGWU). Both unions were countered by the law. In the case of the TGWU the threat was sufficient, but SOGAT was fined £25 000 and had its assets sequestrated by the High Court for persistent attempts to prevent newspaper distribution.

By the following month News International agreed to the involvement of ACAS. The main issue that emerged was that of redundancy payments for those on strike. The company had always maintained that those choosing this course of action forfeited their right to severance pay, and had effectively dismissed themselves. The company did offer the unions the old *Sunday Times* printing plant so that they could set up their own newspaper staffed by the displaced workforce. The offer was rejected by the unions, who insisted on the maximum number of workers being taken on at Wapping and generous redundancy payments for the rest. Increasingly, however, the union position was being undermined by events elsewhere. New technology agreements were being reached with unions at the *Express* and *Mirror* newspapers, and several national newspapers announced their own plans to move to Docklands. In all cases the owners saw the move as an opportunity both to expand and negotiate fresh deals with the trade unions.

By May 1986 the company made what they claimed was a final offer in a bid to end the picketing at Wapping. This comprised a redundancy payment deal totalling £50 million, an opportunity for all workers to apply for vacancies at Wapping as and when they arose, a withdrawal of all legal actions against the unions, and a promise to review the issue of union recognition after a year. The offer was rejected. Picketing was intensified accompanied by a significant involvement of the police and further legal proceedings to prevent the picketing taking place. As a result of these proceedings SOGAT estimated its losses at £1.5 million. The estimated costs of policing the dispute up to June 1986 were £1 million.

In September News International made a revised offer of redundancy payments to the dismissed workers, again rejected by the NGA and SOGAT '82. The mounting costs of the dispute sought SOGAT to appeal for funds among its membership nationwide. The appeal was rejected.

The first anniversary of the strike in January 1987 was accompanied by the largest mass picket to date and extremely violent clashes between the police and the pickets. Part of the violence was undoubtedly attributed to a growing frustration among the workers and a realization that the unions could no longer afford to continue. The cost of legal proceedings, the general cost of running the dispute, and an impending contempt of court action was too much for the NGA and SOGAT to bear and would have resulted in the elimination of all their assets. By February 1987 both unions, along with the journalists' union accepted a redundancy package for the dismissed employees and the dispute ended.

The News International case in a business context

The case illustrates all aspects of our Business in Context model.

Environmental aspects

Economic factors are represented by the highly competitive nature of the newspaper industry. The high potential profit from a national title led to fierce competition for circulation and advertising. Traditionally this resulted in a fierce rivalry and lack of cooperation between the owners. The availability of new technology combined with external competition from television and radio meant that technological changes were sought to reduce costs and maintain profit levels. Furthermore, the relative cheapness of that new technology lowered a significant barrier to entry, thereby increasing competition. This has broken the oligopoly of Fleet Street and led to new national titles as well as major changes in regional newspapers resulting from the growth of the free newspaper industry. In a much broader sense, a high level of unemployment may have increased the resolve of the electricians' union to expand in field of activity, and influenced the lack of wider support for the printworkers in their dispute. (A good summary of such changes and their impact on management strategy in particular can be found in Oram, 1987.)

The State had a considerable influence on events at Wapping both directly and indirectly. There was a direct involvement through the policing of the dispute with extensive costs over a period of a year. The Employment Acts of 1980 and 1982 and the Trade Union Act of 1984 brought about changes in the legal definition of a dispute, and placed restrictions on both picketing and the formation of a closed shop. The unions were challenged on the legality of their dispute and were found wanting. The subsequent clashes between the unions and the courts led to substantial fines being imposed, which eventually brought an end to the dispute. Prior to the events at Wapping, the government of the day had, in 1981, become embroiled in a monopolies issue when News International negotiated to buy *The Times* and *Sunday Times* when it already owned the biggest selling national and Sunday papers. The deal was allowed to go through on the undertaking of editorial freedom for the newly acquired titles. More sceptical observers, like Harold Evans (successively the editor of the *Sunday Times* and *The Times*), saw the acquisition as a reward for News International's editorial support for the government in the previous general election (Evans, 1983). Whatever the situation, this aspect of the case raises the important issue of the relationship between politics and the press.

Technology, or more specifically the introduction of new technology, was a central issue in this case. Changes in the technology of newpaper production brought about the possibility of changes in work allocation. The elimination of traditional printing work through the substitution of direct input and photocomposition challenged the job control of the print workers and ultimately the bargaining position of their trade union. Printing operations could now be performed by journalists and typists, considerably reducing operating costs and presenting much greater scope for editorial changes, allowing newspapers to be much more responsive to changes in the news and hence the needs of the market place. Traditional craft unions like the NGA do not yield their historical controls willingly, hence the intensity and at times the bitterness of the dispute. New technology also gave management a new strategic weapon in dealing with the trade unions and was doubtless seen by some as a means of gaining greater control over costs and workplace practices, especially manning levels. (A much more detailed account of changing technology in the newspaper industry and its impact on labour can be found in Martin, 1981.)

Labour issues, as we can see, are inseperable from those relating to technology. New methods not only mean changes in work allocation, but also an ultimate reduction in the number of jobs. The bargaining position of the trade unions was being challenged on the issue of job control at a time when their response was further weakened by high levels of unemployment. The case is not simply a matter of management versus the unions, but illustrates the complexity of the dispute on the union side. The Fleet Street workers had, for a very long time, considered themselves to be the 'aristocrats of labour', positioned at the very top of the printing hierarchy (Bassett, 1986). This had often rankled with printworkers outside London, and may have explained their reluctance in giving full support to their Fleet Street colleagues. The *Independent* newspaper, launched in 1986, was printed at regional sites away from London, and its management had little difficulty in gaining the agreement of NGA and SOGAT '82 on the use of the new technology. Quite apart from the differences amongst the printworkers themselves, their position was further challenged by the willingness of the electricians to be trained in newspaper operations. This forms part of a much broader debate within the trade union movement, as individual unions, mindful of a declining membership, seek to insure their own future by offering the kind of stoppage–free deals sought by management. In the case of Wapping the EETPU were more than happy to replace the printworkers and on a broader front, to see themselves ideally placed to become the key trade union of the future in workplaces increasingly controlled by computers. Changes in the trade union movement are thus reflecting wider occupational changes. For the future, a weakened NGA and SOGAT '82 may be forced to merge and widen their appeal to attract new members. This would further dilute the traditional power base of the craft union in printing.

The aspect of *culture* is relevant to this case in at least two ways. Firstly we have the issue of the distinctive culture of Fleet Street, brought about by the competitive nature of the industry and the job control of the craft unions. Work practices, manning levels and wage rates have marked off Fleet Street from the rest of the British newspaper industry. The distinctive Fleet Street culture has been especially resistant to change and thus a major factor in the dispute. Secondly, comparative studies of the newspaper industry reveal marked differences between Britain and other countries, notably the USA (e.g., Griffin, 1984). The newspaper industry in the USA has embraced new technology with little union opposition. Moreover, in Britain there is much greater evidence of cooperation and solidarity between print workers, ancillary staff and journalists than exists in most other societies.

Organizational aspects

Whilst the case clearly shows the interaction and influence of the environmental aspects of our model, there are significant organizational influences at work too.

In terms of *size*, though News International's British operation was considerable, part of the motivation behind the move to Wapping lay in the desire to expand. At its previous locations around Fleet Street the opportunities for expansion were denied both by available space, limiting production capacity and distribution, and by manning agreements limiting the size of each edition.

The change to Wapping and the adoption of new printing technology had clear implications for *organizational structure*. A much more flexible structure has emerged for the newspaper industry. The role of the journalist has potentially broadened to assume responsibility for typesetting as well as content. The electricians have emerged as a fast–growing occupational group within the industry. Such changes in work allocation also have implications for management control.

Changes in the newspaper industry have been related to major changes in the *ownership* of national titles. The acquisition strategies of News International led to the grouping of five major titles under a single ownership. More significantly, the ownership style was one that had developed in Australia and the USA, where new technology in the newspaper industry was well established. Ownership changes away from Fleet Street were also having an impact. We have already made reference to the catalytic effect of Eddie Shah, but ownership changes in some local newspapers like the *Notts Evening Post* led to a much more aggressive style by management, especially towards trade unions and the introduction of new technology.

Changes in ownership often went hand in hand with changes in *goals*. Historically newspapers have often been regarded as a special kind of product under the control of individual press barons, such as Lord Beaverbrook at the *Daily Express*. As such, profit goals have co–existed with the less common business goals of political, social or moral reform. Increasingly major titles have come under the control of business groups in which newspapers represent just one of a highly diversified stable of products. An extreme case here would be the holding company Lonrho's acquisition of the *Observer* Sunday newspaper. It is unlikely that such changes have taken place without a corresponding elevation of purely business goals. The case illustrates goal conflict in various ways. At its most obvious this is represented by the unions' need to retain job control in the face of management's desire to reap the cost savings of new technology. The NGA and SOGAT's goal of union solidarity is sharply contrasted with the EETPU's goal of expansion. From an industrial relations perspective the case is interesting in revealing how goals shift as disputes develop; in this case from issues of job control to the negotiation of an acceptable redundancy package.

Strategic aspects

We have seen that changes at News International and in Fleet Street generally have been part of a pattern of inter–related environmental and organizational factors. These changes have resulted in a changed culture within national newspaper organizations. A significant contribution to that changing culture has been the changes that have taken place in management strategy. In general terms Fleet Street management appears to have shifted from a reactive, crisis–induced strategy to one typified by long–term, planned technological and organizational change. A combination of a technological imperative and market and economic conditions has led management to adopt a more confident and, as some would term, aggressive approach in dealing with the trade unions. A widely–voiced speculation concerning the strategic implications of News International's move to Wapping was that it represented a deliberate confrontation with the trade unions as a prelude to changing work practices once and for all. The unions certainly believed that Wapping was never intended for a new evening paper, and that all along it was designed as the operating centre for the company's major titles. Certainly the initial management proposals, effectively removing the union's traditional control of work practices, were ones to which the union were never likely to agree.

Aside from management, the case is an interesting illustration of strategy from a trade union perspective. Trade unions are faced with the problem of declining membership in an unfavourable economic and political climate. Like businesses in a declining market they have to be very careful about their choice of strategic option. In such a situation the case of new technology presents an interesting dilemma; its acceptance by unions would inevitably entail job losses, yet a refusal to negotiate may have far more serious consequences for the future bargaining position of the union. Just as some businesses find declining markets favourable for growth, then some trade unions can take advantage of a seemingly disadvantageous conditions by proposing deals acceptable to management. In this way the EETPU has embarked upon a fairly vigorous growth strategy, not only securing recognition rights, but in doing so creating work for electricians.

Functional aspects

At the heart of management strategy in this case are the implications for the functional operations of business. All our functional areas are implicated by News International's move to Wapping.

Innovation. Changes in News International's operations have obviously been made possible through process innovations in the newspaper industry. Other types of innovation are illustrated by this case, more especially the entrepreneurial activity of industry newcomers like Shah, attempting to break the traditional Fleet Street monopoly on national newspaper titles.

Production. The new site operating under the latest technology offers management a speedier and more flexible operation with a capability of increased capacity. The new location offers all the benefits of a greenfield site, with particular improvements in the supply of raw materials and the distribution of the finished product.

Marketing. In marketing terms, the case illustrates how the need for change has arisen through increased competition and reduced barriers to entry for would–be competitors. The new printing processes offer the reader and the advertiser the potential for a much improved product.

The systems approach is a view of business involving two related concepts. Firstly, businesses are made up of a series of interactions (Key
concept 1.3), involving the various business activities (Key concept 1.2),
the various aspects of the organization (Key concept 1.5), and aspects of
the environment (Key concept 1.7). What we identify as a business is the
sum total of all these influences and interactions. Secondly, the systems
approach views business as a series of inputs from the environment,
internal processes and eventual outputs.

KEY CONCEPT 1.8

**THE SYSTEMS
APPROACH**

Accounting. Major motivations behind changes in the newspaper industry
have been declining readership and reduced profits. The cost of setting up
a new operating plant and its commissioning with state–of–the–art technology represents a considerable short–term investment with a potential
for long–term cost saving. It is however important from a management
perspective that operations commence at the new plant as soon as possible.

Personnel. The case focusses around the industrial relations aspects of
the transfer to Wapping and the introduction of new technology. The
marketing and accounting factors identified above put pressure on the need
for a speedy agreement with the unions. On the other hand the setting up
of a greenfield site has presented management with an ideal opportunity
to introduce a completely new set of personnel and industrial relations
policies.

The systems and contingency approaches

We have stressed both in the editor's foreword and elsewhere in this
introductory chapter that the various elements of our model interact with
one another, and influences go backwards and forwards across the various
levels (see Figure 1.1). We are presenting an interaction–influence model.
The idea of such a model for businesses is not new but forms the basis of
the systems and contingency approaches, which have been developed as
part of organization theory. It is not our intention to present either a
comprehensive review or a critique of these two approaches. Instead we
present a brief summary of their main ideas. Their importance as far as
we are concerned is that they offer the student of business an important
framework for analysis.

The systems approach assumes that all organizations are made up of
interdependent parts which can only be understood by reference to the
whole. As such, organizations may be analysed in terms of inputs, processes, and outputs as we illustrate in Figure 1.2. We can see from this that
there are many similarities with our own model.

The development of systems thinking from an organization perspective
starts with the analogy of the firm as a living organism. To be effective, the
firm, like the organism, must adapt to its environment in order to survive.
The inputs, processes and outputs must be balanced so that the firm can
obtain equilibrium, especially with its environment. The application of

Figure 1.2 A systems view of business.

the systems approach in organizational analysis first gained prominence through the utilization of a socio–technical systems perspective. This is based on the assumption that the social system of the firm and its technical system interact in a complex way. The approach was popularized in the work of the Tavistock Institute and its associated researchers throughout the world (e.g., Trist and Bamforth, 1951, Rice, 1958, Emery and Thorsrud, 1976). Unless the social system and the technical system work in harmony, a firm will be inefficient.

The contingency approach can be traced through the work of Woodward (1965), and Burns and Stalker (1966), although the term itself was popularized in the work of Lawrence and Lorsch who wrote,

> Organizational variables are in a complex interrelationship with one another and with conditions in the environment. If an organization's internal states and processes are consistent with external demands ... it will be effective in dealing with its environment.
>
> (Lawrence and Lorsch 1967 p 157)

The contingency approach starts with an analysis of the key environmental variables which shape the organization. It then proceeds with the assumption that the successful firms are those which adapt to the key influences and achieve some kind of best fit with their environment. This approach has been very influential in the area of corporate strategy. The strategist attempts to match the environmental opportunities and threats with the organization's own strengths and weaknesses, to develop an optimum strategy for the firm in question.

Both the systems and contingency approaches are based on the concept of an organization interacting with several key elements in its environment and adapting to them. Some writers (for example Burrell and Morgan, 1979, pp 164–81) regard the contingency approach as an extension of the systems analysis of organizations. Both approaches have been criticized for focussing on a limited range of environmental variables, for being deterministic, and for ignoring both the influence of the organization on its environment and the values and behaviour of management and the workforce. It is our view that such criticisms place unnecessary limits on the use and value of both approaches. In developing our model of business we wish to use systems and contingency thinking to present a broad analytical framework, enabling us to gain a greater insight into the way businesses

The contingency approach focusses on the relationship between the organization and its environment. It embraces the notion that business activities and the way they are organized are products of the environment in which they operate. The most successful businesses are therefore those which are organized to take advantage of the prevailing environmental influences.

KEY CONCEPT 1.9

THE CONTINGENCY APPROACH

operate. We are concerned to show, however, that businesses, while influenced by their environments, are not wholly determined by them. Business strategies can and do influence environmental contingencies.

The layout of this book

The chapters which follow will analyse each of the various elements of our Business in Context model. After examining these elements students are recommended to return to the Shipping and News International cases presented in this opening chapter.

Chapters 2 to 4 will look at the environmental, organizational and strategic contexts respectively. The variables identified in Figure 1.1 will be examined in turn. In our discussion of these variables certain issues emerge which call for for more detailed consideration. For example, in our treatment of culture as an environmental variable we deal at some length with the phenomenon known as 'Japanese Management', and in viewing size as an organizational variable raise the topic of small businesses. Such issues are chosen for their topicality, but more significantly, that they further illustrate the working of our Business in Context model by drawing together the various activities and their contexts.

Chapters 5 to 9 will focus on the functional areas of business we have chosen to examine; innovation, production, marketing, personnel and finance and accounting. Once again we will emphasize their relationship with each other and with our three levels of interaction and influence. The final chapter of the book will attempt to draw together the key interactions and influences involving businesses in recent years.

Summary

In this introductory chapter we have outlined the workings of our Business in Context model and in so doing mapped out the rest of this book. In the model we identify a number of key variables which interact with business. We have arranged these variables in a series of levels, which we have termed environmental, organizational and strategic. We believe that our understanding of the way businesses and their key activities operate is enhanced by placing them in this contextual framework.

The workings of the model can be seen by reference to two cases. The first deals with the shipping industry and in particular the impact of the recession and increased competition on the shipping fleets of eight indus-trially–developed nations. The second case looks at a single company, News International, and focuses on the events surrounding relocation, technical change and a major labour dispute in 1985. The theoretical underpinnings of the model are discussed with reference to the systems and contingency approaches to organizational analysis.

Further reading

Although they concentrate more upon organizations, their processes and theories, two other texts can be recommended for attempting to integrate their subject matter giving fresh insights into the complexities of business. These are John Child, *Organization: A Guide to Problems and Practice* 2nd edition (Harper and Row, 1984), and Sandra Dawson, *Analysing Organizations* (MacMillan, 1986). Those students seeking more background to the systems and contingency approaches should look at G. Burrell and G. Morgan, *Sociological Paradigms and Organization Analysis* (Heinemann, 1979), and two seminal studies in the area; T. Burns and G. Stalker, *The Management of Innovation* (Tavistock, 1966) and J. Lawrence and P. Lorsch, *Organization and Environment* (Harvard University Press, 1967). More information on the shipping industry case can be found in R.E. Walton, *Innovating to Compete* (Jossey–Bass, 1987), while aspects of the News International case can be found in R. Martin, *New Technology and Industrial Relations in Fleet Street* (Clarendon Press, 1981).

Discussion

1. We have identified five environmental and five organizational variables in our model. By necessity these represent broad categories. What are the possible elements which might be considered under the various headings in our model of business?

2. Using the way we have analysed the two cases as your guide, take in turn an industry, a firm, and a specific issue, and analyse each using the Business in Context model.

3. What is the value of the systems and contingency approaches to an understanding of business?

The environment and business **2** ||||||

In Chapter 1 we introduced the model which forms the basis of our analysis of business. In this chapter we focus on a major element of that model, namely the environment. We define the environment as comprising all factors which exist outside the business enterprise, but which interact with it. As we pointed out in the last chapter, all firms are to a greater or lesser extent constrained by the environment within which they operate, but the activities of businesses themselves also change that same environment. This two–way process is an important theme throughout the book.

In devoting just one chapter to the business environment, the material is necessarily highly selective. Five key areas have been identified, namely the economy, the role of the state, technology, labour and culture. We devote a section to each of these topics and identify issues which illustrate the interactions between the firm and its environment. Each of the areas selected also interacts with the others as the matrix presented in Figure 2.1 shows.

For the business manager, the environment therefore comprises a number of key variables which interact with the business either singly or jointly. The complexity does not end there. These interactions may occur on a number of different levels, as shown in Figure 2.2. Firstly a firm interacts with a local environment, in which expansion plans may need approval from the local council, and where its marketing and personnel strategies will be significantly influenced by firms operating in the same local market. Secondly, interaction occurs in a national environment, influenced by such matters as government laws, bank interest rates, the rate of inflation, and national trade union policy. Thirdly we have the international environment in which the firm may be affected by international money exchange rates, the competition from cheap–labour economies, and the regulations of supranational bodies such as the EEC. As a general rule, the ability of managers to influence their environment diminishes as they move further away from the local environment. As with all such rules there are exceptions, since the ability to influence the environment tends to increase with the size of the firm. We shall see in our discussion of multinationals in the next section that the management of larger conglomerates can exert influences which extend beyond national boundaries to change international economics and politics.

We will deal with each of our five variables in turn. As we stressed in

	LABOUR	TECHNOLOGY	STATE	ECONOMY	
STATE				The extent and direction of state intervention in the economy. The power of the multinationals in influencing policy.	S T A T E
TECHNOLOGY			State support of innovation and technical change and the specific impact on certain industries e.g., defence.	The impact of innovation on economic growth.	T E C H N O L O G Y
LABOUR		The impact of technical change on skills and trade union policy towards such changes.	Government policies to direct the supply of labour. Legislation to regulate trade union activities.	The impact of the economy on the type and levels of employment.	L A B O U R
CULTURE	Cultural influences on personnel and industrial relations strategies.	The impact of changes in technology on society. Cultural attitudes towards technology.	Cultural explanations for the differences between nations regarding state intervention.	The nature of the economy shaping family life e.g., agricultural vs industrial societies. The influence of cultural values on the directions of economic development and specialization.	C U L T U R E

Figure 2.1 The interaction of environmental factors: some illustrations.

Chapter 1, each of them represents broad categories; for example, the role of the state will deal with issues pertaining to the general political environment. The chapter closes with a treatment of 'Japanese management', not only because this is an important topic within any discussion of cultural influence and the diffusion of business ideas, but also in that it represents a fascinating case study of a business community being shaped by and shaping its environment.

The economy and business

With many aspects of our environment we are faced with the immediate problem of deciding where the environment ends and business begins, and vice versa. In looking at the relationship between business and the economy this becomes particularly acute, since much of what we label as the economy is the product of business activity. By the same token, business enterprises are influenced significantly by economic developments. In this section we will look at both these aspects by focussing largely on the experience of Britain in the post–war period. Britain, along with most capitalist countries,

Figure 2.2 Levels of the environment.

is an example of a mixed economy, where free enterprise is mixed with state involvement through public ownership, legal regulation, and various forms of planning and direction. For this reason there is considerable overlap between the economy and the role of the state dealt with in the next section. Obviously a much fuller account of the relationship between business and the economy can be found in the economics text in this series (Neale and Haslam, 1989).

The economy interacts with businesses at all three levels depicted in Figure 2.2. At the local level, immediate competitive issues related to firms operating in the same product market are the most significant. If the Virgin record store in London's Oxford Street reduces the price of all its compact discs by £1.00, then the management of the large HMV store just down the road must determine their most appropriate strategic response. This may involve adopting the same price strategy or it may involve a more selective strategy offering larger discounts on big selling items. In the 1960s labour shortages meant that firms actively competed for labour and often increased pay and bonus rates to attract labour from their competitors. Such competition can reach particularly fierce proportions and many firms prefer to cooperate rather than compete on issues like price or wage rates. In this way businesses form themselves into cartels which may be an effective way of controlling the immediate competitive environment, and perhaps the wider environment too, as in influencing government policy. There are several examples of groups of local grocers being formed to buy in bulk from suppliers in an attempt keep prices down and combat the threat posed by large supermarkets. We deal with the competitive environment in more detail in Chapter 4, and students are referred to Porter's model illustrated in Figure 4.3. For the rest of this section we will illustrate the relationship between the firm and the economy by focussing on issues mainly, but not exclusively, at the national and international levels.

The impact of business on the economy

All businesses produce goods and services and provide employment. In doing so they contribute to a nation's income, its capital assets, and its economic growth. Economies are often compared on the basis of their Gross Domestic Product (GDP), the sum total of the net outputs of each sector of the economy. Key issues for business managers are also key economic issues. These may be identified as products, productivity, markets, profits and the supply of labour. These themes re–emerge when we discuss the role of the economy in the chapters on the various activities of business. For example, in Chapter 5 we examine the view that economic growth is dependent upon product and process innovation.

The impact of the economy on business

There are a variety of ways in which economic changes have affected businesses in this country. We will illustrate these changes through the changing nature of world economies, including structural changes, the supply and price of raw materials, increasing international competition and the emergence of the multinational as a powerful influence. The case of the multinational illustrates the difficulty of isolating business and environmental influences. Many businesses in this country have undoubtedly been influenced by a world economy increasingly dominated by multinational corporations. These same multinationals are themselves businesses with the ability to influence national and international economies.

Changes in the world economy have, for a country like Britain, led to major structural changes involving the decline of the manufacturing sector (de–industrialization) and the growth of the service sector, especially the financial sector. In turn these changes have had a significant impact on levels of employment, causing high levels of unemployment in those areas formerly dominated by traditional manufacturing industry, whilst creating many new jobs in the emerging financial services industry.

The availability of key resources can not only have a significant influence on the fortunes of individual firms, but can also lead to structural changes. In 1973 OPEC representing the oil producing countries decided to restrict the supply of oil, with a subsequent dramatic increase in price. The impacts on businesses in this country were several. Increased costs were passed on in the form of increased prices, or resulted in reduced profits, with some firms unable to compete. Some industries sought substitute products with corresponding increases in demand for products of the coal and gas industries. Rising petrol prices meant increased costs of transport and led to major product changes in the car industry. These changes were even more significant in the USA, with a dramatic reduction in car size and the imposition of a national speed limits on all roads, which stands to this day. Since Britain has become a major oil producer, changes in the price of oil have had an effect upon the exchange value of sterling. An exchange rate strengthened by an oil economy has meant that British exports have been expensive, affecting those businesses who depend for a large proportion of their revenue on exported goods.

Changes in the car industry identified above were not only brought about by increases in the price of oil, but a growing international competition, especially from Japan. The decline in competitiveness of many of Britain's industries, such as shipbuilding, motorcycles, domestic electrical products and cars has been attributed to the rise of cheap–labour economies, especially those in the Far East, or the product superiority of manufacturers such as Japan and West Germany.

The multinational corporation

An important aspect of international competition has been the market dominance of the multinational corporation. Trade and finance have always been international, but it was not until the post–war period that the large American conglomerate with its divisionalized structure was attracted to expanding European markets. While Europe initially provided an open door to American investment, later protectionist policies set up by the EEC accelerated the growth of American susidiaries in Europe. Similar developments took place involving Japan. The coordination of multinational activities was enhanced by developments in communications and especially in information technology.

The multinational has had a significant impact on national economies in a variety of ways. Multinational companies tend to be very large; for

KEY CONCEPT 2.1

THE MULTINATIONAL CORPORATION

A multinational firm is one that operates from bases in a number of different countries. Whilst small businesses can and do operate multinationally, most multinationals are large corporations with diverse interests coordinated by a centrally planned global strategy. Multinationals tend to compete in oligopolistic markets. In recent years there has been a shift in emphasis away from American multinationals to focus on the multinational growth of SE Asian companies, especially the Japanese.

example it is often quoted that Exxon and General Motors have annual turnovers in excess of the GNP of all but fourteen nation states. Whilst they tend to be highly diversified, the multinational tends to concentrate in oligopolistic industries, those dominated by a few large companies, where the general pattern of competition is through expensive product development and expensive promotional strategies. The multinational corporation is able to draw upon a worldwide pool of skilled labour and exploit the advantages of centralized control and a centralized research and development function. Business empires are thus based around a centrally planned global strategy. Such a process has been formalized through the planning process of companies like 3M (Case 4.2).

Certain changes have taken place in the development of multinationals. The USA is still dominant, but has been joined by the expansion of the Japanese and European multinational. The focus for the location has also shifted, from Europe, then to Canada and Latin America, and most recently to South East Asia. Along with this shift in location has gone a marked change in rationale. Initially multinationals grew to exploit local markets and raw materials. The emphasis is now upon manufacture, and especially on specialization, either through product specialization in the case of the car industry or the more general location of labour intensive industries in low wage areas, as with the manufacture of video cassette recorders. Some writers (Adam 1975, Harrison, 1981) see this shift in production as following a set pattern occuring in traditional declining labour intensive industries with a reasonably long product life cycle or in the labour intensive aspects of the more technologically–based industries as with electronics or car manufacture. Both the shift in location and the emphasis on reduced costs have had a considerable impact upon the ability of non–multinationals to compete in manufacturing industry and upon levels of employment in the West, and especially Britain.

Much has been written about the impact of the multinational corporation on the economies of Third World countries (for example Harrison, 1981). Whilst involvement in the Third World is done with the cooperation of host governments, leads to an inflow of capital, provides local employment and improves the balance of payments, there are considerable problems involved. These include the exploitation of natural resources, allegations of bribery and corruption, the expatriation of profits, price speculation, the tendency of multinationals to move both capital and financial assets to gain the most favourable tax and exchange rate advantages and so on. In general, Third World economies become dominated by companies whose primary aim is the maximization of profit, when those countries might benefit more from a planned, local approach to development.

The two cases of resource allocation and the internationalization of capital through multinational expansion show how economic developments can have an impact upon businesses in a single nation state. To these can be added the influence of world financial markets on business investment and, for most countries, increasing attempts to control the economy through state intervention. This aspect will be dealt with in the next section.

The impact of a changing economy on British business

For Britain the major impact of these changes has been the decline of its manufacturing base, the growth of the service sector, and rising unemployment.

The growth of the service sector of the economy also has its roots in the historical development of the British economy. The City has always been a focus of attention due to early British dominance in world trade and the international role played by sterling. Several writers (for example Jessop, 1980 and Armstrong *et al.*, 1984) view the attempts to preserve sterling as a leading world currency alongside measures to protect employment and the welfare state as lending the British economy its peculiar 'stop–go' characteristic of the post–war period. High interest rates to encourage foreign investment to protect sterling have by the same token discouraged industrial investment at home with ill consequences for the development of business and employment.

High levels of unemployment are however a fairly recent phenomenon. Between 1948 and 1966 the average rate in Britain was 1.7%, with only 1.1% in 1966. Along with other industrial countries, levels of unemployment have risen sharply since then, with an official figure of 3.25 million people being out of work in 1982, representing 13% of the working population. (Other figures very considerably, unemployment statistics being very much a part of a wider ideological debate.) Various policies have been initiated to deal with the problem including government training schemes, regional aid, increasing public investment and direct state intervention to support ailing firms. Some of these aspects are dealt with in the next section.

The state and business

Taking his lead from Max Weber, John Scott (1979) defines the state as that body which has a monopoly over taxation, the money supply, and the legitimate use of violence. The state is normally thought of as comprising the executive, parliament, the civil service, the judiciary, the armed forces and the police. It would be wrong to perceive the state as a united body. Tensions can and do occur, as between parliament and the civil service or between parliament and the judiciary. Variations in policy often result from differences in political ideology. These differences are apparent not only between parties, but also within the same party, as revealed in Case

> The state comprises parliament, the judiciary, the civil service, police and armed forces and so on. Traditionally there have been tensions between the State's need to direct the economy and regulate business and the wishes of the business community to pursue their interests with a minimum of State intervention. Nevertheless, State intervention is a feature of business life and is inevitable in a country such as the United Kingdom where the State is a major employer. Intervention occurs through the legal regulation of market transactions, inventions and employment contracts and through the State's attempt to influence demand both as a consumer and via government economic policy. The business community in turn attempts to influence the State by adopting the various tactics associated with pressure groups. Increasingly, business comes under the influence of the policies of supra-national bodies, such as the EEC.

KEY CONCEPT 2.2

THE STATE AND BUSINESS

2.1 at the end of this chapter; or as shown by the policies of the Conservative Government since 1979, which has pursued policies radically different from those of its Conservative predecessors.

We have already noted that the state interacts with business through its management of the economy. The state's influence can also operate at a highly localized and immediate way as the following example shows. In the 1960s the Ministry of Transport had a policy of employing independent firms to act as consultants in the testing of government construction projects such as roads and bridges. The policy coincided with a massive expansion in motorway construction. This resulted in a business boom period for a number of civil engineering firms. Testing contracts were usually given to a small proportion of the large firms in the industry and, for some firms, this government work accounted for 75% of the annual turnover. In 1986 the Government, as part of is policy to encourage greater competition, decided to invite bids for such consultancy work from any civil engineering contractor. The firms which had previously relied on such work as a major part of their income were faced with the prospect of either losing out to new competitors or accepting reduced profit margins through having to lower their consultancy fees. In either case, managements were forced to rethink their strategies significantly.

In this section we will deal with aspects of the state's activity at both national and local levels in terms of the state's attempt to intervene in business and the attempts made by business managers to influence the working of the state. Throughout this book we illustrate the interaction of the state and business by examining the relationship through its impact on the various business activities in Chapters 5 to 9. We extend the concept of state intervention at the end of this section by examining briefly the role of a supranational body, the European Economic Community. We begin our view of the state by looking at two broad theoretical and ideological perspectives.

Theoretical perspectives on the role of the state

We examine briefly two main perspectives on the role of the state. These are the liberal–pluralist and the Marxist perspectives. Both concur that the state is concerned with the maintenance of order and with providing conditions so that business can prosper.

Liberals see the state as a neutral umpire in a pluralist society dominated by voluntary cooperation and exchange, where differences are never fundamental. Under a liberal view of the state, intervention is necessary: to protect the workings of the free market against forces which might otherwise disrupt it, such as excessive monopoly power of either business or trade unions; to provide and/or control goods and services to individuals such as defence and education, where provision by other means would be impossible or inappropriate; and to take a longer–term view of economic, social, and environmental change than individual businesses are capable of doing. The liberal perspective allows wide variation, from a highly directive economy to one in which the free market is encouraged to operate unfettered by government controls.

Marxists on the other hand see the state as the instrument of the ruling class in an essentially exploitative society, where massive inequalities exist. Under a Marxist view of the state, intervention is necessary to maintain the status quo in favour of the dominant class. The state will therefore intervene to protect investments or prevent strikes.

Whichever perspective is adopted, it is clear that this century has seen an increase of state intervention in Britain, much of it aimed specifically at business.

State intervention and business

An examination of state intervention in business this century reveals a progression through three stages; facilitative, supportive and directive. This classification is based on the work of Winkler (1977). We deal with each stage in turn.

The facilitative phase involved minimum intervention, largely through law and order, taxation and currency protection. The primary concern was for the smooth operation of the market. Two factors emerged to challenge this policy; an increase in industrial concentration resulting in large firms being able to override market competition, and increasing economic crises of the 1920s and 30s with sharp rises in the level of unemployment.

Such factors led to the state adopting a much more supportive role towards business. State policies followed the Keynesian belief that the free market was unable to solve the problems of unemployment, and that increasing state intervention was required to redistribute wealth and create employment. The policy was ultimately challenged by a progressively weaker industrial base and the rise of international competition. The state therefore took upon itself to pursue a more directive line.

Increased direction in the 1960s gained broad support, even from groups not normally associated with such a policy, like the Federation of British Industry (a predecessor of the CBI), and the Conservative government in its setting up of the National Economic Development Council in 1962.

Directive policies included attempts to restructure business, the promotion of mergers to encourage both economies of scale and innovation, and incomes policies.

Such state direction in business has been labelled as corporatism. This is essentially an attempt by the government to achieve stability by integration, involving representatives of business and trade unions in the economic decision–making process. Corporatist states tend to favour central planning and the use of extra–parliamentary bodies such as 'quangos' to make decisions. Crouch (1978) has suggested that most countries in Western Europe have set up corporatist machinery at some time in the post–war period, with perhaps Holland and West Germany experiencing most success. In Britain, integration has traditionally been resisted by both business and trade unions, and attempts at corporatism have failed either through the refusal of one or other of the groups to participate or a lack of consensus. One of the more recent attempts at integration occurred when the Labour Government of 1974–9 launched its 'social contract', a device to control the economy with the cooperation of the trade unions through wage restraint. The plan ultimately failed (and the government along with it) with rising inflation being met by ever–increasing wage demands. Some writers are pessimistic about the role of the state in corporatist societies feeling that a failure of consensus may result in an increasingly directive state and the hastening decline of parliamentary democracy. (For an excellent summary of these arguments see Honour and Mainwaring 1982, Chapter 2.)

The lack of consensus highlights one of the major difficulties of state intervention in business. Jessop writes of the British government attempt to influence the direction of business to solve the economic crises of the 1960s and 70s.

> Far from industrial policy being a consensual panacea for solving the British crisis, it is a major focus of economic, political and ideological struggle.
>
> (Jessop, 1980, pp 47–8)

We are able to identify five features which highlight the difficulties of the state's interaction with business.

☐ Differences both between and within political parties have resulted in different approaches to intervention. Norton–Villiers–Triumph, Case 2.1, highlights some of these difficulties.

☐ The business community may oppose attempts by governments to control it. The majority of owners and managers of business have an ideological attachment to *laissez–faire*. In addition, as we saw in the previous section, multinationals tend to have a greater allegiance to their own corporate goals than those of any single nation state.

☐ Labour, as represented by the trade unions, has traditionally resisted any attempts by governments to intervene in the collective bargaining process. Government attempts to control wages in the private sector have been singularly unsuccessful.

☐ Both the business community and the labour movement have weak central organizations and on many issues consensus is lacking. This is a severe handicap in their attempts to influence the state planning process. Unlike their counterparts in most European countries, the employers' associations in Britain play a relatively minor role, and both the Confederation of British Industry and the Trades Union Congress are loose associations and weak policy–making bodies.

☐ Governments of both political persuasions have accorded low priority to the implementation of economic plans, with the Treasury and the Bank of England generally overriding the policies of those institutions set up to deal with economic planning such as the NEDC.

Despite such problems, the state intervenes in business in a variety of ways and an attempt is made to classify these below.

Types of state intervention

Collective Provision. The most obvious form of state intervention is through the provision of those goods and services which would otherwise be too expensive, or too dangerous, or just ineffective if left to private control. Such aspects would include defence, the police, health, welfare and housing. The extent and nature of such collective provision is a matter of political and ideological debate. The British government since 1979 has pursued a policy of reducing its collective provision as illustrated by the sale of publicly–owned housing.

The State as Employer. The proportion of the working population employed by the state has risen from 2.4% in 1851 to 24.3% in 1975 (Strinati, 1982), and has since stabilized at around 25% despite attempts to reduce government involvement since 1979. As a major employer, the state has a profound affect on the labour market. The government since 1979, while formally rejecting incomes policy as a mechanism of control, has attempted to hold down wages in the public sector as part of its policy of reducing public expenditure. This has resulted in major confrontations with such groups as the miners, the nurses, and the teachers. The whole question of the public ownership of business is dealt with in the next chapter.

The State as Consumer. The case of the civil engineering contracts cited in the introduction to this section is a clear illustration of the state operating as a consumer of business services. As a major employer, the state is also a major purchaser of office equipment, and many businesses rely on government contracts as a major source of revenue. The state through its involvement in defence, health and education has a significant influence on the direction of innovation (Chapter 5 has a more comprehensive review of this aspect).

Legal Regulation. The legal regulation of business is extensive and complex, and a comprehensive review is provided by the law text in this series (Cole and Shears, 1989). The law of contract is used to regulate the market place. Company law deals with such issues as the protection of consumers through the regulation of monopoly power, rules governing the provision of company information and so on. Labour law deals with both the protection of the individual worker and the regulation of collective bargaining. Patent law exists to encourage innovation by granting monopoly rights to patent–holders. Illustrations of such legal provisions may be found in the chapters dealing with specific business activities. Some laws operate as constraints while others exist specifically to aid industrial development. The Norton–Villiers–Triumph case is a good illustration of how the Industry Act 1972, was used by the government to assist a single firm in the West Midlands. The government wished to help BSA/Triumph motorcycle manufacturers, but was prevented from giving a grant under regional aid policy as the West Midlands was not designated a special area. Instead, the government was forced by its own laws to aid the entire industry; hence its wish to see all three motorcycle manufacturers merged as one company (Sandberg, 1984).

Demand Management. All governments attempt to influence and control economic growth, the balance of payments, wage and price stability and the level of unemployment. A variety of measures are used including fiscal measures such as taxation, monetary measures such as control of credit, and direct measures such as import controls and assistance to specific firms.

Through its taxation and monetary policies the government is able to raise revenue to finance its activities and also to achieve specific objectives, as through the lower rates of taxation levied on food as opposed to tobacco. Direct intervention was rife during the period 1964–78. In the 1960s the Labour government targeted the nuclear, motor vehicles, and electrical industries for special assistance as well as setting up bodies such as the National Enterprise Board (NEB), the Industrial Reorganization Corporation, and the Ministry of Technology. The 1970 Conservative government targetted the machine tool industry and woollen textiles, and while abolishing all of Labour's machinery bar the NEB, created the Departments of Industry and the Environment.

During that period specific firms were given substantial state aid under what was popularly known as the 'lame duck policy'. These firms included Rolls Royce, British Leyland, British Steel, Upper Clyde Shipbuilders, and Chrysler. While direct intervention in the 1960s and early 70s focussed on larger companies, more recent measures have targeted the smaller firm for special attention. The small firms policy will be discussed more fully in Chapter 3.

Advisory Services. In addition to its policies or regulation and assistance, the state offers various types of advice to businessman. Such advice ranges from overseas trade to dealing with industrial relations problems.

The business community as a pressure group

So far this section has concentrated on the way the state attempts to influence business. We now turn our attention to the ways in which the state can be influenced by the business community acting as a pressure group, or more correctly, as a series of pressure groups.

We have already noted that businesses in this country are traditionally resistant to state control and are generally committed to a *laissez–faire* economy; and that as a pressure group, businesses tend to be fragmented with no powerful central body to coordinate policy. Indeed some evidence suggests that British industry is a singularly unsuccessful pressure group because of this fragmentation, and tends to exert pressure only in response to crises (Grant and Marsh, 1977).

However, as with all pressure group activity, there is both a difficulty in

CASE 2.1

NORTON–VILLIERS–TRIUMPH

In 1972 the Conservative government, worried about the collapse of the BSA/Triumph motorcycle manufacturers, decided to aid the entire industry by assisting the formation of a merger between BSA/Triumph and Norton Villiers. The new company, known as Norton–Villiers–Triumph (NVT) was launched in 1973 backed by £4.8 million from the government and £3.4 million from the Norton Villiers parent company. The new firm employed 1,750 people in three plants, two ex–BSA/Triumph (Meriden and Small Heath) and the other ex–Norton (Wolverhampton).

Faced with intense Japanese competition for the mass bike market, NVT's strategy was to concentrate on larger 'super bikes', mainly for the American market. The company would stress its craftsmanship image. To assist its policy, the decision was made to close the largest production plant at Meriden. The reasons behind this decision were the high cost of overheads, representing 50% of BSA/Triumph's losses, low productivity, a high incidence of industrial unrest, and a lack of space for expansion. The aim was to be in profit within three years and to expand on two sites within six years.

The new company was formed during the July shut–down at Meriden, and faced an immediate strike there over holiday pay. Announcement of the closure was delayed until the strike was settled, when the government pledged its help with shut–down arrangements. The union at Meriden refused to accept the proposals and initiated a work–in, blockading not only their own management but parts and drawings for other factories, in particular affecting operations at Small Heath.

Workers at Meriden wanted to set up a cooperative and in October 1973 offered £1 million in exchange for NVT guaranteeing a market for Meriden bikes. The offer was rejected and redundancy notices were served on the employees in November. The redundancy notices were accepted but the blockade continued amid considerable media attention. The government intervened, resisting NVT's management's request for an eviction order. The Department of Trade and Industry (DTI) acted as facilitator in talks between NVT management and union leaders, and despite much management scepticism, the cooperative were given until the following April to acquire the plant.

The agreement took eight weeks to draft, both sides blaming the other for the delay, by which time NVT and the proposed cooperative faced a number of problems. The affair had drained NVT's working capital, especially as the country was faced with a three–day working week resulting from petrol shortages and a miners' strike. Workers' redundancy money to be used to buy the company was largely spent on living expenses, the company was unable to supply working capital and the government was unwilling to underwrite the exercise. The plan was saved during the General Election campaign of February 1974 when the cooperative agreed to lift the blockade in return for first option on Meriden's assets.

The election of a new Labour government resulted in the reorganization of the DTI. A newly created Department of Industry, headed by Labour left–wingers Benn and Heffer, resulted in increased sympathy

Continued from previous page

for Meriden, backed by an ideology that opposed closures on financial grounds only. Benn proposed further public funding of the cooperative. Meanwhile the blockade continued and NVT obtained a court injunction. The union refused to take action until the government funded the enterprise. However, Benn used his personal influence over the workers, the blockade was lifted and the injunction was not served.

The cooperative appeared to be launched with government financial backing and the appointment of a politically sympathetic manager. The scene now shifted to Small Heath, whose workers opposed the plan, demanding that Meriden's products be sold by NVT, and that jobs be secured with government funding at their plant. Such opposition was grounded in the growth of Meriden at the expense of Small Heath when both were owned by BSA, the lack of solidarity shown by Meriden workers when job losses occurred at Small Heath, and the fact that the recent blockade had seriously affected operations at Small Heath. The Small Heath workers threatened their own work–in and blockade.

The government asked NVT to prepare a three factory plan, but at the same time launched the cooperative with a grant of £5 million. The new NVT plan estimated the need for additional government financial backing to the tune of £12–15 million. The Small Heath workers refused to agree unless job guarantees were made and the investments were made in their plant.

In December 1974, the Meriden cooperative reinstated its blockade and NVT continued to lose money. The managing director of NVT blamed government intervention, and in particular the conflict between economic and ideological motives, from preventing him taking action to solve what he saw as a domestic industrial dispute.

(*Source:* Sandberg, 1984)

observing it and in measuring its effect. We can only make deductions based upon open, formally–reported attempts to influence. The business community tends to be secretive and many attempts to influence government policy are undoubtedly covert and informal. Nonetheless the business community represents an important source of revenue via taxation and borrowing to enable the state to fund its activities, and for this alone constitutes an important political lobby.

We have suggested that, for the most part, firms tend to be reactive rather than proactive as far as the state is concerned and seem more concerned to predict changes in the political environment than to initiate those changes themselves. In this way the tobacco manufacturers predicted increased government regulation of their industry and took measures both to diversify and to transfer attention to growing Third World markets. The same companies reacted successfully to increased restrictions on tobacco advertising by expanding their interests in sport sponsorship to maintain a high public profile. Some companies, of course, are more successful than others in resisting state intervention. Multinationals can use their protected status as members of another sovereign state to limit the extent of intervention in those countries in which they operate, and by transferring funds from country to country can minimize tax liabilities. The Swiss pharmaceutical company Hoffman–la Roche successfully defended itself against the probings of the British Monopolies Commission in 1971 on the grounds that the British government had no legal right of access to information belonging to a Swiss company. The case was considerably hampered by a lack of vital financial information. (For a fuller account of this case see Stopford *et al.*, 1980.)

Real pressure group activity exists where the business deliberately attempts to control the political environment in which it operates. Thomas (1982) has classified business pressure groups into four types.

☐ Sector groups such as trade associations.
☐ Professional groups like the British Medical Association and the Royal Institute of British Architects.
☐ Geographical or Area groups such as chambers of commerce.
☐ 'Peak' groups which are national bodies representing the above, like the Confederation of British Industry.

Such groups operate by lobbying government bodies to secure some kind of advantage or to protect themselves from what they see as unfair competition. Thus the fishing industry in both Britain and the rest of Europe is persistently lobbying for increased protection through the extension of territorial waters.

Not all attempts to influence the state are the products of group pressure. We have already seen the influence of the multinational corporation, and the major firms in any country will make some attempt at influencing government policy and may even be consulted. Individuals too represent an important channel of influence. Many references are made to the 'old boy network' that operates in government and business circles. Several firms take more direct action by enlisting the services of a member of parliament on the board of directors.

In recent years a number of firms have emerged, which operate as professional lobbying consultants. By 1988 there were forty such firms operating in Britain. Clients include local authorities who wish to influence government policy on the dumping of nuclear waste and are resisting proposals to create nuclear waste sites in their areas, and companies such as Britannia Airways, whose management has sought to influence the government's allocation of routes into Heathrow and Gatwick Airports.

We can see that businesses attempt to influence the state in a variety of ways; through personal influence, by gaining media coverage for their views, by taking out expensive advertisements, by hiring consultants, and by submitting letters to the press, often enlisting the support of other interested parties. The timing of such attempts to influence can be crucial. In 1987 two studies emerged with the expressed intention of influencing government policy on the training of managers. The publication of both reports coincided with a general election campaign with a substantial loss of impact.

The European Economic Community

So far in this section we have focussed on the way the state exerts its influence over the business community and vice versa. The EEC operates as a supranational body which increases the complexity of the interaction between the state and business. Britain became a member of the EEC in 1973. The advantages for businesses at the time seemed attractive. The European market was growing while exports to commonwealth countries were in decline. Protectionism was sought both against a buoyant Japanese export trade and in response to increasing protectionism on the part of the USA. In addition, the growing Eurocurrency market was seen as a more attractive proposition than a dollar–dominated economy.

Businesses have been influenced by a certain harmonization that has taken place in company law, employment law, accounting practice, taxation, and the role of financial institutions. There has been significant cooperation over policies concerning industrial development, regional aid, and environmental protection. In the same way that business interests lobby national governments, attempts are made in influence EEC policy.

There would appear to be two major problems for businesses in dealing with the EEC. The first concerns the bureaucracy and somewhat protracted decision–making mechanisms of the Community. The second concerns the conflict of interests between nation states and the EEC which both inhibits decision–making and can cause uncertainty for some firms. In 1987 the merger of Britain's two largest airlines, British Airways and British Caledonian, was sanctioned by the British government, but challenged by the EEC, under pressure from the airlines in other members' countries.

Technology

Technology tends to be a somewhat mystical concept, no more so than when we speak of 'new technology' and 'high technology', overused and underdefined phrases. We hope to shed some light on what technology represents and where it stands in relationship to the firm in its environment.

The concept is popularly used to imply some form of process, invariably machinery–based, so we think of lathes, assembly lines, computers, and cash dispensers. In this way technology represents the application of science and engineering for use in business. However, technology not only refers to the artefacts themselves, but also to the way they are used and the theories governing their application. Human knowledge is therefore an essential ingredient of technology. We often distinguish between manufacturing firms according to the nature of the product, especially its constituent materials and its level of sophistication. We can therefore speak of material and product technology. On a much broader scale we distinguish between societies according to their sum total of knowledge and skills, and the application of these for the benefit of that society. This too is known as technology. From a business perspective we can therefore speak of technology as the application of available knowledge and skills to create and use materials, processes and products.

Technology is closely associated with production systems, representing

KEY CONCEPT 2.3

TECHNOLOGY

Technology is a broad concept referring to the application of available knowledge and skills to create and use materials, processes and products. Technology is often accorded a dominant role in business and is often viewed as determining products, processes, organisation structure and the individual's attitude to work. Whilst there are situations where the prevailing technology is undoubtedly influential, it is the product of human endeavour and many managers do have a choice.

New technology refers to the application through computers of miniaturized electronic circuitry to process information thereby giving managers greater potential flexibility in and control over work operations. *Information technology* links new technology with telecommunications to enhance the quantity, quality and speed of transmission.

both an input and a transformation device. It is also central to the process of innovation. These concepts are developed further in Chapters 5 and 6. In this section we look at more general issues in the way technology and business interact, and focus on the issue of 'new technology'.

Technology: determinant or choice?

A classic view of technology is that it exists as an environmental constraint which becomes the dominant feature of all businesses. Firms operate within certain technological imperatives which shape not only the products and the processes they use, but the structure of the organization, relations between people, and individual job satisfaction. Such a view can be found in the work of Joan Woodward (1965) and Robert Blauner's classic but flawed sociological study of alienation (1964). Galbraith (1972), too, painted a picture of markets being dominated by technological considerations rather than consumer choice.

Woodward in particular has been very influential, her classification of small batch, mass, and process production featuring in most textbook on management and organization since the 1960s, this book being no exception (Chapter 6 has a more detailed description of these three types). To Woodward, technology not only determined organization structure, but the relationship between individual departments and the focus of each business. In small batch firms, product development and technical sales were the key issues; in mass production organizations, fragmentation led to tensions between departments, a source of potential conflict; in process organizations, once the system has been created, high volume sales become the key issue. The relationship between technology and structure was, according to Woodward, crucial to the success of a business. In her study of manufacturing firms in South East Essex she found that the most successful firms financially were the ones which conformed to the organizational type most appropriate for their technology.

Joan Woodward viewed technology as a determinant of both organization structure and the range of possible strategy alternatives. Woodward has been labelled a contingency theorist, yet, as we saw in Chapter 1, the contingency approach puts forward a view of business whereby activities at the level of the firm result from the inter–relationship of a number of variables such as technology, the behaviour of competitors, the role of the state and so on. The end result is supposedly strategic choice for the individual manager following from an analysis of relevant variables. Woodward's view of technology would appear to give the manager no choice at all. Technology is dominant and managers fail to adapt to it at their peril.

We offer two challenges to this view of technology. Firstly we view technology as an element of strategic choice, and secondly look briefly at its relationship with organizational size, an issue taken up again in the next chapter.

We suggested earlier that technology has a certain mystical quality determining the structure and processes of business as the climate and weather determine agriculture. The knowledge, skills, artefacts and processes that make up technology are, unlike the weather, products of the kind of people who operate technological systems. The assembly line is not a technological imperative, but a device created to satisfy the pressures of mass markets and a product of the foresight to entrepreneurs like Ford and the skill of designers who made the process work. Viewed in this way, technology is not a determinant of business, rather a product of the way managers respond to other environmental influences. Furthermore, the kind of technology employed by businesses may be a matter of strategic choice. The application of socio–technical systems analysis offers managers the possibility of changing the prevailing technology to suit the needs of their own particular workforce and the prevailing social situation in which they operate.

Another challenge to the notion of an all–pervasive technology is offered by those who champion size as a more influential variable than technology (for example Hickson *et al.*, 1969). Studies such as these conclude that technology may well be an important determinant of the structure and work patterns in smaller plants, but as firms increase in size, it is size itself which becomes the more dominant influence. We examine the variable of size more fully in the next chapter.

Whilst we cannot afford the space for a full academic debate on the role of technology, nor offer a complete critique of contingency and socio–technical systems theory, we may conclude that the relationship between technology and business is highly complex, certainly involving the inter–relationship of other variables like size, and one which cannot be reduced to a simple notion of determinism. A good illustration of this complexity is provided in Chapter 5. Using Rothwell's illustration of the development of railways, we conclude that innovation is neither technology–led nor market–led, but a complex inter–relationship of these and other variables, such as the availability of finance and cheap labour (Rothwell and Zegveld, 1982).

New technology

New technology represents yet another elusive and imprecise term, used in a variety of different ways. In this book we take it to refer to the application through computers of miniaturized electronic circuitry to process information. We therefore find 'new technology' in a variety of business and non–business settings. In banking and finance, it has enabled money markets all over the world to be linked with instant access to information and especially market changes. The speed with which changes can be registered with the subsequent speed of response has been cited by some as a major contributory factor behind steep stock market falls in all major markets during the latter part of 1987. In retailing, 'electronic point of sale systems' (EPOS) provide instant information on sales trends, cash flows and stock levels. In manufacturing, computer–controlled machines, robotics, and entire computerized flexible manufacturing systems have greatly enhanced a firm's response to changing market demands and improved product quality. In the office, the introduction of word–processing systems can greatly speed up typing operations, especially where large numbers of standard letters are involved. The case of Surrey County Council, Case 2.2, focuses on some of the advantages of new technology in an office setting.

The concept of new technology is often linked to that of information technology. The above illustration from banking and finance shows how miniaturized electronic circuitry has been combined with developments in telecommunications to broaden the information–processing capacities of a single computer system.

Child (1984b), gives us some clues to the popularity of new technology for businesses in the 1980s, in that it offers the following.

☐ The opportunity of reducing operating costs through the reduction in manning levels and the relatively cheap price of many computer systems.
☐ Increased efficiency through improved information and diagnostic systems with speedier operation and relatively low energy costs of many systems.
☐ Improved quality in both system operation and the outputs.
☐ Improved management control through the provision of immediate and consistently accurate information.

To these advantages of Child's we might add improved service to the user and consumer. There are however a number of problems which may be created by the introduction of new technology. While desktop computers and word–processors can be relatively cheap labour–saving devices for the office, the introduction of entire manufacturing systems based on new technology can be prohibitively expensive. In general terms, the introduction of new technology in the office incurs much lower costs than in manufacturing. We have made reference to the use of computer control, robotics and flexible manufacturing systems in Chapter 6. Likewise the

CASE 2.2	In the early 1980s, Surrey County Council set up a centralized word-processing unit to undertake much of the work done by existing typing pools in a number of different departments. The council had two main stated objectives.
SURREY COUNTRY COUNCIL	

Continued from previous page

☐ The centre was designed to meet user needs more effectively than previous systems. After consultation with department heads as part of a two year planning process, work systems were introduced which included the standardization of text layout; the creation of a centralized file of standard letters and paragraphs; the facility to combine reports emerging from a number of different sources into one document; and the creation of small work teams each specializing in a particular aspect of the council's work.

☐ The council wished to create a more satisfying work environment, and consultations were held with other local authorities, ergonomics experts, union representatives, and the staff likely to be involved. Apart from the obvious attention to the hardware and software elements of the system, consideration was given to the physical nature of the work environment and the way work was organized. Five offices were combined into one large open–plan room. Attention was paid to lighting and work station arrangement; rest areas were provided; and the noisy print room was separated from the main work area. The creation of small specialist teams was intended to give operators a greater identification with the work and a closer relationship with users than had been the case hitherto under the typing pool system. Within this specialization the intention was that there would be flexibility of operation in dealing with urgent items and the boring task of printing out was rotated among the operators.

Whilst the system was being set up, negotiations were held with the Trade Union involved, NALGO. The union's wish for a comprehensive agreement covering all aspects of new technology was rejected by management. An agreement was reached on the introduction of the word–processing unit, including provisions for no compulsory redundancies and the involvement of NALGO in all matters pertaining to redeployment and on the health and safety issues of the word–processing systems.

The new centre was staffed using existing typists. The main selection criteria seemed to be desire on the part of the typists themselves to retrain as word–processor operators. Fifty per cent of the workforce opted for retaining, and all had the option of a return to their old typing jobs if things did not work out.

The benefits of the new system were estimated by Surrey Council to be worth £20 000 a year and comprised the following.

☐ A much quicker turn–round of work, particularly on standard items.
☐ An improved quality necessitating less time in checking and correcting.
☐ A closer relationship between operator and user with a clearer identification of priorities and a better understanding of user needs.
☐ More flexible working allowing peaks of work to be smoothed and priorities to be dealt with.
☐ Increased job satisfaction among the staff involved.

(*Source:* Smith, 1982)

problems of skills–training and industrial relations are dealt with in Chapter 8. Students seeking information on these aspects are advised to refer to the relevant parts of these chapters. The one area where there is considerable controversy is the impact of new technology on labour, and it is to this we now turn.

New technology and labour

There would appear to be three perspectives on the impact of new technology on labour. Firstly we have the kind of view associated with such writers as Braverman (1974). New technology is seen as a deskilling agent reducing the amount of discretion an individual has over his job, at the same time increasing management control over both work process and the worker. The labour force has been reduced with the greatest effects of both deskilling and job losses being felt by skilled craft workers. The second perspective offers an optimistic scenario. New technology is seen as creating new opportunities for the workforce in the form of new and different types of labour with opportunities for existing workers to learn new skills. The third perspective is also optimistic, viewing new technology as a liberating device, eliminating the need for human labour in repetitive, dangerous or unpleasant tasks. The evidence supporting these three perspectives is mixed. We will view the effect on the numbers employed, on the type of jobs involved, and on the content of those jobs.

In terms of the numbers employed, the introduction of new technology in manufacturing industry has resulted in some job losses (Daniel, 1987). Predictions of actual numbers vary but most studies stress that actual losses occur mostly in lower–skilled jobs and are generally fewer than envisaged. A survey of the period 1981–3 estimated a net loss of 34 000 jobs but at the same time stressed that this represented only 5% of all job losses in manufacturing (Northcott and Rogers, 1984). This view is reinforced by Daniel (1987). He acknowledges the difficulty of isolating the impact of new technology and claims that its impact on job losses is much less than other forms of change, notably declining markets. He also found that actual dismissals were very rare and that reductions were generally met by redeployment, early retirement and (in some cases highly attractive) voluntary redundancy schemes. In the service sector, predicted job losses have not occurred. The introduction of new technology has been used to increase productivity and provide an improved service retaining existing employment levels or, in the case of banks, by providing new types of customer service requiring more, not fewer staff (Williams, 1984). The study by Daniel (1987) found that the use of computers and word–processors in offices led to a general increase in staff.

The impact of new technology varies greatly according to the type of job. In general, the demand for unskilled labour has fallen whilst that for skilled labour has risen. Far from causing mass unemployment, this has led to job shortages in some areas, notably computing, and renewed attempts to raise skill levels through training opportunities (Chapter 8). This uneven impact has in some cases led to a transfer of skills from one group of workers to another. Wilkinson (1986) points out that the introduction of the computer control of manufacturing equipment (known as 'numerical control' and 'computerized numerical control') has shifted the skill from the craft jobs on the shop floor to the computer programming skills of the office. There are variations within manufacturing industry; Northcott and Rogers (1984) found that where microprocessors were part of the manufacturing process then job losses resulted, but in those industries which used microprocessors as part of the product, then job gains were made. The same study found that the introduction of new technology generally called for more flexible skills and work practices.

The debate about job numbers is matched by that concerning job content. The implication of the point made by Wilkinson in the last paragraph is that for *some* shopfloor workers deskilling has taken place. However, the PSI survey from 1980–4 concluded that on balance advanced technology has enriched the jobs of those affected in both manual and office settings, with greater possibilities being afforded the latter group. In deference to Braverman the survey does make the distinction between enhanced satisfaction in terms of job content, and reduced autonomy through the centralization of management control. In manufacturing, automation has greatly enhanced the work environment of jobs like paint–spraying. In the office the use of word–processors has reduced the drudgery of typing numerous addresses. Nevertheless the benefits derived through the introduction of such advanced systems can be offset by the cost in manufacturing, and by the time taken to encode information in the office, before such benefits can accrue.

The main point to be taken from all the studies is that new technology should not be viewed deterministically. Its impact is based on a number of different factors including the nature of the product and service, the type of organization involved, the management strategy employed, and the attitude of trade unions and employees. The case of Surrey County Council highlights a number of these points. In this case, the introduction of word–processing was carried out in the context of introducing new methods of working through the introduction of work teams; the union was involved in the planning process; and the employees themselves were largely self–selecting.

We end this section on new technology by raising two related and fundamental issues.

Firstly we may conclude that the job losses arising directly from the introduction of new technology are much less than originally envisaged and must be viewed in the context of job losses resulting from other causes, and in the light of job gains in skilled occupations and service industries. Three notes of caution have been sounded.

☐ Whilst there has been a transfer of labour from the manufacturing to the service sector, it remains to be seen how long this will continue (Wilkinson, 1986).
☐ New technology is generally associated with growth industries. Rather than focus on job losses perhaps we should be more concerned about the lack of job gains (Daniel, 1987).
☐ In terms of job losses the hardest hit group has been the low–skilled

workers. Since female labour is over–represented in such jobs, the introduction of new technology may have a significant impact on un-employment levels among women workers (Williams, 1984).

Secondly the point has been made that whatever the effect upon labour through the introduction of new technology, the failure to embrace it will be much more wide–ranging (Williams, 1984, Wilkinson, 1986). Williams writes as follows.

> if the United Kingdom introduces new technology more slowly than other industrialised nations, there will be a real danger of job losses through declining competitiveness without the wider benefits which new technology can bring.
>
> (Williams 1984, p 210)

Labour

Labour interacts with business through the workings of the labour market and through the activities of trade unions. Aspects to consider are the changes in both the level and nature of employment and the role played by trade unions in the operation of business. The labour factor itself interacts with other elements in our environment, so levels of employment are also affected by state intervention and the introduction of new tech-nology. The type of employment in a particular labour market is a product of these and cultural factors. Firms themselves influence the workings of the labour market through various management strategies of recruitment, training and payment. Variations in management strategy also account for the way different companies handle issues of industrial relations. In this section we will look at two aspects of labour; employment trends, and the power of trade unions in influencing management decisions. A more detailed discussion of personnel and industrial relations strategies may be found in Chapter 8.

Employment trends

We have seen elsewhere in this chapter that changes in the economy have significant effects on both the type and levels of employment. The changes affecting Britain, and indeed many other industrialized nations, may be summarized as follows.

☐ In the 1960s and 1970s considerable job losses were experienced in the primary sector (mining, agriculture, fishing etc.). During that period the work force was cut by one half, although, largely through mechani-zation, its share of total output was increased.

☐ The process of de–industrialization has led to considerable job losses in the manufacturing sector, the workforce falling by over 3 million since the early 1960s.

☐ Job gains have been experienced in the tertiary sector of the economy, particularly in the financial sector, catering, the professions and pro-fessional services.

1913	23%	Density = Trade union membership as
1920	45	a percentage of the working
1933	22	population.
1945	38	
1964	44	
1974	50	
1979	55	
1983	50	
1985	46	

Sources: Price and Bain, 1983, *Department of Employment Gazette*

Figure 2.3 Trade Union density, 1913–85.

☐ Many changes in the nature of employment are attributable to changes in technology. References to this are made throughout this book and aspects of new technology have been dealt with earlier in this section.
☐ There is some evidence that firms in this country and elsewhere are following the Japanese practice of establishing a dual labour market comprising a trained core of employees supported by workers on a less permanent basis. Several firms already express a preference for part–time employees. (The Orlake Records case in Chapter 6 illustrates this.)

Trade unions

Trade unions are formally organized groups of employees with the aims, among others, of job protection, the improvement of pay and conditions, and the widening of industrial democracy. Such aims often bring unions into conflict with their employers, a conflict normally resolved by a process known as collective bargaining. We will examine first the changing nature of trade union membership before assessing the power unions can use to influence business decisions.

Trade union membership has grown considerably as we see in Fig 2.3. Within this overall growth there have been several changes, summarized as follows.

☐ There are marked variations in union membership in different types of employment. In coal mining, union density has consistently stood at over 90%. A high density can also be found in local government and the engineering industry. Low levels of membership are found in retailing, and hotel and catering.
☐ Through the process of almalgamation the number of unions has declined from 1323 in 1900 to 393 in 1983. These figures mask an even greater concentration. In 1986 the number of unions affiliated to the TUC and carrying the majority of membership stood at eighty–eight (TUC, 1986). The growth of the firm has been matched by the growth of the large trade union. At the peak of membership in the late 1970s, the biggest union, the Transport and General Workers Union, almost topped two million members.

☐ Unions in older–established industries such as coal mining and the railways have suffered large membership losses as employment has declined, whilst union growth has been most marked in the white collar sector and among public employees. More recent membership increases are to be found among part–time workers and female employees of all types.

☐ In the 1980s there has been a marked decline, with a 19% fall in membership between 1979 and 1984, representing 2.3 million members (Bassett, 1986). Figures are not available for 1987, but predictions indicate a much lower density than the 1985 figure. The statistics may hide an even greater decline, since there is always a tendency for membership figures to be presented in the most favourable light.

Union growth and decline have mirrored economic, political, and social changes. Increasing levels of unemployment have not only led to a reduction in trade union membership, but undoubtedly weakened their bargaining power. Two other developments may be noted. Firstly the influence of unions has been further weakened by the dismantling of many tripartite forums, associated with the labour governments of the 60s and 70s, and hence the removal of unions from the political arena and the development of economic policy. Secondly, following the pattern set by American and Japanese multinationals, it is not unusual to find firms with no trade union representing the workforce, or where a union does exist, it operates under single union, no–strike agreements. These strategies are analysed in Chapter 8. Despite this weakening of trade union power there is still a concern that unions often operate against the interests of private property and the public at large. It is to this we now turn.

Trade union power

Any debate about trade union power seems to be based upon assumptions about a balance of power and management's right to manage. At an obvious level trade unions do have influence. For example, wage rates are higher in unionized firms than non–unionized firms in the same industry, and certain groups such as the Fleet Street printworkers have resisted technical change in their industry. The union supporter would doubtless claim that the trade union acts as an important check and balance in management decision–making, preventing management from acting unreasonably and improving the quality of the decisions made.

Some, however, view trade unions as being too powerful, that they disrupt the mechanisms of the free market, particularly by pricing jobs according to bargaining strength rather than demand. This favours only a minority, pricing jobs out of the market and adding to the problems of unemployment. In addition, individual freedoms are challenged by strikes affecting the supply of goods and essential services. The belief is that unions are privileged members of society whose power needs to be curbed. The Employment Acts of 1980 and 1982, and the Trade Union Act of 1984 were introduced to effect such controls. (Those seeking further analysis of this position are referred to Shonfield, 1968, Hayek, 1984, and Conservative Government policy 1979 onwards.)

A trade union is a group of employees who formally come together to achieve mutual goals. Such goals normally include job protection, improving pay and conditions and attempting to influence management decision-making. In the United Kingdom, trade union membership cuts across individual firms and entire industries, although different patterns exist in other countries, notably industrial unions in West Germany and company unions in Japan. There is considerable ideological debate concerning the influence of trade unions in business decisions.

KEY CONCEPT 2.4

A TRADE UNION

This view in turn has been challenged on the basis that unions are only concerned with marginal issues, such as minor changes in rates of pay and conditions, or the resistance of change in highly specific areas. The challenge further argues that unions are relatively unconcerned about wider issues of management control and industrial democracy. By contrast, it is believed that managements wield considerable power, which is actually strengthened by the formal procedures used in dealing with unions; most procedures attempt to protect the staus quo, thereby favouring management. The introduction of formal procedures tends to push the conflict away from its source, away from the traditional basis of union strength, the membership, so that it is dealt with by top management in negotiation with full–time union officials, not involved in the original dispute. (A further analysis of this position may be found in Hyman, 1972, Fox, 1974b, and Goldthorpe, 1974.)

The debate about union power will doubtless run and run, since it is all a question of ideology. Many of the arguments above have their roots in different values and party politics. This influences not only the position taken, but the way facts are selected and interpreted. As with all influences on the management decision–making process, there are insuperable problems of measurement. Even then we have to be content with observing the formal procedures when so much influence is undoubtedly the product of informal communication.

Cultural influences and business

Culture may be defined as that part of human action that is socially as opposed to being genetically transmitted. It comprises ideas through which we perceive and interpret the world, symbols we use to communicate these ideas, and institutions which enable individuals to become socialized and satisfy their needs. Culture is a highly complex subject and interacts with business in three different ways.

☐ Our socialization, the influences which shape our behaviour in a particular social setting, will determine our individual orientations to work.
☐ We tend to see organizations as societies in microcosm, with their own specific cultures and ways of transmitting these cultures to their members. In some companies, like Hewlett–Packard, the creation of a

corporate culture is seen as a priority and a great deal of time, effort, and expenditure is given to induction and training (Case 3.5).

☐ We use culture as an analytical device to distinguish one society from another. Hofstede (1980, 1985) believes that there are significant national differences in the way people approach work and organizations, and that these differences could be explained by reference to four variables.

   ☐ *'Power distance'*, which is the extent to which members of a society accept that power is distributed unequally in organizations.
   ☐ *'Individualism'*, which represents a preference for looking after yourself or your immediate family group.
   ☐ *'Uncertainty avoidance'*, which is the degree to which members of a society feel uncomfortable with uncertainty.
   ☐ *'Masculinity'*, which represents a preference for achievement, assertiveness and material success.

☐ These variables shape the values and hence the behaviour of people operating in work organizations, and enable us to explain differences in the way different countries conduct their business affairs. They may also explain why work systems developed in one country will not work in another. For example, Hofstede reported that American car workers from Detroit working at the Saab–Scania plant in Sweden disliked the work system which placed a great deal of emphasis on group work. The Americans, with the exception of one woman, were much happier with a system which stressed individual achievement.

All these aspects of culture are dealt with in greater length in the organizational behaviour text in this series. We deal with the concept of organizational culture in the next chapter, and focus here on the third meaning of the term, viewing the wider cultural environment as one of the influences which shape business. Culture is of course the most pervasive of our five environmental factors in the model, having an impact on the other four. Factors such as the role of the state, the application of technology, and the orientations of the labour force to their work can all be viewed as being culturally determined. As with the other elements of the model the relationship with business is not just one–way. The way businesses conduct their affairs affects and often changes the particular culture in which they operate; the operation of the multinational corporation in the Third World being a case in point.

Interest in cross–cultural research blossomed in the 1960s following the popularity of the convergence thesis; a claim that the imperatives of industrialization would eventually cause all industrialized liberal democracies to become more like one another. This has been called the 'culture–free' hypothesis, and claims that business organizations the world over have converged on the same dimensions with increasing size, complexity, specialization and formalization (Harbison and Myers, 1959). Undoubtedly, part of this process was the assumption that theories and approaches to management and organization were universal, and that the same recipes (usually American) could be applied irrespective of the cultural context.

KEY CONCEPT 2.5

CULTURE

Culture represents all human activity that is socially, as opposed to being genetically, transmitted. Cultural influences therefore pervade all areas of business life. A particular interest in business is the extent to which we can learn from the business experiences of other cultures and transplant ideas developed by businesses in one culture and use them in a totally different setting. It is this reason that many people have sought to understand the reasons for postwar business growth in Japan and Germany and, in particular, the interest shown in Japanese management methods.

By comparison, the 'culture–specific' hypothesis claims that cultural influences in different societies will result in different styles of organization behaviour and different patterns of organization structure, as well as variations of influence in the business environment, such as the role of the state or trade unions (Granick, 1972).

While convergence as an idea represents a somewhat superficial analysis, its practical implications are that all advanced societies are moving in the same direction and we may therefore learn from the mistakes of others further along the route. The supporters of the 'culture–specific' hypothesis believe that specific aspects of business are especially susceptible to cultural and national influences. Studies have identified the most likely as attitudes to work, management behaviour, organization structure, industrial relations, recruitment and training (Brossard and Maurice, 1976, Child and Kieser, 1979, Sorge and Warner, 1981). If we accept the culture–specific hypothesis then we need to be cautious in our approach to managerial panaceas. Useful ideas and methods may be transplanted but care must be taken to see that they have been adapted to the new cultural setting and that there is an understanding of the supporting conditions needed for their development.

Reality of course never fits neat conceptual explanations. Both our models may be used to explain the rapid emergence of Japan as an industrial nation. Elements of its business organization, mangement techniques and state machinery have been imported from other cultures, while other elements are clearly products of its own cultural past. Its late start to industrialization enabled businesses to learn from the mistakes made in more advanced countries such as Britain, the USA, and West Germany. The specific elements of the Japanese culture undoubtedly gave these ideas a fresh impetus, so much so that the West has in the 1980s become fascinated by Japanese business methods. This is the reason that books on business and management have, since the 1970s, paid homage to the phenomenon we call 'Japanese Management'. This topic has assumed great importance in academic, business and political circles and we devote much of our review to it. For this we make no excuses, for a study of Japanese business and management practices is truly a study of Business in Context, for nowhere is the inter–relationship between business activities, management strategies, organizational culture and environmental factors more clearly illustrated.

In illustrating the relationship between culture and business we examine specific aspects of Britain and West Germany, and offer a cautionary note on the dangers of cross–cultural comparison. We end the chapter with our analysis of Japanese business and management.

The British and business

A popular topic in the 1980s is the search for an explanation of Britain's economic decline (for example, Wiener, 1982 and Gamble, 1985). Wiener uses cultural variables to explain an economic phenomenon. He believes that the British are no good at business because their hearts are not really in it. The prevailing values in Britain are those espoused by the land–owning gentry and as a consequence, business and especially industry are rejected as being representative of something fairly unpleasant. The consequences of this prevailing attitude are that the pursuit of economic gain is half–hearted and talent is directed away from industry. Government and the professions are favoured as occupational routes, capitalists aspire to be land–owning gentry, and the education system is dominated by a public school ethos which shuns science, technology, business and industry. Our half–hearted approach to business is consolidated by leaving management to the sometimes gifted but most times untrained amateur.

While it is not the job of this text to examine contending theories of Britain's economic decline, views such as those expressed by Wiener have a certain appeal. They are easy to understand and focus on easy targets, such as the public school system and the land–owning gentry. However, the hypothesis is highly speculative, difficult to verify and probably represents an exaggerated and idealized view. There is no explanation for the success of British entrepreneurs, the energy which accompanied the industrial revolution, nor the economic growth of the banking and finance industries in the post–war period. While it is true that the best products of our education system tend to be attracted not to industry but to the civil service and the professions, that situation is also true of Japan, a country we tend to hold as our economic role model.

Despite such criticisms of hypotheses such as Wiener's, there are cultural elements which seem to have a significant impact on business. The class structure of this country provides us with greater insights into the relationship between management and workers. Certainly we assume that anyone with the 'right' background and a reasonable level of education can assume managerial responsibilities with no professional qualifications or training, a view taken up in recent reports on the state of management training in this country. On average, a manager in this country will receive one day of formal training per year. Charles Handy has referred to the British view of management as 'something that happens to decent people at a certain stage in their life'. On a more general level, the British labour market has experienced a continuous shortage of technically skilled manpower ever since the last war, despite attempts to remedy the situation through legislation (the Industrial Training Act 1964) and a considerable amount of political rhetoric. A country which appears to take its training more seriously is West Germany and it is to this we now turn.

West Germany: a training ethos

Compared to their British counterparts managers in West Germany are qualified to higher educational levels. Approximately 80% of German managers are graduates, while Britain boasts fewer than 50%. The degrees of German managers are vocationally oriented, with engineering and other technical subjects predominating. Generally the managers better qualified educationally hold the more senior positions in the hierarchy, and have risen through the ranks rather than by switching companies as is the norm in Britain and the USA (Lawrence, 1980, Child et al., 1983). It is quite common to find German managers who have preceded their degree by some kind of technical apprenticeship, and if we include compulsory national service for men, it is understandable that management positions may not be assumed until the age of thirty.

West Germany lays great store by its system of youth training referred to as the 'dual apprenticeship system'. A very high proportion (around 85%) of all school leavers who do not go on to higher education enter a three year apprenticeship across a range of occupations (Casey, 1986). The apprenticeship involves training in a mixture of job–specific and general work skills, with one day a week spent in a specialist vocational college. The scheme has been successful in supplying the labour market with skilled workers that are easy to retrain because of the presence of general work skills and the emphasis on attitude training. The scheme is supported by government, employers, the education system, and trade unions. Not least in this support is that of the trainees themselves, whose acceptance of initially low wages helps fund the scheme. For example, a sixteen–year–old trainee in Germany can expect to receive only 25% of the adult wage for the job, compared to 50% in Britain (Casey, 1986). It is this social acceptance of training costs against likely future benefits that does much to underpin the system. No such ethos exists in Britain, and attempts at introducing youth training schemes have met with a consequent unenthusiastic response.

The difficulties involved in using culture as a variable

Culture remains a fascinating concept but a difficult analytical tool. The following points attempt to give some indication of the difficulties involved.

☐ Many studies which use culture as a central concept tend to define culture in rather broad, generalized terms. In many instances it is a kind of residual variable, a catch–all to explain away differences that cannot be explained by differences in the economy, technology, role of the state, size of the firm and so on.

☐ Comparisons with other countries are often difficult because of the different rules governing the collection of data. Thus, strike statistics are notoriously difficult to compare because different countries use different yardsticks to define and measure a strike.

☐ Cultural comparisons tend to be made from the perspective of one culture only. We may make conclusions about another culture based on our own values. A study of the car industry worldwide showed that

European and US manufacturers outperformed the Japanese on criteria they deemed most relevant; profitability measured by accounting ratios. The Japanese however laid greater store by market penetration and growth, and on these criteria easily outperformed the European and American manufacturers (Bhaskar, 1980).

☐ In many cases language presents a serious barrier to full understanding. Certain concepts do not translate easily. 'Technik' is a central concept to German manufacturing, yet has no direct translation in English.

☐ We have seen that we possess preconceived notions about other cultures, often expressed as stereotypes. These can creep into our analysis and become self–fulfilling prophecies; we see what we expect to see. Our ready acceptance of such stereotypes prevents us from digging more deeply. For instance, an analysis of German management will reveal a much greater formality in superior–subordinate relations than exists in Britain or the USA. We may conclude from this that the Germans have less interest in man–management, when all evidence points towards good working relations existing in German firms.

Japanese business and management

Explaining the heady success of Japanese manufacturing has, in recent years, virtually replaced baseball as our national pastime. The trouble is, however, that American managers cannot agree among themselves on the rules of this new competition, the current score, or even the precise type of game in which they are involved.

(Wheelwright, 1981 p 65)

The quotation by Steven Wheelwright is appropriate for two reasons. Firstly it introduces the notion of Japanese industrial success, and secondly identifies the problems that we in the West have of understanding and interpreting that success. These problems have done little to deter those willing to offer us an explanation. Management literature of the 1980s seems preoccupied with Japan. Serious and popular newspapers alike have jumped on the bandwagon, and television documentaries have followed the fortunes of British recruits to Japanese multinationals as they exchange Newcastle Brown Ale for sake. Despite such exposure, our knowledge of Japanese management, while much greater, appears to have done little for our real understanding. In many respects Endymion Wilkinson's quote is still valid.

I examine the European image of Japan and find it composed of an arsenal of stereotypes founded on the shifting sands of indifference, ignorance, prejudice, and fear, rather than on any effort to seriously understand the Japanese.

(Wilkinson, 1983 p 17)

The stereotypes to which Wilkinson refers have changed dramatically over the years from a manufacturer of cheap, unreliable products, to a menacing military and then economic imperialist, to a currently fashionable view of Japanese management science as the panacea for the ills of western capitalism.

Even allowing for the difficulties of comparing the economies of different nations, it is clear that Japan has emerged in the post-war period as the world's second largest economy behind the USA. There is a widely held view that this is some kind of post–war miracle in which a modern Japanese economy arose from the ashes of a completely devastated country. A similar view is often proffered for West Germany. Indeed, respective accounts of the two countries sometimes vie for the greatest extent of devastation, and hence a claim to the greater 'miracle'. In both cases, the foundations of a strong economy were laid much earlier. Nevertheless, post–war growth has been significant and in Japan's case, particular advances were made in the period 1955–61 (Armstrong *et al.*, 1984). That growth has since slowed dramatically, causing considerable concern to the Japanese. Nevertheless there remains such a fascination in the way that the Japanese organize their business affairs that we will attempt to give just a flavour of the complexity and paradoxes of that area known as Japanese management. We will do this by looking at various explanations that have been offered for Japanese economic success, ending with a brief look at the experience of Japanese firms in Britain.

The various explanations that we will deal with are cultural, political, economic, and organizational in nature. Additionally a more radical explanation will be offered, but first we turn to attempts which focus on the social and cultural background of the Japanese themselves.

Cultural factors

According to Ronald Dore in his excellent book *British Factory — Japanese Factory*, Japan has benefited greatly from the 'late industrialization effect', whereby the diffusion of ideas from advanced industrial societies into totally different settings gives those ideas a new impetus (Dore, 1973). In the case of Japan, Dore believes, the system has developed to permit a culturally conservative society to adjust to rapid technical change. The core values that are often quoted as shaping Japan's particular response to industrialization are 'loyalty', 'dependence', and 'duty' resulting in an importance being attached to vertical relationships. This would explain the Japanese loyalty to the group, be it the country, the family, or their company. Both historically and emotionally Japan is a closed society, due largely to a sense of isolation and a lack of resources. The resulting insecurity has led the Japanese to place more emphasis on bank savings than their counterparts in other industrial nations, and to adapt quickly to changed conditions. When we view these characteristics alongside the core values it may well explain the tendency of the people to give their whole-hearted support, be it to Imperial decree, government decisions, or company initiatives.

The role of the state

Historically the state has always had a significant role in the development of the Japanese economy. The big five companies known collectively as the

'Zaibatsu', and which dominated the Japanese economy in pre–war times, developed with the specific assistance of the government. Their legacy today is in the large holding companies at the heart of the Japanese economy.

A central feature of the state's influence is the role played by the civil service, in particular the two departments known in the west as MITI (Ministry of International Trade and Industry) and MOF (Ministry of Finance). Between them they help coordinate and direct Japan's economic strategy. Specifically, MITI targets those industries that are internationally competitive as in the case of cars and micro–electronics. Industries operating in preferred sectors are offered prime locations, are allowed to expand, receive tax relief on modernization programmes, and MITI ensures that such industries get first priority as far as foreign investment is concerned. The department has been especially active in encouraging cartels, both for purposes of rationalization and for exploiting world trading conditions, both occurring in the case of the shipbuilding industry. As part of this strategy there is marked lack of assistance for those businesses operating in non–designated sectors of the economy.

MOF controls the Bank of Japan, which in turn has significant influence over the twelve major commercial banks and hence the direction of investment. It is important to know that in Japan, banks are the major shareholders in industry and commerce, individual investment playing a very minor role indeed. This system is actively encouraged by the intervention of MOF. Additionally, with MITI, MOF assists in the process of channelling foreign investment to high priority companies, especially when capital is short, and targets Japanese investment abroad, in particular to those areas rich in the kind of natural resources coveted by Japan.

The activities of the civil service take place within a highly stable political framework, the Liberal Democratic Party having held power since 1955. The state in Japan represents a network of influence between politics, the civil service and business, operating a system of targeted development and trade protection at home, with selective investment overseas. Elites within this system tend to circulate; the civil service recruits top graduates from the best universities, the most successful of which tend to move at a later stage in their careers to politics or business. Such relationships are ripe for those who favour conspiracy theory and images have been painted of a mafia style command economy. However, the images do not bear close examination. Conflict exists, not only between business and the state, but also between companies themselves competing for the same markets. The ruling party, the LDP, is far from a cohesive body, and consists of different factions competing for power. The view of a highly directive state is also challenged by the success of industries outside the favoured sectors, such as Hi–Fi, pianos, television manufacture, and above all motorcycles. Nevertheless, the state has played an influential role in the development of the Japanese economy, particularly in accelerating market forces. A legacy of this is the continued dominance by big business, which could well benefit from their influence with MITI and MOF to the detriment of the small business sector.

Economic organization

Duality is the central theme which dominates Japanese economic life. This duality operates both in the organization of the manufacturing sector and in the labour market. Every large firm in Japan uses a large number of smaller firms as subcontractors. For example, Nissan uses 150 different subcontractors within a 50 km radius of its plant at Oppama, with the result that only 30% of the Nissan car is actually manufactured in its own plant; this compares with 40% at Austin–Rover (Hetherington, 1986). Other writers have noted that it is not unusual for a firm employing 1000 workers to have 160 subcontractors (Armstrong *et al.*, 1984). In this way a hierarchy of manufacture is built up, with larger firms subcontracting to smaller and so on. In every case, the relationship between the firm and its supplier is carefully specified, with deliveries being requested not by the week or even day, but by the hour. Furthermore it is quite usual for the purchasing company to get involved in work organization and job design in the subcontractor's factory, often in an attempt to reduce costs and hence the price of supplied parts.

Such a system tends to favour the large corporation, and the Japanese economy is indeed dominated by big businesses operating as giant holding companies controlling a number of (often) highly diversified firms. For example, the Sumitomo Group has divisions dealing with mining, cement, chemicals, electrical goods, and heavy industries; the Mitsubishi Group deals with chemicals, glass, rayon, paper, automobiles, steel, and heavy industries. Additionally, both these groups along with the other large holding companies have banking, insurance and real estate divisions (Sato and Hoshino, 1984). The role of banks as major shareholders has already been mentioned, but here we have a case of banking operating as yet another division of the holding companies. This not only gives such firms access to sources of investment, but places them at the centre of a network of information. The relationship with subcontractors is further cemented in that the bigger firms, often through their banks, are major shareholders in the smaller companies.

As for the labour market, a great deal of publicity has been given to the Japanese concepts of lifetime employment and seniority payment systems. However, such benefits only apply to the *minority* of Japan's workforce and a dual labour market operates. The system works as follows. The labour force is divided into 'permanent' and 'temporary' workers. The 'permanent' workers have tenure and receive the pay and welfare benefits normally associated with Japanese firms, while those classed as temporary workers have no such security, have few employment rights and enjoy none of the benefits of their permanent counterparts. According to such rare accounts as Satoshi Kamata's experience as a temporary worker for Toyota, the lot of the temporary worker is far from idyllic (Kamata, 1983). Precise statistics concerning the proportion of workers in each category are difficult to obtain, but various accounts estimate the 'permanent' group to represent around 35% of the total workforce, although this varies considerably according to the size and nature of the organization. A major firm like Nissan will have 'permanent' employees in the majority, perhaps around 75%, the remainder being made up of workers who are classed as temporary. Nissan's major subcontractors will likewise have a large proportion of 'permanent' staff, but the further down the subcontracting hierarchy the proportion of 'temporary' workers rises sharply, many smaller firms having no 'permanent' workers whatsoever. No farm workers and very few women in Japan have 'permanent' status.

We will look at the negative aspects of this dual system later. From the point of view of the country's economy there would appear to be some advantages to this economic organization, not least of which is a built–in elasticity to cope with changing demand. A firm like Nissan will cope with increased demand by taking on more temporary workers and either increasing its number of subcontractors or placing greater demands on its existing supplies. Reduced demand will be met by lay–offs of temporary workers and a corresponding reduction in orders to suppliers. The system would appear to succeed because of the privileged position and economic strength of the larger companies and the ready supply of temporary workers, a proportion of whom aspire to 'permanent' status, and a proportion who are basically farm workers seeking seasonal work.

Organization style and management strategies

A number of aspects of Japanese company life have been identified by various writers as playing a significant role in the economic growth of Japan (for example, Dore, 1973, Pascale, 1978, Ohmae, 1982, Sethi *et al.*, 1984). These aspects are identified below.

Personnel policies. These are often the most publicized aspects of Japanese firms, but as we have seen, they only really apply to about a third of the workforce. They include lifetime employment, pay based on seniority, an attention to employee welfare, and fringe benefits such as company housing and holidays. Recruitment and selection tend to be rigorous even for comparatively low level employees. As we will show in the case study of Nissan, the selection of supervisors is a highly competitive affair, candidates being subjected to a battery of tests and strenuous interviews. The selection process for all workers is followed up by an equally rigorous training programme where employees are expected to master most aspects of a particular process. The emphasis is clearly on flexibility, reinforced, in most cases by an absence of organization charts and job descriptions.

Industrial relations. All Japanese trade unions are company unions, and employees have no choice as to which union they join. Not suprisingly, plant level industrial relations are comparatively harmonious and are more akin to joint consultation than collective bargaining. Disputes do occur at national level, but they tend to be highly predictable affairs based on annual pay negotiations (referred to as the 'Spring Offensive') or about the size of the autumn bonus. Since the early 1980s the unions have been increasingly opposed to Japanese investment overseas, but carry little political clout to affect policy.

Decision–making. 'The process of communication within a Japanese organization is very much akin to the mating dance of penguins' (Sethi *et al.*, p 37). As this quotation implies there is considerable ritual and a great deal of consultation. Much attention has been focussed on consensus and collective decision–making ('ringi sei'), when, in practice there would seem to be considerable initiatives and decisions taken by top management alone. However, the consultation process ('nemewashi') is very important and large numbers of workers do in fact participate. The consultation process is part of a corporate culture, which is typified by an absence of class divisions and which is reinforced by the trappings of egalitarian society, including company uniforms for all, compulsory exercises for all at the start of the day, and a sharing of the same canteen facilities.

Production orientation. For many, the attention paid to the production function is the key to Japanese manufacturing prowess and export success (White and Trevor, 1983, Hayes and Wheelwright, 1984). Whilst attention has been focused on specific techniques such as 'Quality Circles' and 'Just–In–Time', the essence is almost certainly a meticulously planned, integrated system, in which attention to quality plays a central role. To this we must add an orientation to product innovation which pays particular attention to the needs of the customer. A pivotal figure in this production system is the first line supervisor, which perhaps explains the attention paid to his selection. The production orientation is supported by a system which places considerable emphasis on rules, regulations and discipline. Dore's comparison of Hitachi with English Electric noted, in the Japanese case, the emphasis placed on attendance and timekeeping and the willing participation by Japanese employees in the widely–found practice of sacrificing holidays in favour of the company (Dore, 1973). A more detailed review of Japanese production methods can be found in Chapter 6.

The result of these organizational features and management strategies has been the creation of the firm as a community and a high level of identification with the company on the part of individual employees. There is however an alternative explanation for Japan's economic growth.

Japanese management: an alternative view

The cultural, political, administrative, economic, organizational and strategic factors identified above have all been cited as explanations for Japanese economic superiority over the West. Kamata's view of life as a temporary worker for Toyota, with accounts of production speed–ups, excessive overtime and the oppression of the bachelor dormitory paints an entirely different view (Kamata, 1983). Other analyses, some of them Marxist in their approach, conclude that Japan's economic success is based on carefully planned exploitation (especially Armstrong *et al.*, 1984).

This exploitation takes several forms. Firstly, the 'temporary worker' is exploited in terms of his lack of security and must bear the brunt of any recession; a case could even be made for the exploitation of the 'permanent' employee through an employment system which ties him to a single employer. Secondly, the larger firms exploit the dependent position of the smaller firms through the system of satellite subcontractors. Thirdly, we have the suppression of independent trade unions which render plant–level collective bargaining somewhat meaningless. The particular system of company unions has its origins in a four–month dispute in 1953 involving workers at the Nissan car factory. The dispute led to a lock–out by mangement that was backed by the major shareholder, the bank, and the USA authorities. The stipulation for a return to work was the acceptance by the workforce of a company union with the motto 'Those who truly love their union love their company' (Hetherington, 1986). Other companies took Nissan's lead and set up their own unions. Finally it has been argued that the economic system exploits the cultural characteristics fo the Japanese people themselves, namely their loyalty, discipline, and commitment to national goals.

It is difficult for someone brought up and operating in a particular culture and value system to draw accurate conclusions about the exploitation that is supposed to occur in an entirely different cultural context. More accounts like Kamata's would be welcome, especially since it dates from the early 1970s.

We do however have experience of Japanese methods in the United Kingdom through the operation of companies such as Nissan, Sony, and YKK, many of which have been manufacturing from British bases for a number of years. It is to this aspect we now turn.

Japanese firms in Britain

A study of Toshiba Consumer Products (UK) Ltd revealed specific features about their operation including the absence of job descriptions at any level, a periodic review of the company plan with *all* employees, a much greater application of planning techniques than is normally associated with a British firm, with a much closer relationship between manufacturing and sales, and a corresponding attention to consumer needs, product design and quality (Taylor, 1984). Whilst there was no company union, there was recognition of a single union only (the EETPU) and an agreement for pendulum arbitration, a system referred to in Chapter 8, and in the case study which follows.

A series of studies of Japanese manufacturing plants and financial concerns in the United Kingdom concluded that many features associated with Japan, namely a stable, highly committed workforce, complete co-operation in change, and low levels of conflict, simply do not exist over here (White and Trevor, 1983). Nevertheless these Japanese firms do exhibit higher levels of productivity than their British counterparts. In achieving these levels of productivity, White and Trevor found that typically Japanese employment practices such as the lifetime employment and the seniority principle were not used, but that great attention was paid to selection and training. They found no real difference in levels of employee satisfaction, but the real distinction lay in certain work practices. These were a highly organized approach with an emphasis on fine detail, the elevation of quality as the top priority and a much greater sense of discipline throughout the various organizations. They noted a quite exceptional acceptance of management authority, which tended to be more favourable the greater the Japanese presence, almost as if employees were more willing to legitimize the position of Japanese managers than their British counterparts. White and Trevor attributed this to the greater egalitarianism displayed by the Japanese and the greater willingness on the part of the Japanese manager to get involved in the operations. As the authors note: 'The predominant response of employees was one of approval and often some pride at being part of such an exceptional effort' (White and Trevor, 1983 p 130).

Studies of the introduction of Quality Circles in British factories tend to reinforce this view (Bradley and Hill, 1983, Collard and Dale, 1985). It is not the shop–floor employee who is resistant to 'Japanese' methods, but the reasons for the failure of Quality Circles is often attributable to a mixture of management fear and scepticism, resulting in a lack of support on the part of the managers and suspicion on the part of the employees.

The conclusion drawn from such studies is that successful transfer of certain Japanese methods is possible to British institutions. The main elements would appear to be a careful attention to detail in the production process, a greater investment in training and a much more egalitarian approach to management. White and Trevor believe that the essence of the Japanese system shifts the emphasis to micro issues at the shop floor level. In so doing, the system fits in with the prevailing industrial relations culture in Britain.

While the expansion of Japanese multinationals in Britain is part of the general process of the internationalization of the Japanese economy, two additional factors stand out. Firstly, the interest Japanese firms have shown in Britain is seen as a mechanism to circumvent EEC trade restrictions on Japanese imports. This has resulted in many joint ventures between British and Japanese firms, as between Austin–Rover and Honda in the development and manufacture of the Rover 800 series, and the Triumph Acclaim before that. Secondly, those Japanese firms that have established themselves in Britain have tended to favour development areas where government grants and other advantages are available. There is however an alternative and perhaps more cynical interpretation that has more to do with the exploitation hypothesis, previously mentioned. The development areas, such as the North East of England and Scotland, have high levels of unemployment. It is undoubtedly much easier to ensure the compliance of a work force and the cooperation of trade unions, even to somewhat alien work practices, when the alternative is long–term unemployment. There is no doubt that the situation also favours the company in its relationship with its local suppliers. When suppliers are struggling to survive in a harsh economic climate, it is much easier for the purchaser to negotiate contracts that are highly favourable to him in terms of price and delivery.

However, there is evidence in the North East of England that many of the workers taken on by Japanese firms are neither unemployed nor refugees from the most depressed industries such as mining and shipbuilding (Tighe, 1986). There is also little evidence to suggest that the Japanese are treating English suppliers any differently from those in Japan, where exacting cost, quality and delivery requirements are the norm. Moreover there is significant evidence that Japanese companies are giving customers what they require, with a growing trend towards the customization of products for local markets.

Further insights into the Japanese in Britain may be found in the Nissan case later in this chapter.

Japanese management: some conclusions

The specific nature of Japanese culture, state intervention, the subcontracting system, the dual labour market, management strategies and practices, company unions, and the exploitation hypothesis have all been used individually or in combination to explain the post–war growth of the Japanese economy. All contain elements that are highly plausible, and in all probability the real explanation is a complex interaction of all factors, with some factors being more important than others at particular times.

Many in the west, including business leaders, politicians and some academics would like to reject the cultural hypothesis, since this offers us little hope of practical gain, unless we all become Japanese. Interest in Britain centres on two phenomena.

☐ The expansion of Japanese multinationals, the subsequent employment of British workers, and the introduction of Japanese management practices.
☐ The use of 'Japanese management' practices by management in British firms.

The conclusion drawn by such writers as White and Trevor and Hayes and Wheelwright is that there is nothing peculiarly Japanese about the way they run their businesses. The emphasis is on high growth and market penetration; a concern for long–term as opposed to short–term profits; a concern for labour productivity and costs; a concern for quality, employee selection and training; and an emphasis on incremental product improvement. Commitment on the part of employees is based largely on the egalitarianism of factory life, which leads to an acceptance of a highly disciplined regime. The implication is that British firms could follow suit with economically beneficial results.

Three factors temper this enthusiasm. Firstly, the factors mentioned above may well represent excellent management practice, but their successful application in Japan may be due to a supportive state, a particular form of economic organization, and draw upon specific characteristics of the Japanese people. Secondly, such methods have assumed greatest interest in the west at a time of high unemployment and the weakened bargaining position of employees and trade unions. Thirdly, the system would seem to be under threat in Japan itself. The world economic recession and competition from Korea and Taiwan have led to rising unemployment, resulting in early retirement programmes and redundancy of some 'permanent' workers. At the other end of the scale, there are labour shortages created by the introduction of labour mobility in some high–technology sectors. All these factors lead to a weakening of the ties that bind the Japanese worker to his company. Increasingly in Japan the system is challenged by women, the older and younger workers.

Undoubtedly time will tell whether the phenomenon we call Japanese management represents a new era in management strategy and employment practices, is simply exploiting favourable conditions, or is merely yet another passing management fad.

Nissan, the major Japanese car manufacturer, produced its first British–built car at its plant in Tyne and Wear in April 1986. The firm was coveted by several county councils seeking to stimulate business and employment in their areas, and competition to attract a major company like Nissan was fierce.

The plant uses robots for welding and has a fully automated paintshop, but these are hardly unique features in modern car manufacture. For many the real differences at Nissan lies in its approach to industrial relations and its personnel policies.

Acknowledging the traditional labour relations problems with the car industry in Britain, and a strike frequency of over seven times the norm for manufacturing industry, the company on the advice of personnel director, Peter Wickens, opted for the recognition of a single union only. The policy alternatives of either a non–union shop or the recognition of several unions were felt to be recipes for antagonism and chaos respectively. The competition for union recognition among Trade Unions hungry for members was considerable. Nissan represented a potential of 2700 new members when most Trade Unions were losing members at an alarming rate. Recognition was eventually achieved by the Amalgated Union of Engineering Workers (AUEW), and a deal embracing terms and conditions of employment was signed between the union and company representatives before production started in 1985. The deal was unique both for the car industry and for the AUEW.

The agreement between the union and the company lists certain key principles upon which it is based. These include mutual trust and cooperation; a commitment to quality, productivity, and competitiveness, using modern technology; a need for change and flexibility to maintain the competitive edge; a belief in open and direct communications. Most significantly there is an adherence to the avoidance of any action which interrupts the continuity of production, and the union's recognition of management's right to make the final decision in the best interests of the company.

These principles have been reinforced by several mechanisms. Firstly, terms and conditions form part of a two–year agreement, which is binding on both sides and includes a no–strike clause for the duration of the agreement and during any negotiation or arbitration. Secondly, in exceptional circumstances, when agreement cannot be reached ACAS will be called upon to arbitrate, but a straight choice must be made between the two alternatives in a system of pendulum arbitration. Thirdly, negotiations are made between the company and the Works Council, not the Trade Union. The Works Council is made up of elected representatives, each representing part of the plant. Although the election is supervised by the union, representation is open to all employees. In fact one estimate has put union membership at only 18%. As well as negotiating salaries and conditions, the Works Council concerns itself with issues of productivity, quality and planned change.

The personnel practices are also new to the car industry. All em-

Continued over page

CASE 2.3

NISSAN UK

Continued from previous page

ployees are treated as single status, share the same canteen, wear the Nissan blue uniform, and all receive annual salaries paid in equal monthly installments. Employees are not required to clock on and are only asked to clock off when overtime is being worked so that a record may be kept. Workers are paid a guaranteed week of thirty-nine hours. Management has retained the right to review both the clocking on procedure and the guaranteed week in the light of operating experience, and to lay workers off without notice should production be disrupted by industrial action either at Nissan itself or one of its suppliers.

Competition for jobs at Nissan has been high. In an area of 20% unemployment, an estimated 3500 applied for the first twenty-two supervisory positions. An estimated 11 000 applied for the 240 production jobs. Selection processes were exacting. The potential supervisors were all put through a series of psychological tests, whilst the production workers were narrowed down through successive hurdles including pencil and paper aptitude tests and at least two interviews for short-listed candidates. The emphasis was on seeking employees with a strong positive commitment to the goals of the company, thereby reducing future potential conflict. Apart from the management, nearly all recruits were under forty years old, few had previous experience in the car industry and only a minority were unemployed. By comparison, the senior management nearly all had motor industry experience and were recruited from such companies as Ford, Austin Rover and Rolls Royce. In total the company started with three British and four Japanese directors.

Peter Wickens has claimed that Nissan's policies are not peculiarly Japanese, and feels them to be a distillation of American, German, and British as well as Japanese methods. Indeed, he operated similar policies in his previous employment with a North Wales–based American company. Whatever the origins, the novelty of Nissan's approach lies in its single union, no–strike deal and in its insistence on absolute commitment to the goals of productivity, quality and continuity. The approach has formed the basis of its advertising campaign, orchestrated by Saatchi and Saatchi under the slogan, They don't half work.

(*Sources:* Burrows 1966, Tighe 1986)

Summary

In this chapter we have identified five key aspects of the environment, namely the economy, the state, technology, labour and culture. For each of these we have selected issues which highlight the interaction between business enterprises and the environment in which they operate.

The *economy* is viewed as a product of its constituent business activity, as well as exerting considerable influence upon the way businesses operate.

These influences work through resource availability and allocation, international competition, especially via multinational enterprises, the extent of state direction and levels of employment.

The *state* is examined from the perspective of increasing intervention as an employer, a collective provider, an advisor, a legal regulator, and most significantly for business as a demand manager. Business interests for their part attempt to influence government policy through pressure group activity with mixed results. Businesses also interact with supranational bodies such as the EEC.

Technology is viewed as the application of available knowledge and skills to create materials, processes and products. It is viewed both as a constraint and an opportunity as well as a product of innovation by business. New technology is seen as an opportunity for businesses to reduce costs, while increasing the quality of their products and the effectiveness of their service. Evidence concerning its impact on both job content and levels of employment is mixed.

The relationship between business and *labour* is seen through the workings of the labour market and the influence of trade unions. Changes in the economy have resulted in changes in the type and availability of jobs. Trade unions are seen both as a constraint and an aid to management decision–making, but the debate on their ultimate power and influence founders for lack of evidence and the inevitability of ideology.

Culture is viewed as a pervasive factor shaping the entire environment of business. Dominant cultural aspects of society leave their mark upon businesses operating in that society and lead to certain generalizations about the value different societies place upon business. Interest in culture has been stimulated by the prospect of learning from others and transplanting business methods from one society to another, as with the popular pastime of analysing Japanese business methods. This book joins in that pastime by giving its own account of Japanese business. This is not only illustrative of the cultural debate but also represents an extended case of the way businesses in a particular society interact with key elements of that society.

Further reading

The relationship between the economy and business and the role of the state are well treated by P. Armstrong *et al.*, *Capitalism Since World War II* (Fontana, 1982), R. Scase ed., *The State in Western Europe* (Croom Helm, 1980), C. Crouch, *The Politics of Industrial Relations* (Fontana, 1982), R.E. Thomas, *The Government of Business* (Philip Allan, 1982). Although dated, J. Woodward *Industrial Organization: Theory and Practice* (OUP 1965), is a good account of the influence of technology on business organization, while illustrations of the impact of new technology can be found in B. Wilkinson, *The Shopfloor Politics of New Technology* (Heinemann, 1983). Good sources for labour and trade union issues are G.S. Bain ed., *Industrial Relations in Britain* (Basil Blackwell, 1983) and M.P. Jackson, *Trade Unions* (Croom Helm, 1982), whilst a more contemporary account is offered by P. Bassett, *Strike Free* (Macmillan, 1986). An interesting account of the impact of culture on business in Britain can be found in M.J. Wiener *English Culture and the Decline of the Industrial Spirit 1850–1980* (CUP, 1981). Good treatments of Japanese management include R. Dore *British Factory — Japanese Factory* (University of California Press, 1973) and M. White and M. Trevor, *Under Japanese Management: The Experience of British Workers* (Heinemann, 1983).

Discussion

1. In what ways can a business influence its immediate economic environment through its R&D, production, marketing and personnel strategies?

2. Using the illustrations of a) a mass producer of cars, b) a university, and c) a small accountancy practice, examine how a firm interacts with its economic environment at the local, national and international level.

3. To what extent is the state a facilitator and to what extent a constraint in the operation of a business? Using the three illustrations offered above identify how management could influence the state and the directions this influence might take.

4. What reasons can you give for the state's involvement with Norton–Villiers–Triumph (Case 2.1)? What does this case tell us about state intervention in business?

5. Using Case 2.2 of Surrey County Council as a starting point, identify the various types of change that are likely to occur from the introduction of new technology. What opportunities and threats exist for management and the workforce? What problems will be created and how may they be overcome?

6. What changes do you forecast for the 1990s in the labour market in Britain and in the way labour is utilized?

7. Is the British Government in the 1980s justified in introducing laws to restrict the freedom and powers of trade unions?

8. How useful is the concept of culture in explaining the way businesses operate in different countries?

9. To what extent is it both desirable and feasible for Western firms to adopt Japanese methods of business and management?

10. Examine the environmental influences which lay behind Nissan's decision to open a new plant in the North East of England (Case 3.3). What does the case tell us about Japanese management methods?

Organizational aspects of business 3 ‖‖‖‖

In the last chapter we examined aspects of the environment which interact with business. Such aspects constitute the outer level of our model. In this chapter we examine a second level of interaction and influence belonging to the organization itself. We will consider five aspects in our model; goals, structures, size, ownership, and organization culture. Students seeking further exploration of these organizational issues are referred to the companion organization behaviour text in this series.

As with other aspects of our model, there is considerable interaction and overlap between these organizational issues. As well as pointing out the areas of overlap in each individual section, the way that issues relating to goals, ownership, structure and size come together is examined in more detail through the concept of organization culture. In addition, we highlight two specific issues, the public sector and small businesses, both of which illustrate the complex nature of these organizational relationships. The public sector has been chosen since it is a good illustration of the interaction and tensions both within the organizational elements, as well as those operating between the organization and its environment. The distinction between public and private concerns is becoming increasingly blurred, further justifying our focus. The treatment of small business raises contemporary economic and political debates as well as highlighting the very specific nature of business problems found in this sector.

Goals

In this section we shall examine the nature of goals, the purposes they serve and how they emerge. We shall also consider the potential problem arising from a number of different goals operating in the same organization. We often speak glibly of organizations like Marks and Spencer, British Rail, or even our own college as having goals. However, we ought not ascribe behaviour to abstract entities such as organizations. Goals should always be attributable to some person or group. Case 3.1 later in this chapter illustrates the goals of three organizations, two explicitly stated (Sainsbury, the supermarket chain, and Rank Hovis McDougall, the food processors) and the third extracted from the Chairman's statement (Rhône–Poulenc, a French multinational with interests in chemicals, fertilizers, pharmaceuticals and computer tape and discs).

There has been a recent renewal of interest in the role played by goals in influencing the behaviour of organization members. This has been high-lighted through the concept of the 'excellent company' (see for example Peters and Waterman, 1982). In companies like IBM, Hewlett–Packard, and Boeing you will find clearly–articulated goals which are so dominant that they appear to have a life of their own, irrespective of the personnel involved. Closer examination will certainly reveal that such goals are carefully formulated by the chief executives of such companies as as part of a policy of establishing a set of dominant values which guide the behaviour of every organization member. As with all organizations, the main purpose of goals is to give members a sense of direction and to reduce ambiguity and conflict.

Managers who use goals in this way make the assumption that the clear formulation of goals will influence performance. This assumption has been translated into a set of techniques aimed at influencing the behaviour of individual members, known as 'Management–by–Objectives' or MBO (Drucker, 1964). Where MBO is used, the goals for the organization as a whole are generally broken down into individual goals or targets for each manager, forming an entire network of interconnected and internally con-sistent goals. The most effective MBO schemes tend to be those where there is some measure of negotiation between manager and subordinate over the precise nature of the goals to be achieved by the subordinate. This raises two points; that goal formulation is part of a political process and that goal achievement is undoubtedly related to the extent to which goals are shared by members of the organization.

However, the evidence on the influence of goals on performance is mixed, and even where such a relationship can be shown, it is unclear how it works. The use of goals to determine performance is easiest to under-stand where jobs are straightforward so that clear targets can be set and performance measured. Many jobs are more complex and performance measurement is difficult to achieve. Furthermore, employees may be ex-pected to achieve a number of different goals which could conflict with one another or with those of other workers. We shall see that for some organizations internal consistency is difficult to achieve in the face of considerable inter–personal and inter–departmental conflict. The extent to

KEY CONCEPT 3.1	The stated goals of an organization exist to give direction to the activities of its members. In many companies, goals comprise both an overall state-ment of intent, sometimes referred to as a mission statement, and a set of more detailed objectives to guide strategic planning. Since many organi-zations are made up of different interest groups the formulation of goals can be a highly political process. This can cause conflict but the goals of most businesses are generally accepted as being those of the senior management team. There has been a renewal of interest in the role of goals to shape the culture of an organization. We deal with this aspect in our discussion of organizational culture (Key concept 3.6).
ORGANIZATIONAL GOALS	

which goals can be used to motivate performance is also a function of management behaviour and individual expectations.

Not every company has such clearly identified goals. For many small firms (as well as some larger ones), goals remain the unstated intentions of the owners; they may be thought of only in the vaguest of terms; employees may be completely unaware of them, and may give priority to their own personal goals, sometimes bringing them into conflict with management. A review of most companies' annual reports will reveal that the explicit statement of the goals is usually marked by its absence (the cases of Sainsbury and Rank Hovis McDougall are the exception rather than the rule). Instead the various missions, objectives and strategies must be extracted or at best implied from the various statements by company chairmen and operating reports (the case of Rhône–Poulenc providing a much clearer exposition than most).

The nature of goals

'We consider goals to be the ultimate, long–run, open–ended attributes or ends a person or organization seeks' (Hofer and Schendel, 1978, p 20). Allowing for the contention that organizations can engage in goal–seeking behaviour, this definition sees goals in terms of the further orientation of the company, but stated in rather loose, broad terms. The examples in our case illustrate this point. A popular notion is that business firms should possess some superordinate goal, namely the maximization of profit. This view has been challenged. Some, like Handy (1976), see profit as a by–product of other goals like survival, market expansion and enhancing reputation. Marris (1964) sees profit as less important than growth. In any case the profit notion is entirely inappropriate for those public sector organizations where goals of service take precedence over all others.

Hofer and Schendel (1978) make the distinction between goals, objec-

---

To discharge the responsibility as leaders in our trade by acting with complete integrity, by carrying out work to the highest standards, and by contributing to the public good and to the quality of life in the community.

To provide unrivalled value to our customers in the quality of the goods we sell, in the competitiveness of our prices and in the range of choice we offer.

In our stores to achieve the highest standards of cleanliness and hygiene, efficiency of operation, convenience and customer service, and thereby create as attractive and friendly a shopping environment as possible.

To offer our staff outstanding opportunities in terms of personal career development and in remuneration relative to other companies in the same market, practising always a concern for the welfare of every individual.

CASE 3.1

ILLUSTRATIONS OF COMPANY GOALS

A STATEMENT OF COMPANY OBJECTIVES BY J. SAINSBURY PLC

Continued over page

Continued from previous page
(Source: Annual Report and Accounts, 1986)

To generate sufficient profit to finance continual improvement and growth of the business whilst providing our shareholders with an excellent return on their investment.

THE STATED AIMS OF RANK HOVIS MCDOUGALL

The business of the Rank Hovis McDougall Group of companies is to process and market a wide range of food products in the United Kingdom, Europe, the United States, the Far East and Australasia.

Our aims are:
☐ to provide attractive and wholesome food products at prices which represent good value for money:
☐ to provide our employees with worthwhile jobs in safe working conditions at fair levels of pay:
☐ to provide our shareholders with an acceptable return on the money they have invested in the Group:

(Source: Annual Report and Accounts, 1988)

☐ to provide for the long–term growth and stability of the Group in the interests of customers, employees, and shareholders alike.

RHONE–POULENC: EXTRACTS FROM THE CHAIRMAN'S MESSAGE, 1986

In this changing world our ambition is to lead the Rhône–Poulenc group along exceptionally vigorous lines to place it among the world leaders in each of the fields in which it excels. Our strategy can be summed up in three points. They are concomitant and complementary.

We must first increase the high–value added activities where Rhône–Poulenc already holds considerable know–how and strong markets... To succeed in these fields means continuing to pursue our capital expenditure program as well as continuing our substantial commitment to Research and Development ... to sign research agreements ... with the international academic world ... seizing every opportunity for external expansion through acquisitions.

Secondly we reinforce our upstream activities ... our chemical business in major intermediates, both organic and inorganic, areas in which we hold positions of leadership and where we have been able to set extremely competitive cost prices. To do this we must unceasingly pursue the improvement of our manufacturing processes. We must maintain here high levels of investments in productivity and capacity, and exercise a particularly rigorous industrial management policy.

Lastly we want to free ourselves from activities which are too far removed from our fundamental business or facing severe economic problems.

(Source: Company Report and Accounts, 1986)

tives and strategies. Goals themselves are seen as being unbounded, generalized statements of intent, whereas objectives represent those intentions that can be measured within a certain time frame. Strategies are seen as the processes by which goals are determined through the adoption of certain courses of action and the allocation of resources. We examine strategies more thoroughly in Chapter 4.

Richards (1978) distinguishes between closed and open–ended goals.

Closed–ended goals are those which have clearly defined and measurable targets to be achieved within a stated time period. By contrast open–ended goals are the type which include some broad statement of intent such as the pursuit of excellence. This broader view of goals has sometimes been defined as a firm's 'mission', which would seem to equate with Hofer and Schendel's concept of a goal. A mission has been described as a master strategy which has a visionary content, and which overrides all other types of goal (Richards, 1978).

Despite the confusion over terminology we can therefore see a kind of hierarchy developing which comprises different types of goals, as follows.

MISSION

OBJECTIVES

STRATEGIES

Another classification made by Perrow (1961) distinguishes between 'official' and 'operative' goals. 'Official' goals are the statements of intent which occur in official documents and are the type illustrated by our case illustrations. 'Operative' goals on the other hand reflect the behaviour that is actually occurring, and which may in fact conflict with the official intention. To Perrow the development of a package of operative goals was the process or corporate strategy formulation. This process is developed in the following section.

How goals are developed

Our understanding of how goals develop owes much to the work of Cyert and March and their *Behavioural Theory of the Firm* (1963). They see organizations as being formed around individuals and groups who combine to pursue mutual interests as coalitions. The interests need not be shared but the coalition is recognized by all participating interest groups as the most effective way of achieving their goals.

An interest group may be an entire department, such as marketing or research and development, or it might be a particular section within that department such as a project team. It may even be a less formal grouping of managers within a department who collectively wish to pursue a specific policy. The creation of such interest groups may be a deliberate structural device. For example, senior management at Procter and Gamble felt that its interests could best be served through the creation of teams based around a single product or groups of products. The aim was the creation of healthy competition between product teams, and a competition and justification of resource allocation which would operate in the best interests of the firm as a whole. A more detailed discussion of the relationship between goals and structure may be found in the next section.

Interest groups can emerge due to the complexity of the organization's task and/or its environment, requiring a degree of internal specialization, to deal with specific problems, such as product development, or external bodies such as banks. Interest groups may also develop informally, cutting across formal structures.

Each interest group will determine its goals by reference to the information it collects. Such information generally includes comparative data on other organizations on such issues as price, product design, and criteria for success. Many interest groups for example establish their goals in relation to competing groups in the same organization. The important point made by Cyert and March is that groups deliberately limit strategic choice by selecting information from the range available and having decided upon a course of action, often fail to consider alternative strategies. This is perfectly understandable given the range of information and the time available to make decisions. Such a process is sometimes referred to as 'bounded rationality'.

Interest groups combine to form coalitions, and in any one organization there will be a number of such coalitions. They are created by a process of influence, negotiation and bargaining between different interest groups. It is out of this process that the goals emerge which guide the behaviour of organization members. However in any one organization there is usually a group that may be identified as a dominant coalition. Once established, the dominant coalition will set up procedures to ensure that their goals are pursued by the organization as a whole. Such criteria will normally include establishing the procedures for staff selection, promotion, and reward as well as laying down the rules of operation. The dominant coalition usually comprises, therefore, the senior management of an enterprise. However, certain groups align themselves with top management to ensure their goals are well represented. Even in those organizations where decision–making proceeds along more democratic lines, as in institutions of higher education, the various coalitions will compete for membership of key committees at which decisions about such issues as resources are taken.

In short, the ability of groups to pursue their goals depends upon the power they wield in the organization, which may depend on a number of variables; such as their position in the hierarchy; the skills of group members; the resources they command; whether or not their role is seen as legitimate by the rest of the organization members.

It is inevitable that different coalitions will pursue different interests and that some will compete. The process of influence, negotiation and bargaining may be termed organizational politics. Such a concept tends to be viewed pejoratively and political activity in business firms is often seen as a problem. Yet if we subscribe to the views of Cyert and March the process is an inevitable prelude to goal setting. Nonetheless the potential problem of goal conflict will now be explored through the examination of multiple goals.

Multiple goals

In any organization made up of different interest groups some conflict over goals is inevitable. This has been illustrated by many writers. Marris (1964) speaks of the goal conflict emerging from the separation of ownership and control. He found that while shareholders were concerned primarily about profitability, the professional managers acting as the directors of companies were more concerned with growth. In this instance profitability is a by–product, for it is growth which expands the director's sphere of influence and hence his personal power and reward. Despite such potential conflict between director and shareholder goals, some compromise is usually made by directors to protect their own position. Handy (1976) presents several examples of goal–conflict including that between the sales and production departments. The goals of the sales department are normally measured by volume turnover, whilst those of the production department are measured by cost–efficiency. We return to this particular problem in Chapter 6, when we depict the classic dilemma of the production department as that of satisfying the twin demands of customer satisfaction and operating efficiency.

In some cases such conflict can be seen to operate against the best interests of the organization. A study by Selznick (1949) of the Tennessee Valley Authority is viewed as a classic of its kind. An emerging organization formed to solve the problems of irrigating and redeveloping a vast area in the Tennessee Valley, tackled its job through delegation and specialization. In this case, each specialist division within the organization (Selznick refers to these as sub–units) developed a greater commitment to its own sub–unit goals than those of the organization as a whole. This fragmented the total effort and resulted in groups devoting a great deal of their time to legitimizing their activities and competing for resources. This set up conflicts with other groups which further strengthened the resolve of each sub–unit to pursue its own goals. Selznick referred to this process as the 'bifurcation of interests'. Burns and Stalker (1966) noted how a similar conflict developed between the production and research and development departments in certain Scottish electronics firms with the subsequent decline in their competitive standing. In Pettigrew's (1973) study computer programmers saw their status threatened by an emerging group of systems analysts. In response they attempted to control information to preserve their exclusive position and prevent their work being down–graded.

In such cases, activities move away from dealing with customers or even coping with external changes in the market to focus on the resolution of internal tensions, and management becomes the management of internal coalitions.

We have already noted that it is quite normal for multiple goals to exist in most organizations. Not all conflict of this kind is necessarily a problem. It would appear to be limited by four factors.

☐ Most groups in an organization will agree to those goals formulated by senior management as a means of achieving their own goals. This is the result of the bargaining and negotiating process between interest groups.
☐ Most organization members would appear to accept the goals of top management with little question. This would seem to be an implied element of the employment contract.
☐ The dominant coalition normally sets up a series of controls to ensure compliance to their goals. Such controls have been alluded to earlier and include selection procedures, induction and training to ensure that rules are followed. In addition, management can use technological

controls in the form of work design and job allocation, and financial controls in the form of budgets and reward systems. In such ways as these, the management of organizations ensure at least a minimum level of compliance with their chosen goals.

☐ In many firms senior management acknowledge that different groups may have their own goals which need to be satisfied. This is illustrated in Case 3.1.

In this section we have depicted the formation of goals as a complex process involving the resolution of external influences and internal politics. As such, the system is highly dynamic and changes in the goals will occur with changes in the external environment, such as market demand, technology and government policy, as well as changes that take place between interest groups within the organization. A change in ownership or top management may lead to a shift in emphasis of the firm's operations. The acquisition of the department store chain Debenhams by the Burton Group led to a change in operation as well as image. More franchises were awarded to established retailers to operate within each Debenhams store and there was considerable investment on internal refurbishment in all locations.

Goals are not formalized, meaningless statements but the products of a highly interactive and dynamic process. The changing of goals in the face of external and even internal changes is seen to be a prerequisite for the survival of the organization. Those managers who cling to inappropriate goals would appear to place their companies at risk. However, simply changing goals may be an inadequate response by itself, since the relationship between goals and performance often demands some consideration of the organization structure. It is to this we now turn.

Structure

A dominant theme in our discussion of goals was that organizations are made up of different interest groups formed as coalitions. One of the factors which may facilitate or inhibit the way these groups pursue their goals and whether such goals may be achieved is the structure of the organization. In this section we will examine how structures develop, the variations that occur in structural type, and their impact on performance. You should note however thay any discussion of structure is biased towards the large firm, and most of the studies in this area are of large corporations. This is inevitable in that structural problems tend to be associated with size and complexity. The balance is redressed later in this chapter when we devote an entire section to the problems of small businesses.

A structure is concerned with the grouping of activities in the most suitable manner to achieve the goals of the dominant coalition. It is concerned with the organization of work around roles, the grouping of these roles to form teams or departments, and the allocation of differential amounts of power and authority to the various roles. It is associated with job descriptions, mechanisms for coordination and control, and management information systems.

An organization structure is a grouping of activities and people to achieve the goals of the organization. Considerable variation is possible in the type of structure employed and the influences at work include technology, size, the nature of the environment, management strategy, the behaviour of interest groups, the firm's history and wider cultural factors. In general terms a particular structure emerges to maximize the opportunities and solve the problems created by these various influences. In practice however the evidence concerning the influence of structure upon performance is very patchy indeed.

KEY CONCEPT 3.2

ORGANIZATION STRUCTURE

In much of the writing there is an implicit assumption that senior management seek a structural elegance for their organizations to enhance performance. This in turn assumes that managers have a choice and that structures can be deliberately created to affect overall performance. We will now examine those factors which can influence a firm's structure to determine the extent to which structures can be manipulated by management.

The factors which influence structure

There are a number of factors which may influence the structure of an organization. We have identified them under six main headings, placed in no particular order of importance.

Technology. For some, technology is the most important, if not the sole, determinant of a firm's structure. This is part of the concept known as 'technological determinism'. Much of the work in this area is indebted to Joan Woodward's (1965) work on the impact of technology on a hundred manufacturing firms in South East Essex (also mentioned in Chapters 2 and 6). She and her research team found that differences in manufacturing, from small batch to mass production to process technology, resulted in corresponding differences in such factors as the extent of the management hierarchy, the proportion of management to other employees, the proportion of direct to indirct labour, and the number of subordinates controlled by any one manager (the span of control).

Size. Other researchers find size to be a more significant variable in influencing structure than is technology. This was a particular theme of a group of academics at Aston University in the 1960s and 70s (see for example Pugh *et al*. 1969). As firms increase in size, additional problems are created in terms of coordination and control often necessitating structural changes. For example, as the business expands, the owner of a small business often faces increasing pressures on his time. No longer is he able to maintain a close control of operations, act as the major representative to customers, as well as managing administration and wages. In such cases some formalization and delegation is inevitable and a stage is reached when small businesses take their first steps towards bureaucratization. Such changes in structure with increasing size can be viewed in large as well as in small firms. We can see with Dow Corning in Case 3.2 that significant structural changes were made as the company expanded its product range and its markets. The way firms respond to size may vary, resulting in different types of structure, which we identify in the next section. While there are obvious connections between size and structure, Child (1984) points out that the complexity of an organization's operations may have a more significant impact on its structure than sheer size.

Changes in the environment. In the last chapter we saw how the contingency approach saw organizations as needing to adapt to their environment in order to survive. An important feature of that adaptation is structural. Burns and Stalker (1966) noted that technological and market changes in the post–war electronics industry were best served by a less bureaucratic, more flexible kind of organization. Such organic structures were an essential element in the firms' ability to cope with a highly changing environment, and firms which retained their traditional bureaucratic or mechanistic structures were much less successful. The IBM case at the end of this section illustrates the relationship between structure and a rapidly changing product market.

This theme of the structure fitting the dominant aspects of the firm's environment is the major plank in the work of Lawrence and Lorsch (1967). They believe that different tasks in the organization are confronted by different environmental problems and demands, differences which should be reflected in the structures of the departments carrying out those tasks. In their study of the plastics industry they found a highly uncertain technological environment which called for a flexible R&D function, whilst the demands imposed on the production department were more predictable, enabling a more traditional, bureaucratic structure to operate. The structural implications of Lawrence and Lorsch's analysis do not end with what they term the 'differentiation' of functions. In order to operate effectively all organizations so differentiated must establish integrative devices, which might include a committee structure or designing special coordinating roles.

An interesting illustration of a firm adapting to a predominant environmental condition is given by Child (1984). He cites the example of the Americal multinational ITT operating in a highly volatile political environment in Chile in the 1970s. As part of its coping strategy, the firm set up a political intelligence unit.

Strategy. The influence of strategy on structure is related to the way management perceive their environment. A firm wishing to be a product leader in a technologically sophisticated product market will have a correspondingly large R&D department both in terms of investment and employees. A firm that places a grest deal of emphasis on cost controls may have a larger than average accounting department.

The relationship of strategy to organizational structure owes much to the work of Alfred Chandler (1962, 1977). He based his first work around an in–depth case study of the development of four companies; DuPont, General Motors, Standard Oil and Sears Roebuck. His work, however, had a much broader perspective; that of charting the development of American capitalism and especially the role played by the professional manager. One of the major conclusions of his work is that structure is a product of managerial strategies. The relationship between the two is more complex than many summaries of Chandler acknowledge. He found that structure did not automatically follow strategy, and that managements often needed a crisis before they would agree to structural change. This point emerges in Case 3.3 with IBM.

As might be expected of an economic historian, Chandler viewed the relationship between strategy and structure as dynamic and evolutionary. He identified several stages in the development of American capitalism. These were cycles of growth and consolidation, each with its own implications for the organizational structures of the emerging large corporations in his study. The growth of mass markets and the development of the techniques of mass production was accompanied by vertical integration to ensure the supply of materials and secure distribution channels, and horizontal integration through takeovers to maintain growth. Expansion brought its own problems of coordination and control and subsequent inefficiency. These were solved by the growth of professional management and the development of organizations structured around specialist functions, such as marketing and finance. As existing markets became saturated and the benefits accruing from organizational restructuring slowed down, new markets and products were vigorously pursued by overseas expansion and R&D respectively. Once again these developments brought their own problems of coordination and control. This time a new form of structure emerged. All four firms in Chandler's study had adopted a multidivisional structure by 1929, with DuPont and General Motors leading the way. The essential qualities of this structure will be identified in the following section.

Similar cycles of expansion and consolidation through structural change can be found in studies of British companies (Channon, 1973). While such works offer strong evidence for the influence of strategy over structure, we have already noted the complex nature of the relationship. Chandler noted that the motivation for structural change emerged not only from changes in strategy but that it needed the catalyst of an organizational crisis. We can see cases where structural change may be unnecessary or at least delayed by the sheer market power of the firm, as in the case of IBM. There may even be a case for arguing that structure can determine strategy. For example, once a company has adopted a multidivisional structure, this could well give divisional managers the incentive, confidence and resources for even greater expansion. This interplay of strategy and structure reappears in Chapter 4 and is illustrated by changes in the US multinational 3M depicted in Case 4.2.

Culture. The influence of culture on structure should not be underestimated. There is evidence that different structural forms are favoured in different countries. For example, American firms developed initially through the adoption of divisional structures, while in Britain we favoured the holding company (Channon, 1973). Firms in different countries often reflect different emphases, so it has been noted that whilst American firms stress the finance and marketing functions, those in Germany have a production orientation (Hayes and Wheelwright, 1984); industrial relations management plays a much more significant role in Britain than either of those two countries. Studies on such aspects as the shape and extent of the management hierarchy have also noted differences between countries (Brossard and Maurice, 1976). Structure may also reflect specific organizational cultures; for example, those firms favouring the involvement of employees in decision–making may set up participative forums to facilitate this.

Interest groups. Although Chandler noted the resistance on the part of some managers to structural change, the whole issue of interest groups and organizational politics was largely overlooked. The preferences of the dominant coalition can exert considerable influence on the structure as can the demands of major stakeholders. Those firms where the owners play a major role in management tend to be highly centralized. In the public sector the pressure for accountability often results in elaborate financial control mechanisms and bureaucratic procedures. In some manufacturing firms, the pressure from banks on lending may, in times of recession, lead to reductions in development activites, with a corresponding impact on the size of the R&D function.

Cases 3.2, 3.3 and 4.2 all show structural changes following management changes. While size, maket and other environmental influences inevitably played a major role in Dow Corning, IBM and 3M, the catalyst for new structures in all cases would seem to be changes at the top.

Two important points emerge from our consideration of the six influences above. Firstly, there is considerable overlap between the various factors. For example, the structural changes of firms like Dupont and General Motors link technology, size and strategy; the different structural routes taken by firms in different countries are both a function of cultural differences and variations in environmental factors. In short, the structure of an organization can only be explained by reference to a number of interrelated factors. Once again this is amply illustrated in both the Dow Corning and IBM cases. Secondly our analysis raises the issue of the extent of choice senior managements have in determining the structure of their organizations. Are structures creative innovations to implement changing strategies or are they the inevitable consequences of adaption to prevailing influences? Such issues were raised in the shipping industry case in Chapter 1; structural changes were an important factor in the implementation of strategic change in a highly competitive environment, but they were also determined by technical innovations in such areas as cargo handling and telecommunications. In short the structure of the shipping companies would appear to be the result of both prevailing economic and technological conditions and management choice.

If managers do have a choice of structure for their organization, then it may include one of the following structural types.

Types of structure

In this section we present a brief review of the major structural types. Very few organizations conform precisely to a particular type. In some organizations a particular kind of structure predominates, while others display a variety of types. We will explain the basic characteristic of each type and present in Figure 3.5 a summary statement of the supposed advantages and

CASE 3.2

DOW CORNING

Dow Corning was formed in 1942 from Dow Chemical and Corning Glass. The original focus of the firm was R&D, and the firm was highly centralized around technology and products. At this stage of its development the products were closely related and the firm operated under a traditional functional management structure.

By 1962, several changes had taken place. The company had grown, largely through product diversity, and central control of product development was no longer appropriate. In addition, there had been a change in top management and the new Chief Executive established five product divisions as profit centres, each with its own functional structures. The new structure was seen as successful in integrating the functions, and a contributory factor in the firm's continued growth and increased profitability.

Within a short time further international expansion brought its own problems. There was conflict between the demands of the home and foreign markets. Conflict also arose over the central supply of raw materials and the mechanisms for transfer pricing. The impact of an economic recession meant that profit levels fell. These problems were met by a further change in management along with a major structural change to a matrix organization.

The ensuing matrix comprised two major elements; specialist functions and ten business profit centres, newly created from the existing five divisions. Employees reported to a business centre manager and a functional vice–president. Each business centre comprises different product boards. Each product board is led by a particular functional manager and leadership tends to change with the product life cycle, from R&D at the early stages to marketing as the product develops.

Structures and processes have been developed within the matrix to enhance coordination and deal with conflict. A great deal of attention has been focussed on modifying individual behaviour by such techniques as MBO and group goal–setting. The firm is helped in its search for goal congruence by having a management structure dominated by chemical engineers.

(*Sources:* Galbraith and Nathanson, 1978)

problems associated with each one. In this summary we group the divisional and holding company type together, since each represents a different method of achieving decentralization As we mentioned earlier, structure does not emerge as an issue until a firm reaches a certain size. Many small firms have no apparent structure at all, beyond a centralized control system, but even this is not inevitable as in the case of partnerships between professional people. We identify five types of organization structure.

Functional. The main criteria guiding this type of organization is functional specialization. As we can see from the illustration in Figure 3.1, employees performing related specialist tasks are grouped together under

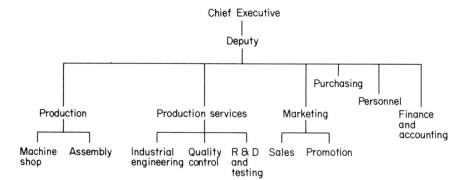

Figure 3.1 A functional structure: an engineering components business.

a single management structure. Most firms as they develop adopt this form of structure and it is especially suited to single–product firms. The structure was widely used by British firms, even very large companies, up to the 1960s, but became less common in larger firms especially, as it was superseded by divisionalization (Channon, 1973).

Divisional. The development of the divisional or, as it is sometimes called, the multidivisional company, is associated with market expansion and product diversification. In both these cases traditional functional structures showed themselves to be inadequate in coordinating and controlling the firm's activities. Divisionalization was a particularly American development and is associated with 'pioneer' companies like General Motors and DuPont in the 1920s and with the multinational expansion of American firms in the 1930s (Chandler, 1962).

An illustration of a divisional structure is shown in Figure 3.2. Under such an organization structure each division is self–contained and operates as a profit centre. Divisions can be grouped around products or markets or a combination of the two, as in the case of Ford. The activities of the various divisions are directed by a central headquarters unit who take a global view of corporate strategy. Other central activities might include R&D and purchasing, to benefit from economies of scale. The dual existence of divisional profit centres and central units is a source of tension for many firms operating this structure, especially in the allocation of the costs of these central untis to the individual divisions. In one case, a divisionalized engineering firm operated a central foundry, which also had to act as a profit centre in its own right. As well as serving the needs of its own organization, the foundry, having spare capacity, was encouraged to seek contracts outside the firm. This set up two sorts of tension; firstly, the various divisions complained about having to pay the 'going rate' for foundry products, and secondly, the divisions always demanded priority over external contracts, which hampered the foundry from achieving its own profit objectives.

Once divisions have been established a decision still have to be made about grouping within each division. In some cases this is done along traditional functional lines, whereas in others staff are organized around products.

A multidivisional company comprises a number of different business units which may pursue markedly different types of business activity. The various business units operate as profit-centres and are centrally coordinated by a corporate headquarters, which may also control certain central services such as research and development and finance. This kind of structure developed in the USA is response to business growth. In Britain many large, diverse organizations have tended to favour a somewhat looser holding company structure with possibly less central coordination of strategic planning. In reality there is much overlap between the two kinds of structure.

KEY CONCEPT 3.3

THE MULTIDIVISIONAL COMPANY

Figure 3.2 A divisional structure: Unigate – a divisional structure organized around product groupings. (Source: *Company Report and Accounts,* 1988).

The holding company. This form of organization is associated with the growth of the firm by acquisitions and a high degree of product diversification. It comprises, as we can see from the illustration in Figure 3.3, a group of independent companies controlled by a coordinating group usually made up of the chief executives of the constituent companies. At its extreme form, as exemplified by a company such as Lonhro, this structural type represents as much a form of ownership and investment as it does a kind of organization. Holding companies can be highly diversified, as in the case of Trafalgar House, or built around loosely related products as with the TI Group. Ultramar on the other hand represents a holding company of highly related activities in oil and gas exploration and the production, shipping and refining of crude oil and petroleum products.

As we saw in the previous chapter, the holding company is the prevalent structural form for large Japanese companies. It has also been described as the peculiarly British route to divisionalization (Channon, 1973). Although there are similarities between divisional and holding company structures, Channon believed that the reluctance of British firms to adopt divisionalization was a contributory factor in their relative failure in competitive world economies; a case of structure influencing performance.

Figure 3.3 A holding company: Royal Dutch/Shell. (Source: *Company Report and Accounts*, 1988).

The project team. These comprise units specially created, often to cope with a highly unstable environment. In essence they are temporary structures formed around a particular task or problem, and reflect technical expertise rather than any notion of management hierarchy. Such structures are commonly found in high technology firms and some types of service organizations, especially consultancies. In advertising agencies, teams are usually created to deal with specific client accounts. In R&D departments the research work may be organized around several teams, each handling a different problem. In construction companies project teams may be created to deal with a particular job such as the building of a new office block. The membership of teams can be highly fluid; different specialists may be brought in at different times and one employee may be a member of several teams.

The approach reflects a close identification with the needs of the client and is an extension of the kind of client–based structure found in professional firms such as solicitors, accountants and the like. While focusing specifically on the needs of the client does have its advantages, there can be some unnecessary duplication of resources and there can be scheduling

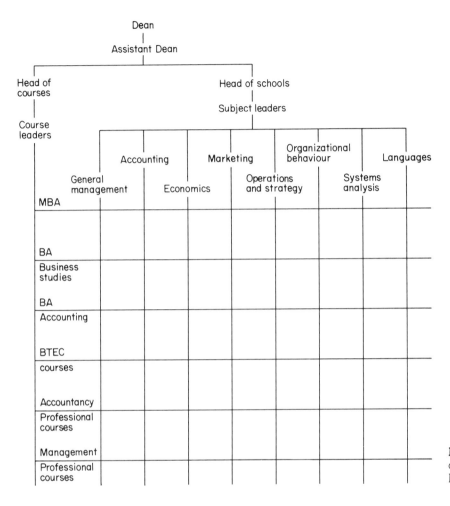

Figure 3.4 A matrix organization: a polytechnic business school.

and logistics problems. These become more severe as the organization gets larger and a stage may be reached where project teams need to be supported within a functional or divisional framework. The matrix structure was developed especially with such problems in mind and it is to this we now turn.

The matrix. Essentially the matrix is an attempt to combine the best of all worlds, the customer orientation of the project team, the economies of scale and the specialist orientation of the functional organization, and the product or market focus of the divisional company. The matrix is an attempt to devise a structure that can effectively manage at least two different elements, be they size, products, markets or customers. The essence of the matrix is presented by the Dow Corning case; the work is controlled in two directions, by a functional specialism and by a product grouping, committees are set up to coordinate the two orientations, and attention is given to training the staff towards goal congruence. The illustration of a matrix in a polytechnic business school is presented in Figure 3.4.

The matrix became very popular in the 1970s and owed much to the work of Lawrence and Lorsch (1967) and Galbraith (1971). It was embraced by companies such as Dow Corning (see the case later in this section), General Electric, Ciba Geigy and Citibank. The popularity was short–lived and of all the structural types the matrix has attracted most criticism. In a later work Paul Lawrence referred to the matrix as an 'unnecessary complexity', which was only justified in certain situations (Davis and Lawrence, 1977, p 21). Firstly, if two or more of a firm's dimensions, like products and markets, were especially critical to its performance. Secondly, if employees needed to carry out highly complex, interdependent tasks in an uncertain environment. Thirdly if economies of scale were needed, espcially in the use of scarce or expensive resources. Unless such conditions are present then the matrix can cause more problems than it solves. It is interesting to note that at a time when most business organizations were finding the matrix wanting, it was emerging as perhaps the most popular structure in university and polytechnic business schools.

Students should always remember that the structural types identified above represent fairly broad categories. In reality a firm may display a mixture of structures. We have already seen how many divisionalized companies have functional specialisms within each division. In a functional organization we may find that different departments are organized along different lines; the operations department may well extend the functional structure, whilst the R&D staff may well be organized as project teams. New structural forms are emerging all the time, adapting the traditional approaches to suit their own needs. The Philips factory in South London is still organized along functional lines but management has re–drawn the organization chart to place the production function at the centre of a network of supporting activites, in an attempt to establish manufacture as the core activity.

A currently popular concept is that of networking. This type of structure has been made possible by developments in computer technology whereby computer systems can interact. Such a system enables people to operate from home and has been heralded as the organization structure of the future. Networking has attracted considerable publicity both in academic journals and the popular press. This attention however tends to exaggerate the real extent of networking. Even in pioneer networkers such as Rank Xerox, those employees operating under this system are but a very small percentage of the total employed. Of course, a form of networking has been around for some time in certain types of manufacturing industry in the form of homeworking. In this case individuals or even families engage in simple assembly work (as with electrical components) or in such activities as dressmaking and alteration. Homeworking has become a way of life in some countries such as Japan and is a particularly low–cost form of labour.

Whilst the publicity surrounding networking outstrips the reality, this is not the case for franchising, an emerging form of organizational structure akin to the holding company. Under a franchise agreement a parent company will assist in the start–up of a new business enterprise. The terms of that agreement usually involve an initial investment on the part of the franchisee and an undertaking to deal exclusively with the franchisor in

ADVANTAGES	PROBLEMS
1. Functional Organization	
☐ Specialization.	☐ Conflicting departmental objectives.
☐ The logic of custom and practice.	☐ Conflicting management values.
☐ A clear chain of command.	☐ A lack of coordination.
	☐ A lack of consumer orientation.
2. Divisional organization and Holding company	
☐ The operation of businesses as profit centres.	☐ Cooperation and interdependence.
☐ The encouragement of entrepreneurship.	☐ Accounting procedures, especially transfer pricing.
☐ Reduces upward dependency on top management.	☐ Increasing diversity of operations.
☐ Economies of scale by centralization of common functions like R&D.	☐ Overall management control.
3. Project teams	
☐ The ability to cope with an unstable environment.	☐ A costly duplication of resources.
☐ The use of individual expertise.	☐ Scheduling.
☐ The ability to cope with diverse problems.	☐ The participants have no functional home.
☐ Deal directly with the customer.	☐ What happens when the project is finished?
4. Matrix organization	
☐ Emphasizes the strengths of the functional and project types.	☐ Coordination and control.
☐ Flexibility of labour.	☐ A proliferation of committees and meetings.
☐ The ability to transfer expertise where it is most needed.	☐ Too many bosses.
☐ Dual control via function and project.	☐ Conflicting loyalties for staff.
☐ Closeness to the customer.	☐ Can be slow to adapt.

Figure 3.5 A summary of advantages and problems associated with different types of structure.

the marketing of his products. The purchase of the franchisor's products invariably involves the payment of a mark–up in return for the advertising and promotional support of a larger company. A good illustration of franchising is presented by the fast food industry, such as Kentucky Fried Chicken, although there are more than three hundred different franchise operations in Britain including such diverse operations as the British School of Motoring, drain clearage and wedding dress hire. A recent growth in franchise operations has taken place in the financial service sector, as in the case of insurance broking. In this case the franchisee, instead of buying goods from the franchisor, buys access to a computer data base. The main advantage to both parties in a franchise agreement is the spread of risk. As such it has become a popular form of small business venture.

The two illustrations of networking and franchising focus on criteria of flexibility and cost and bring us back to the relationship between structure and performance.

Structure and performance

We can see from Figure 3.5 and our discussion of the various structural types that some structures are more suited to some situations than others.

Conversely a firm that adheres stubbornly to a structure that is totally inappropriate to the contingencies that it faces may be creating problems for itself. However the evidence on these matters is far from convincing. The major difficulties in establishing a correlation between structure and performance would appear to be firstly, identifying appropriate measures of performance and secondly, proving causality. We can make some general points.

☐ Whatever the relationship between structure and performance, Johnson and Scholes (1984) point out that once a structure has been installed, it is often very difficult to change it. Equally, frequent structural changes could be damaging in terms of the disruption that takes place and the requirement on the part of staff to learn new systems.

☐ It is extremely doubtful whether structure alone can lead to improvements in performance. However sound the structure may be, it is unlikely that it can totally overcome problems created by staff incompetence or even divisive internal politics. In some cases a high degree of specialization or divisionalization can lead to a worsening of relationships. We might even speculate that there is more evidence for suggesting that structure can affect performance in a negative way than there is for its having a positive impact. There is some evidence that structure in harness with other variables can lead to improvements in performance (Child, 1972). This point was taken up by Galbraith and Nathanson (1978), who argue that effective financial performance is obtained by achieving some kind of congruence between strategy, structure, processes, rewards and people.

☐ Child (1984) also points out that performance can influence structure, citing the example that more successful companies financially tend to have fewer cost controls. This fits in with the one of the key assumptions of our Business in Context model; that influences operate in more than one direction and while organizational factors such as structure can affect the outcome of a firm's activities, that outcome in turn affects the organization.

Ownership

We might assume quite logically that ownership is an important variable in that the owners of a business will wish to determine the goals and the way that business operates. In support of our assumption we could cite illustrations of influential founders such as Henry Ford, Thomas J. Watson of IBM, and the Sainsbury family of supermarket fame. We could also refer to numerous cases of small firms where the owner, often single-handedly, controls the destiny of the business. In the case of the small firm the owners can be clearly defined and their impact easily assessed. Discovering who actually owns and controls businesses becomes much more difficult with large corporations like the major oil companies, or even an organization like British Airways, where privatization has been accompanied by widespread share issue. It would appear that the greater the size of the organization and the greater the dispersal of share ownership, then the more

In 1988 the senior management at IBM implemented significant structural changes, following the appointment of a new chairman in 1985. These changes were seen as a product of several inter–related factors, not least of which was an unacceptable fall in profits since 1984.

Before 1988 the organization structure reflected a high degree of specialization between the various functional departments (known somewhat confusingly for our purposes as divisions). Clear distinctions were drawn between the technical division, which designed the computers, the manufacturing division, which made them, and the marketing division which was responsible for sales. In addition, IBM had no separate department concerned with software development. As a result of this type of structure, management concluded that counter–productive internal conflicts were set up, new designs were delayed by as much as two years, and new models when they were introduced lacked supporting software, enabling competitors to increase their market share in key areas.

In a way IBM had been lulled by their dominant market position and early technical leadership in the field. The company firmly established its leading position throughout the 1960s and 70s. Current management thinking suggests that the company became complacent, highly bureaucratic, ultra–conservative and missed the essential entrepreneurial spirit associated with its early days.

While IBM still dominated the mainframe market, helped significantly by its US government contracts and supplies to many major companies throughout the world, it had not responded to important changes in other markets. The computer market has become technically very diverse and there have been many aggressive new entrants. Such new entrants have not been held back by a large bureaucracy, they have operated with flexible organization structures that have enabled them to respond more effectively to technological change and be sensitive to the needs of the customer. The resulting market has become highly fragmented and price competitive. IBM mini systems have been losing out to Digital and the personal computer market has been swamped by IBM compatibles like Amstrad, selling at considerably cheaper prices and offering a more comprehensive range of software.

The structural response of IBM has been divisionalization and decentralization. Five divisions have been created; mainframes, mini computers, personal computers, telecommunications, and new technology. Each division is autonomous, and is responsible for its own product design, manufacture, sales, and ultimately profits.

CASE 3.3

IBM

(*Source:* John Cassidy and David Holmes, IBM Spreads Workload for Quicker Pace, *Sunday Times*, 14 February 1988)

we can question our original assumptions and need to examine the relationship between the ownership and the control of businesses.

The degree of private and public ownership is another issue which holds significant interest for students of business in this country. Organizations that are wholly or partly state–owned, like Austin–Rover or the local hospital, raise important issues of management control and public accountability.

In this section we will focus on these two aspects of ownership and examine the implications for the way businesses operate. We deal firstly with the traditional debate surrounding ownership and control. Secondly we examine the issue of the public ownership of organizations. The two elements have been brought much closer together in the latter half of the 1980s in Britain. Since 1980, many organizations like British Telecom, Jaguar, and British Aerospace have passed from public to private ownership or to a mixture of public and private ownership. This has been accompanied by a massive increase in the proportion of the population owning shares and a highly dispersed ownership pattern for those concerns. It is this dispersal that is at the heart of the ownership and control debate.

Ownership and control

The issue of ownership and control is one of continuing interest for academics, more especially among economists and sociologists. It is also a debate which raises significant questions for businesses in practice. How committed to the future of an enterprise are managers who have no stake in its ownership, or shareholders who have no interest beyond a return on investment? Are the resulting strategies in the best interests of all concerned; owners, managers, employees, the state, the public at large? How much freedom do managers have in developing business strategies?

The debate around these issues originates from the separation of ownership and control through the creation of the joint stock company and the subsequent dispersal of share ownership. With increased investment businesses grew in size and complexity, and control by professional managers became a necessity. The complexity of such growing businesses led to a specialization within the management group and the separation of the firm into different specialist functions and activities. Bureaucratic rules and procedures were developed to coordinate and control such activities. Both the specialization and bureaucratization reinforced the control of the management group with a supposed weakening in the power of the owner to influence decisions. The owner's main source of control was through the possession of capital stock.

This phenomenon was highlighted in the seminal study of Berle and Means (1932) and developed in later work by Berle (1954). Berle and Means in a study of the two hundred largest non–financial corporations in the USA classified the firms by their mode of control. They concluded that 44% of the firms were management–controlled and that this trend was increasing. The Berle and Means study has been replicated in both the USA and Britain with similar results, although both the data and conclusions of such studies have been the subject of significant controversy (Scott, 1979 has a reasonable summary of these studies).

Berle and Means used their data to develop and support their own view of a 'managerial revolution'. To them management control was 'better' in that it resulted in more effective decisions both for the profitability of the firm and for the general good of society; it was more professional and more socially responsible. The concepts of a 'neutral technocracy' and a 'soulful corporation' have stemmed from such value assessments of management control. We can see a clear link between Berle and Means's notion of 'managerialism' and the earlier work of F.W. Taylor on 'scientific management' (published in 1947). For both Taylor and Berle and Means, management should use a professional approach based on the application of science to solve the problems facing the firm. According to Berle and Means, management control would be truly professional in that strategies would be guided more by scientific analysis and be more answerable to society than the potentially narrow self–interest of the owner–manager. This concept of a managerial revolution was popularly espoused by Burnham (1941), whose ideas have attracted perhaps more attention than his analysis deserves. Burnham, writing at the time of Roosevelt's 'New Deal' saw similarities in many nations through the increased state control of the economy. He believed that through this managers, as the controllers of capital, would be able to assume a powerful role in society and direct businesses to serve their own ends.

There is a tendency to view such debates as purely academic. This would be wrong since the questions that emerge are central to the way businesses operate and the control of organizations has implications not only for the survival and prosperity of the organization itself, but also for the people who work for it, firms who deal with it, and society at large. We therefore examine some key issues in the ownership and control debate and raise a number of questions around the conclusions drawn by Berle and Means.

☐ Do managers really have more power and control than shareholders? Even with a dispersal of share ownership, shareholders needs still have to be satisfied, which may place constraints on management decisions. There is always a danger that shareholders, in the face of what they perceive as unpopular management decisions will sell their shares creating instability in the firm's stockmarket position. In any case, the distinction between managers and shareholders has become increasingly blurred. Whilst in many companies there clearly has been a separation of ownership and control, there is an increasing tendency, especially in the larger firms, to offer senior management shares in the company as part of their annual remuneration deal. In this way, managers may well identify with shareholders' own aspirations. This argument has been extended by the Marxist analysis of ownership and control, which views shareholders and managers not as being separate but as different forms of the same animal; no real distinction is drawn between managers and capitalist owners. In addition to such arguments, we can see that management freedom to make decisions is often held in check by banks, governments and Trade Unions. This complicates the ownership and control debate, and we return to the role of the financial institutions later.

☐ In addition to the above arguments it has often been pointed out that many large and influential companies are both family–owned and controlled and no separation has in fact occurred. In the retail trade in Britain such family–run businesses as Sainsbury, Asda, and Dixons have grown and prospered in relatively recent times. Empirical work from the USA suggests that family ownership and control of major businesses is still a significant feature; Sheehan (1967) found that of the largest five hundred American firms, 150 could be designated as having a significant family interest in terms of management and control.

☐ Has the ownership of shares really been dispersed? The data presented by Berle and Means (1932) showed that 86% of the largest two hundred US companies had a minimum of 5000 shareholders, with 22% having over 50 000. Putting such data in perspective, Miliband (1969) cites evidence which reveals that in Britain in 1961 only 4% of the population owned shares and 1% of the population owned 81% of all shares. Others, notably Child (1969), interpret the evidence that while there may be some evidence of share dispersal, the majority of shareholders own relatively small numbers of shares and tend to be extremely passive. This can result in minority shareholders owning a substantial proportion of all shares, with considerably more interest and potential influence in management decision–making. It is not just the dispersal of shares which should concern us, but the pattern of that dispersal.

Most of these data are of course fairly old, and the entire pattern of share ownership in Britain at least, has been confused by the large number of share issues in the 1980s resulting from the government's policy of privatization. Many of these share issues, like British Telecom, have been significantly oversubscribed. Whilst it is undeniable that large numbers have been brought into share ownership for the first time, it is however much too early to assess the situation. Many of those who have bought shares have done so with the prime intention of a quick sale for profit. This whole business has been summed up by the humourist Miles Kington as follows.

> The British public has learnt how to fill in forms they didn't quite understand, send them off at the last possible moment, receive negligible numbers of shares in public companies they are not interested in, flog them off immediately for a tiny profit.
>
> (extract from an article in the *Independent* 30 July 1987)

The shares of such public sales may well find themselves consolidated among a much smaller group of traditional shareholders within a relatively short space of time.

☐ Are professional managers more effective and more socially responsible than the traditional owner–manager? Recent assessments of management in Britain have raised serious doubts about the competence of those managers. Degrees of social responsibility are in particular difficult to gauge. In any case there is some logic in suggesting that the career–motivated professional manager would show less not more paternalism towards staff and less concern for social issues in general than the traditional entrepreneur, who would often have strong connections with the local community.

The contemporary plausible interpretation of the ownership and control debate focusses on the role of financial institutions. We can always cite the case of small firms and even large corporations where owner control is the norm. However, in both Britian and America a substantial shareholding of many of the major firms has passed to the hands of financial institutions, including banks, insurance and pension companies. (Scott, 1979 provides an excellent summary of the supporting evidence.) Their presence changes the nature of the Berle and Means debate. There is an acknowledgement of a separation between shareholders and managers, but a serious challenge to the concept of the passive shareholder. Such financial intermediaries not only tend to hold a significant minority stockholding, which gives them both power and influence, but they also take an active interest in important strategic decisions. Their credibility with their current clients and their ability to attract future investors rests upon the ability of their investment managers to ensure that yields are both attractive and secure. The sale of large numbers of shares by a bank or pension fund could well undermine the confidence of the stockmarket in a particular firm. Scott (1979) argues that large financial investors have become the dominant form of strategic control in British companies. They possess the mechanisms to be well informed and the power to make their views known to management. They become particularly active in crises and may be instrumental in not just dictating the policy of top management, but determining the composition of that group.

The clear inference from such an examination of the stockholding role of financial institutions is that the envisaged separation of ownership and control has not taken place. However, as Scott points out, the influence of financial institutions on business is far from being just financial. He propounds the notion of a 'constellation of interests', whereby the representatives of financial institutions are elected or appointed to the Boards of Directors of those companies where they hold a substantial minority interest. The senior officials of a bank may each hold a number of such directorships, as do the senior officials of other financial institutions. A pattern is thus built up of interlocking directorships representing a very important network of information, which supersedes finance as an instrument of power. Such directors will influence the recruitment of other directors and will inevitably favour those with access to vital information.

We can see that management decisions in a single firm may be influenced and even significantly constrained by directors representing the interests of other institutions altogether. A similar pattern of influence and constraint occurs in the management of public sector organizations and it is to this we now turn.

Management and control in the public sector

We often refer to the public sector as if it were a homogeneous group of organizations. This is highly misleading, for the public sector encompasses a wide range of institutions. At least three broad types may be identified. Firstly we have the nationalized industries; these are wholly owned and controlled by the state, and include such organizations as the National Coal Board and the Post Office. Secondly we have those companies which are controlled by the state acting as a majority shareholder and holding company; currently this operates through the British Technology Group (incorporating the National Enterprise Board). Both these types of enterprise have business objectives in that they sell their goods and services in the market place, in many cases with the profit motive in mind (although nationalized industries are theoretically bound by statute to break even).

The third type of public sector organization, such as the health, education and social services offers its services to the population and is funded indirectly through the taxation system.

The rationale for a public sector can be explained in political, economic and social terms, although we can make a broad distinction here between the business and non–business institution. In terms of the provision for health, education, social services, and especially the police and armed forces, there is a broad consensus that public ownership and control is socially and indeed politically desirable, but even here there is fierce political debate on the extent of public provision in areas such as health and education. The major political contention concerns a public sector business presence, brought sharply into focus by the privatization of many public sector concerns in the 1980s. The commitment to public ownership has been a major ideological strand in the constitution of the Labour party enshrined in Clause 4. Indeed the nationalized industries have their goals defined by statute; to provide a specific service, to break even and to operate in the interests of employees and the public at large. Other arguments are made in support of the business public sector; that it supports the growth of other industries by providing such needs as energy; that it can both prevent and ease the decline of industries, significant either for the product or numbers employed or both, as in the case of British Leyland; that the state is in an ideal position to develop new technology. (For an illustration of this final point you are referred to the INMOS case in Chapter 5.)

The major opposition to the public sector focuses on issues of efficiency and effectiveness, as well as control. Heald (1985) senses that the pro–privatization lobby of the 1980s views the public sector organization as inherently flawed, which no amount of attention paid to efficiency and control can cure. According to Heald, the privatization enthusiast's case rests upon two major assumptions. Firstly, public sector organizations are seen as less effective instruments of public policy than those of the private sector and secondly, the political objectives of public ownership are seen as less valid than the market critera of private enterprise.

It is not the intention of this text to discuss the particular arguments surrounding the privatization debate as these are well documented. There is, however, no escaping the conclusion that the public sector is faced with a number of serious problems arising from the tensions between public ownership, political control and day–to–day management. These tensions may be viewed in terms of goals and objectives, finance and control.

Despite the statutory responsibilities of nationalized industries, the goals of public sector organizations have often been ill–defined and conflicting. For example, there was never been a clear policy coordinating the activities of the coal, gas and electricity industries, when all three were under public ownership. Moreover, many public sector operations have found conflict between the provision of a service and the necessity to break even, the railways being a good illustration. Such confusion over the goals led Sir Peter Parker to comment on his time as Head of British Rail, 'I'd never before been in a job where no–one could tell me what winning means' (Quoted in Foy, 1983, p 68).

The superordinate goal of the public sector to operate in the public

KEY CONCEPT 3.5

THE PUBLIC SECTOR

This is a broad term covering a range of organizations in both the manufacturing and service sectors. Despite the differences, public sector organizations share many problems. These include the extent of State control over management decisions, the public accountability of management decisions, levels of government spending and conflict over goals. The Government in Britain since 1979 has attempted to solve such problems by taking organizations out of the public domain and establishing them as private enterprises.

interest is itself open question. Who defines the public interest and is it possible to satisfy all elements of the public at the same time? The National Coal Board, British Steel and British Rail have suffered possibly the greatest losses of any public sector industry, but would the public be best served by making reductions in the services they provide?

Financially the public sector operates under considerable constraints. Pricing policies are often dictated by government in attempts to tackle inflation, as under an incomes policy, or to direct consumption, as in the case of energy use. Public sector enterprises often find investment difficult; they are often prevented from borrowing from the government to hold down the public sector borrowing requirement (PSBR), and the sources of external funding are severely restricted. As we have seen, many public sector enterprises are required only to break even, yet there remains a strong belief among senior management that the greater the profit, then the greater the freedom to operate free of government interference. Variations in profit margins have certainly led to inconsistencies in the treatment of public sector concerns by successive governments, the relatively prosperous gas supply industry enjoying considerably more policy–making freedom than the coal industry.

Excessive intervention has been a frequent complaint among public sector managers. The very structure of the public sector demands answerability to different groups within government itself, to politicians, civil servants, appointed governing bodies, and to various consumer groups, all of whom may have differing expectations and impose conflicting demands upon management. The whole issue is invariably complicated by the organizational politics that develop in the relationship between the heads of public sector organizations and their respective government masters.

The privatization policy vigorously pursued by the Conservative government of the 1980s has its roots, as we have indicated, in an ideological commitment to the free market, and a belief in the inherent inefficiency of the public sector. This has not only resulted in the selling of entire industries, but in the privatization of certain services within the public sector, such as the laundry in hospitals and rubbish collection in some local authorities. Could such a policy liberate management from excessive constraints on their freedom to manage as illustrated above? It is much too early to assess fully the impact of such measures and there is considerable difficultly in disentangling the ideological, political and economic aspects of the argument. Apart from the social issues at stake there is at the moment little evidence to suggest that the private sector is any more efficient or effective than the public sector. More significantly, the privatization of such vast concerns as British Telecommunications and British Gas seems not to have influenced the market place at all, but merely changed the ownership status of a monopoly.

Size

The influence of size as an organizational variable interacts across all levels of our Business in Context model. Many of the issues relating to size are dealt with elsewhere in this book, and in this section we simply present a summary of those issues. We do however develop the concept further by examining the issues relating to small business.

We have already seen earlier in this chapter how size is an important determinant of structure. Hickson *et al.* (1969) noted that with increasing size the technological imperative gives way to the size imperative. Increasing formalization and bureaucratization are inevitable consequenes of the growing firm, and the organization structure and management procedures are shaped by the need to coordinate and control large numbers of people. In our earlier discussion we saw how the growth of firms, especially through diversification was an important element in companies such as General Motors adopting a divisional structure.

With size comes the development of specialist activities. In Chapter 8 we see how the development of personnel management as a specialist function is closely related to the increasing size of organizations. The employment of large numbers of people invariably calls for specialist expertise in the areas of recruitment, training, job evaluation, payment systems and industrial relations. In Chapter 5 we see a relationship between size and the R&D function. In this case it is not simply a matter of the numbers employed, but also a function of the need to maintain a powerful market position through investment in both product and process development and, of course, the ability to attract that investment.

Size is also related to dominance in the market place, as illustrated by the brewing industry in Britain. The industry is dominated by a handful of very large firms who maintain their market position not just by their ability to invest in product and process development, but also by the amount they are able to spend on nationwide advertising campaigns. Their position is further strengthened by their strategy of acquiring smaller independent breweries who find themselves unable to compete. The growth of lager sales at the expense of the traditional bitter beers has attracted the attention of the international brewing industry, who are investing heavily in the British market.

The ability of the larger firm to dominate the market place is only part of its relationship with its environment. The size of a firm may be an important buffer in dealing with the demands imposed by its environment. We saw in Chapter 2 how the multinational corporation is able to dominate its environment, including influencing and in some cases overriding the policies of nation states. Size has also been a factor in attracting government support, not only in terms of R&D investment; the numbers employed by such firms as British Leyland have necessitated government rescue attempts during financial crises for political and social reasons as much for economic ones. In the 1970s in particular, size was often a vtial protection against enforced closure.

Size, structure and market position are themselves important variables in the determination of organization culture, which we deal with in the next section. At the micro level there has been a great deal written about the impact of organizational size on the individual by focussing on the concepts of bureaucracy and alienation. Students are referred to the Organizational Behaviour text in this series for a full discussion of these issues. Large organizations can undoubtedly present behavioural problems in terms of both management control and individual motivation. Such problems have been tackled by a range of devices, including the creation of autonomous work groups in an attempt to break up the organization into more easily managed units. Despite such behavioural problems it should not be forgotten that, at the management level at least, many employees actively seek out large firms for the career opportunities they offer.

Whilst there is considerable evidence supporting the dominant position of the large firm, the problem of control in particular questions whether large firms actually make the best use of their resources. The relationship between size and performance has been challenged by the small firms' lobby, elevated from a 'small is beautiful' campaign in the early 1970s to a near political crusade for the future of Western capitalism in the 1980s. We now deal with the issues and arguments surrounding small firms.

Small business

The small firm has played a key role in the development of the business enterprise, particularly in the nineteenth century, when economic growth owed much to the activities of individual entrepreneurs. The role of the small firm was overtaken by the development of mass production, mass markets, and above all the creation of the joint stock company which created investment and effectively removed a major constraint to the growth of businesses. Throughout this century the focus has been on the increasing size of businesses and the market domination by big business and the multinationals in particular.

The watershed came in 1971 with the publication of the *Report of the Committee of Inquiry on Small Firms*, generally referred to as the Bolton Report, after the Committee's chairman. The Committee's investigation was born out of a concern that the small firms' sector was being neglected, but also out of a disillusionment and fear of the economic and social consequences of domination by big business. The conclusion of Bolton and his colleagues was that the small firms' sector in Britain was in decline, both in terms of its size and its contribution to the nation's economy, and that the decline was more marked in the United Kingdon than in its major economic rivals. The report concluded that despite the decline the small firms' sector 'remains one of substantial importance to the United Kingdom economy' and that 'the contribution of small businessmen to the vitality of society is inestimable' (*Report of the Committee of Inquiry on Small Firms,* 1971, p 342).

The Report's importance lay not just in its conclusions, but as the first serious and subsequently influential attempt to define the small firm and in its stimulus to later research, much of which takes Bolton as its base point. The stimulus of the 1970s became the academic growth area of the 1980s, with many business schools setting up special small firms' units, both for the purposes of academic research and to provide support for the regeneration of the small firms' sector. The stimulus was fuelled in the 1980s by a government increasingly determined to publicize the small business as the key element in the nation's economic revival. A report published in 1983 by a group of conservative MPs and researchers states,

A high small firms ratio is consistent with high levels of growth and output. The malaise of our small business sector is a symptom and a cause of our comparative decline as an industrial nation.

(Bright *et al.*, 1983, p 15)

Such statements were reinforced by a host of measures aimed at supporting the small businessman including special loans for business start–ups and special extension of welfare benefits to stimulate self–employment. In addition changes were made in the stock market through the creation of the Unlisted Securities Market whereby small firms could raise investment capital. The entrepreneur became the hero figure for the 1980s and people such as Clive Sinclair and Eddy Shah became household names. The rationale for government support was more than a belief in the economic importance of the small firm. At a time of high unemployment the small business start–up offered a practical, and to some, a highly attractive solution. Moreover it was a solution that was ideologically compatible with the government's views on economic management, welfare, and self–help. It would be wrong of us to view the support of the small firm as the sole prerogative of the 'New Right' in British politics. Support for the small firms sector has come from all sides of the political spectrum and it is one area where a Conservative government has met with agreement in many Labour–controlled urban areas (with a notable exception of the now de-funct Greater London Council, of which more later).

In this section we will look at the extent and nature of the small businesses in this country and assess their value, focusing particularly on the economic arguments for continued state support. Many of the points are illustrated by in the case study later in this section which summarizes a study of several small firms in the Nottingham area.

The extent of the small firms' sector

Any student of small businesses is immediately confronted with two problems. Firstly there are serious difficulties in defining a small business. The Bolton Report's working definition included those firms employing fewer than two hundred people. The Committee identified three primary characteristics of a small firm; these were having a small market share, being owner–managed, and being independent of any larger concern. The Committee, whilst acknowledging the difficulties, recognized the need for a

Industry	Statistical definition of small firms
Manufacturing	200 employees or less
Retailing	Turnover £50,000 p.a. or less
Wholesale trades	Turnover £200,000 p.a. or less
Construction	25 employees or less
Mining/Quarrying	25 employees or less
Motor trades	Turnover £100,000 or less
Miscellaneous services	Turnover £50,000 or less
Road transport	5 vehicles or less
Catering	All excluding multiples and brewery managed houses

Figure 3.6 The Bolton Report definition of the small firm.

(*Source: Bolton Report* 1.9 p 3)

numerical definition of a small business, but also recognized that the criteria used for manufacturing (numbers employed) would be inappropriate for construction, where much smaller firms were the norm, and for retailing, where the totally different criterion of turnover was seen as more appropriate. Some kind of quantitative definition is essential to the effective administration of government support and the law, small firms being exempt from certain aspects of employment law. The criteria used by Bolton are shown in Figure 3.6.

Secondly, a difficulty arises in estimating the size of the small business sector. Official statistics are incomplete as far as small firms are concerned. For example, the Census of Production excludes firms of less than twenty employees and has only limited data on those of less than a hundred employees. In addition there is a marked preference on the part of some small businessmen to remain outside official statistics for the purposes of tax avoidance. It has been noted that this area of small business development, known as the 'Black Economy', has increased quite dramatically during the 1980s, with estimates of its contribution to the GDP as anything from 3% to almost 15% (Curran, 1986).

Because of these problems the estimates of the extent of small business activity and the contribution to the economy can vary considerably. Nevertheless a recent attempt to summarize the current position, as a review of the Bolton findings fifteen years on, paints a much more optimistic picture than the original report. By 1986 it was estimated that 10% of the population worked for themselves and there was an increase in the number of small firms in all sectors, with the exception of retailing, where small businesses have declined. In addition, new types of small firm have emerged such as producer cooperatives and franchise operations (Curran, 1986). All these developments led Curran to conclude,

The official data does indicate that, for a wide variety of small enterprise, there has been a remarkable increase since 1970 so that the overall total and proportion of small scale activity in the economy has increased.

(Curran, 1986, p 15)

Small businesses still predominate in the distribution, hotel and catering, repair, and contruction sectors, but between 1963 and 1980 there was a 25% increase in the numbers of small manufacturing concerns (source Department of Employment, quoted in *New Society*, March 1986). The same source points to an increase in the numbers of ethnic minorities setting up small firms.

In addition to the increase in the number of firms, the survival chances of of small firms appear to have improved. Although the problems of data accuracy are as acute here as elsewhere, estimates of the failure rate of business start–ups in the 1970s ranged from 50 to 75% within the first two years (Bannock, 1981). More recent and perhaps more reliable data suggest a figure of around 50% for the first two years, but that the chances of survival over ten years are 40–50% (Ganguly and Bannock, 1985). More significantly it has been found that the death rate of small firms has actually slowed down during one of the worst period of the recession, although it is felt that business owners are intent on survival only in the absence of other opportunities (Stewart and Gallagher, 1985 have a fuller explanation). Other studies however remain more sceptical (Binks and Jennings, 1986 summarized in the case study).

However incomplete the database on small firms may be, there is considerable evidence that the United Kingdon has fewer self–employed than many other comparable industrial nations, and it has fewer small firms making far less of a contribution to the economy. The small firms' sector here is smaller than that in the United States and West Germany, and significantly smaller than that in Japan (Ganguly and Bannock, 1985).

The value of small businesses

The value of small businesses may be viewed in terms of the benefits to the owners, their impact on economic growth, the number of jobs they provide, and their service to the consumer. We will deal with each of these aspects in turn.

In terms of the individual, the small firm offers a number of assumed advantages. A Gallup Poll finding in 1986 cited the desire to 'be your own boss' was the main motivation behind small business start–ups, and more significant than unemployment (*New Society*, March 1986). Certainly self–employment offers the individual far greater opportunities for control, and perhaps greater satisfaction through direct involvement, than working for someone else. The small business has for many been the pathway to real wealth, social mobility, and perhaps political power in the local community. Some owners doubtless see their own business as a source of security for their family and as a kind of immortality via family succession. Against such values is the very real risk of failure, and serious financial loss for the owner and their family, and romantic tales of individualism, wealth, and job satisfaction should be set alongside the long working week, the frustration and the stress that many small business owners inevitably experience. The reality for many is that self-employment is less lucrative than working for someone else (*New Society*, March, 1986), and those that are successful either become prime candidates for a takeover bid by a larger firm or fear a loss of control that inevitably comes with growth.

We have already noted that the Conservative government of the 1980s sees the small firm as an essential ingredient of a healthy economy. The most obvious role for the small firm in this respect is to act as a 'seedbed' for future big business, and in so doing secure the future of the economy. In addition, the small firm is seen as filling gaps in the market place by offering specialist products that would be uneconomic for the larger firm to offer. More significantly the small firm is seen as a force for change by being inherently more flexible and innovative than the larger business. This image of the small firm has been strengthened in the 1980s by the publicity given to the success and growth of certain small firms in the computer industry, although the majority of small businesses are decidedly 'low' rather then 'high' tech. In particular the small firm is seen as a useful vehicle in a recession; small firms are seen as price–takers and therefore offer no threat to inflation rates, and are able to plug the gaps left after larger firms have rationalized their operations. The rationalization of bus routes by the major companies together with the government deregulation of bus services paved the way for a number of smaller companies to enter the market, especilly in rural areas and on the larger housing estates. These bus companies were able to operate routes that were uneconomic for the larger companies.

Many writers (for example Scase and Goffee, 1980, Rainnie, 1985) are more sceptical of the economic contribution of the small firms' sector, feeling that the small firm is exploited by big business and the main economic advantages of a small business presence accrue to the larger company. Certainly large manufacturing concerns could not survive without the components supplied by a host of smaller companies, but this could be seen as a symbiotic rather than an exploitative relationship. However we did see in our examination of Japan in the last chapter and the spread of Japanese type subcontracting methods to this country that the purchasing power of the larger firm can have a significant impact on the profit margins of smaller companies. Certainly there is evidence of larger firms taking over markets created by smaller companies when those markets prove successful, the activity of IBM in the personal computer market being a case in point.

There is an assumption that small firms are first to the market place because they are inherently more innovative. Supporters of this view cite inventions such as air–conditioning and cellophane that originated from individual entrepreneurs and that small businesses often emerge from ideas for new products or clever adaptations of existing products. Big business on the other hand is often accused of channelling R&D along predictable lines and being less cost effective in its use of R&D expenditure. Apart from the difficulties of measuring such things, the evidence for these claims is very mixed (Rothwell and Zegveld, 1981 have a good summary of the research). More recent research suggests that even if small firms are inventive they often lack the development capital for successful innovation. (The distinction between invention and innovation is drawn more fully in Chapter 5.) Moreover there is evidence to suggest that a high proportion of small business start–ups do not involve new products but involve the owner in replicating his previous employment (Binks and Jennings, 1986). This trend becomes especially critical where buy–outs are concerned and may be a primary cause of small business failure among buy–outs. In this case an ailing firm either sells out or divests part of its operation to a group of existing employees, usually management. Their experience and skills give them the optimism to continue operations in the same product market, perhaps ignoring the lack of demand or excessive competition operating in that same market, and they merely repeat the failure of the original firm.

There are obvious benefits of a thriving small firms' sector for the labour market. As we see in Case 3.4, redundancy and unemployment are big push factors towards self–employment. Small firms have been started and operate successfully in growth areas of the economy such as computer software and consultancy and the service sector in general. Moreover, self–employment is a valuable source of work for those groups, such as ethnic minorities, who are discriminated against in the labour market. In certain communities an overdependence on a few larger firms for employment can have serious consequences when those close, as the people of Skelmersdale found when Courtaulds decided to cease trading in the town. Under such circumstances a healthy small business presence may provide employment diversity and help counter the worst effects of mass redundancy. This view was taken by the government with the experience of mass redundancies at the nationalized British Steel Corporation in the Sheffield area. The company took advantage of tax advantages by providing venture capital to business start–ups in the area.

However, the small firm is hardly a great provider of employment. A study of the Hi–tech industry, one of the flagships of the small firms lobby, in the Cambridge area from 1971 to 1981 concluded that only eight hundred new jobs had been created during the entire period (Gould and Keeble, 1984). Rainnie (1985) points out that whatever new jobs are created, they can easily be overshadowed by job losses in a large organization and cites a report of 10 000 redundancies at Britain's largest computer firm, ICL, in 1984. Moreover we have already seen from the high proportion of start–up failures that small firms are a source of job losses too. Outside the arguments about the small firm as a source of employment, the Greater London Council was especially critical of the small firm as an employer, citing exploitation through low wages, long hours and an absence of trade union recognition as the main reason for their lack of support for small business development (GLC, 1983). This view of small firms was also taken by Scase and Goffee (1980) who saw their main contribution to employment as solving the problems as defined by employers. Obviously not all small firms exploit their workforce, and many employees prefer the informal working environment that the small firm can provide.

We have already seen in our example of the deregulation of the bus industry how the small firm can benefit the consumer by filling the gaps left by the larger company. There is also the argument that the smaller firm is also closer to its customers and can provide them with a more personalized, responsive and specialized service. There are certain highly specialized product markets, such as precision scientific instrumentation, which tend to favour the small concern. Whether the smaller firm offers a 'better' service to the consumer is impossible to generalize or even judge. When buying expensive wine for keeping several years, a small specialist firm may be the most appropriate consumer choice, whilst a supermarket chain

A survey was carried out of a hundred small firms in the Nottingham area. The firms were all wholly new businesses that had come into existence since 1977 and were independent, owner–managed and engaged predominantly in manufacturing. The main findings concerned the motivation behind setting up, the choice of product, the advice sought by small businessmen, and the labour costs involved.

The attraction of setting up in business was seen in terms of both pull and push factors, often operating together. The main push factors in order of significance were: redundancy; job insecurity and unemployment; disagreement at a previous firm; and the closure of a previous venture. The main pull factors in order of significance were; the desire for independence; the possession of specialist knowledge; the development of a product idea; and the incentive of financial reward.

The product chosen by the new company was invariably derived from the owner's previous experience, hobby or working skill. Seventy-eight per cent set up in businesses that were the same or similar to a previous employment, and only 4% were classed as having innovated a new product or process. The advice available to small business concerns was seen to be not particularly helpful or attractive to the potential entrepreneur. Over 40% took no advice at all prior to starting up, and only 4% attended any type of training course. Labour costs were typified by the owners working long hours for little remuneration, especially in the first two years, and the relatively low wages accepted by employees. The labour cost policy was related to a competitive pricing policy for market penetration.

The researchers conclude that such small firm growth in manufacturing is a response to economic recession and occurs in established industries with little contribution to product or process innovation, and as such is unlikely to contribute towards economic recovery and growth. Moreover, the pricing and wages policies of the new entrants is likely to have a depressing effect on the local economy by threatening the livelihood of established enterprises. As such, government policies aimed at increasing the number of small firms 'may simply be increasing the throughput of firms rather than the stock'.

CASE 3.4

SMALL FIRMS IN THE NOTTINGHAM AREA

(*Source:* Binks and Jennings, 1986)

may offer the best value on less expensive purchases. The situation becomes particularly blurred when you consider that a number of larger firms of all types pay particular attention to customer sales and after–sales service. At a broader level, a small firms' sector may be of considerable benefit to the consumer in challenging the power of monopolies.

The small firm as a case for government support

We believe that the health of the economy requires the birth of new enterprises in substantial number and the growth of some to a position from which they are able to challenge and supplant the existing leaders of industry.... We cannot assume that the ordinary working of market forces will necessarily preserve a small firm sector large enough to perform this function in the future.

(*Committee of Inquiry on Small Firms* 8.5 p 85)

Bolton and his committee were clear that government support was necessary to secure the future of the small firm and hence the economy. In spite of its commitment to market forces the Conservative government of the 1980s reveals its support of the small business by a large number of different measures.

One of the intentions in our analysis of small businesses was to look behind the current popular support for the small firms' sector and attempt to challenge the view that the encouragement of small business development is a valid strategy for economic recovery and growth. It is indeed difficult to draw any firm conclusions at all, for despite the growth of research data and the space devoted to small businesses in the serious as well as the popular press, many difficulties remain.

Confusion still reigns over an agreed definition of what actually constitutes a small business and the evidence that we do possess is highly contradictory in its findings. The main danger is certainly one of politics and ideology, which was as much a part of the Conservative government's support as the GLC's condemnation.

What we do find is that the small firm provides some jobs, offers some hope for the unemployed and meets the subcontracting needs of big business. However there is very little evidence that a policy of the encouragement of small firms will either solve the problems of mass unemployment or result in substantial economic growth. Behind the rhetoric of politicians there is considerable criticism aimed at those very measures designed to support the small firm. The sheer number and complexity of such measures, and the different sources of advice have been shown to be as confusing as they are helpful. Moreover the cost of much government support such as the Loans Guarantee Scheme has proven much too expensive for many small firms. Outside the government schemes the banks appear keen to provide services for the small firm, but even here the picture must be seen in perspective. German banks on average lend twice as much for longer periods and at lower interest rates than their British counterparts (Bannock, 1981).

Bannock's vision of a healthy economic future involves small and large business in a kind of optimal balance, with small firms as the 'motivators of growth' and large firms as the 'consolidators and accelerators'. In this way the small firm may play a significant role in the recovery from recession (quoted in Curran, 1986, p 44). Curran himself remains less optimistic.

The fashionable concern with the contribution of small enterprise to economic restructuring should not be allowed to obscure the dominating presence of the large enterprise.

(Curran, 1986, p 46)

Concern for the small firm may well be, like the interest in Japanese management, a fashion born out of recession. Certainly small business development is important in the future of any economy, but current political interest owes as much to ideology as it does to sound economic

In recent years the notion of organizational culture (Key Concept 1.6) has been used to develop a set of principles which mark out the so-called excellent company from those that are less successful. Elements of excellence which are assumed to contribute towards business success include clear objectives, customer orientation, workforce involvement and commitment, strong values developed by top management and accepted by all employees and a commitment to entrepreneurship, irrespective of the size of the firm. As with all attempts to establish universal principles, considerable debate has been aroused.

KEY CONCEPT 3.6

THE EXCELLENT COMPANY

argument. For our purposes the case of the small firm is again an excellent illustration of the interplay between the various elements of our Business in Context model.

Organizational culture

We have already encountered the concept of culture in our treatment of the environmental context of business in Chapter 2. Our emphasis there was on broad cultural distinctions between different groups of people, particularly in the comparisons of business in different countries. In this section we focus upon culture in a more localized setting, that of the organization itself. The goals, structure, patterns of owernship and size of an organization both reflect and are reflected in its culture. Other influences on the culture of an organization include its history and all those aspects we have identified as belonging to the environmental level of our Business in Context model. The importance of the organizational culture is that is sets the scene for the determination of strategy and hence the operational aspects of organizational life. The concept assumes therefore a central position in our model of business.

Interest in the workings of an organizational culture were heightened in the USA during the 1970s as American companies searching for a solution to the problems of the economic recession looked to the role models of Japanese firms and the more successful firms within their own country. In turn, academic research in business shifted its focus away from individual management techniques to examining the business as a complete entity and viewing the way people responded to their own organization. A more subjective view of organizations began to emerge.

In this section we will examine the precise nature of organizational and corporate culture, examine the concept of the 'excellent company', and assess its value as a business tool. We will illustrate these points by reference to Hewlett–Packard, the American computer and electronic instrument firm, presented as Case 3.5.

The nature of corporate culture

Perhaps the most straightforward and often quoted definition of organizational culture is offered by Deal and Kennedy (1982) as 'the way we do things around here'. In more academic terms it is seen as 'an amalgam of beliefs, ideology, language, ritual and myth' (Pettigrew, 1979, p 572), which enables people to function in a given setting. Similar elements to Pettigrew's crop up in Deal and Kennedy's treatment. 'The way we do things around here' comprises the following.

☐ The business environment, created by competitors, customers and the prevailing technology.
☐ Values, which are usually those of top management and communicated to the workforce.
☐ Heroes, meaning those who best typify the organizational culture.
☐ Rituals which emphasize and reward the type of behaviour expected.
☐ A cultural network, comprising a system of communication to spread the values, create the heroes and generally tie everything together.

The main difference between the two treatments of organizational culture is the more specific context of Deal and Kennedy. To them organizational culture has a function, that of establishing values and creating a cohesive unit. There is a clear link between Deal and Kennedy's analysis and the notion of the 'excellent company' attributed to Peters and Waterman (1982). In this way the concept of organizational culture becomes entwined with the much more normative and positive concept of a corporate culture, and the notion that it can be created and fashioned to increase productivity and profitability. In short, organizational culture is both a set of distinguishing features that mark of one organization from another, and more popularly used has become a set of universal principles guiding best practice. The concept has both descriptive and normative elements. In the case of the latter, writers like Peters and Waterman and Ouchi believe they have discovered those elements of culture which contribute towards success in business which management can then develop in their own organizations.

The processes of creating such a 'positive' organizational culture would appear to operate as follows. The senior management of a company sets goals and issues guidelines which promote strongly–held shared values; there is normally an emphasis upon enthusiasm, diligence, loyalty and service to the customer. To ensure that such guidelines are passed on to all employees there is usually a high investment in the procedures of communication and integration. A number of techniques are commonly used to create and maintain a specific corporate culture. Some firms pay particular attention to the physical environment; the layout in Hewlett–Packard is designed to encourage communication and they try to maintain the same layout in all their establishments throughout the world; in IBM layout is equally important as is the use of a corporate colour, blue. The goals of the company are invariably written, explicit, communicated to all employees and tend to stress the contribution that employees can make to the firm. Heroes and myths play in important role in communicating the core values as illustrated by the 'Bill and Dave' stories in Case 3.5. The same role is ascribed to important rituals such as presentations to successful employees and social gatherings; in companies such as IBM, employees are encouraged to participate in our–of–work activities, with non–participation being frowned upon.

The culture is also strengthened by more formal procedures such as training and induction and the design of the organization structure. There is usually a deliberate attempt to create clearly–defined autonomous units to enhance group identity and loyalty, together with an emphasis upon informality and avoidance of bureaucratic controls. In recruitment and selection procedures a great deal of care is usually taken to select only those individuals who would fit in with the prevailing culture.

At its most influential the corporate culture is seen as having replaced organized religion and the family as the most important focus in a person's life (Ray, 1986). In a recent television documentary about the establishment of the Japanese firm Komatsu in Britain, one of its senior Japanese employees listed his priorities in order as the firm, the state, and finally his family. Not surprisingly the Japanese firm is often held as the prime example of an organizational culture.

Those who subscribe to this view of organizations claim that such ideas constitute a new management theory and a return to the universal principles approach which typified the earlier but essentially different theories of people such as Fayol and Taylor. The type of firms which embody such principles better than most are the so–called 'excellent companies'.

The notion of the excellent company

Peters and Waterman (1982) may not be the only writers to attempt to identify the features of the excellent company (Ouchi attempted much the same a year earlier), but their attempt proved to be the most successful by far with their book *In Search of Excellence* selling almost three million copies. Peters and Waterman carried out an investigation of sixty-two top–performing American companies. Six measures of long–term productivity were devised and only firms which ranked in the top twenty of their industry on four out of the six criteria were included in their in–depth study. Their final sample numbered forty-three firms including IBM, Hewlett–Packard, Boeing, Digital, Caterpillar, Eastman Kodak, Walt Disney, and 3M. The sample was not intended to be representative of all types of firm and banks are notable by their exclusion.

In all eight attributes of excellence were identified. These were, using Peters and Waterman's own terminology, as follows.

☐ 'Bias for action', being typified by clear objectives and a marked absence of committee procedures.
☐ 'Closeness to the customer', typified by processes and procedures aimed at identifying and serving the customers' needs.
☐ 'Autonomy and entrepreneurship', which are best achieved through the creation of small cohesive teams.
☐ 'Productivity through people', with workforce involvement at all times.
☐ 'Hands on; value driven', involving the fostering of a strong corporate culture by top management who are seen to be in touch with all employees.
☐ 'Stick to the knitting', which involves limiting activities to what the firm does best and avoiding diversification into unknown territory.
☐ 'Simple form, lean staff', avoiding complex hierarchies and large administration sections.

☐ 'Simultaneous loose–tight properties', which means that organization structure should display a combination of strong central direction with work group autonomy.

Throughout their work Peters and Waterman stressed the importance of excellent companies socializing and integrating individuals into a clearly defined corporate culture. The firm becomes much more than a place of work, 'by offering meaning as well as money, the excellent companies give their employees a mission as well as a sense of feeling great' (Peters and Waterman, 1982, p 323).

How useful is organizational culture as a concept?

We need to distinguish between organizational culture as a means of differentiating between companies, and organizational culture as a set of principles which shape 'excellent' companies.

The development of organizational culture as an analytical device leaves much to be desired. There are problems of defining the elements which comprise organizational culture, and, in a review of the literature, Hofstede (1986) is disappointed by the apparent lack of empirical research. Until we develop some systematic measures of organizational concept then its utility as an analytical tool must be limited. Given such problems it is difficult to prove links between culture and performance, let alone understand how such a relationship operates.

The major controversy concerns the concept as a set of principles to guide 'good' management practice. Advocates argue that they have analysed successful companies and found links between organizational culture · and performance. There are a number of difficulties with this approach which we identify below.

Several writers feel that the importance of culture has been overstated. Carroll (1983) considers that the important effects of technology, market dominance, the influence of the state and the control of critical·raw materials have all been ignored in the analysis. Dawson (1986) takes this a stage future. She feels that what people such as Peters and Waterman have uncovered is not a set of universal principles of management, but strategies that only work in certain types of company. She writes:

> Their 'slim consensual organizations' of the future are probably applicable to firms employing professionals and technicians from the primary labour market in the development and operation of new technology or highly fashionable products and processes. They may however be less successful in other technological, product and labour market conditions.
> (Dawson 1986, p 137)

It is interesting to speculate whether the kind of processes and procedures illustrated in our Hewlett–Packard case would have any relevance for an inner city local authority or the health service, or assist management in older industries such as British Steel.

The focus of research has been on 'excellent' companies. Child (1984) speculates what would happen if the very same attributes were found in less than excellent companies. There has been little or no comparison with

the cultural characteristics of poor performers. In fact, immediately following Peters and Waterman's study three of their excellent companies,
including Texas Instruments and National Semiconductors suffered serious
set–backs in their performance and there was evidence of a reversion to
more bureaucratic types of control.

The above paragraphs may be summed up by the difficulty of proving a
relationship between the features of excellence and company performance.
More significantly, we could argue that the features displayed by these
excellent companies are a direct result rather than a cause of company
performance. It is much easier to gain employee consensus and focus on
customer needs when profits are healthy.

Situations might be envisaged where a strong commitment to a corporate
culture could lead to resistance to change, when major reorganization is
called for in response to market, technological or other changes. If all
employees are selected in the same image, where will the organizations
find the 'deviants' to initiate change? This view would doubtless be challenged by representatives of such as Hewlett–Packard, who would point to
the emphasis placed in their organization on innovation. Moreover, given
the commitment to corporate values in such 'value–driven' firms, change
could well be initiated through a series of top management exhortations.

The type of processes and procedures used by 'excellent' companies do
have certain similarities with techniques of conditioning and even brain-
washing and may be morally unacceptable to some. Nevertheless, whilst
there are personality types who would find working for such companies
difficult, there are countless others who enjoy their association with them.

Despite such criticisms the development of an organization culture to
enhance performance can be appealing to management and workforce
alike. For management it is an important source of control through the
moral involvement of the workforce (Ray, 1986). In this respect there is a
similarity with the techniques associated with the 'human relations' and
'organizational development' schools of management thinking. Moreover
the popularity of *In Search of Excellence* is in part testimony to the optimism
it portrays and its morale–boosting effects on managers. As far as employees
are concerned, they are given clear guidelines about the kind of behaviour
expected of them, which has been estimated as saving up to two hours a
day (Deal and Kennedy, 1982). In addition, there is no doubt that many
employees enjoy working in the deliberately–created integrated atmo-
spheres of the IBMs and the Hewlett–Packards, and successful, 'excellent'
companies do tend to pay well!

Summary

In this chapter we focussed our attention on the organizational elements of
business which we identified as goals, structure, ownership, size and organizational culture. As befits our model, all elements interact not just with
each other but with aspects of the environment, business strategy and
operations.

We view *goals* as the products of a highly interactive and dynamic
process, such that changing goals may well be a prerequisite for business

CASE 3.5

HEWLETT–PACKARD

Hewlett–Packard is an American multinational operating in most major countries of the world. It was founded in the late 1930s in Palo Alto, California by Bill Hewlett and Dave Packard, both of whom still have considerable influence on company philosophy. The firm operates in four main divisions, each representing different product groupings. The divisions are; the Computer Systems Group, the Measurement Systems Group, the Medical Products group, and the Analytical Instrumentation group.

The central element in all their activities is the 'HP Way', a set of beliefs, objectives and guiding principles, and described by Bill Hewlett as follows.

> The policies and actions that flow from the belief that men and women want to do a good job, a creative job, and that if they are provided with the proper environment they will do so. It is the tradition of treating every individual with respect and recognising personal achievements . . . You can't describe it in numbers or statistics. In the last analysis it is a spirit, a point of view. There is a feeling that everyone is part of a team and that team is HP. As I said at the beginning it is an idea that is based on the individual. It exists because people have seen that it works, and they believe that this feeling makes HP what it is.
>
> (Quoted in Peters and Waterman, 1982, p 244)

The HP Way is probably best illustrated from a number of words and concepts extracted from Hewlett–Packard's own publications. These are love of the product, love of the customer, innovation, quality, open communication, commitment to people, trust, confidence, informality, teamwork, sharing, openness, autonomy, responsibility.

It is not just the communication of such sentiments that appears to be important in Hewlett–Packard, but that such sentiments appear to be shared by a majority of employees and felt with a certain intensity.

The sentiments are reinforced by a series of processes and procedures which we identify below.

Communication is the key underlying theme behind all activities in Hewlett–Packard and is an important ingredient of the company's attitude towards innovation and quality. Informal communication is encouraged between all employees of different levels and functions. The physical layout of the offices and work stations has been deliberately created to encourage ad hoc meetings and brainstorming. The use of first names is almost obligatory and is the norm even in the West German operations, where employees are used to a much greater degree of formality in personal relationships. Management assists the informal processes by engaging in what Hewlett–Packard term MBWA ('management by wandering around'). At a more formal level there are frequent announcements to the workforce on such matters as company performance, and all employees are given a written statement of the company goals, stressing as they do the contribution which individuals can make. The communication policy is assisted by the company's commitment to decentralization.

Continued from previous page

An important aspect of communication in Hewlett–Packard is the various stories and myths that are a continual feature of management training, retirement parties, company speeches and in–house journals. These stories generally tell of key moments in the company's history, or recount the exploits of the corporate heroes, usually Bill Hewlett and Dave Packard. These stories serve an important purpose of stressing a collective identity and underlining the goals of the founders.

Quality, according to Peters and Waterman, is pursued with zealotry. The company certainly sees its prime objective as a commitment to the design, manufacture and marketing of high quality goods. Commitment to quality is viewed as ongoing with continual product improvement as a major goal. All employees are involved in the definition and monitoring of quality, a process reinforced by procedures such as MBWA and ceremonies to recognize, reward and publicize good work.

Innovation, like quality, is regarded as the responsibility of all employees. Following the espousal to 'stick to the knitting' there is a clear commitment to products related to electrical engineering and the company's existing product portfolio. Openness is encouraged and prototypes are often left for other employees to test and criticize. Employees are free to take company equipment home with them. In relations with their customers the company is guided by yet another principle and mnemonic, that of LACE ('laboratory awareness of customer environment'). A central strategy in R&D is the design of products to customer specifications and the LACE programme gives customers the opportunity to make presentations to the company. Such procedures stress the strong emphasis on customer service.

Personnel policies are carefully designed to reinforce the HP Way as well as ensuring that it works. Most HP employees have no requirement for clocking–on and many operate on flexible working hours. All employees attend a detailed induction programme with communication of the HP Way as a key ingredient. It terms of selection care is taken to select only those who meet the criteria of being high calibre and possessing flair, adaptability and openness. Most recruits are young. As we have seen, considerable attention is paid to the environment and the general well–being of employees is a major consideration.

There is a somewhat traditional and conservative approach to finance and accounting. There is an emphasis on careful management of assets, self–financing investment, and minimal long–term borrowing.

The overall impression is often that Hewlett–Packard is too good to be true. 'We tried to remain sober, not to become fans. But it proved impossible' (Peters and Waterman, 1982, p 246).

Certainly on most measures of performance and employee satisfaction, Hewlett–Packard emerges as a highly successful company. A measure of the employees' commitment occurred in 1970 when in the middle of a recession and bad time for the company financially, a 10% pay cut was agreed rather than lay people off.

(*Sources:* Peters and Waterman, 1982, Beer *et al.*, 1984, Needle, 1984) survival. Goals give a sense of direction to a firm's activities and may be presented in a hierarchy involving a mission, objectives and strategies. The formulation of goals is closely related to the way power relations are worked out in organizations, and often involve highly political processes of influence, conflict and compromise between different interest groups. A number of goals may operate at any one time. These may conflict, but in general the goals of a business follow closely those of the dominant coalition.

The factors which influence *structure* are identified as technology, size, environmental changes, strategy, culture, and the behaviour of interest groups. We identify various models of organizational structure including, functional, divisional and matrix, but acknowledge that very few firms confirm to such ideal types. Many firms have mixed structures and new variations are emerging all the time. The relationship between structure and performance is of obvious interest to businessmen, but as yet the evidence is inconclusive.

Ownership is important because of its potential impact on the way business are managed. We examine this relationship by focussing on the traditional debate of ownership versus control, and the freedom of managers to make decisions in the face of the growing influence of institutional shareholders and the power of interlocking directorships. The dilemmas that can arise in the relationship between ownership and control are examined with reference to the public sector.

We examine the influence of *size* on such factors as structure, market power, relationship with the state, and the impact on the individual. The main focus of this section is the small firm. The case for government support of the small firm is examined in light of the potential contribution of small business to the economy and society. We conclude that the current enthusiasm for small firms owes more to ideology than it does to economic analysis.

Organizational culture is viewed as the product of goals, structure, ownership and size, as well as company history, technology, its product–market environment and several other variables as well. The sum total of those influences distinguish organizations from one another. The main argument surrounding organizational culture is that a particular culture can be created to enhance performance and the debate has focussed on the notion of 'excellent' companies. Despite the enthusiasm for 'excellence', the research is inconclusive, and culture may be less important than technology or the product market.

Further reading

A good insight into the complexities of goal formation may be found in R.M. Cyert and J.G. March *A Behavioural Theory of the Firm* (Prentice Hall, 1963). Discussions and illustrations of structural considerations are probably best found in J. Child, *Organizations: A Guide to Problems and Practice* (Harper and Row, 1984), although another good source is J.R. Galbraith and D.A. Nathanson, *Strategy Implication: The Role of Structure and Process* (West Publishing, 1978), and those students seeking an historical perspective are advised to look at A.D. Chandler, *Strategy and*

Structure: Chapters in the History of American Capitalism (MIT Press, 1962). Probably the best summary of the ownership and control debate is offered by J. Child, *The Business Enterprise in Modern Industrial Society* (Collier–Macmillan, 1969) and a good review of the key studies as well as the role of financial institutions can be found in J. Scott, *Corporations, Classes and Capitalism* (Hutchinson, 1979). A good summary of the research and debates about the role of the small firm is found in J. Curran, *Bolton Fifteen Years On: A Review and Analysis of Small Business Research in Britain 1971–86* (Small Business Trust, 1986) whilst a good focus on the problems facing small firms can be found in R. Scase and R. Goffee, *The Real World of the Small Business Owner* (Croom Helm, 1980). No examination of organizational culture would be complete without a look at T.J. Peters and R.J. Waterman *In Search of Excellence: Lessons from America's Best-run Companies* (Harper and Row, 1982) and a more academic treatment is offered by The *Journal of Management Studies*, May 1986 which devotes a whole edition to this topic.

Discussion

1. What purposes are served by the kind of goals and statements presented in Case 3.1?

2. How are goals formed and what are the major difficulties encountered in goal formulation and implementation?

3. Identify the various strategic, organizational and environmental factors which led to structural changes in Dow Corning and IBM as illustrated by Cases 3.2 and 3.3. What problems will the new organization structures solve, and what new problems may emerge?

4. What purposes do the various structural types identified in this chapter serve? What are the major influencing factors which may cause management to favour one structural type over another?

5. How significant is the separation of ownership and control to the way business operate?

6. To what extent will privatization solve the problems of managing public sector organizations?

7. Examine the rationale behind the government support for the small firms sector. Will small firms be economically relevant in the 1990s?

8. What is the relationship between the type of corporate culture envisaged by Deal and Kennedy and by Peters and Waterman, and company performance in terms of profitability and job satisfaction? Can the internal culture of an organization act as a buffer against environmental influences?

9. What are the advantages and disadvantages of the Hewlett–Packard style as illustrated in Case 3.5? What threats could challenge the effectiveness of such a style?

10. Examine the relationship between organizational culture and the other organizational variables of the Business in Context model.

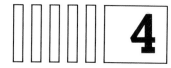

4 Management strategy

Management strategy as a linking process between environmental and organizational variables is a fundamental aspect of our Business in Context model. We are able to observe the functional operation of R&D, production, marketing, personnel and accounting only through their relevant management strategies. In our introduction to this book we highlighted the case of the shipping industry and News International, both representative of the exercise of strategic options in the face of external and internal opportunities and contraints in the two industries concerned.

Management strategy contains a number of inter–related elements. Firstly, it involves a consideration of environmental changes which bring about new opportunities and pose new threats. Secondly, it is concerned with the assessment of the internal strengths and weaknesses of the institution and in particular its ability to respond to those opportunities and threats. Thirdly management strategy is the product of a decision–making process influenced by the values, preferences and power of interested parties. Finally, management strategy is concerned with generating options and evaluating them. Management strategy is therefore an all–embracing term dealing with goals and objectives, the firm's environment, its resources and structure, the scope and nature of its activities and ultimately the behaviour of its members.

In this chapter we deal with all these elements. We begin by examining the nature of strategy, through the way strategy is formed. We refer to this as the strategic process. We then look at the different contexts in which strategic decisions are taken, and go on to identify the various environmental and organizational aspects of management strategy. We end the chapter by examining a number of common strategic options, and a brief look at the criteria for strategic choice.

We prefer to use the term 'management strategy' since most strategies in organizations originate from the management group. The concept crops up in many guises and is sometimes referred to as 'business policy', 'corporate strategy', 'corporate planning' and so on. Although attempts have been made to formulate distinctions between such terms, the general inter–changeability of their use indicates a similarity in approach.

The strategic process

An examination of how strategy is formed gives us useful insights into the

The strategic process refers to the way in which management strategy is formed. In most organizations this involves a mixture of scientific and rational analysis together with more subjective and political considerations.

KEY CONCEPT 4.1

THE STRATEGIC PROCESS

nature of strategy itself. We identify five different approaches, which we have termed, rational, flexible, creative, behavioural, incremental and a sixth which suggests that some managers operate without a conscious strategy. We deal with each in turn.

The rational approach. Strategy formulation is often portrayed as a scientific and highly rational process, assisted by a range of techniques such as technological forecasting, portfolio analysis, environmental impact analysis and sensitivity analysis. The rational approach owes much to the development of contingency theory. In Chapter 1 we noted that the contingency approach stressed the importance of a strategic fit between the firm and its environment. Analyses are made of a firm's environment to assess likely opportunities and threats, and of its internal resource position to identify strengths and weaknesses.

This process is sometimes referred to as SWOT analysis, a mnemonic for strengths, weaknesses, opportunities and threats. An illustration of the kind of analysis that can be made is offered in Figure 4.1. The approach is based upon the assumption that information is readily available to the strategist and an accurate assessment can be made of its likely impact on the firm. As we shall see later, this is not always the case and the entire process is subject to behavioural influences. The so-called rational techniques illustrated above have been criticized as 'pseudo-science'. Nonetheless this is the basic approach used by many texts (for example, Ansoff, 1968, Glueck and Jauch, 1984).

In the 1960s and 1970s the emergence of an increasingly complex and turbulent business environment called for modifications in the rational approach.

The flexible approach. The complexity and volatility of the environment may mean that a detailed SWOT analysis is both difficult and inappropriate. The environment may be changing so rapidly that many of the historical and current data are meaningless. This kind of situation led the oil companies, like Shell, to adopt a different approach to strategy formulation known as 'scenario planning'. The approach recognizes that uncertainty can never be eliminated, but it can be reduced by plotting different scenarios, each responding to alternative visions of the future. Managements are therefore prepared for a number of possible changes that may occur.

The creative approach. This takes the flexible approach one step further by stressing the importance of imagination in the strategic process. The idea that such an approach to strategy formulation is actually *better* has been taken up by management writers in the 1980s. Peters and Waterman

KEY CONCEPT 4.2

SWOT ANALYSIS

SWOT stands for strengths, weaknesses, opportunities and threats. It is normally associated with more rational approaches to strategy formulation but perhaps its greatest contribution lies in providing the management strategist and student of business a broad framework for analysing the position of a firm at a particular moment in time. It can also be useful in the development of a number of strategic options which attempt to tackle opportunities and threats and build on corporate strengths and weaknesses. An important consideration is that for most management there is a choice of strategy.

OPPORTUNITIES

Promotion to other divisions.
Increased revenue from success in cup competitions.
Sale of town–centre site and redevelopment on the outskirts.
Development of a membership squash club and fitness centre attached to the ground.
Use of ground for other functions, e.g., rock concerts.
Development of retailing activities.

THREATS

Seven other professional clubs operating in a twenty–five mile radius.
Rising costs of wages and transfer fees; bank interest charges; policing; equipment.
Local authority refusing planning permission.
Government proposals to introduce a compulsory membership scheme for attendance.
Best players will leave.
Competition for spectators' time and money from other sources e.g., cinema, DIY.
Increased levels of unemployment in the area.

The club owns its own ground and car-parks in a good town-centre site.
Good housekeeping and relatively low wages.
A hard core of 2000 loyal supporters.
A successful and well established youth development policy.
The image of a 'friendly' club with good connections in local industry.

Large bank overdraft.
Ground facilities in poor order, especially seating and toilets.
Insufficient funds to invest in higher wages and transfer fees.
A relatively small population to support so many clubs in close proximity.
Poor image compared to first division neighbours.

Figure 4.1 An analysis of the strengths, weaknesses, opportunities and threats of Swot United, a third division football club.

STRENGTHS

WEAKNESSES

believe that the more formal approaches to strategy formulation with the emphasis on complex environmental and organizational analysis can lead to 'paralysis through analysis' (Peters and Waterman 1982, p 31). The resulting policies are often too conservative, insufficiently adventurous and positive, and ignore the human contribution. Their 'excellent' companies are typified by a strategic planning approach which recognizes the values of the decision–makers as one of the driving forces giving the firm its competitive edge.

The more complex and changing the business environment, and the more difficult the problems facing managers, then the more creative they need to be. Such situations have been termed 'messy problems'. These have serious implications for the firm involved, but the problems are difficult to identify, and information is incomplete or of dubious value to the strategist. It is thought that such situations are becoming more commonplace, calling for a greater creativity in strategy formulation (McCaskey, 1982 has a fuller discussion).

The behavioural approach. There is strong support for the view that strategy formulation is far from being a rational, logical process (Cyert and March, 1963 and Child, 1972). Instead, strategic choice is the product of the organization's dominant coalition, invariably senior management, and is based upon its values, ideologies and personalities, and upon the process of organization power and politics. The process invariably involves some negotiation between senior management and other groups. The most overt of these processes take place at shareholders' meetings and in collective bargaining with trade unions. However, the most significant negotiations generally take place between competing factions within management itself, over such issues as the allocation of scarce resources, and are consequently much more difficult to observe.

Behavioural analyses of the strategy formulation see management values and objectives as more than individual inputs to the planning process. They influence the way the environment is perceived and hence, the choice of opportunities and threats and the assessment of strengths and weaknesses.

The incremental approach. This sees strategy not as a carefully prepared plan with clear goals, but a process by which the organization gradually comes to terms with its environment. Limited objectives are constantly modified in the light of experience and through the process of negotiation between interested parties. As a consequence, strategies are continually being changed. The incremental approach has been put forward as a more realistic and more effective method of dealing with complex and changing situations. The concept originated from the work of Lindblom (1959) in an article appropriately titled 'The Science of Muddling Through'. Although his work was mainly concerned with large public sector organizations such as hospitals and universities, there are strong parallels with larger private sector firms.

An absence of strategy? Finally, we present the view that strategy formulation is not a conscious management activity. Strategy is not an issue when firms appear to be operating to the satisfaction of management. It becomes an issue only in times of crisis when any attempt at strategy formulation may be too little and too late. There may be several reasons for this. Management may be complacent and reluctant to rock the boat, or they may have myopic vision and hence a limited view of alternatives (see Levitt, 1960, and a discussion of the concept of 'marketing myopia' in Chapter 7). It may be that managements are too distracted by the daily business of survival and see themselves too weighed down by resource constraints to contemplate strategic options.

The various approaches we have identified reveal a mixture of rational and non–rational approaches to the formulation of management strategy. Nevertheless, strategies are more than management hunches played out in an information vacuum. More likely, managements select that information that is appropriate for their purposes, and this invariably involves consideration of both environmental and organizational variables. Management values and organization politics are important not only in the choice of strategy but in the selection of information upon which that strategy is based. The following illustration reveals this mixed approach to strategic decision–making.

One of the partners in a firm of solicitors is keen to establish a computerized client record and accounts system. He spends several months persuading his fellow partners that this may be a good idea. The process of persuasion is accompanied by a gathering of information to show the growth of the firm over the past few years and illustrations are well chosen to show the advantages of faster information retrieval and better management information on the current status of client accounts. Information is also collected on the type of hardware and software systems currently available and their price. Quotations are sought from a few computer firms with experience in servicing professional firms. The partners agree to go ahead with the project and a more recent convert to the idea, one of the senior partners, uses his influence to promote and eventually engage a firm of computer consultants. This firm has been set up by the brother of a senior partner in another law firm and he has successfully installed a system in that firm.

The above illustration reinforces the notion of strategy as both as intellectual exercise in information gathering and presentation and a political exercise involving values, power and influence. In this case the situation was a relatively straightforward investment decision with implications for office practice. Strategic decisions to enter a new product market or change radically the structure of the organization involve even greater complexities.

Apart from these six approaches, we can identify three broad planning styles; formalized planning, consultation and negotiation, and entrepreneurship (a similar model is offered by Mintzberg, 1973). In Figure 4.2 we show how these different planning styles interact with the first five of the strategic approaches.

The suitability of a particular planning style may depend on the size and nature of the firm. For example, a formal planning system is more likely to be found in a large firm, smaller firms by their very nature will favour an entrepreneurial style, and a high degree of consultation will be found in larger public sector organizations. Moreover, different styles may be appropriate for different functions. Whilst formalized planning may be a key feature of production strategy, an R&D strategy may benefit more from an entrepreneurial approach. Where trade union influence is considerable management may need to proceed more through consultation.

APPROACH	STYLE		
	Formalized planning	Entrepreneurial	Negotiation and consultation
Rational	X		
Flexible	X	X	
Creative		X	X
Behavioural			X
Incremental			X

Figure 4.2 Approaches and styles of management strategy.

Both the approaches and styles may change over time. A polytechnic which has operated through a mixture of an incremental approach and a consultative style, may when faced with the kind of threats identified in Case 4.3, need to operate in a much more entrepreneurial way. Indeed, at certain stages of their development, all organizations may require such entrepreneurial inputs to survive (Mintzberg, 1973). The role of the entrepreneur is usually associated with discussions of small businesses. It is our contention that entrepreneurial activity is equally important in large firms too, a theme we develop in Chapter 5.

Strategic contexts

We have identified how managers may employ different approaches to the task of strategy formulation. In addition we can identify various contexts in which the strategic process operates.

Firstly, strategy is not the sole preserve of the profit–making organization. All organizations have strategies, formalized to a greater or lesser extent. We can see strategies at work in such diverse organizations as businesses, schools, the police, charities, professional football clubs, and the church. In recent years there has been a focus on management strategies in the public sector. The health service has actively recruited its area managers from industry and commerce in an attempt to introduce a more businesslike approach, including a greater emphasis on strategy formulation. In Case 4.3 we present the case of British polytechnics operating in a changing environment and their need to formulate a different kind of strategy.

Secondly we may differentiate between those strategies pertaining to entire industries, such as shipping or machine tools; strategies employed by firms operating in a number of different business markets, such as Unilever and General Motors; and strategies pertaining to those operating in a single or restricted product market. Cases 4.1 and 4.2 illustrate the strategic process at the level of an entire industry and also within a multinational corporation. The distinction is sometimes drawn between a 'corporate' and 'business' strategy. A corporate strategy is employed by those firms operating in a number of different businesses and focusses on issues relating to

the overall business mix and helps identify the type of businesses management could pursue. A business strategy deals with a single business and
concentrates on issues relating to successful competition. A multi–divisional
firm like General Motors therefore operates both corporate and business
strategies.

Thirdly we may identify strategies operating at different levels of the
organization, from broad strategies at the top, moving through a series of
successive stages towards strategies for specific functional areas like personnel and marketing, and finally to individual targets and budgets.

The uses and value of strategy

We can identify several reasons for management to engage in strategy
formulation.

☐ Strategy assists in the formulation of goals and objectives, and enables
  them to be modified in the light of information and experience.
☐ Strategy is a form of management control. It is a plan which guides
  behaviour along a predetermined route. At the operational level it
  results in budgets and targets.
☐ A clear strategy both assists in the process of allocating resources and
  may provide a rationale for that allocation so that it is perceived to be
  fair by organization members.
☐ It enables management to identify key strategic issues which the firm
  may face in the future and prepare appropriate action.
☐ Strategy performs a useful role in both guiding the action of the constituent parts of the organization as well as acting as an integrating
  mechanism ensuring units work together. The integrating power of
  strategy is a central feature of 'strong' corporate cultures as illustrated
  by firms such as IBM and Hewlett–Packard.
☐ Leading on from that, strategy formulation can be an important element in the process of social change. Strategic objectives are achieved
  by changing the behaviour of employees. This is the essence of organizational development programmes used by such companies as Shell,
  and part of the current vogue for the creation of a strong corporate
  culture.
☐ The formulation of strategy is seen as a useful training ground for the
  development of future managers.

We have already questioned the extent to which formalized strategy is
used by firms. An even more important consideration is the extent to which
the existence of a formalized strategy contributes to organizational success.
Studies suggest that those companies using some form of strategic planning
process perform better than those who do not, and where data are available they tend to show that the introduction of strategic planning methods
leads to improvements in performance. (A good summary of a number of
studies in this area is presented in Hofer and Schendel, 1978, Chapter 1).

The difficulty with such claims and indeed such studies is the problem
of isolating and measuring the effect of strategic planning on performance,
be it return on investment, market share or some other criterion. A firm's

The machine tool industry provides manufacturing firms with the means by which the products are made, including tools for such operations as metal cutting, stamping and drilling. Larger manufacturing companies with highly specialized machining needs, such as Austin–Rover, will make some of their own tools, but most will buy from specialist machine tool manufacturers for at least some of their requirements. According to Hayes and Wheelwright (1984), a healthy machine tool industry is an essential prerequisite for a successful manufacturing industry. It is only by using custom–designed tools that innovative products can be made, and only through such products can firms gain a competitive advantage.

The machine tool industry in Britain has been in decline for a number of years. Its share of the world market fell by 50% from 1965 to 1982, whilst imports rose from 26% to 61% over the same period. A number of reasons have been forwarded to explain the decline. These are as follows.

☐ The general decline in manufacturing industry.
☐ The competitive threat posed by Japan and West Germany.
☐ A lack of graduate engineers in Britain.
☐ Overdiversification resulting in short production runs.
☐ A general lack of automation and computer application.
☐ A vicious circle of decline resulting in a lack of investment.
☐ Poor marketing.
☐ Low volume production at high cost.

Several strategic options for the industry have been identified.

Industry extinction. This involves allowing the industry to die a natural death by starving it of investment and relying solely on imported machine tools. Such a strategy may be detrimental to manufacturing for the reasons outlined above.

State intervention. Attempts have been made at state intervention, including special provisions for the development of state–of–the–art tools in computer–aided design and manufacture, and flexible manufacturing systems. Other measures have included attempts to encourage merger amongst smaller manufacturers to pool development ideas and achieve some economies of scale. The problems of state intervention lie in possible policy changes with shifts in political ideology and a danger of management complacency. The ultimate form of state intervention would be nationalization, a somewhat remote possibility in the current political climate. A suggestion has been made that the government imposes some form of import control. This could be a dangerous strategy in that other countries may retaliate, and despite its declining market share, British industry does depend on its exports. Furthermore import controls may speed up the process of Japanese machine tool firms operating from British or other European bases.

Rationalization. Not suprisingly this is the most common strategy. The suitability of such a strategy would seem to depend on a number of mergers also taking place. This may achieve some kind of product

Continued over page

Continued from previous page

standardization, longer production runs and subsequent cost reductions. The still declining market suggests that this strategy is not working, and it may be a route to eventual extinction.

Foreign investment. This is already occurring in that British firms are being bought by USA and Japanese interests. Investment would only be attractive in the case of highly specialized firms with attractive market niches or to get around the kind of import controls suggested in the second option.

Licensing. Under this arrangement British firms would manufacture products designed by firms in other countries. The current success of the Japanese machine tool industry supported by a large manufacturing base, would make the Japanese attractive partners in such joint venturing. It is not clear what the Japanese would gain from the licensing arrangement beyond a fee for British firms manufacturing Japanese patented products. Licensing can be valuable if it generates innovation on the part of the licensee. The Japanese however are very restrictive on what they will allow licensees to do, and this may well preclude innovation.

(*Sources:* Eilon, 1985, Lane, 1985)

financial and market performance, even over time, may be influenced by so many variables outside the control of management that causal links between strategy and performance may be difficult to show. Furthermore, the relationship is complicated in that performance may well influence strategy rather than the other way around. A firm which has been highly profitable may well be stimulated into seeking new investment opportunities either through new product development or acquisition. Conversely a firm incurring significant losses may well be limited in its strategic options and may well have them determined by people external to the firm such as bank managers or appointees of the Official Receiver. In this case the firm's performance is the reason for pursuing a divestment strategy, involving the closure or sale of the least profitable parts.

The environmental aspects of strategy

In the last section we suggested that it was often difficult to establish a clear link between strategy and performance because of the great number of influences at work. Much of that complexity may be attributed to the firm's environment.

The firm's environment is of course a key aspect of our Business in Context model. In Chapter 1 we introduced the notion of contingency theory and the belief that a firm's performance was dependent upon it achieving a strategic fit between itself and the environment in which it operates. In Chapter 2 we identified, with the use of selected examples, significant aspects of the business environment. We noted how these aspects influenced and in turn were influenced by businesses. We further suggested that these elements not only interact with business but with each

The Minnesota Mining and Manufacturing Company, better known as 3M operates in thirty different countries producing around 50 000 different products using many different technologies. By most definitions it is regarded as a very successful company. It is truly multinational and multi–divisional, although the company was relatively slow to diversify both internationally and in terms of its product range.

The company was founded in 1902 to mine corundum, but quickly switched its attention to the manufacture of sandpaper, its only product for twenty-one years. In 1923 the company developed masking tape for paint shops in the car industry, and this was followed by domestic adhesive tape and other tape products, such as sound recording tape. Tape products account for some 17% of output, but the company also produces office and photographic equipment, pharmaceuticals and chemicals. Only in 1951 did the company set up operations outside the USA, which remains its biggest market.

It fitted Peters and Waterman's model of an excellent company along several dimensions. Firstly, it was a highly innovative company supported by a corporate goal that 25% of annual sales should come from products developed in the last five years, and a senior management dominated by scientists who encouraged R&D staff to follow through their own ideas. Secondly, the company was committed to high quality goods design to fulfil customers' requirements. Thirdly, a considerable emphasis was placed upon communication throughout the company, and management processes were dominated by a network of meetings; in Peters and Waterman's terms it was a 'loose, consensual organization'. Finally 3M was based around a strong central culture based on a traditional USA midwest work ethic. Wherever they operated, small town locations were favoured as best embodying the core values, and management recruited staff who best fitted the culture.

In best Peters and Waterman tradition the company had no complex planning mechanisms. By 1980 the firm was undergoing change. The firm had grown considerably in a short period, especially in terms of overseas expansion. A new chairman was appointed and there was a belief that the company had become too committed to short–term goals. In particular the environment in which the firm was operating was changing in a number of different ways, which included an increased variability in interest rates, high rates of inflation in some operating countries, shorter life cycles for some products, scarcer and more expensive resources, and a declining demand in its traditional markets of office products and magnetic tape.

A major discontinuity was occurring, involving changed senior personnel, and both organizational growth and an increasingly threatening environment. The priorities identified by management were as follows.

☐ An even greater effort to be expended on product innovation.
☐ An improved control and coordination of the firm's global resources.
☐ A great concern for the future by establishing a more comprehensive approach to long–term planning.

Continued over page

Continued from previous page It was decided that new arrangements for strategic planning would accompany a major structural reorganization. This is shown in Fig. 4.3.

Figure 4.3 3M's new organization structure and planning system (Case 4.2). (Source: Kennedy, 1988).

The main elements of the new system may be identified as follows.

It is an attempt to build upon the existing loose consensus by emphasizing the exchange of information and ideas, but facilitating this by more formalized systems. A database was set up to generate information about the company. In particular managers were encouraged to analyse and discuss the strategic options pursued in other parts of the company. This enabled managers to learn from the actions of others as well as being an excellent method for training new managers.

A new formalized planning system was introduced whereby global strategies were worked out by the SBCs, the SPC and top management, and individual business strategies were worked out by each division using the global strategy as a template. The division was able to set realistic performance measures based on detailed knowledge of its own product market.

The SBCs acted as centres for the generating of ideas by integrating information and ideas from each of the operating divisions. It was hoped that some form of synergy of ideas would take place. The SBCs focussed specifically on product development issues. The generation of ideas was supported by an annual event, during which each operating unit must submit plans outlining where it will be in fifteen years' time. This event acted as a forum for creativity outside the normal planning framework and deliberately adventurous ideas were encouraged. In addition to these systems the firm holds regular brainstorming sessions throughout the year.

Since the new system has been introduced there has been greater international activity and an expansion of R&D work in Japan and Europe through the establishment of new laboratories and joint ventures with universities. Several unproductive business have been sold and the company attempted to establish a higher international profile through corporate advertising and the sponsorship of the 1988 Olympics. The new arrangements have also attracted some internal criticism on the basis that whilst the company has a greater knowledge of and direction over its existing businesses, no significant new ideas have been generated.

(*Sources:* Peters and Waterman, 1982, Kennedy, 1988)

other, resulting, for most firms, in an environment that was highly complex and changing. In this and the previous chapter we have already noted how that complexity is further complicated by the values of decision–makers and the internal structures and politics of organizations. The strategist's task of making sense of the environment is therefore a very difficult assignment.

We can identify two aspects of the environment which may influence strategy. Firstly there are those issues which affect all firms operating in a given business environment. These are many of the issues we raised in Chapter 2 and may include the state of the economy, the nature of the labour force, changing technology, government policy and social and cultural influences. We call this the 'general environment'. Secondly, there are those factors which have direct bearing on the firm's competitive position, which we will call 'the immediate competitive environment'. An analysis of both these environments will enable management to arrive at some assessment of the major opportunities and threats facing the organization.

The general environment

An analysis of a firm's general environment is sometimes known as environmental scanning, and usually comprises some sort of assessment of the key environmental influences, how they interact with the firm and with each other and how they change over time. There are many difficulties with such an analysis. Some managers tackle the sheer complexity of the environment by generating masses of information, not all of which is relevant and not all of which is accurate. The use of computers has increased the capacity for information handling and in some firms, managers can be submerged in a sea of data, most of which have only marginal relevance to their needs. At the other extreme their are some who either ignore the environment completely or who have a very blinkered perception of the firm's relationship to it. In such a situation key trends can be missed, and the firm either cedes opportunities to its competitors or is unprepared for changes when they occur.

Our analysis of the general environment is based on a model which classifies the environment as: simple and static; dynamic; and complex (Johnson and Scholes, 1984). We deal with each in turn.

A simple and static environment. Firms operating in a relatively simple and static environment can generally rely on management strategies that are based on historical data. Customer needs and hence sales forecasting can generally be predicted from past records. A company producing fireworks knows precisely that demand will peak dramatically prior to November 5th and will have a good idea of the size of that demand. However there is a danger that managers become complacent and the survival of the business may be jeopardized by sudden and unexpected changes as with a change in the law making the sale of certain types of firework illegal.

A dynamic environment. A dynamic environment changes quickly and frequently. Managers operating in this environment generally need to be sensitive to the environment and predict those changes that are likely to occur. The home computer market has been particularly dynamic. Those firms, such as Amstrad, that have been sensitive to, and even helped create, changing consumer needs, have outperformed others, such as Sinclair, who, though first to the market, failed to maintain the required product development. Businesses which fail in dynamic environments are generally those where managements have failed to see the changes which are occurring or are either unable or unwilling to take appropriate action. The case of professional soccer in England and Wales is one where an entire industry has lost ground to a variety of competitors for its customers' time and money, and the general trend towards declining attendance and hence revenue now seems irreversible. The result is that most of the ninety-two professional clubs suffer operating losses each year. There are many contributory factors, but the main one is that the clubs have under-estimated the changing needs of the market and offer a product, particularly the facilities at grounds, which is largely unacceptable to an increasingly sophisticated clientele. The problem has been compounded in 1988 by a government which sees soccer as the focus for violent, anti–social behaviour and has plans to introduce a restrictive membership scheme for attendance at matches. Attendances are likely to fall even further and so limit investment which might lead to an improvement in facilities.

Such environments require entrepreneurs who perhaps have the vision to spot opportunities and the motivation to pursue them. They are also suited to more creative approaches to strategy. However, there may be a danger that management could respond unnecessarily to changes in a dynamic environment. For example, some firms, when threatened by new entrants offering much cheaper products in the same market, respond by launching a cheaper version of their own product. This not only shows a lack of faith in the quality of the firm's original product, but it will inevitably take sales away from that product and have a potentially damaging effect on the firm's reputation.

A complex environment. This is one in which different demands are placed upon different aspects of the firm's operation. A firm producing a range of different products for different markets could be said to be operating in a complex environment. Most firms in such situations reflect this complexity in their organization structures. We saw in the last chapter how the development of the multi–divisional firm was a direct response to the problems faced by emerging multinational corporations like General Motors in the 1920s. The problem facing firms in a complex environment is the extent to which the complexity needs to be accommodated by organizational changes. The TI Group, which operates in a number of different product markets attempted to reduce the demands placed upon it in a difficult economic environment by selling some of its individual divisions, including Raleigh bicycles.

Figure 4.4 The model of competitive rivalry. (Source: M.E. Porter, 1980.)

In the case of dynamic and complex environments a firm faces a number of interconnected problems related to the degree of change, the speed of change, the complexity of its environment and the corresponding complexity of the organization. Managers tend to seek to reduce such uncertainty as much as they can be a variety of measures.

Firstly the uncertainty may be reduced by collecting relevant information. We have already noted the problems associated with collecting accurate information and with information overload. Secondly, as we saw in Chapter 2, managers will attempt to influence and control the environment. This can be done by a variety of measures such as technological innovation, forming coalitions with other organizations, political lobbying, acquiring raw material suppliers or retail outlets, stockpiling materials and equipment, training staff in rare skills, and so on. Thirdly, new structures and procedures such as planning and forecasting may be set up to cope with uncertainty. There are however dangers with setting up new structures. A common reaction to developments in computer technology has been the establishment of a specialist computing department within the organization. The establishment of such specialist units can create its own problems of cooperation and integration which override the benefits of specialization in the first place (Selznick, 1949 and Pettigrew, 1973 have two good case illustrations).

The immediate competitive environment

We will attempt to locate a business in its immediate competitive environment using the model devised by Porter (1980) as shown in Figure 4.3. Porter has identified four forces which have immediate bearing on a firm's competitive position. We explain and illustrate these forces in turn.

The threat of potential entrants. The threat of entry is related to the ease with which a new business can establish itself in the same product market. The relative ease with which new restaurants emerge in a large urban area like London, suggests that the threat to existing restaurateurs is very real. However the ease of entry means increased competition and can result in a highly volatile market, to which the death rate of new restaurants will testify.

The threat posed by potential entrants is reduced if there are barriers to entry. These can operate in a number of different ways. Equipment and associated capital requirements place heavy burdens on investment and firms may have to withstand considerable unit cost disadvantages initially. Such difficulties would be presented to firms attempting to enter mass car production or oil refining. It would be difficult for newcomers to achieve sufficient economies of scale to recover their outlay in a reasonable time.

These difficulties can be increased where access to raw materials is an additional problem. In some types of industry breaking into a market is difficult due to the considerable customer loyalty to existing products and brands. A soft drinks manufacturer attempting to launch a 'cola' type product would have considerable difficulty persuading the market to switch from Coca Cola or Pepsi Cola. In the industrial components industry getting customers to switch may pose the additional difficulties of part compatibility. Such barriers may be further compounded by the difficulty of obtaining access to channels of distribution. Our soft drinks manufacturer may have considerable difficulty persuading the major supermarket chains to stock his products. Patents held by existing manufacturers can pose a significant obstacle to those wishing to enter the market with imitative products.

The patents on the drugs librium and valium owned by Hoffman–La Roche have enabled the firm to establish a monopoly position in the tranquillizer market. Similarly, patents held by Polaroid posed difficulties for firms such as Kodak to enter the instant camera market. In a more general way the operating experience gained by existing firms over a number of years can place the newcomer at a significant disadvantage.

Apart from from the threat of new entrants, competitive rivalry can be heightened among existing competitors if the general growth rate of the industry is slow and if there are many firms of similar size with a relatively undifferentiated product range.

We should not forget that there are barriers to exit as well as barriers to entry. A large manufacturing company with considerable operating losses, but with many employees and a significant investment in plant and machinery, will undoubtedly face pressures to stay in business. Such pressures will be related to the extent of the firm's assets which may not be recoverable if the firm closes. This fear of lost investment may only be one factor. Senior management may be particularly attached to the company, emotionally as well as financially, and place a high value on its survival, despite market and financial evidence to the contrary. Pressures will undoubtedly come from the local community and, in the case of some firms, from the national government, fearing the effect of closure on local and national economies and on levels of unemployment. In the case of some firms such as British Leyland and Rolls Royce in the 1970s, government pressure was accompanied by significant government investment to ensure the survival of these companies. Barriers to exit operate in small firms as well, where there is likely to be an even greater ego involvement on the part of the owner managers and a subsequent reluctance to accept forced closure in the face of market forces.

The threat of substitution. Substitution occurs where a consumer is able to replace your product with a different type of product performing the same service or satisfying similar needs. The cotton textile industry in Briain was not only threatened by new entrants from cheap labour economies, but also by the development of substitute products in the form of man–made fibres. We have already identified some of the threats facing the professional football industry. A major threat has been the growth of substitute activities such as sport on television, active rather than passive participation in sport, and the growing popularity of DIY.

The bargaining power of buyers. Buyer power increases where there are a large number of firms offering the same or substitute products, especially where there is little or no cost involved for the buyer in switching from one supplier to another. A restaurateur in Central London faces considerable competition from the large number of other restaurants operating in that area, as well as other attractions competing for the potential client's disposable income. In such situations the product/market strategy of the restaurant becomes of utmost importance. Such strategies will include considerations of product differentiation and quality, market segmentation, price and promotion, (Chapter 7 has a fuller account of these strategies). In the industrial components industry, particularly where specialist components are involved, then the relationship may be different. There may well have been a mutual accommodation of product changes over a number of years, and such a strong relationship forged that the cost of switching would be high. Components suppliers often invest time and energy building up such relationships with customers. In such situations a threat still exists if the customer firm's acquisition strategy takes in a similar components supplier.

The buyer–supplier relationship is highly complex, and involves most facets of our Business in Context model. The complexity of the technology plays a major part as does the competitiveness of the market. We saw in our discussion of Japanese management in Chapter 2 that a mix of cultural and economic factors was also significant. As part of their normal business strategy, Japanese industrial firms operating in Britain rely heavily upon subcontractors to supply components, and tend to build up close relationships with these suppliers. With British government backing, Japanese manufacturing companies have tended to locate in areas of low economic activity. This automatically places such firms in a strong bargaining position with respect to the local components industry.

The power of a buyer generally increases the more he buys. This power can be exercised in the demand for discounts or the expectation of preferential treatment in the supply of goods. A factor to consider here is the relative size of the two parties. Buyer power normally only exists if the volume purchased forms a high proportion of the selling company's total sales. The larger supermarket chains have considerable buyer power, particularly over such as the smaller food suppliers. Smaller foodstores have attempted to secure greater buyer power by banding together for bulk purchases, as with associations like Spar, Mace and VG.

The bargaining power of suppliers. Our illustration of the bargaining power for buyers in the industrial components industry works equally well for suppliers. In this and other cases supplier power is stronger where the component is highly specialized and few suppliers exist. Supplier power is also strong where the cost to the buyer of switching allegiance would include major product adaptations. A computer manufacturer can gain additional market power where it develops popular software that can only be used on its own machines. A larger firm that has no central policy for the purchase of computer hardware and software may see the benefits of having a single operating system when it finds that much of its existing equipment is incompatible.

Most firms act as both suppliers and buyers, and the bargaining power can be a two–edged weapon. A restaurant operating in an affluent area where there are no other restaurants probably does not face strong bargaining power from its customers and therefore maintains a strong competitive position. However if there are equally few suppliers of meat, fish and other foodstuffs then these firms have supplier power over the restaurant.

The use that mangements can make of Porter's model is to establish a position for their firms in the market to maximize defences against competitive forces, and where possible turn them to best advantage. Porter identifies three generic strategies of particular advantage in this respect. These are product differentiation, market segmentation and seeking to obtain the lowest costs. A further explanation of these strategies may be found in Chapters 6 and 7.

The strength of a model like Porter's is that it focuses on the immediate operating environment of the business and avoids prescription by enabling management to examine the forces acting upon their firm. The analysis does however depend upon a level of knowledge about competitors which may just not be available.

Aspect of the environment	Opportunity	Constraint
Economy	Growth in the market and demand for the product.	Increased foreign competition with rising interest rates at home and an unfavourable foreign exchange rate.
State	Tax concessions for small manufacturing firms.	New laws on safety and design necessitating a costly product modification.
Technology	Making more effective use of the computer system for administrative and financial control and information.	The high cost of new manufacturing technology to meet increased demand.
Labour	Local supply exceeds demand and there is a regular supply of past–timers and casual workers.	A shortage of workers in certain key skills and the relatively high wage demands of those workers.
Culture	A traditional small–firm community with a tradition for hardwork and company loyalty.	An influx of newcomers to the area from industries with a long history of management–worker mistrust.

Figure 4.5 Examples of environmental opportunities and constraints using the Business in Context model, as they affect a small manufacturing firm.

Environmental threats and opportunities

An assessment of the general environment and the firm's immediate competitive position should enable management to identify the major threats and opportunities facing the firm. In Figure 4.5 we present an illustrative list of the environmental opportunities and threats using the elements of the Business in Context model. This is usually the first stage in selecting appropriate strategic options. For a firm like Orlake Records (Case 6.1), producing gramophone records in a declining market, or a restaurateur opening in central London, the threats and opportunities may be very clear. However, we can identify several complicating factors.

A threat to one part of an organization may represent an opportunity to another. Thus in the 1970s when the post and telecommunications service in Britain were part of the same organization, a postal workers' strike led to increased revenue through telephone calls. The closure of some courses in a polytechnic due to falling student demand may divert resources to other areas.

Defending yourself against a threat or capitalizing upon an opportunity is a function of both the firm's standing in its environment and its internal resource position. Survival in a declining market may be easier if you have a large market share to begin with, and raising finance to invest in new products is often easier for larger established firms than the small business. Small firms often face the particular dilemma of spotting a market opportunity but lacking the resources to take full advantage. Laker Airways was relatively successful at breaking into the charter airline market by offering cheaper flights than those currently available. As the firm expanded by introducing flights to the USA, it faced direct competition with the larger state–financed airlines. Laker was ultimately unable to compete with the larger firms, who adopted price–cutting tactics, and the company over-reached itself financially through the purchase of a large number of new aircraft in anticipation of increased revenue from the new routes.

Managements differ in their ability to identify opportunities and threats. The management of a firm doing particularly well in a declining market may ignore the longer–term implications of their position. Even when opportunities and threats have been identified, managements may differ as to their relative importance and may develop different perspectives, based perhaps on their attitudes to risk. Careful analyses of market opportunities may come to nought in the face of a preference for inaction rather than entrepreneurial risk–taking. Failure to take action in the light of environmental change is one form of management myopia. Perceiving the environment as presenting more of a constraint than it need is another.

We can therefore see that the perception of an opportunity or threat is a highly subjective process. It is partly for this reason that strategy formulation is as much a behavioural and political process as it is analytical. There is another important point. We have tended to focus on the environment as offering the management decision–maker opportunities or constraints. A major contention in this book is that the manager can influence and shape the environment. This means more than simply recognizing that big business can dominate. There is increasing recognition that creativity in strategy formulation is the ingredient for giving firms a competitive edge (McCaskey, 1982, Earl, 1984). It is not simply the analysis of the environment that provides the answer, but the ability of managers to see more in that environment than their competitors and in so doing create their own opportunities.

The organizational aspects of strategy

In this section we will explore the relationship between management strategy and the organizational aspects of our model, and focus on particular issues of resource assessment such as portfolio analysis. Organizational analysis is traditionally an integral part of strategy formulation, and serves two related purposes for management.

☐ Some kind of resource profile is needed to establish whether the various opportunities, threats, and management expectations can be met by the organization in its present state. A knowledge of the resources an organization possesses, and what can be done with them, is a prerequisite for determining future plans, and establishes whether a gap exists between what management would like to do and what they can do. This is sometimes referred to as 'gap analysis'. For example, the management of a manufacturing firm would need to know if it would accept and meet a new, large order using its existing product range and its existing machine and labour capacity. The gap analysis will identify for management those resource aspects which may be lacking and which will have to be rectified if opportunities are to be realized or threats are to be successfully fought off. The completion of new orders by our manufacturing firm may be dependent upon product modification, the purchasing of new equipment and the hiring of new staff. This in turn may involve the raising of new loans from the bank and setting up programmes for the recruitment and training of staff. Expansion of this nature has further implications for the size of the supervisory and maintenance teams.

☐ An internal analysis will enable management to assess the attractiveness of the organization, its activities and its products in its current markets and assess their potential for future investment. This is the particular contribution of portfolio analysis.

A rather narrow, traditional view of strategic planning sees strategy as the result of environmental analysis, and the organization factors are seen either to facilitate or inhibit the chosen strategy. Such a view runs counter to the major contention of our Business in Context model, which sees all elements as interacting with one another. Organizational changes are brought about by changes in strategy, but strategic changes are also the product of aspects of the organization. We have already noted in Chapter 3 that it is possible for structure to influence strategy. We can also see that expansion plans will undoubtedly build on strengths, a case of the firm focussing strategy around a key resource, such as the skills of a particular group. We deal with more general issues of strategy and organization before turning to the more practical questions of resource analysis and portfolio analysis.

The interaction of strategy and organization

All the organizational elements of our model, goals, ownership, structure, size and culture interact with the process of strategy formulation. We have already seen how the *goals* of an enterprise set targets for strategy to follow. We have also emphasized the behavioural nature of this process in that both goal and strategy formulation are the products of management values, and the processes of organizational power and politics, which have a major influence upon management decision–making.

The process of goal setting and strategy formulation is greatly influenced by *ownership* variables. A group of professional accountants in partnership may each have their own views about the growth of the firm, the recruitment and training of new staff and so on. In a partnership these views are generally resolved by discussion or through the dominance of a particular partner. Our discussion of ownership and control in Chapter 3 showed that for larger companies with diffuse share ownership and professional managers, strategy formulation was more complex and often dependent upon the influence of some shareholder groups. There are numerous illustrations where small business owners may deliberately resist growth strategies in order to retain personal control over the firm. However, the reverse is also true, in that strategies involving merger and acquisition have a significant impact upon patterns of ownership and control. Managers may actively pursue acquisitions which give them more power and enhance their own career aspirations.

We noted in the previous chapter that, according to Chandler (1962), *structure* followed strategy, and this was a dominant feature in the expansion of American multinationals and in particular the development of multi–divisional structures. We also suggested that strategy can be influenced by structure. For example, a company with a large and active R&D department would almost certainly pursue vigorous strategies of new product development. The 3M case in this chapter shows how top management were concerned that their existing procedures for strategy formulation were inadequate and set about creating a new structure precisely to give the firm a new strategic impetus. At the operational level the organization structure can facilitate or inhibit strategy formulation and implementation. Two aspects appear to be important here; the authority structure of the firm and the procedures for making decisions. Burns and Stalker (1966) studied the post war electronics industry and saw differences in the strategic responses of firms to changing market conditions. Those firms which had responded most effectively to changed market demand were firms typified by a more flexible, open structure, which they termed organic. The firms which struggled in the changed environment and failed to adapt were by contrast more bureaucratic, with often lengthy and inappropriate procedures for making decisions, and where structural divisions between departments inhibited cooperation. Organizations, particularly those in the public sector, which rely heavily on committees for the formulation of important decisions, may find the process too cumbersome when a quick strategic response is needed. In similar way participation, which can facilitate employee motivation and commitment, may inhibit decision–making through the inherent slowness of the procedure.

The authority structure of a firm usually determines the person or group with the ultimate responsibility for strategic choice. A study of how strategies were formed in five companies, including Cadbury Schweppes and Manganese Bronze, concluded, not suprisingly, that strategy was decided by a small group at the top of the hierarchy. What interested the researchers was the part played by entrepreneurship, even in large organizations, and that strategy was greatly influenced by the individuality and personality of the senior executive (Minkes and Nuttall, 1985).

Such considerations of structure are inevitably linked to *size*. In very large organizations strategy formulation may be cumbersome for the reasons given above. There is also a danger that strategy can become fragmented through the diverse nature of operations and locations. It was these conditions which led 3M to reconsider its procedure for strategy formulation as illustrated in Case 4.2. Another handicap of large size involves the control of a strategy once it is formulated. The larger the organization then the more filters there are to interpret and perhaps distort a central strategy.

We have already discovered that an important element in the core management strategies of firms such as IBM and Hewlett–Packard is the creation of an *organizational culture*, with an emphasis upon shared values. We have stressed the importance of management values in both formulating and evaluating strategy. In this case the creation of a value system to embrace the entire organization is seen by some to be more significant than strategy itself. We have already noted how traditional approaches to strategy have been down–graded by such as Peters and Waterman (1982). Nevertheless, the care with which such firms as Hewlett–Packard embark upon staff recruitment, selection and training to develop such shared values (Case 3.5) would indicate the influence of a very distinctive strategy indeed. The culture of a particular organization may act as a constraint against strategy implementation. For example, strong trade union organization may resist management's proposals to sell off part of the organization in an attempt to safeguard the jobs of its members.

Resource analysis

At the beginning of this section we explained the importance of the current resource position to the formulation of management strategy. A manager needs to know what resources the organization possesses, how those resources are used and how they are controlled. The analysis will cover physical resources such as land, plant and machinery; financial resources; and human resources. In the case of the last category some analysis of the skill mix is important.

For example, the staff running a business course at a polytechnic may wish to change the curriculum to give much greater time and emphasis to computing. An analysis of the current position may reveal a shortage of available personal computers and terminals, a shortage of funds to increase the provision, and staff with insufficient skills and experience to teach this subject. Even if funds could be diverted or revenue raised from running extra courses, there may be physical constraints on the establishment of new computer laboratories. In addition, recruitment may be difficult in a highly competitive labour market, so the management may need to seek substitute skills from its existing workforce. In this case an analysis of the resources may reveal that achieving the goal of increased provision by expansion is not possible. Consequently the utilization of the existing provision needs to be examined to reveal the existence of slack and to see what could be achieved using the existing resources.

In many firms resource analysis is accompanied by the use of a variety of accounting ratios such as return on capital employed, profitability and so on. Different ratios have more relevance at different stages of the firm's development than at others, so that whilst profitability may be appropriate for established firms, productivity and sales may be more useful for newly established companies, and cash flows may be more significant when firms are in decline.

The value of resource analysis lies not only in assessing the viability of a particular strategic proposal, but also in assessing the ability of the organization to adapt to change. Can the firm deal with changes in demand or can it withstand a price war with its competitors? Has it the financial backing to invest in new technology? Is the age profile of its staff sufficiently balanced to ensure succession? Many such questions deal with issues of resource balance. We now turn to the question of maintaining an appropriate balance in terms of products and markets.

CASE 4.3

BRITISH POLYTECHNICS IN 1989

By the middle of 1989 polytechnics in England and Wales will achieve corporate status, disassociating them from the control of local authorities and causing significant changes in the way they are funded and managed. Such changes have been brought about as the result of government education policy and accompanying legislation. A declining population of school–leavers will affect traditional patterns of student recruitment, but the effect is likely to be uneven as some courses such as business studies continue to grow in popularity, whilst others, such as some engineering courses, decline. Continued government pressure to hold down public sector expenditure has resulted in reductions in staffing and the resourcing of facilities such as libraries. Since the majority of polytechnic courses are vocationally oriented, they need to respond to such changes in business as the use of new technology, and the creation of the European market in 1992, and may well require extra resources to meet the challenge.

Polytechnics therefore face a rapidly changing environment. Many have responded by creating new posts in finance and marketing to meet the new challenges. Most have placed an emphasis on income generation through the winning of research grants, hiring out staff as consultants, and setting up courses to bring in extra fees. For example, the government policy of charging full–cost fees for overseas students

Continued over page

Continued from previous page

has resulted in many polytechnics (and universities) seeing such groups as an important source of income and actively searching new overseas markets. Some colleges have established special units to maximize opportunities in these areas. More attention is being paid to the marketing of courses and the attraction of students from non–traditional sources, especially mature students, to counteract the impact of falling school rolls.

Whilst the environment may be similar for all polytechnics, there is considerable variation in the way each is responding. Colleges differ in their financial position, their resources, their own particular areas of excellence, and their perceived attractiveness to potential students, to businesses and to their central government paymasters. This may cause some to seek greater strength through merger and others to consider their portfolio of courses to build on strengths and eliminate weaknesses. The route that each goes down will inevitably be decided by a mixture of careful analysis, inspirational management, ideology, value judgement, pressure brought by interested parties, and good fortune.

(a) The Boston Consulting Group Matrix

(b) The General Electric Business Screen

Figure 4.6 Illustrations of portfolio analysis. (Source: Hofer and Scherdel, 1978).

Portfolio analysis

Portfolio analysis is a technique normally associated with those firms operating in a number different businesses and markets, as is the case with the larger multinational corporations. It may also be applied to those firms who operate in the same market with a number of different products. The technique enables management to assess the attractiveness of its business and products in their current markets, and assist decisions on the direction of future investment. Through such an analysis the manager may reach conclusions on the particular mix of products and markets, the growth and profit potential of those products and markets and the level of risk involved with each one. As a result, a clearer idea emerges regarding priorities for corporate effort and resource allocation.

There are several models which may be used in portfolio analysis and two are illustrated in Figure 4.6. The most famous portfolio technique is the matrix developed by the Boston Consulting Group (BCG). This was specifically designed to analyse individual businesses in a company with a range of different business interests. The matrix enables the analyst to plot the position of that business (or product) with reference to the growth of the market and the company's share of that market. We can see from Figure 4.5 that the matrix has been divided into four sectors, each with different product/market characteristics. The products located within these sectors have been labelled 'question marks', 'stars', 'cash cows' and 'dogs' respectively. We will deal with the characteristics of each.

Question Marks represent products which have a low market share in a market of high growth. The market offers clear potential but the firm invariably needs significant financial and other resource inputs to compete. This may involve product modification, increasing output capacity, increasing promotional activity, recruiting extra staff and raising the level of bank borrowing. Investing in question marks carries a high level of risk, as can be seen through the British Government's excursion into microchip development by funding the firm INMOS (Case 5.1). The gains may be significant but the market tends to be highly competitive and the costs of improving market position are invariably high.

Stars are those products that have achieved a high share of a still expanding market. A company with a number or even one of such 'stars' is generally envied by its competitors. Nevertheless, the cost of maintaining this position is usually high. A growing market tends to attract a number of competitors, and 'stars' usually need continuing investment in product development and promotion. The personal computer market in the last few years has maintained a high growth but the increased competition, particularly in terms of product development and price, has meant that several of its 'stars' have risen and fallen in a relatively short time. Other markets where 'stars' have risen and fallen rapidly include cameras and video cassette recorders.

Cash Cows are products with a high market share but market growth has stabilized. These provide the firm with its greatest return on investment. The market is generally much less competitive and the market position is generally less costly to maintain than with 'stars'. Overall costs are generally lower and economies of scale can be achieved. The surplus funds generated by the 'cash cows' can be used to provide funds for the development of 'question marks' and the maintenance of 'stars'. The Volkswagen Golf has maintained its position as the best–selling car in Europe and is an undoubted 'cash–cow' enabling the company to develop a new luxury sports model and thus break into new markets.

Dogs are products with the poorest profile on the matrix. Such products tend to be a drain on resources and can be candidates for being dropped altogether or being sold off. This was the reason behind the TI Group's sale of Raleigh Bicycles to Derby International. 'Dogs' are not necessarily worthless. Product ranges and indeed entire companies can be revitalized by perhaps a change of management and some fresh ideas. A 'dog' to one company may experience a new lease of life when sold to another. For example, a highly diversified company may find itself unable to devote sufficient attention to those products which are more peripheral to its central activities, as in the case of a manufacturing firm with a subsidiary whose primary activity is property development. The property business could be enhanced if it were sold to a firm specializing in that area.

The BCG matrix implies that management should seek to establish a balanced portfolio and carries with it a notion of progression. It assumes that 'question marks' should become 'Stars' which will eventually turn into 'cash cows' to fund the next generation of developing product/markets. Plotting a firm's products in this way may be a useful guide to acquisition and divestment strategy. These options will be discussed in the next section.

The BCG matrix is not without its critics. Much of the criticism is concerned with the imprecise nature of the four categories. For example, 'stars' can differ considerably in their rate of growth and size of market share and the positioning of some products may be an inaccurate reflection

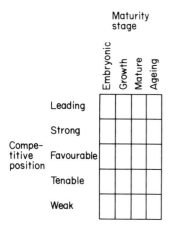

Figure 4.7 3M product and market portfolio matrix – this matrix is used to analyse both products and markets. (Source: Kennedy, 1988).

of their value, simply because the category may be too broad. Mercedes–Benz has a low share of the total car market, but a high share of the luxury car market (Hofer and Schendel, 1978). In this case a number of matrices will have to be plotted to represent the different market segments. More complex matrices have been developed so that products can be plotted more usefully. An illustration of the General Electric Business Screen is shown in Figure 4.6. In this case the concept of industry attractiveness is used instead of market growth and nine categories have been identified to achieve greater accuracy.

In spite of the problems of plotting and measurement, such methods of portfolio analysis are of use both in planning future product/market strategy but also raising important questions about how business interests are handled. We have already seen that by analysing a 'dog', changes may be possible to improve its position. One company to make use of this type of analysis is 3M. They have developed a matrix to analyse both products and markets, as illustrated in Figure 4.7. The management of 3M is concerned that each of its products and markets is capable of being maintained or improved. It was this method of analysis which led the company to sell off its photocopying equipment business (Kennedy, 1988).

Strategic options

So far in this chapter we have discussed the various components of strategic analysis; the environment, resources and dominant values. We have also suggested that strategy may be formulated by a variety of methods which may involve a highly formalized planning procedure or may simply be no more than the stated perferences of the chief executive. Whatever the process, the outcome is a particular strategic option or range of possible options. In this section we have identified four types of strategic option and how they might be achieved. When there are several options to choose from, some criterion is needed to select the most appropriate strategy, and we end this chapter by identifying examples of such criteria. Case 4.1 examines the type of strategic options that may be available to declining industry and should be compared with Case 6.1, which examines the types of strategies employed by a firm in a declining market.

Types of strategic option

There is an assumption in many management texts that the superordinate goal of most businesses is survival, and this may only be achieved by pursuing strategies of growth. Whilst it is difficult to argue against the first assumption, it is clear that not all businesses pursue growth strategies, and for those like the British steel and coalmining industries drastic contraction may be the only chance of survival. Our four strategies depict different approaches to growth and contraction. These options are not discrete categories and in some cases, especially between the first two, the distinction can be blurred.

Diversification strategies. Diversification is undoubtedly the most radical growth strategy open to management in that it represents a deliberate attempt to change the nature of the business. We can identify two types of diversification, related and unrelated. Related diversification can be further classified into backward, forward and horizontal integration.

☐ *Related diversification* occurs when the new business is related in some way to the old one. Several firms have sought to gain greater control over the source of raw materials or the supply of components by some form of *backward integration*. As we saw in Chapter 2, the larger Japanese manufacturing firms depend on a network of subcontractors for the supply of components. In many cases the larger company has a controlling financial interest in the supplier. In the restaurant business it is becoming more common for some restaurant owners to grow their own herbs and perhaps their own vegetables, or bake their own bread, to ensure both the quantity and the quality of the supply. This also provides the restaurant with an additional promotional strategy. *Forward Integration* occurs when producers diversify to control the onward processes of delivering their goods to the consumer, as in the case of a manufacturer setting up a transport or retail operation, or a group of actors leasing a theatre to stage their own work. British Rail has always been a major source of transport for Post Office letters and parcels. In recent years British Rail have extended their own delivery service, Red Star, which has taken business away from the Post Office by offering a speedier and guaranteed delivery service. Together, backward and forward integration are known as vertical integration. *Horizontal integration* occurs when the product range is extended to incorporate similar items, as with the case of a firm supplying fitted kitchens diversifying its operation to include fitted bathrooms and bedrooms as well. Laura Ashley began by selling furniture fabrics, moved into dress fabrics and eventually diversified into selling dresses themselves. Horizontal integration may be a valuable way of using a firm's spare resources or capacity. The fibreglass operations of Pilkington Glass found that the waste created in cutting standard widths of fibreglass could be put to good use through the setting up another operation which compressed the material into insulating bricks, thereby creating a different but related product. Case 6.1 shows how a record company has used related diversification into specialized products as a major strategy of survival in a declining market.

☐ *Unrelated diversification* occurs when management expand its business into a totally different product market. At the time of writing Marks and Spencer have announced plans to diversify by selling financial services, a totally different operation from their core business of clothes and food retailing. Many diversified companies have a mixture of both related and unrelated products. The London Rubber Company main product range of contraceptives has been augmented by a range of surgical and household rubber gloves, but the company also produces soap and cough medicine. As with many forms of classification, the difference between related and unrelated diversification is often a matter of degree. The 3M case in this chapter is a good illustration of both types. The company switched from the mining of corundum (an abrasive) to the manufacture of sandpaper (using abrasives as a raw material). The company then began producing masking tape which led to the related products of adhesive tape and all other kinds of tape product.

The concept often associated with unrelated diversification is synergy. This refers to the collective influence of the various activies of the company producing an overall effect that is greater than the sum of the parts. Synergy is often cited as a major benefit of diversification, although its impact is often difficult to identify and measure.

We have seen how diversification can provide managers with greater control over supplies and distribution and exploit resources. A highly diversified firm may also be one where risks are spread across a range of products and markets. The motives for diversification may be complex and may include the desire of senior management to extend their power and influence as the firm grows larger. In the USA, the diversification of many companies into totally different areas of business was a direct response to anti–trust laws which put severe restrictions on the creation of monopolies. There are problems with diversification strategies. A highly diversified company often presents special problems of communication, and control and resources may be duplicated. It is for this reason that many diversified companies have adopted a structure involving a mixture of autonomous units sharing some central services, such as R&D. (A fuller discussion of structural devices may be found in Chapter 3).

Many of the illustrations of diversification presented above represent activities which have grown out of the firm's existing business. Firms may also add new products and markets through acquisition. This has the advantage of being a much faster method of diversification than internal development. The company is gaining an 'off–the–peg' business with the experience, knowledge, resources and markets already in existence. Much has been written about acquisitions and mergers, and such activity presents consistently good copy for the financial journalists, particularly when it is accompanied by accusations of insider dealing on the stock market.

The evidence suggests that acquisitions and mergers tend to occur in cycles (Channon, 1973). Another cycle appears to be occurring in the mid to late 1980s, especially amongst firms in the retail and the food and drink industries. Why such cycles occur has not been fully explained, and may represent yet another business fashion. The overwhelming evidence is that acquisitions are rarely successful. In their study, Peters and Waterman (1982) cite the case of ITT and the difficulties the firm encountered when it diversified out of telephones by acquiring banking and hotel interests. They claim that synergy rarely happens through acquisition, and the whole exercise takes up a disproportionate amount of management time and effort. As befits two proponents of firms adopting a strong central image and consensus culture, Peters and Waterman see great difficulties in achieving a cultural fit between two different enterprises and advise managers to 'stick to the knitting'.

Other research echoes Peters and Waterman's concern and tends to warn against unrestrained diversification. A study of two hundred companies in the USA from 1949 to 1969 concluded that the poorest performers were those operating in a number of unrelated businesses and those that had attempted vertical integration. The best performers were those that had diversified only in related areas around a set of core activities and skills

(Rumelt, 1974). It is interesting to note that whilst vertical integration is a complementary extension of a firm's core activites, it often requires totally different skills from that core activity. For example, a succesful manufacturer of domestic electric appliances may turn out to be a very poor retailer and provider of repair services.

Changing the Competitive Position of an Existing Business. Whereas diversification and rationalization represent fundamental changes in the nature of a firm's business, strategies in this category attempt to improve the market position of the existing range of products and services. There are a number of strategic options available.

☐ New product development (Chapter 5).
☐ Improved market penetration by deploying the various elements of the marketing mix, such as promotion or price strategies (Chapter 7).
☐ Seeking new markets by aiming the product at new market segments or by export (Chapter 7).
☐ Improving the quality of the product or service (Chapter 6).
☐ Seeking cost reductions through an improved utilization of resources such as improvements in productivity.

Many of these strategies are related. A firm which wishes to move 'up market' and aim its product at a more quality conscious but less price–sensitive consumer group may need to accompany product changes with an intensive promotion campaign. We pursue this theme in more detail in our discussion of marketing strategies in Chapter 7.

Attempts to change the competitive position of the business can be made through acquisitions which improve the product range and gain access to new markets. Such strategies carry the same advantages and disadvantages outlined above. A growing type of competitive strategy involves franchising (examined in Chapter 3). Through franchising its products or services to individual small businesses, a firm can reach a wider market, and, at the same time, spread the risk of that expansion.

All five options of improving the competitive position of the firm by focussing on existing products and services can be achieved by internal change strategies. Expansion into new markets may be accompanied by increased promotional and sales activity in that area. However, the more successful change strategies take time and involve more than simply exercising another strategic option. Moves to effect changes in product quality and productivity may involve industrial relations strategies (Chapter 8), and attempts to change the organizational culture (Chapter 3).

Deleting Operations. The decisions to cut back and/or sell off part of the operations of a firm is referred to as rationalization or divestment. As its ultimate level this will include liquidation and closure.

Such strategies can pose enormous difficulties for the firm involved. The cutting back of activites such as R&D and training to achieve short term savings may have damaging long term repercussions. Reducing product lines and services may alienate customers. Cut–backs and closures are generally vigorously opposed by trade unions. The National Coal Board's plans in 1984 to close the Cortonwood Colliery in Yorkshire precipitated one of the longest and bitterest disputes in the history of the industry. On a more general level, rationalization strategies may cause a lowering of employee morale to such a level that existing operations are endangered.

Nevertheless, for some firms, rationalization is the only viable option and may, as successful management buy–outs have shown, offer a new lease of life to part of an organization. In 1981, the shoe manufacturer Norvic was forced to go into liquidation, and one of its sudsidiaries, the Mansfield Shoe Company was faced with closure and most of its workforce were made redundant. The Mansfield subsidiary was saved by a management buy–out which raised extra capital from local industry and from employees exchanging their redundancy payments for shares in the new company. Freed from the financial burden of helping to support an ailing parent company, the newly formed organization found new markets and became reasonably successful, expanding its operations by acquisitions in other parts of the country.

Consolidation. A consolidation strategy involves the firm operating in the same product market at existing levels. It is however far from a 'do nothing' strategy. Even to stand still firms must keep pace with their competitors. This may involve all the kinds of strategies outlined above, and will certainly involve considerations of product development, quality improvement, marketing and cost reduction.

Strategic choice

Faced with a number of strategic options a manager must make a choice. We have already indicated that the process involves consideration of a number of factors which we may summarize as follows.

☐ An analysis of environmental threats and opportunities.
☐ An analysis of company resources.
☐ The stated objectives of the company and those of the management team.
☐ The values and preferences of management decision–makers.
☐ The realities or organizational politics.

Johnson and Scholes (1984) use a checklist for the evaluation of strategic options. This involves testing various options for their suitability, feasibility and acceptability. The suitability of a strategy would include such considerations as its ability to tackle major problems, improve competitive standing, exploit strengths, and the extent to which it meets corporate objectives. The feasibility of a strategy is the extent to which that strategy can be achieved given the financial, physical and human resource base of the company. Even if a strategy is both suitable and feasible it must still be acceptable to various interested parties, such as management, employees, shareholders and customers. Shareholders may be particularly sensitive to strategies of acquisition. The ultimate acceptance of a particular strategy might depend on the attitude of senior management to risk.

The Strategic Planning Institute in Britain and the USA offers assistance in strategic choice by identifying those strategies most likely to result in increased profit levels. They have set up a scheme known as PIMS (Profit Impact of Market Strategies). In essence PIMS is really a huge database generated by those companies participating in the scheme. A record is kept of strategic options and their links to profit levels. Firms participating in the scheme have access to the data generated by other companies and may therefore learn from their successes and failures. Analysis of the information to date suggests a positive relationship between profitability and market share, but a negative relationship between profitability and the intensity of investment. Suprisingly the PIMS data have uncovered that investment is not such a safe option as many assume. Intense investment usually occurs in highly competitive businesses and companies tend to engage in damaging price wars or find that excessive investment proves a barrier to exit (Beasley, 1985).

The way a strategic choice is made will depend very much on the power and authority structure of the organization. In some firms the strategy may be highly detailed with little scope for interpretation by functional managers. In other firms a great deal of freedom is given to functional management to develop appropriate strategies within broad guidelines. We deal with specific functional strategies in Chapters 5 to 9. A theme stressed throughout is that R&D, production, marketing, personnel and financial strategies should achieve a high level of internal consistency, irrespective of where in the firm the strategy was formulated.

Summary

In this chapter we have portrayed the formulation of management strategy as a complex process involving the consideration of environmental and organizational factors as well as management values and organization politics. As a result the process is a mixture of rational techniques and subjective decision–making processes, including a consideration of management values and negotiations between interested parties.

We have identified a range of approaches and styles, which may operate at the same time, although at different stages of the firm's development one type of strategy may be more appropriate than another. The formulated strategy has several functions, not least of which is to anticipate the future by coordinating activities and focusing resources towards chosen objectives.

An analysis of the general environment and a focus on the immediate competitive environment will enable management to identify significant opportunities and threats, although how these are interpreted is a function of the values and creative ability of management. We identify four kinds of resource; product, physical, financial and people. All are important in enabling management to formulate strategy around the organization's strengths.

We examine four generic types of strategic option and suggest that each option should be assessed in terms of its suitability, its feasiblity and its acceptability. The final criterion stresses the central theme of this chapter; the importance of management values and organization politics in the strategic process.

Further reading

Three texts are worth particular consideration. G. Johnson and K. Scholes, *Exploring Corporate Strategy* (Prentice Hall International, 1984) offer probably the best British text currently available with good case illustrations. At the time of writing a new edition is about to emerge. W.F. Glueck and L.R. Jauch, *Business Policy and Strategic Management* 4th edition (McGraw Hill, 1984) and C.W. Hofer and D. Schendel, *Strategy Formulation: Analytical Concepts* (West Publishing, 1978) are both American texts, the former following a very clear model and offering some good meaty cases, and the latter providing some useful research material. A book which examines a variety of approaches and styles used in management strategy as well as offering some good illustrations is A.L. Minkes, *The Entrepreneurial Manager* (Penguin, 1987). At a more specific level, a good analysis of the competitive environment is offered by M.E. Porter, *Competitive Strategy: Techniques for Analysing Industries and Competitors* (Free Press, 1980). A somewhat different approach to strategy is presented by M.B. McCaskey, *The Executive Challenge* (Pitman, 1982) and T.J. Peters and R.H. Waterman, *In Search of Excellence* (Harper and Row, 1982) offers good case illustrations, although as we note elsewhere in this book, the approach has its critics.

Discussion

1. Examine the role of the scientific method in the process of strategy formulation. What role do entrepreneurship and creativity play?

2. What is the purpose of strategy, and how might a particular strategy be evaluated?

3. Identify the major environmental opportunites and threats faced by a city centre restaurant, a large retail store, a high street bank, a polytechnic, and a firm manufacturing television sets.

4. Using Porter's model identify the specific competitive forces operating in the five situations defined in the previous question.

5. In what ways can management use resource analysis and portfolio analysis to guide strategy? What are the major strengths and weaknesses of the models for portfolio analysis identified in this chapter?

6. Assess the relative contribution of environmental influences, resources and management behaviour to strategy formulation. In what situations may one of these influences predominate?

7. Make a critical analysis of the different approaches to diversification. In what situations would such strategies be appropriate?

8. With reference to Case 4.1, what strategic options would be most useful for the machine tool industry? What other strategic alternatives can be suggested?

9. Identify the environmental, organizational and management considerations which led 3M in Case 4.2 to rethink its planning procedure. What further threats might the company have to face?

10. Using Case 4.3 as a starting point, what strategic approaches, styles and options would best fit a polytechnic for the 1990s? What problems do you foresee with these approaches, styles and options?

Innovation **5**

In the second half of the 1970s innovation became a household word, mainly because it was apparently lacking.

(Van Duijn, 1983, p 93)

The quote by Van Duijn is typical of a fairly widespread belief that innovation will lead to economic growth, both at the level of national economies and at the level of the individual firm. This theme has recurred at intervals throughout the twentieth century, and more specifically in times of economic depression. The theme is popular in the United Kingdom in the mid to late 1980s as we compare ourselves unfavourably with countries like West Germany, Japan, the USA and France.

Innovation is a key function of business since it is related to entrepreneurship, the driving force behind business growth and development. In this chapter we attempt a broad–based view of innovation. We will start by examining the differences between the related concepts of innovation, invention, research and development, design and entrepreneurship. We move on to examine the relationship between innovative business activity and the environmental aspects of our model, in particular its impact on economic growth, the role of governments in stimulating innovation and entrepreneurship, and especially differences in government policy of different nation states. Much of government policy focuses upon the encouragement of new technologies, yet it is our contention that the development and design of new products needs to be accompanied by corresponding developments in marketing. In the latter part of this chapter we extend this view of innovation still further by examining how it operates within organizations, and in particular the relevance of organizational structure and culture to innovative activity. We end the chapter by focussing on a number of generic innovation strategies.

We can therefore see that innovation is not confined to the technological hardware of products and processes. We believe that successful product innovation invariably requires accompanying innovations in marketing and organization structure. There is a particularly close association between innovation and marketing. Peter Drucker sees these two activities as the basic functions of business, as he regards them as the only truly entrepreneurial functions (Drucker, 1968).

The link between innovation and entrepreneurship is important, since

KEY CONCEPT 5.1

INNOVATION

Innovation is the process through which new ideas and inventions become a business reality in the form of new products, processes, marketing strategies, and new methods of organization and management. Its importance to business survival and growth is acknowledged by many firms through the creation of special units such as research and development departments in manufacturing industry.

it establishes innovation as a function of all businesses. Many people associate innovation with the process of new product design in manufacturing industry. Yet, examples of innovation can be drawn from every conceivable organizational context. In the financial services industry, banking has been transformed by the introduction of automatic cash dispensers, giving the general public much greater access to their accounts. In an increasingly competitive market the banks have developed mortgage services and the building societies have begun to offer a range of services we normally associate with banks. In the entertainment industry, the innovation of multi–screen cinemas offers the public a wider choice and has contributed to significant increases in attendance and hence revenue. In education, innovations occur through the development of new courses or new methods of presenting those courses, such as distance learning.

What all these various forms of innovation have in common is the difficulty facing management in implementing such changes. These difficulties can include raising the necessary finance, ensuring that the firm is staffed by people with the required skills, being able to persuade the consumer to buy the new product or service, being able to deliver in sufficient quantity when demand is created, and invariably coping with the political processes within the organization which accompany any form of change. Factors which may add or detract from the difficulty involve the time scale required for the change to take place and people to see the returns and the attitude of the people involved towards risk and their ability to cope with uncertainty. A major product change or the installation of new equipment can take five years and longer before the development costs are recovered, a reason why major innovations are apt to make both management and financial backers nervous. We examine the management and organization processes related to innovation later in the chapter. Firstly we make an attempt to sort out the various terms.

Identifying the concepts

The terms 'invention', 'innovation', 'research and development', 'design' and 'entrepreneurship' are all used in a variety of contexts, often interchangeably. There is a further confusion in that whilst all are processes, 'research and development' or 'R&D' as it is popularly known, is frequently used in an organizational context to identify a department whose primary objective is the creation and development of new products and new ways of making them. We will now look at the concepts themselves in a little more detail.

Type of innovation	Extent of the innovation	
	Basic	Modification
Raw material	The use of plastic in place of glass in bottles.	Changing the components of the plastic in the bottles to make them tougher.
Product	The use of integrated circuits on microchips to replace transistors.	Employing electronic controls in a washing machine.
Process	Introducing robots to perform the welding operation in a car assembly plant.	Increasing the number of stages in a car painting process to gain a better finish.
Marketing	The opening of a high street shop by a mail order bookclub to widen sales.	Using television personalities instead of politicians in a televised political broadcast.
Organizational	Creating a matrix form of organization to replace the traditional arrangement based on specialist functions.	Creating a separate training function within the Personnel department.

Figure 5.1 Different types of innovation.

Invention and innovation

These terms are often confused, yet if we take Schumpeter's line there is a very clear distinction between them.

> As long as they are not carried into practice, inventions are economically irrelevant.
>
> (Schumpeter, 1961, p 88)

Invention is the creation of something new, be it a new computer, a new method for painting cars, a new form of selling, a new university course, or a new form of organization structure. An invention becomes an innovation when the idea becomes a reality; when the new computer goes into manufacture and starts selling; when the new university course begins to recruit students.

This reinforces the notion that innovation operates in a variety of forms and in a variety of contexts. We present these various forms together with appropriate examples in Figure 5.1. We are also able to distinguish three broad categories.

A distinction can be drawn between product innovation and process innovation. Product innovation is the development of a new product such as a new model of car, a new form of insurance policy, or a restaurant offering a new special vegetarian menu. Process innovation is concerned

Type of innovation	Number of innovations
Basic innovations	7
Radical innovations	29
Very important improvements	62
Important improvements	145
Minor improvements	239
Minor product or process differentiation	760

Figure 5.2 A classification of innovations, 1953–73.

(*Source:* Van Duijn, 1983)

with how the product is made or delivered to the customer. The development of robots in manufacturing industry is a form of process innovation, as is a restaurant opening a self–service section in addition to an existing waiter service operation.

We have already noted that innovation may occur in every aspect of the organization's operations. We may therefore identify innovations in the selection and use of raw materials, in the way goods and services are produced, in the marketing activities and in the way the organization is structured and managed. For example, the introduction of work group participation in management decision–making is a form of innovation, as are types of job enrichment to enhance worker motivation.

We can also make a distinction between basic innovations and innovations that are modifications and improvements on existing products and processes. In fact the great majority of innovations are not major breakthroughs but modifications, often of a very minor nature. This was the conclusion drawn by a panel of experts who examined product and process innovations that had taken place between 1953 and 1973. We present their conclusions in Figure 5.2.

In addition to the various types of innovation, we might add a fourth category. This has been termed 'pseudo–innovations' (Mensch, 1979). These are often introduced to revitalize a stagnant market, but in fact no real change has taken place. Such pseudo–innovations are often the product of marketing campaigns to change the fortunes of a flagging product. The product may be relaunched under a different brand name, repackaged to suggest product changes or advertised as containing a 'new improved formula' when no significant change has taken place. A case in this area is that of the washing powder 'Square Deal Surf'. Its forerunner, 'Surf', was experiencing a declining market share in a market where every new product appeared to come with a new formula for washing whiter. The company aimed the product at a segment of the market that they had identified as 'anti–gimmick'. To emphasize this point they offered the product with a changed name, which suggested to consumers that they were getting a better deal than those offered by competitors. The change and repositioning of the product in the market was highly successful and sales increased. We deal with aspects of market segmentation and positioning in more detail in Chapter 7.

The case of 'Square Deal Surf' illustrates the complexity of innovation. To Mensch it undoubtedly represents a pseudo–innovation in terms of product, yet the marketing strategy employed was highly innovative. Moreover, not all innovations are visible. Where washing powders have radically changed their formula this is not instantly apparent to the consumer, and the company relies upon its marketing effort to convey this information, reinforcing the importance of an integrated innovation and marketing strategy.

Research, development and design

We can define research and development as the organization of innovation at the level of the firm. It is that activity of an organization that both seeks to satisfy a market need by developing new products and methods and find uses for scientific and technological inventions. This introduces the concepts of demand pull innovation (fulfilling a market need) and technology push innovation (applying existing knowledge). R&D is clearly associated with science and technology, although the R&D function can be performed in all types of industry. We have seen that the process of new product development occurs in non–scientific and technical situations. In many organizations there is a group of people whose primary task is the generation of new business ideas, as in the case of television companies which have a department for new programme development.

In some industries, especially those involved in complex, competitive environments, R&D is a vital part of the business. Firms like IBM and Hewlett–Packard in the computer industry, and Ciba Geigy and Bayer in the pharmaceutical industry, have large teams of staff engaged exclusively in R&D work. In the case of Hewlett–Packard, innovation is part of the organizational culture and is stressed as a responsibility of all employees (Case 3.5). The institutionalization of R&D can bring its own problems, which are raised when we look at organizational aspects later in the chapter.

R&D is an incremental process. We illustrate this by using as a framework the classification of R&D developed by Burns and Stalker (1966). Although their classification is biased towards technological industries it gives us further insights into the innovative process.

Pure research. This is concerned with advancing the state of knowledge in a particular field with little immediate concern for its commercial application. Very few firms engage directly in this kind of research, and on the whole it is generally left to the university sector. Business concerns are involved indirectly so far as some of them sponsor research activity in some universities and polytechnics.

Basic research. Here firms do get involved since this kind of research is directed at advancing the state of knowledge in a particular applied field with the very real hope that it will prove useful. The managements of these firms hope that such research will lead ultimately to those product and process innovations that will give the business its competitive edge. In some firms, like 3M, the active encouragement of staff to develop their own research projects is an important part of company policy, and many ideas generated from the staff's own programmes have been turned to profitable use by the company (Case 4.2).

Industrial research. Industrial research stands in relation to basic research as invention to innovation. Industrial research attempts to transform pure and basic research into some form of profitable use.

Development. This takes research a stage further by translating the outcome of research into something more tangible. At this stage in the design of a new product, a prototype or a sample would be produced.

Design. This is the final stage in the R&D process which translates the development into the final product for the consumer. The design stage attempts to fuse certain elements which are referred to as the 'design mix'. These elements are effective operation, safety, easy maintenance, value for money and aesthetic considerations. These are all focussed on satisfying customer needs.

The design aspect of research and development is an obvious area of overlap with both the production and marketing processes, to the extent that product design is seen as an essential element in both fields. Design and styling assumes particular importance in industries such as car manufacture, where products are often sold as much on their appearance as their inherent product qualities. A firm like Bang and Olufsen produces televisions and Hi-Fi equipment to high technical specifications, yet its distinctiveness in the market place owes much more to its visual appeal. Making their products look very different from their competitors' is a deliberate Bang and Olufsen strategy.

The British government targetted design for special consideration by businesses in 1985. Part of this targetting was an encouragement to schools and colleges to seek ways of incorporating design in the curriculum. A major concern has been the place of design in manufacturing industry. An underlying assumptiom behind such developments is undoubtedly the view that Britain as a manufacturing nation is falling behind its rivals, notably West Germany and Japan, in the perceived quality and desirability of its goods. We discuss the importance of quality in Chapter 6.

It is not only in manufacturing industry that design is important. A good illustration is presented by the clothing retail chain Burton. The company had always been fairly successful catering for the needs of a middle-of-the-road male market segment. However the firm suffered a serious decline of its market share and profitability. The styling of their clothes had not kept pace with the needs of an increasingly fashion-conscious market, particularly those in the younger age group who spend a good proportion of their income on clothes. Moreover the image of their shops and store layout was decidedly old-fashioned and unappealing to the new consumer. As a result of a very detailed research programme to identify and meet the specific design needs of different consumer groups, the management introduced a completely new range of clothes to capture the growing market and invested in a modernization programme to give their stores a new image. The management has attributed a great deal of their rise in profits from £16.4 million in 1981 to £80.22 million in 1985 to a conscious effort in design management.

KEY CONCEPT 5.2

ENTREPRENEURSHIP

The entrepreneur is responsible for creating new products, services and markets and the means through which these products are made, services produced, and markets reached. Entrepreneurs are often responsible for creating new forms of organization and new ways of managing people. The entrepreneur operates by introducing such changes directly and by having the ability to organize physical, financial, information and human resources to bring about innovation.

Entrepreneurship

We noted at the beginning of this chapter that the activities of the entrepreneur were crucial to the process of innovation. Innovation happens because the entrepreneur has initiated it, as illustrated by the work of Ronald Hickman and the 'Workmate' in Case 5.2. The entrepreneur creates new products, new markets, and new means through which products are made and markets reached, based around new forms of organization and new means of managing people. Entrepreneurs have therefore been key figures in business history.

The centrality of entrepreneurs to business development has led researchers to seek out those characteristics which make a successful entrepreneur. The research has shown that entrepreneurs are hard workers, risk–takers, outsiders, but, not surprisingly, no distinctive set of personality traits has emerged, which adequately define entrepreneurs. Perhaps the most significant finding was that which suggested that successful entrepreneurs had a high need for achievement and a moderate need for power, whilst the less successful had a low need for achievement and a positively high or low need for power (McClelland, 1961). The message from this research is clear; entrepreneurs are achievers but those seeking entrepreneurial activity only as a means of achieving power over others are likely to fail.

For a time, the role of the entrepreneur in business was understated as the focus turned to the growth and activities of the large corporation. However, the entrepreneur re–emerged in the 1980s as a hero figure, when the media highlighted the success of certain businesses when those around were failing. Success through a general recession made household names of such as Alan Sugar at Amstrad, Anita Roddick at the Body Shop and Richard Branson at Virgin.

We see interest in entrepreneurship taking two directions.

☐ The success of certain entrepreneurs to rise above the recession has prompted a government, already committed to a free market, to encourage even more entrepreneurial activity in the form of small business development. We deal at length with issues pertaining to small business development in Chapter 3. Suffice it to say here that not all small businesses are entrepreneurial, since many merely replicate existing forms of business. Becoming self–employed to run a newsagency business has little to do with innovation and entrepreneurship.

☐ The focus upon small firms and the entrepreneur as a small businessman has detracted from the importance of entrepreneurship in
large businesses. In his study of General Motors, Sears, Dupont and
Standard Oil, which we referred to in our discussion of structure in
Chapter 3, Chandler stressed the importance for managers to be able to
see beyond the daily problems of controlling a large corporation and
develop new business ideas for the future. More attention is now being
paid to the role of the entrepreneur in large firms.

It is our view that all firms irrespective of size need the introduction of
new ideas of survive. In Chapter 4 we introduced the concept of entrepreneurial decision–making as a type of strategy employed by all organizations at some stage. Whether innovation through entrepreneurship is most
successful in a small or a large setting, or how it is best organized, are questions we leave to our discussion of organizational aspects. We turn now to
environmental issues in innovation.

The environmental aspects of innovation

Four aspects of our model are particularly significant here. We will look
first of all at the relationship between innovation and the economy, which
leads logically to a discussion on the role of the state in encouraging
innovation. This in turn leads to the differences in the way nations
approach innovation, which we examine by looking at cultural influences.
There is a clear relationship between technology and innovation, which
we acknowledge in our assessment of the contending influences of tech-
nogical development and the market place. We will not discuss the relationship between innovation and the labour force here. It is an important
relationship as the skills of the workforce and their attitude towards change,
more especially changes in technology, are crucial to the successful implementation of innovation. These themes are developed in Chapters 2 and 8.
A core element in all these discussions is the role of the economy, and the
belief that innovation stimulates economic growth.

The role of the economy

There have been many attempts to link innovation with economic growth.
In general, innovation is perceived as the means through which economic
regeneration occurs. As such it has held a particular fascination for those
who see government investment in research and development as a positive
strategy for tackling the problems of economic decline. More specifically
economists have attempted to prove links between innovation and such
factors as per capita growth and export competitiveness. In this section
we will view briefly the general debate which sees innovation as the key
mechanism in long–wave economic cycles and then examine attempts to
identify more specific relationships.

Innovation and long–wave cycles

The relationship between innovation and economic activity owes much to
the work of the Russian economist Kondratieff. He put forward the view

KEY CONCEPT 5.3

**INNOVATION AND
ECONOMIC GROWTH**

There is considerable debate concerning the relationship between innovation and economic growth at the level of both national economies and the firm. Several theories have been based around innovation as a prerequisite for economic growth and more especially its role in leading economies out of depression. Despite the plausibility of several of these claims it is difficult to measure the precise impact that innovation has upon the economy and establish clear causality. As with many aspects of business, the isolation of a single factor such as innovation can present a misleading view of the complex nature of business interactions. Nevertheless, the importance accorded by governments to innovation as the stimulus for economic growth has resulted in considerable state intervention in this area.

that economic activity exhibits regular long–term cycles of growth and depression, followed by a further period of growth and so on (Kondratieff, 1934). Each cycle is characterized by a particular form of economic activity; thus the period 1785 to 1842 was dominated by iron ore, coke and the cotton industry, whereas the following period to 1897 centred around the development of the railways. If we extend the cycles to the present day then we can see periods of economic activity based around electricity, chemicals and the automobile and more recently focussing upon aerospace, electronics and computers.

The explanation for the operation of these cycles has been taken up by a number of economists. For Schumpeter the key was innovation. Each phase of economic recovery can be attributed to clusters of innovations, enabling capitalism to evolve and usher in a new period of prosperity (Schumpeter, 1939). He thought that most innovations occurred when the economic climate appeared more favourable, thus acting as a stimulus for entrepreneurial activity. However, some believe that innovations only occur in the depths of depression, when profits are so low that entrepreneurs are stimulated into risk–taking ventures (Mensch, 1979).

The notion of economic cycles has generated considerable debate among economists and others, who, despite the absence of hard data have felt more than capable of contributing to the debate as to when the cycles begin, how long they last, and what the key innovations are. The problems with long waves are the task of identifying and dating the major innovations and the highly deterministic nature of cyclical activity, leaving some economists to view the theory as convenient rather than meaningful.

The belief that mankind is in the grip of mysterious forces which it is powerless to change recurs in period of stress and difficulty

(Brittan, 1983)

This may explain the resurgence of interest in long wave theory at the end of the 1970s.

Rank	Corporation	No. of Patents
1	Canon K.K.	847
2	Hitachi Ltd	845
3	Toshiba Corp.	823
4	General Electric Corp.	779
5	US Philips Corp.	687
6	Westinghouse Electric Corp.	652
7	IBM Corp.	591
8	Siemens A.G.	539
9	Mitsubishi Denki K.K.	518
10	RCA Corp.	504
11	Fuji Photo Film Co., Ltd	494
12	Dow Chemical Co.	469
13	E.I. du Pont de Nemours & Co.	419
14	Motorola, Inc.	414
15	AT&T Co.	406
16	Honda Motor Co., Ltd.	395
17	NEC Corp.	375
	Toyota Jidosha K.K.	375
19	Bayer A.G.	371
20	General Motors Corp.	370

Figure 5.3 The top twenty corporations receiving US Patents, 1987.

(*Source: Intellectual Property Owners, Inc.*, March 1988)

Innovation and specific measures of economic performance

A number of studies have been carried out in an attempt to provide hard data linking innovative activity and some measure of economic performance at both the level of national economies and the individual firm. An excellent summary of the various types of research that have been carried out in this area can be found in Rothwell and Zegveld (1981). A number of linkages have been found, as summarized below.

☐ Investments in R&D, particularly those relating to technical change, are the major cause of improvements in productivity and output.
☐ A correlation exists between the number of registered patents and export performance. Between 1937 and 1975 West German patents registered in the USA outnumbered those from any other foreign country. During the same period West Germany was the leading exporter to the USA. Since 1975, West Germany has been replaced by Japan on both counts. In 1987, the top three companies receiving patents in the USA were all Japanese. In fact, eight Japanese firms feature in the top 20. (Figure 5.3)
☐ There is some evidence to suggest that consumers appear willing to pay more for goods of superior technical quality. Once again West Germany features, this time in comparison with Britain. Between 1971 and 1975 West Germany's share of exports to OECD countries was 22% compared to Britain's 10%, despite the fact that the unit value of West German exports was 40% greater. The assumption here is that investment in improving the quality of goods will pay back in the form of increased sales.

Despite the research findings and the persuasive pleas for investment in R&D, the links between innovation and economic performance remain speculative. The major difficulty is our inability to measure innovation. Indicators that have been used, such as patents and the amount of money a firm has invested in its R&D activities, can at best be considered a rough guide. For example, a patent may be registered and then never used to produce anything of value; improvements in products and processes can originate as much from individual inventors and equipment users as they can from organized R&D departments.

More significantly, the attempts to isolate innovation may give a false impression. The export success of 'upper range' West German cars such as Mercedes Benz and BMW may well be attributed to the technical superiority of the product when compared to other cars in the same range. Such an explanation fits the research findings identified above. There is another explanation. Both firms have been particularly active in carefully targetted advertising campaigns which not only stress the technical superiority of their product, but also attempt to give the product an image of exclusivity and high status. How much of their sales are attributable to technical innovation and how much to an effective advertising campaign? This illustration confirms the inter–relationship of innovation and marketing that we identified earlier. It also emphasizes a key theme in this book; that business activities are inter–related and there are dangers in viewing one activity, such as innovation, in isolation.

Throughout this section we have made reference to the role of state intervention, and it is to this aspect we now turn our attention. We will view the role of governments in general terms and we then explore how governments in different countries operate with respect to the stimulation of innovation.

The role of the state

The state is involved in innovation in a number of different ways. It invests in R&D in individual firms, government research establishments and in universities and polytechnics. It has established the legal protection of inventions through the patent system. Various state departments are actively concerned in the stimulation of innovation; currently the Department of Trade and Industry proudly announces itself as 'The Department for Enterprise'. The state's financial support is clearly biased towards technological innovation in the manufacturing and defence industries but exhortations for innovation and enterprise are usually aimed at all firms in all sectors. Occasionally such exhortations are transformed into government policies and schemes, such as those aimed at innovation through small business development (Chapter 3).

The activities of the state in subsidizing, protecting and encouraging innovation provide an excellent illustration of the inter–relationship between the state and business at a more general level. In this section, we attempt a classification of the types of intervention specifically concerned with innovation and examine the associated problems. Firstly we identify the motivation behind this involvement.

□ Using the kind of economic evidence presented above there would appear to be a clear belief that innovation and entrepreneurship are major factors in economic expansion and export competitiveness.

□ We have already noted that investment in innovation is both long term and high risk. The mechanism of the free market may be inadequate in generating those basic innovations upon which economic expansion is based, hence the need for state subsidy when individual companies are reluctant to invest.

□ Intervention is often necessary for political and strategic as well as for social reasons. In Britain and the USA defence spending forms a major part of all expenditure on innovation. Many countries have seen space exploration as a goal of national importance and prestige, and the same could be said for the British and French Governments' involvement with the development of the supersonic jet airliner, Concorde. Investment in the nuclear fuel industry is viewed by several governments as a desirable energy strategy.

Since 1945 successive British Governments have invested heavily in innovation, although not as much as in some other countries and certainly not as much as some critics would like. Those countries with the biggest post–war growth in research and development expenditure are those countries where costs have been significantly underwritten by governments. The greatest subsidy occurs in the USA where much of the funding supports defence and aerospace projects. These two areas have become increasingly intertwined as seen in the 1985 proposals for the Strategic Defence Initiative, popularly known as the 'Star Wars' project. This aims to set up missile defence systems in outer space and its implications for government involvement in the R&D of individual firms have already extended beyond the States.

The British Government has agreed a set of rules under which British firms and universities will accept research contracts from the American Government. One of the stated aims of such projects is that technology transfer will occur; that the products, knowledge and skills developed in such research will have a use in other areas of application. Not least here is the view that work carried out in defence and aerospace will be widespread in its application to other industries and thus be of great benefit to the economy. A stated aim of the United States Government is that involvement of firms in the Strategic Defence Initiative should have particular benefits for the American computer industry thereby assisting in the competition against Japanese firms. The British Government, by formally pledging its support, also hopes that benefits will accrue to its own industries. However, any estimation of the economic impact of such developments is not only highly speculative but raises important ethical arguments concerning the direction of government intervention in private industry and the universities. We shall return to these difficulties at the end of this section, but first we need to identify the various types of intervention.

Types of state intervention in innovation

We examine state intervention under four main headings; procurement, subsidies, regulation, and education and training. These types of innovation occur even where the government has expressed its ideological opposition to interference in the workings of the free market.

Procurement. The need of the state for certain products has stimulated research in many areas. The clearest illustration of this is to be found in government defence contracts, with implications not only for the armaments industry itself, but also in electronics, computing and aerospace, as identified in the SDI case mentioned above. Businesses in the USA have seen the armed forces as a very large and very stable market. There is a view that the goals of business and the military have become intertwined and form an important part of the image–building that goes on between ideologically opposed nations in a cold war (Galbraith, 1972).

In Britain the needs of the National Health Service have stimulated developments in the pharmaceutical industry, and in most nations the fear of disappearing natural resources has led to government–backed research to find synthetic materials.

Subsidies. Subsidies to individual firms occur in the form of investments, grants and tax concessions. We have seen how special policies exist, such as those to encourage innovation through small firms. Most subsidies aim to support a particular form of research and development. In 1981 the British Government made available £80 million to promote the use and awareness of information technology. This was deemed necessary as Britain was seen to be falling behind its major competitors, and was followed up by 1982 being officially designated as 'Information Technology Year'.

The coordination of Britain's policy of selective intervention has been placed in the hands of the British Technology Group. This body was set up in 1981 to incorporate both the National Research and Development Council and the National Enterprise Board. It seems clear that the Government wishes to align itself with more progressive industries and establish a more proactive role. The National Enterprise Board was often viewed as reactive and was all too often identified with policies to prop up ailing industries, as in the giving of financial support to British Leyland and Rolls Royce. The development of INMOS presented in Case 5.1 illustrates the role of British Governments in subsidizing R&D and the dilemmas which often accompany it.

Regulation. There are various types of state regulation which serve to support, encourage and even limit the innovative activity of businesses. A more detailed review of the laws relating to innovation can be found in *Law in a Business Context* (Cole and Shears, 1989). We classify regulations in terms of patents and licensing, restrictive and enabling laws, and import restriction.

(a) *Patents and licensing.* A patent is a legal device which enables the holder to maintain a monopoly in an invention for a stated period, which in Britain stands at twenty years. In exchange for granting this monopoly, the owner of the invention must make available its details to the general public. The patent system operates in almost every country in the world including the Soviet Union and the People's Republic of China. The stated benefits of such a system are, firstly, that it actively encourages new developments by offering protection to the patent holder against others copying the invention. Secondly, by revealing the details of the invention, it en-

CASE 5.1

INMOS

'The Inmos saga ... provides 1980s evidence of Britain's still un-bridged 'two cultures' gap, through politicians' ignorance of techno-logy and technologists' naivety about politics.

(*Guardian*, 3 December 1985)

Inmos has been a hostage of political incompetence, City misunder-standing and corporate chaos.

(*Financial Guardian*, 31 March 1987)

In 1978 under a Labour government, the National Enterprise Board (NEB) in its role as an industrial holding company, invested £50 million in a newly formed company, INMOS, to develop, manufacture and market semi–conductors, popularly known as microchips. The company was formed by a small group of capitalist entrepreneurs, including an Englishman and two Americans, and was based originally in the USA. NEB accepted the proposals of the new company even though it had no product or even design for one at the time. The motivation behind the government's involvement was the desire for Britain to develop its own semi–conductor industry, not only because this was seen as a valuable and growing market, but also as part of a wider strategy for the develop-ment of the government–backed electronics industry, including such firms as Ferranti and ICL, an industry identified as central to the country's economic development through the 1980s. An important factor was the decision to join a race for the development of a new form of microchip, one which would perform the functions of several types of semi–conduc-tors on a single chip. This creation of a 'mini–computer' on a single chip was seen as the next development in 'Very Large Scale Integration' (VLSI) technology.

At the time, the semi–conductor market was dominated by the Ameri-cans with Texas Instruments leading the field. The Japanese, however, were launching a collaborative effort by leading companies to develop the next generation of VLSI. By contrast, European firms had a weak position in the market and prospects looked none too good. The man-agement of INMOS decided that its main stategy was to push ahead and be the first company to produce the revolutionary chip, its particular version to be known as the Transputer. In the meantime it was decided to design and manufacture conventional semi–conductors and the com-pany set up two production plants at Colorado Spings in the USA, de-signated the corporate headquarters, and at Newport in Wales. The British operation was controlled from a research base in Bristol. INMOS saw its success in a highly volatile industry as being based upon, firstly the development of an entirely new product acceptable to the majority of users as the best, and secondly on high volume sales to offset the high development costs.

At the outset INMOS faced a number of difficulties. There was sceptic-ism in the City, among the civil servants, from some trade unionists and from potential American customers wary of a state–controlled company. There was opposition from within the ranks of the Labour party, espe-cially left–wing members who objected to the three founders acquiring

Continued from previous page

such a large stake in the company and in particular to the large amounts of money being paid to the two Americans. More significantly several experts in the field felt that insufficient investment had been made given the nature of the company's strategy. Worse problems were to follow with the defeat of the Labour Government at the hands of the Conservatives in the 1979 election. The incoming Government were less than enthusiastic about INMOS, preferring to give support to those companies like ICL that were already established in their field. Moreover, there were proposals to limit the activities of NEB and an ideological commitment to privatization. This not only placed the future of INMOS in some doubt, but there were delays in necessary funding at a crucial time in the company's development.

In 1984, after investing an estimated £100 million into the company, the Government sold its interests to Thorn EMI for £95 million. This followed a well–established pattern in the microchip industry; that of small innovative companies being bought up by large multinational organizations. In Thorn's case it was seen in the City as a hasty acquisition, after the company had been refused in its attempts to merge with British Aerospace. The following year the microchip market suffered a downturn and INMOS was forced to cut back its activities by 20%, with lay–offs in both Britain and America. Later in 1985, Thorn EMI announced that it was looking for a development partner for INMOS, possibly from Japan, and was willing to relinquish up to 49% of its shares.

There can be little doubt that the ideological and political differences, the selling of INMOS at a crucial stage in its development, and the continued uncertainty of its role within the Thorn EMI stable, has arrested the company's growth. However, the Transputer was developed successfully, it was ahead of its rivals and began to sell well.

(*Sources:* Stopford *et al.*, 1980, *Financial Guardian* 31.3.87. A much more detailed account can be found in *The INMOS Saga: A Triumph of National Enterprise?* by McClean and Rowlands, 1985.)

courages further inventions and innovative activity along similar lines. Thirdly, it prevents the duplication of research, and fourthly, it ensures that the benefits of research are passed on to society. A real benefit to the patent holder is the opportunity to issue manufacturing licences, as illustrated in Case 5.2 by the licence bought by Black and Decker to manufacture and sell the 'Workmate'.

A firm holding a patent on a particular type of manufacturing process may allow another firm in the same business to use that process upon the payment of an agreed fee. In the case of major inventions this can be an important source of revenue for the patent holder. The revolutionary method for the production of glass, the 'Float Process', was developed by the St. Helens firm of Pilkington Brothers Ltd in the early 1960s, since when licences have been granted to glass manufacturers all over the world enabling them to use the same process. In certain cases the law has had to intervene to enforce the issue of licences where it was felt that some companies were operating an unfair monopoly. This occurred in the case of Hoffman–La Roche, the Swiss pharmaceutical company. In 1971 the

CASE 5.2

THE WORKMATE

In 1973 a Design Council Award was made to Ronald Hickman, the inventor of the 'Workmate'. This was only the third time such an award had been made for a tool. The 'Workmate' is a combination of a work bench, a sawing horse and vice, but whose versatility as a tool is much greater than the sum of its parts. It is small, lightweight, and easily stored. The device is bought in great numbers by DIY enthusiasts, but also by professional carpenters and building firms.

Hickman, who had received only a high school education and possessed no technical qualifications came to Britain in 1955, working first as a bookkeeper in a music store and then with Ford Motor Company in the styling department. By 1958 he had been doing freelance design work for Lotus cars and eventually joined them as a designer. He was entirely responsible for the Lotus Elan, and in five years had become the design director of the company. He reached the stage where the job was taking all his time, and in 1967 he left Lotus to form his own company Mate Tools.

The idea for the company arose during his time at Lotus. He had moved house and had invented a device to assist him in building fitted furniture to his own design. After various modifications the Workmate Mark 1 emerged, which he patented and sold through mail order advertising in such magazines as *Do-it-yourself, Homemaker, Radio Times* and newspapers such as the *Daily Mail*. Sales started in 1968 and the product became an instant success. The demand for the product was greater than Mate Tools could satisfy. As a result several imitators appeared and Hickman began to look for a larger firm to take on manufacture and sales.

The patent protection saw off the imitators, sometimes after court action and damages awarded to Hickman. In 1972, Hickman granted Black and Decker an exclusive licence to manufacture the 'Workmate' which was now redesigned as Mark 2.

When the Mark 2 was launched in 1972 the demand was so great that all stocks were immediately exhausted. The Mark 1 had achieved an annual sales growth of 120%, and under Black and Decker sales of the Mark 2 were growing at over 138% per year. By 1976 over one million had been sold and by 1983 the product was being manufactured in Britain, France, Italy, Spain, Canada, Japan and Eire. Mate Tools still sold the 'Workmate' itself but bought them ready made from Black and Decker.

(*Sources: Reports of Patent Cases*, 1983)

British Patent Comptroller ordered Hoffman–La Roche to grant licences to two British firms, Berk Pharmaceuticals and DDSA Ltd for the manufacture of the tranquillizers librium and valium. Despite frequent requests the Swiss drugs company had repeatedly refused manufacturing licences on the grounds of the safety standards of the finished product. However the British Patent system held that the refusal to grant licences gave the Swiss company an unfair monopoly in the drugs industry (the Hoffman–La Roche case in Stopford *et al.*, 1980, has further details).

Since that time the law relating to licensing has been amended, and compulsory licences may now only be issued in the case of the non–manufacture of the product by the patent holder, or in cases where the product is not manufactured in this country. The main idea behind such laws is to stimulate the development and use of the invention in that country and hence assist local businesses.

(b) *Restrictive and enabling laws*. Most countries possess laws which control manufacturing standards and relate to such aspects as safety and pollution. Not only do these laws ensure that innovations conform to certain standards, but they aim to encourage research into socially desirable end–products such as car engines with low fuel consumption or car exhaust systems which restrict pollution into the atmosphere. The ends are not only socially desirable but can have an effect on business performance as well. A firm which meets Government standards of product quality enters the market place with additional competitive edge. As we see in Chapter 6, there is a growing trend in Britain for firms to show that they have met British Standards of quality assurance. There is a strong prediction that firms with strong policies on quality, like Marks and Spencer, will, in the future, only deal with suppliers that have met these standards.

Whilst such regulations may well encourage certain types of innovation, they may restrict others. This benefits some firms but handicaps others. The use of restrictive laws has been greatest in the USA bringing forth calls for deregulation, as happened in the 1970s. Although in practice very little actually changed, there was undoubtedly a belief among the American business community that excessive government regulation was holding back technological innovation and hence the country's economic growth.

As we saw with the relationship between innovation and economic growth, there is a difficulty in establishing a direct causal link between such laws and innovative activity at the level of the firm. As an illustration, we can see that increases in the price of oil in 1973 resulted, in both Britain and the USA, in new laws relating to speed limits and exhaust emission. However, the ensuing trend in motor manufacture towards the design and manufacture of smaller cars would almost certainly have occurred in response to increased oil prices irrespective of any legislation.

(c) *Import controls*. The theory here is that restriction on the imports from other countries will have a beneficial effect in stimulating research in the home country or intensifying the search for a substitute product or process. Import controls enforced by Japanese governments since the second world war have often been cited as the major impetus to considerable innovations by Japanese businesses. The danger in such a strategy however is that other countries may well retaliate and impose their own restrictions. In 1987 both the British and American governments have considered the initiation of a trade war with Japan, and the Americans considered proposals to implement an import tax on Japanese goods to cause price increases of up to 100%. The Americans themselves have in the past been fond of using import controls, and the development of the synthetic fibre industry in the USA owes much to restrictions on the import of woollen products.

Education and training. There is an underlying assumption that state investment in education and pure science will have a significant impact in increasing the level of innovation and thus benefit both the economy and society. The relationship between primary research and the knowledge–based activities of higher education institutions is supposedly one of the key features of the modern age. Galbraith observed of educators and scientists that they 'stand in relation to the industrial system much as did the banking and financial community in the early stages of industrial development' (Galbraith, 1972 p 283).

There are certain well publicized developments in both Britain and the USA that lend substance to the post–industrial society thesis. Developments in 'Silicon Valley' in California, 'Route 128' in Massachusetts and around Cambridge in England all show the relationship between industrial research and major universities with a reputation for science. The growth of some American high–technology companies such as Hewlett–Packard in Palo Alto, California is clearly associated with this phenomenon, as is the development of a network of businesses in computing and related fields in the vicinity of Cambridge. This networking of businesses around a university is referred to as a 'Science Park'. Businesses which locate there feel that substantial benefits will accrue from their association, both with a university and with other progressive industries. This is an illustration of potential synergy that we referred to in the discussion of strategy in Chapter 4.

In spite of such developments, British institutions of higher education have in the 1980s been subjected to a series of financial cuts as part of the government's determination to reduce public expenditure. The resulting debate has identified both positive and negative aspects. On the positive side it has, in many cases, pushed industry and universities much closer together. Some universities like Salford rely heavily on the outside funding of research by private companies, which has enabled many universities and polytechnics to generate income for re–investment. The critics of this type of development see a danger of weakening the primary research base and restricting university research to projects related to the very specific requirements of a limited number of companies. This could restrict opportunities for breakthroughs in basic technology considered essential for industrial regeneration.

The state sometimes intervenes in skills training (Chapter 8 has more information). The question of skills shortages becomes particularly crucial when emphasis is placed on innovation and technical change. This aspect illustrates the interaction between innovation and the labour force in our model. Any innovation can only be effective if it is matched by a labour force having the requisite skills. The development of new processes may prove even more costly if they remain idle waiting for the skills of the work-force to catch up, as Rolls Royce found to its cost in the early 1970s. The development of the high performance jet engine, the RB 211, encountered many problems. Although the focus was upon the mounting costs of the project, costs which almost forced the company out of business, a contributory factor was the lack of expertise to overcome the many technical difficulties which arose at the development stage. In the 1970s many firms invested in computer hardware and software in the belief that this would change their business overnight. In some of these companies the systems were under–utilized, as insufficient consideration had been given to training the employees.

Some problems with state intervention in innovation

We have seen that the main motive for state intervention to encourage and support innovative activity is the desire to improve economic performance. We have also seen the difficulties of showing a direct relationship between investment in innovation and economic growth, whether measured at national or organizational levels. There are other difficulties with the state's involvement and we identify these below.

A major difficulty lies in the ability of government employees to make decisions in highly specialized technical and scientific areas, and decisions which are in the best interests of the business community as a whole. Government support may well be important in stimulating innovation but the critical skills and knowledge reside in the firms themselves or the higher education sector. For intervention to be successful, extensive consultation is required and there needs to be freedom for individuals to pursue their own research goals, otherwise there is a danger that intervention can be misdirected. Several highly publicized government–backed ventures such as Concorde or gas–cooled nuclear reactors have not met with the success predicted for them as a result of these difficulties. Similarly, measures to support small firms have been criticized for being insufficiently geared towards the specific needs of the small entrepreneur.

The issue of freedom raises the most fundamental questions of an ideological kind, and is especially troubling for those governments committed to *laissez–faire* economic policies. As we see in the INMOS case, the British Government was at the same time pursuing a policy of support through the British Technology Group, whilst planning to sell the company to the private sector. Such conflict of interests may well be detrimental to innovation since political considerations may come to dominate business development.

Underpinning many of the difficulties outlined above is the view that governments have the power to constrain innovation and entrepreneurial activity by bureaucratic interference and restrictive legislation. Although many policies have been aimed at the small firms sector, much of government support for innovation tends to be more beneficial towards larger companies with established R&D departments. The effectiveness of such institutional research has been questioned. In a study of major inventions in the twentieth century it was concluded that the majority were made outside the departments of research and development (Jewkes *et al.*, 1970).

The direction of state intervention may raise conflicts within the agencies of the state as well as raising certain ethical issues. Proposals by one department such as the Department of Trade and Industry may be opposed by another, such as the Department of the Environment. For example, new developments in air travel, in particular the increased passenger carrying capacity of aircraft, have necessitated airport expansion. This can be of benefit to the local economy by stimulating the job market and offering opportunities for local businesses. The same proposals will almost certainly be opposed by local residents and environmentalists. Such debates have surrounded the siting of London's third airport and the expansion of the airport at Heathrow to incorporate a fourth terminal complex. Issues like these deal with aspects of business ethics and question the purpose, direction and outcomes of innovative activity. Kumar is especially sceptical and he sums up the whole argument most appropriately.

> There are the familiar examples of the atomic bomb, other weapons of the biological and chemical kind, space exploration and large scale capital intensive technology with its propensity to pollute the environment and exhaust the world's supply of fossil fuels. Then there is the ingenious and expensive gadgetry of the mass consumer industry with its built–in principle of planned obsolescence and marginal technical improvements ... medical research seems equally skewed in the direction of people with power to persuade and pay ... and 99% of the knowledge effort of the industrial societies is devoted to the problems of the developed world.
>
> (Kumar, 1978 p 230)

Cultural and national differences

> So convinced have we become of the dependence of the total social, political and economic order on technical development that national output of scientific discoveries and the rate of technological advance have begun to appear as the ultimate criterion of culture and different political and social systems are compared as facilitators of this kind of achievement.
>
> (Burns and Stalker, 1966 p 19)

We have seen in the previous sections that the state in Britain has shown considerable interest in the innovative activity of private business. Nearly all governments in the major industrialized countries have attempted to influence the direction of innovation in some way. Whilst there is a danger of creating cultural stereotypes and perpetuating myths, the response of different governments has varied, and different areas have been targeted. Not only this, but investment in R&D has been taken as an indicator of a nation's economic health and future prosperity. We will explore both these issues.

Britain has always been typified as placing emphasis on basic research with its application in defence, nuclear energy and space research. The spin–offs have been few and limited to a small range of companies, but making little impact on the manufacture of commerical products. The USA too has been criticized for emphasizing big projects in defence and aerospace, usually with government backing, and consequently with a corresponding reluctance on the part of private companies to invest in their own long–term projects. France on the other hand is typified as giving strong central direction and significant financial support to private industry in a bid to achieve scientific and technological independence, by creating a domestic supplier in every major world industry. The West Germans conform to a less directive model but give specific assistance to those areas where market success is guaranteed; a policy particularly successful in the machine tool industry. We have seen in Chapter 2 how much emphasis is placed in Germany upon supporting businesses through a national system of training, thus ensuring the workforce possesses the required skills.

When national myths and stereotypes are being voiced, the greatest number usually relate to Japan (see the section on Japanese management in Chapter 2). Japanese economic success has been linked to the import of key innovations and technologies from other industrialized nations, imperative for such a late industrial starter. The widespread belief soon developed that Japanese businesses could not innovate. Whilst there is little doubt that Japan has gained from bought–in technology, there is also clear evidence that Japan is now probably the most innovative industrial nation (Figure 5.3). The Japanese have made significant advances in machine tool technology and in particular in developments in automated plant and robotics, and in modifying existing technologies. Japan has more of its workforce engaged in industrial R&D than Britain, France or Germany (Peck and Groto, 1982). Furthermore, the Japanese Ministry of International Trade and Industry (MITI) has organized six of the largest computer companies into two research associations to collaborate on new developments. The government also appears to have been successful in the specific targeting of certain key industries. Japan's policy focus has therefore shifted from steel to shipbuilding to cars and then to computers.

An underlying theme in the comparative analysis of national attitudes to research and development, is one developed in our earlier section on economic aspects of innovation; that trends in R&D investment are correlated with national economic growth. Underinvestment in R&D has been cited as the main reason for the decline in American competitiveness (Hayes and Wheelwright, 1984). A similar view can be taken of Britain. In comparison with other major industrial countries not only do we spend less on R&D as a proportion of GDP, but Britain is the only country to reduce expenditure since 1980 (*Sunday Times*, 16 Feb. 1987)

This picture is even more revealing if expenditure on defence is removed from the calculations. Figure 5.4 with data from 1983, shows expenditure on *civil* R&D.

The same source makes an implied criticism that where money has been spent, it has concentrated in a limited number of industries, notably, electronics, aerospace and chemicals, which spend on average £2500 per employee on R&D. By comparison the rest of manufacturing industry spends only £250 per employee. The implication is that Britain must step up expenditure on R&D not only to improve the nation's technical competitiveness, but also to generate more jobs in the manufacturing sector. This introduces a social as well as an economic objective for the investment in R&D. Whilst figures such as these are revealing, we repeat our caution, that it is difficult to show precise links between R&D expenditure, innovation and economic growth. Furthermore, whilst criticism is voiced at the British Government for pursuing an apparent selective policy, Japan is often held as a shining example for doing much the same thing.

Our discussion of cultural and national differences has focussed almost exclusively on the role of technology. Differences exist in other forms of

CASE 5.3

**INNOVATION AND
MARKETING;
TWO CASES**

□ *The Brownie 127 and the Canon Autofocus*

Throughout the 1950s and 1960s one of the most popular cameras was the Brownie 127, made by Kodak, the British subsidiary of the American company. Its simplicity and ease of operation made it a market leader. The camera was produced from 1952 to 1964 and underwent just one model change involving a slight modification of the lens. A comparable camera today is the Canon Autofocus made by the Japanese company Canon. It has the ease of operation of the Brownie 127 but is much more complex technically. Introduced in 1979, there were five model changes in the first six years of its life. This was deemed necessary not only because of the rapid technological advances in electronics but also because of the intense competition among Japanese camera manufacturers, causing Canon alone to spend 10% of its turnover on R&D in 1985. The market expects regular product changes reflecting new developments in photographic technology and each new technical development, in the form of improved performance, styling and new features, is eagerly paraded through advertising to give camera producers that significant edge over their rivals.

(Sources: The Sunday Times, 16.2.87)

□ *The 3M 'Post–it' notes*

The R&D department of the American multinational 3M had developed a partially adhesive glue, but had found no commercially viable application for the development. The development waited five years until one of the team devised the idea that a noticeboard coated with this adhesive would provide a much more convenient means of fixing and removing notices than the conventional drawing pin. This innovation was compatible with 3M's considerable interests in office equipment. The idea failed at the test–marketing stage. One of those responsible for the project then turned the idea around. The glue on the notice board was changed to glue on pieces of paper which could then be used on notice boards and other places where messages were fixed. The product was refined and the end result became the 'Post–it' note; a pad of readily detachable adhesive labels. Once again the marketing test failed, but it was thought that the product was not reaching the potential user. The company persevered and in a risky marketing venture introduced a mass trial of the product by giving away large numbers of pads to secretaries, typists, receptionists, bank clerks, and anyone else who might possibly use the product in the company's home town of Minneapolis–St.Paul. The 'Post–it' notes soon became addictive, and a massive local demand was created which soon spread both nationally and internationally.

(Source: Kennedy, 1988)

Britain	1.6% of GDP
France	1.7%
USA	1.9%
West Germany	2.5%
Japan	2.5%

(*Source: Guardian*, 21 November 1986)

Figure 5.4 Expenditure on civil R&D as a % of GDP.

innovation too. Whilst big business in America might fight shy of investment in R&D in favour of short–term profits, entrepreneurial activity is clearly a part of American life. This has its roots in the historical development of the USA and in particular the expansion from the Eastern seaboard. Individualism and enterprise have become key features of American culture, and probably explains why more people are engaged in self–employment as a proportion of the total population than in any other industrialized nation. We should however treat such comparisons with caution since we have already noted that self–employment should not automatically be equated with innovation.

We return to the theme of technology, but the theme is used to further illustrate the inter–relationship between innovation and marketing.

Innovation and technology

There is an obvious relationship between technology and innovation. Numerous illustrations exist where developments in state of the art technology result in business innovations and the development of new products and processes, the microchip being a good example. There are some, like Schumpeter, who see technical breakthroughs as *the* force which changes the whole nature of business, and the ability of firms to respond is crucial to their survival (Schumpeter, 1961). The emphasis on the role of technology is referred to as 'technology push'. There is an alternative view in which demand plays a leading role in determining the direction, extent and impact of inventions. Whilst some industries undoubtedly have a richer knowledge base than others, notably chemicals and electronics, the profitability of the application of that knowledge was predominantly a question of demand. This process is referred to as 'demand pull' (Schmookler, 1966). Several attempts have made to support the primacy of demand pull over technology push and vice versa, and illustrations can be given on both sides. The development of synthetic fibres is clearly a case of demand pull, whilst the growth of the mass market in electronic calculators is clearly a case of the successful use of developments in integrated circuits and hence technology push.

In most instances the debate is highly simplistic. The growth of sales of the compact disc player is the product of both the application of laser technology to produce consumer goods (technology push) and a function of rising discretionary income and market segmentation (demand pull). The two forces would appear to operate side by side. The development and rapid expansion of 'International Direct Dialling' by British Telecom was a direct response to a growing market demand among the business community for telephone communication with overseas associates. Having developed the technology, British Telecom found that the resources were being underutilized outside peak business periods. The company therefore launched a successful advertising campaign to increase private and domestic use of the available technology. The initial development was demand led, while subsequent developments were clearly a case of technology leading the market, and a company anxious to obtain a healthy return on a not inconsiderable investment.

Another interesting example is provided by Case 5.3 concerning innovations in camera technology and the development of 'Post–it' adhesive note pads. Both illustrations reveal the close relationship between innovation and marketing. In the case of the Canon, technical developments are used as a selling feature to give companies an edge over their rivals. For their part, consumers, through the media of persuasive advertising, have come to expect regular product changes which improve the performance or add on extra features to existing models. The 3M product would not have seen the light of day were it not for some lateral thinking on behalf of some staff, and the product would have failed but for an aggressive marketing effort and a persistent faith in its utility.

We can see from these illustrations that the marketing function is both an important guide and support to the direction of innovation. Marketing activity helps in the selection of R&D projects by providing information on the probability of their commerical success. It then assists in persuading the consumer that change is desirable (Simmonds, 1986).

We can see then that invention, innovation, research and development, manufacturing, and marketing have a complex relationship that is not always fully explored by those seeking to prove a correlation between innovation and economic growth. The illustration of the development of the railways in Britain is a good example of this complexity. In 1814 the technology for the development of the railways was available. However, it was several years before a number of factors converged. These were the technological know–how, the availability of cheap labour, an expanding export market, the need for rapid access to ports, a growing mobility among the middle classes, and the available investment from the profits of industrialization. In other words the innovation of the railways was a product of technology, market need, available capital, together with encouraging social and political conditions (Rothwell and Zegveld, 1981).

The picture becomes even more complex if we take organizational factors into consideration, and it is to these we now turn

Organizational aspects of innovation

When we examine innovation at the level of the individual organization, the most significant aspects to emerge are those of size, structure and organization culture. Ownership variables do not appear to be particularly significant, and despite the obvious interest of the state in the innovation process, there is certainly no evidence to suggest that innovation in publicly owned companies is any more significant than that in private firms. Indeed, critics of public ownership may well argue, citing the INMOS case as a good illustation, that political involvement slows down the process of innovation. We shall see that the question of goals is invariably tied up with issues of size, and we deal with these aspects together in our next section.

Organizational size and goals

Not only does the impact of organizational size upon innovation present us with some rather conflicting evidence, but, in this country at least, public policy appears equally confused. From the 1970s onwards we may be forgiven for thinking that the attention of the policy makers has focussed largely on small firms, possibly as a reaction to the merger activity of the previous decade. In practice however, R&D expenditure in Britain is concentrated in relatively few large firms. In 1978 five firms accounted for 41% of all expenditure on R&D and received 76% of all government R&D funding. We will examine some of that evidence and attempt to show both the relationship of size with changing goals as well as illustrating the dynamic process of innovation at the level of the firm. However, we must remember the major difficulty in our assessment of innovation; that of measurement. Whilst R&D expenditure is clearly some indication of inno-vative activity, firms can be highly innovative in their products, marketing and organization without having an organized R&D function.

There is a clear line of thinking going back through such writers as Galbraith to Schumpeter, which believes that developments in technology depend upon expensive research programmes of the kind that can only be found in the large corporation. Accordingly big firms are deemed to be best and monopolies even better. The complexities of modern technologies and the corresponding development costs set up irrevocable pressures towards the growing scale of organizations. Evidence in the 1960s was fairly clear in that large manufacturing firms spent proportionally more on R&D, had a larger share of innovation and were quicker to adopt new techniques of manufacturing (Mansfield, 1963). Findings such as these led to the assumption that R&D could only be economic once a certain size of firm had been reached. Certainly this line of thinking influenced British public policy in the 1960s with its encouragement of merger activity.

There can be little doubt that the large firm is able to invest in projects which carry a higher element of risk. The Convair Division of the General Dynamics Corporation was able to ride a loss of $425 million on its pro-duction of jet aircraft because of the highly diversified nature of its opera-tions (Galbraith, 1972). However, there are two pieces of evidence which appear to favour the smaller company.

☐ Small firms spend more on R&D as a proportion of total sales and employ proportionally more staff in R&D than the larger firms (Child, 1969); though this could be a case of economies of scale operating in favour of the larger firm, rather than any significant differences in their innovative capacities.
☐ Firms of less than 1000 employees account for more than 20% of innovations in Britain, far greater than their share of R&D investment, but less than their share of employment or net output (Pavitt, 1983).

Those who subscribe to the small firms lobby would argue that the smaller company is much more adaptable, much closer to the consumer, and hence, the source of far more significant innovations than the big firm. We deal with such arguments in more detail in the section on small businesses in Chapter 3.

Jewkes has consistently championed the cause of the small inventor, but found that size is a far less significant factor than the competitive nature of the market in which the firm operates (Jewkes *et al.*, 1970). We may conclude from this that highly innovative firms are more likely to be found in very competitive markets, as illustrated by the previously mentioned case of Canon cameras, and that this occurs irrespective of the size of the firm.

There are however important variations according to the nature of the sector in which the firm operates. Most innovations in the electrical, electronic, food, chemical and vehicle industries occur in large companies. In the case of mechanical engineering, instrumentation, leather and foot-wear, it is the smaller firm that tends to dominate (Pavitt, 1983). There is a danger with such analyses in that they confine innovation to products and processes. Significant innovations in such as retailing and financial services tend to be overlooked.

We may conclude from all this that there is no clear relationship between size and innovation, but we are able to make the following observations. The investment required in some types of innovation, and the need for high volume production for a return on that investment, clearly operates in favour of large companies. A good example here would be the chemical and pharmaceutical industries. An influencing factor would seem to be the sector of operation. Some sectors, like chemicals, tend to be traditionally dominated by large companies, while in others, especially instrumentation, the small firm still plays a significant role. There are cases of breakthroughs being made by small firms in all sectors, but they may have to align them-selves with larger companies to obtain the necessary development capital, production capacity, or access to markets, the 'Workmate', Case 5.2, being a good example. However, where markets are especially volatile, any firm, irrespective of size, may have to keep innovating to maintain market share. It is in such situations that entrepreneurial activity becomes most important.

The main difficulty with analyses of this nature is that they tend to view relationships at one point in time, when in reality the innovative process and the size of firms can be viewed as highly dynamic. Henry Ford pro-duced five different engines in quick succession prior to the Model T in a relatively small, jobbing–based organization. No product change then took place for fifteen years, as the emphasis shifted to the develop-ment of mass production process technologies and incremental product improvements (Abernathy and Utterback, 1978).

Examinations of business histories show us that the most fundamental product innovations usually take place at a relatively early stage of a firm's development, when it is still relatively small. As the firm develops, more emphasis is placed on process innovations. A stage may well be reached where the growth of mass markets and the need for economies of scale in the production process mean that fundamental change is resisted as being too costly. In other words the goals of the company change over time with changes in size and the nature of the innovations. A longitudinal study of the development of Computer Aided Design (CAD) systems in manufacturing found that from 1969 to 1974 initial innovations took place in small computer software companies. From 1974 to 1980 the main developments were taking place in much larger companies. Either the original firms had expanded, or they had been bought out by firms such as General Electric, wishing to buy into the new technology. In both cases, size was seen as an important factor in the attraction of venture capital. From 1980 onwards, smaller firms once again entered the market, concentrating on the development of highly specialized CAD systems, with a limited field of application (Kaplinsky, 1983).

We have noted in this section the need for some small firms to align themselves to larger companies for access to development capital and markets. There are some larger firms who pursue a deliberate strategy of innovation through acquisition. This can be a useful strategy where the acquired firm operates in the same product market, but, as we saw in the last chapter, difficulties can arise where diversification is totally unrelated.

In recent years the phenomenon of corporate venturing has emerged. This involves a larger established business collaborating with a smaller, less established but entrepreneurial firm to exploit business opportunities. The large firm offers finance, management expertise, access to markets, an established financial control system, and perhaps the benefits of an established reputation. The entrepreneurial firm offers new ideas and perhaps a greater ability to respond to changing markets and technologies. The French–based multinational, Rhône–Poulenc invested in Calgene, a small American firm operating in the biotechnology market. The market was developing, but Calgene was in serious financial difficulty. Rhône–Poulenc's investment gave them instant access to a new technology and Calgene obtained much–needed finance. The firm recovered, went public and provided Rhône–Poulenc with a tenfold return on its original investment (*Sunday Times*, 14 August 1988).

Innovation and organization structure

> When novelty and unfamiliarity in both market situation and technical information become the accepted order of things, a fundamentally different kind of management system becomes appropriate from that which applies to a relatively stable commercial and technical environment.
>
>   (Tom Burns, in the preface to the second edition
>   of *The Management of Innovation*, Burns and Stalker, 1966 p vii)

The starting point is appropriate, since it was Burns and Stalker's study of the post–war electronics industry, and in particular the failure of some of the Scottish firms in their study to set up effective research departments, that has been so influential, not only in the development of organization theory, but as a practical guide to innovative firms on the development of appropriate structures. In this section we will examine why such a 'fundamentally different kind of management system' is necessary, the problems encountered in setting up such a system, and the attempts that have been made to provide solutions to those problems. We illustrate the arguments by focussing on the R&D department in typically science–based industry. The same arguments apply for any group within an organization with the primary responsibility for initiating innovation. For example, in an advertising agency, tensions often arise between those staff who manage client accounts, and who have to adopt a business orientation, and those staff whose primary responsibility is the generation of creative ideas.

The R&D function and those connected with it have various claims for different treatment from the rest of the organization. There is a fundamental belief that the creativity inherent in the function requires its workers to communicate freely both within and outside the organization and to be free of the kind of bureaucratic controls to which other departments are subjected. The very nature of the work demands that there be flexibility as far as the allocation of priorities, patterns of working and normal management control systems are concerned. Specifically there is a demand for the relaxation of hierarchical controls and need to see investment in R&D as a long–term issue.

Those companies where innovation is a key activity have tended to respond by creating special R&D departments. The kind of problem that tends to arise most frequently is that this sets up a clash of cultures between R&D and the other departments. The need for flexibility as outlined above challenges the existing bureaucratic controls and with it, the existing power base. The old order with its allegiance to the organization and the status quo can be shaken by a group of scientists and technologists with their allegiance to a knowledge base whose source lies outside the organization. In such a situation it is often convenient for top management to isolate the R&D department both politically and sometimes geographically. In this way it presents less of a challenge to the status quo and can be conveniently amputated when costs need to be cut. It is not uncommon in times of economic recession for firms to cut back or close down altogether their R&D function. This sets up an interesting paradox between the need to reduce expenditure and the central role ascribed to innovation in economic recovery.

However it is often the scientists themselves who support this isolation within the organization. It absolves them of responsibility and gives them the kind of freedom they seek to pursue their own goals. This can involve role–playing to a widely held image of the eccentric scientist. As Burns and Stalker note,

> A reputation for eccentricity may be helpful not only in creating a complaisant attitude in industry towards the transgression of normal rules and towards a claim for privileges but also in furthering a career ... also taken to imply in some degree abdication from claims to leadership in the general management of business concerns.
>
> (Burns and Stalker, 1966 p 176)

The result for the organization is invariably a lack of coordination between R&D, and other activities like production and marketing, a situation which, as Burns and Stalker found, retarded the innovative process and was detrimental to the effective operation of the firm as a whole. A great deal of time can be wasted on internal politics and the situation can lead to a proliferation of committees and intermediaries to operate in a coordinating capacity, creating jobs like methods engineers.

In many ways, the R&D department *needs* to be different because its goals are different, the time horizon on which it is evaluated is different, and it has different needs with regard to the formality of its operations. An R&D department needs an informal structure because of the uncertain nature of its work and its need for a flexible response to both technological and market changes. Specialists may need to be brought in from outside, possibly on a temporary basis, decision–making and responsibility may have to be decentralized, and there will usually be a very loose specification of jobs and work procedures. Integration may be achieved through the management information system, by creating cross–functional teams, or by using some managers in special integrating roles.

There are dangers with this approach. Catering to the special demands of the R&D function can lead to the kind of isolation we have already discussed and the various attempts at integration can all too often result in paperwork jungles or the creation of supernumerary roles whose sole reason for existence is to act as go–between. In his study of the management of innovation in eight different firms, Parker found that a great deal of attention had been paid to structural considerations, setting up departments, creating special teams, training and coordination. What he found to be lacking in most instances was an effective strategy for innovation (Parker, 1982).

A more effective device may be to organize the entire firm around its dominant competitive issue. In this way, if innovation were identified as the priority then the firm should locate its centre of power and influence around that activity. Successful innovative firms not only see innovation as a priority but build an entire organization culture based on innovation. In the next section we reinforce this theme.

The role of organization culture

In the previous section we dwelt at length on the structural issues pertaining to the operation of an R&D function. We have maintained throughout that innovation is not the sole prerogative of science–based manufacturing industry, nor does it depend on the existence of a formally established R&D department. We have already established that innovation applies to all forms of business, and many firms are entrepreneurial and innovative largely because it is seen as a responsibility of all staff, irrespective of their function.

A culture of innovation may be built up in a variety of ways, such as through the recruitment of entrepreneurial staff, and by using training programmes to develop creative thinking. More significantly the lead normally comes through the activities and energy of senior managements, and their creation of an organization to foster innovation.

Deal and Kennedy's (1982) innovative organization of the future is highly decentralized, in which each member of staff is allowed to be his or her own entrepreneur. They refer to this as the 'atomized organization'. We came across a similar phenomenon when we discussed networking as a structural form in Chapter 3. For most organizations their vision is far in the distance or has only limited application. Nonetheless, effective changes in operation can be achieved using less revolutionary methods, as illustrated by Case 5.4 of the Baystate Banking Corporation, which successfully used the introduction of automatic teller machines as a catalyst in the creation of an organization with a much stronger central identity.

Innovation and management strategies

Throughout this chapter we have seen that both management and representatives of governments have operated on the clear assumption that innovation is linked to increased productivity, market share and profitability, as well as being an indication of the state of a nation's economic health. At the level of the firm we can see that managers have a choice of strategies. Four stategic types have been identified by Ansoff and Stewart, and we will use this classification as the basis of our analysis (for more details, see Ansoff and Stewart, 1967).

'First to the market' strategy. Organizations pursuing this this type of strategy see research and development as a central part of their operation. There is a strong commitment to basic research, technical leadership and hence a willingness to take risks with comparatively large investments. Research tends to be close to the state of the art, and the organization employs a high proportion of top rate research scientists. There is considerable coordination between research, production and marketing, and planning is usually long–range.

An example of such as innovative company is the Oxford Instruments Group (Parker, 1982). In addition to the above features, the company maintains very close links with universities and other research establishments. Research is encouraged in different discipline areas, in a bid to increase the product range, which at any one time comprises a limited number of high cost items. The large pharmaceutical companies like Hoffman–La Roche and Ciba Geigy would also fit into this category. They use R&D and a 'first to the market' strategy as a deliberate attempt to dominate the market.

'Follow the leader' stategy. This type of firm emphasizes development rather than research. It relies very heavily on good technical and market information and has the capacity to respond rapidly to change. Again there is a high level of integration between the various functions, but whereas a company like the Oxford Instuments Group would employ a high proportion of pure scientists, this company tends to carry more development engineers. Several companies operating in the domestic electrical market would come into this category. A firm like Philips will take state–of–the–art technical knowledge and apply it to its product range or use it to develop new products.

'Application engineering' strategy. A firm with this type of strategy would tend to avoid outright innovation. The firm is keen to use new technology, but would introduce it somewhat behind the state of the art and then somewhat cautiously. They tend to be highly cost–conscious and will only develop products that have been seen to work in other firms. The emphasis is very much on design and improvement rather than innovation. Again we can see firms in the domestic electrical product market operating this type of strategy. Firms like Hotpoint are not so much concerned with

developing new products, but with making design modifications to their existing range.

'Me too' strategy. Whereas the application engineering company will make its own developments, companies subscribing to this strategy have no R&D function as such. They exist largely on a strong manufacturing base and have the ability to copy others' products quickly and effectively. Successful firms of this type operate on low costs, have a comparatively low selling price and the ability to deliver on time. They rely on being highly competitive as opposed to innovative. Firms operating in this way do not tend to be well known but quite often entire economies are placed in this category, as is currently the case with Taiwan. However, a 'me too' strategy is followed by well–known companies in specific circumstances. When Rank Xerox's patent on the photocopier expired, several companies including Canon and Gestetner used the available technology to manufacture their own versions.

According to this classification we may conclude that any firm has a choice of strategic options. There is however a lobby which promotes the idea of innovation as a prerequisite to survival and growth, subscribing very strongly to the kind of assumptions we identified at the beginning of this section. The latest of these is a fairly convincing argument put forward by Hayes and Wheelwright. They maintain that firms must innovate to survive, since strategies which depend on imitation and following market trends will ultimately lead to a saturation of the market. Whilst some firms will survive better than others by clever marketing strategies and introducing the kind of 'pseudo–innovations' we discussed at the beginning of the chapter, real growth is dependent upon the development of new products. An important feature of the Hayes and Wheelwright hypothesis, as far as manufacturing industry is concerned, is the primacy of individual machine–tool technology. Only through this will firms be able to manufacture products that are distinct from those of their competitors (Hayes and Wheelwright, 1984). We will return to this argument when we discuss manufacturing in the next chapter and refer you to Case 4.1, which deals with the decline in the British machine–tool industry. For the meantime, we may conclude from these, other authors and various case histories that the stategic implications for a firm wishing to be innovative are as follows.

☐ In general there needs to be a risk–taking ethos that is supported by top management. There ought to be a willingness to experiment and therefore a freedom to fail.

☐ This should be supported by the recruitment of people with creative talents and, where appropriate, with technical and scientific backgrounds.

☐ Recruitment policies need to be reinforced by training and development programmes which place emphasis on innovation and the acquisition of the required technical knowledge. Promotion strategies should include technical know–how and a commitment to innovation as key criteria.

☐ The exchange of ideas should be encouraged, not just within the firm, but especially for those operating in science–based industries, by fostering links with universities and other research establishments.

☐ Mechanisms can be set up which facilitate communication, such as suggestion schemes and more radical methods of employee participation, but more generally, innovation may be encouraged if the organization is flexible and decentralized.

☐ Whether a special R&D department is created or not, attention needs to be paid to integrating the function of innovation with rest of the organization's activities. As Johnson and Scholes claim,

> R&D strategy is a particularly good example of an area in which consistency with more general levels of strategy and with other functional strategies is very important. It is easy to be seduced by the development of new ideas and products without paying enough attention to the practical considerations of the likelihood of pay–off.
>
> (Johnson and Scholes, 1984, p 258)

☐ The above comments raise the importance, not only of generating sufficient income to fund innovative activity, but of developing accurate and acceptable methods to choose and evaluate projects.

Probably the most significant feature to emerge from the points made above is the need to create a particular organization culture or climate that is supportive of innovation. This in turn needs to be supported by an environment where emphasis is placed on developing the skills of the workforce and where innovation is encouraged by banks and by effective political policies instead of rhetoric.

Despite the central role ascribed to innovation, there are considerable constraints which may significantly limit its effectiveness. For any new idea there is a high probability of failure. If we add this to a tendency on the part of many managers to underestimate the costs involved, then it is easy to see why some companies have found innovation a particularly risky strategy. Lockheed and Rolls Royce in the aerospace industry are good illustrations of this. This is compounded by yet another problem. Managers in many industries faced with the pressure for career development and pressures from shareholders for a generous dividend, may opt for safer short–term investments, which preclude more radical innovative strategies. The time lags between development and commercial exploitation can be highly variable, a process taking an estimated twenty-two years as far as television was concerned.

In addition to all these problems, economic, social and political conditions may militate against effective innovation. We have already been the importance of a skills infrastructure and supportive political policies. Objections by trade unions fearing losses in job security, either real or imagined, can set back the introduction of process innovations as we have seen in the newspaper industry (Chapter 1). High interest rates offered by banks as a result of high inflation can add to the reluctance on the part of managers to invest in new ventures.

Difficulties of the kind identified above have led to the preference of some firms to seek alternative strategies. A common alternative is the use of the patent and licensing system, identified earlier in this chapter. Instead of developing products and processes itself, a firm will manufacture a product or use a process that has been developed elsewhere, on the payment of a license fee to the patent holder. This is not only a strategy for the avoidance of R&D costs, but can save a great deal of time in the

CASE 5.4

**BAYSTATE
CORPORATION**

Baystate Corporation is the third largest bank in Massachusetts. In 1974 it had the largest network of banks in the state with 173 locations and its financial performance was good. However, several problems were perceived.

☐ Interest rates had fallen, and hence revenue.
☐ Bad loans had increased.
☐ Inflation had risen.
☐ Competition had increased especially from smaller, independent banks offering interest on current accounts.

Most significantly, the company's response to these threats was handicapped by its structure. Baystate Corporation was in fact a holding company of twelve different banks, all trading under different names. Attempts had been made to centralize operations with the introduction of a central computer. The individual banks had resisted any move towards a corporate identity and the issue had become one of intense political manoeuvring amongst senior management.

A new chief executive was appointed who supported the idea of the twelve banks operating in a coordinated fashion to compete more effectively. The vehicle chosen was 'electronic funds transfer'. This system had been in existence for a number of years and had operated mainly through cash dispensers. In 1974 it was not popular with account holders who preferred personal service. Despite this, developments in electronic funds transfer, especially the 'Automatic Teller Machine' (ATM) offered Baystate an opportunity to unify operations. An account holder would be able to gain access to that account through any one of the bank's 173 outlets at any time, for cash, or simply account information.

McKinsey's the management consultants were hired and initiated the following innovations.

☐ 'The Greater Boston Task Force', a group made up of the chief executives of the largest banks to study ideas for consolidating operations and marketing. This group as supplemented by specially-selected staff members, picked out for their youth and their ability to generate bright ideas.
☐ The implementation of the ATM system in all banks to give the company a marketing edge on the independents and the savings banks.
☐ The selection of a new corporate name. 'Bay–Bank' was chosen, and each of the constituent banks would now be called by this name, followed by their own, as in Bay–Bank Norfolk Trust.

(*Source:* McCaskey, 1982)

development process by eliminating duplication of effort. The high cost of development in the electronics industry was considerably reduced for many firms, by using as their starting point the original patent for the transistor owned by the Bell Telephone Corporation. Licensing may not be totally passive and may in fact be a spur to modifications, resulting in a company developing its own innovations.

In addition to licensing, the costs of innovation may be reduced by undertaking joint development with another company, buying in specific research work as needed from a specialist research consultancy firm, or even through acquisition strategy. In this way a firm can add to its stable of new products, processes and patents by purchasing particularly innovative companies, operating in their chosen direction of diversification.

In discussing innovation strategies, students should always remember that the strategies are never as discrete as textbook models would like them to be. A firm may well have a strong R&D department with a record of successful innovation. At the same time it could license developments from its competitors and even pursue an acquisition strategy of buying up certain highly specialized units. The model of Ansoff and Stewart, discussed earlier, does not preclude mixed strategies. So a firm can be first to the market place with some of its product range while following other firms in other types of product.

What does appear to be important is an integrated strategy, a theme that appears central to the innovative process. A good idea may be wasted without corresponding policies in production and marketing, the respective themes of our next two chapters.

Summary

Invention, innovation, research and development, design and entrepreneurship are all related concepts. For businesses it is the process of innovation that is the key concept, turning an invention into something profitable. Innovation can relate to products, processes, marketing and organization, and can range from the most fundamental to the most minor changes. It is seen as the key to increased productivity, increased market share, and hence profitability and the firm's continued survival. The theme has been translated to the scale of national economies, and we have seen how some regard innovation as the source of economic recovery out of a recession. These relationships are difficult to prove, but there can be no denying that without innovation there can be no new products or processes.

The importance of innovation has been recognized by governments all over the world, although there are considerable variations in the extent and direction and intervention. Government support for innovation is seen not only for economic, but for political and social reasons too, although there can be significant ideological and practical difficulties in the state's involvement. All societies need to support innovation by ensuring that the workforce is educated and trained in the required skills.

There are clear links between innovation and technology, although in practice it is difficult to determine whether an innovation is a result of 'technology push' or 'demand pull'. Most important innovations in business are the product of a range of different factors. An understanding of the market place is particularly important, and innovation and marketing are inter–related activities.

At the level of the individual firm there is no clear evidence linking the size of a company with its propensity and ability to innovate, although very expensive research tends to be concentrated in large companies. The sector in which the firm operates and the volatility of the market all interact with the size of establishment in a rather complex way. What is fairly clear is that firms with an R&D department have special problems in the integration of R&D with other activities and in particular, production and marketing. The most successfully innovative companies tend to be those that have paid attention to the creation of a particular organization culture and the encouragement to all staff to be creative.

Some firms clearly see themselves as technical and market leaders and invest a high proportion of their income in developing new ideas, products and processes. Other firms are more content to sit behind the field and rely upon minor developments or strategies of copying. There are a range of possible strategies that can be adopted either singly or together.

Further reading

For an environmental approach to innovation, students are advised to read J.J. Van Duijn's *The Long Wave in Economic Life* (George Allen and Unwin, 1983). This book is particularly good on the economic aspects of innovation. In a similar vein, but concerned more with the role of the state, students should consult R. Rothwell and W. Zegveld's *Industrial Innovation and Public Policy* (Frances Pinter, 1981). Both the above books are biased towards technological innovation. A broader–based view of entrepreneurship may be found in most of the books written by Peter Drucker, especially P. Drucker, *Innovation and Entrepreneurship* (Heinemann, 1985). Although the study is over twenty years old, there are very few better books on the organization of innovation than T. Burns and G.M. Stalker's *The Management of Innovation* (Tavistock, 1966). A series of good cases may be found in R.C. Parker's *The Management of Innovation* (John Wiley and Sons, 1982).

Discussion

1. Which can have the greater impact on businesses; product or process innovations?

2. Examine the ways through which the state can subsidize, encourage and protect innovation in private firms. Why should the state get involved, and what difficulties arise with such involvement?

3. Assess the relationship between innovation and economic growth. Which criteria would you use to show such a relationship?

4. Select a range of consumer domestic products which illustrate the relationship between technology push and demand pull Which of these two is the more significant?

5. What contribution can the size of the firm make to innovative activity?

6. What steps would you take to develop a greater awareness of innovation amongst employees in a firm?

7. Identify the major problems associated with the existence of a special function responsible for the initiation of new business ideas, such as an R&D department. What structural devices would you employ to reduce these problems?

8. Assess the innovation strategy alternatives for a manufacturer of consumer electrical goods, a major computer firm, a package holiday company, and a polytechnic or a university.

9. What can we learn from the INMOS case about state intervention in innovation? How could INMOS have been more effective?

10. What aspects of innovation do Cases 5.2, 5.3, and 5.4 reveal? what lessons do they contain for other companies?

Production $\boxed{6}$ |||||||

The production function is concerned with the creation of the goods and services offered to consumers. In this chapter we use the term production in its widest context. We clearly associate production operations with manufacturing industry, but we can also see a production function operating in department stores, restaurants, banks, local government, schools, and hospitals. The term operations is occasionally used to denote this broader approach, but since that concept has so many different connotations, we use the term production throughout. To reinforce this broad view of production, we will, where appropriate, cite illustrations from the non–manufacturing sector, and devote Case 6.2 to an examination of the production function in a firm of patent agents.

We begin by examining the central role played by production in all organizations and examine two specific aspects of that role; the design of production systems and the operation of those systems. For the purposes of this text we deal with the important function of purchasing in this chapter, under the heading of materials management. The production function is sometimes portrayed as the function that is most isolated from the environment in which it operates. We refute that idea, and examine the relationship of production with its environment by looking at the influences of changing economy and government policy towards manufacturing industry, factors pertaining to the labour force, the impact of technological developments and cultural differences in the way societies view and organize production. A particular reference will be made here to Japanese manufacturing industry. Our analysis of organizational aspects also explores cultural differences, but at the level of the firm and how they interact with the other variables of the Business in Context model, especially the role of organization size and structure. We close the chapter by exploring some common production strategies.

A central function
The production function has a central role in most types of organization. According to some estimates it accounts for some 70 to 80% of a firm's assets, expenditure and people (Hill, 1983). In addition, it is central to the firm's success by providing what the customer requires either at a profit in a private company, or within budget in a non–profit organization. It is therefore concerned with issues that are crucial to the consumer, issues of

KEY CONCEPT 6.1

THE UNIVERSALITY OF PRODUCTION

The production function exists in all types of organization; service industry as well as manufacturing. It is concerned with the transformation of a variety of inputs such as information, people, materials and finance into a variety of outputs such as goods, services, customer and employee satisfaction. Viewed in this way, all organizations can be shown to have a production system irrespective of their primary objective. The centrality of the function means that its operation has a singificant influence on organization structure.

quantity, quality, availability and price; and issues that are crucial to the management of an enterprise, issues of productivity and cost.

Despite its centrality it is often regarded as the 'cinderella' subject of management, and, certainly as far as production management in manufacturing is concerned, an area to be avoided by aspiring managers. As Wickham Skinner writes,

> Manufacturing is generally perceived in the wrong way at the top, managed in the wrong way at plant level, and taught the wrong way at business schools.

> (Skinner, 1969, p 137)

There are signs that this view is being reappraised. The growth of the non–manufacturing sector has encouraged our rethinking of the production concept. Significant production problems exist in managing an airport as busy as Heathrow. Planes must take off and land safely and on time. In order for this to occur, key operations must be coordinated, including air traffic control, ground crews, baggage–handling, passport and customs, aircraft cleaning, refuelling and catering. Production problems also have to be faced in large hospitals with busy operating schedules. Operations must be carefully timed and scheduled, patients transferred to and from wards, equipment prepared and the various support systems from nursing to catering properly briefed. Production techniques, originally developed in manufacturing are now commonplace in non–manufacturing contexts, and senior staff in these organizations assume the role of coordinating production operations. It is the importance of the production function in solving this type of problem that led Drucker to define production as 'the application of logic to work' (Drucker, 1968, p 122).

Furthermore, production management is making a comeback in manufacturing. The oil crisis of the 1970s, the rising cost of raw materials and labour, concern for the level of productivity, and the success of those countries with different approaches to manufacturing system design and management have all conspired to raise the level of interest in the production function in both the USA and Britain. There are signs that a former complacent attitude and a view of production management as simply a set of techniques is giving way to the elevation of production as the key management strategy, which, alongside innovation and marketing, can give firms a distinct competitive advantage, as well as making a significant contribution to export and the economy in general.

Despite the application of production techniques to manufacturing and non–manufacturing firms alike, some differences can be found. We examine these briefly before looking at the various elements which make up the production function.

Some differences between manufacturing and non–manufacturing industries

Both these sectors are concerned with the production of goods and services, but differences do exist between different types of organization operating in the same sector. An oil refinery has little in common with a small business making hand–crafted furniture, yet both are lumped together as manufacturing concerns. By the same token, an organization like Barclays Bank would be classed together with a small hairdressing business, as non–manufacturing concerns. We can see that the differences within each of these sectors can be as significant as those between them. When we examine the organizational aspects of production later in this chapter, we make an attempt to classify different types of production system in each sector. At this stage, however, it is worth pointing two major differences between manufacturing and non-manufacturing.

☐ A major difference concerns the part played by the customer. In a non–manufacturing concern the customer is generally more of an active participant in the process. This is especially true in education and hospitals and those organizations offering a personal service, such as hairdressers, solicitors, financial advisors, and counsellors. The interaction of the customer means that the process is often less predictable, and production systems correspondingly more complex.

☐ This unpredictability means that the production process is more difficult to control in the non–manufacturing sector. The degree of contact with the customer can affect the efficiency of the operation. For example, a doctor may not be able to plan her work as effectively as she would like due to the variability in the consulting needs of patients. Productivity therefore becomes more difficult to measure and quality becomes much more a matter of subjective assessment.

We examine the implications of these differences when we look at the various elements of the production process in the next two sections.

Identifying the production function

We have seen that a production system exists to provide goods and services, which it does by transforming inputs into different kinds of output. This represents a systems view of production, comprising inputs, process and outputs, which we illustrate in Figure 6.1. (See also the section on the systems approach in Chapter 1.)

We can see clearly from Figure 6.1 that the production function transforms the various resource inputs into the required goods and services. Three aspects of the model need further explanation.

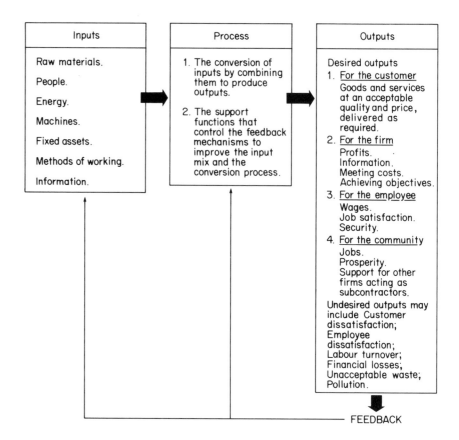

Inputs	Process	Outputs
Raw materials. People. Energy. Machines. Fixed assets. Methods of working. Information.	1. The conversion of inputs by combining them to produce outputs. 2. The support functions that control the feedback mechanisms to improve the input mix and the conversion process.	Desired outputs 1. <u>For the customer</u> Goods and services at an acceptable quality and price, delivered as required. 2. <u>For the firm</u> Profits. Information. Meeting costs. Achieving objectives. 3. <u>For the employee</u> Wages. Job satisfaction. Security. 4. <u>For the community</u> Jobs. Prosperity. Support for other firms acting as subcontractors. Undesired outputs may include Customer dissatisfaction; Employee dissatisfaction; Labour turnover; Financial losses; Unacceptable waste; Pollution.

FEEDBACK

Figure 6.1 The production process as a system.

Not all the outputs of the system are necessarily desired outcomes. Waste, either in the form of substandard products or unused raw materials, can be a costly item in manufacturing and waste in the form of polluting chemicals can constitute an environmental hazard. Customer dissatisfaction can be an unintended output. The consequence of diners at a restaurant receiving bad service may well mean they decide never to return.

The concept of environmental pollution introduces the notion that outputs of one system are invariably inputs to other systems. The manufactured outputs of a car components factory are clearly inputs to other firms. In the 1960s delays and industrial disputes in the car components industry caused production stoppages at the major car manufacturers and led them to rethink their purchasing strategies. Wages paid to workers will invariably be passed on to shops and supermarkets, and also to such as building societies in the form of mortgage payments, which are then used to fund further investments.

Outputs may also be considered as inputs to the same system. In this way, information gained during the production process can be used to improve the operation of the system, such as changing the supplier to improve the quality of parts and reduce the number of rejects. A large number of dissatisfied customers at a restaurant or a hairdressers is an indication that some element of the process needs attention. This is known as feedback. Another type of relationship can be built up between output and input when materials are recycled. In the manufacture of float glass at the Pilkington plant in St. Helens, the smoothing of edges, the cutting of glass to size, and the generally fragile nature of the product, mean that there are always quantities of broken glass. Whilst measures are taken to keep this waste to an acceptable minimum, it is broken up to form 'cullet', a vital raw material in glass production.

We can see from the systems model that production is a transformation process resulting in the creation of goods and services. This provides us with a means of classifying different types of production system. Wild has identified four types, each based predominantly on a different kind of transformation (Wild, 1985).

☐ A transformation in the form of raw materials or components is typified by manufacturing firms, but also by such as builders and landscape gardeners.
☐ A change in the nature of ownership is primarily the concern of suppliers, wholesalers and retailers.
☐ A change of place is the focus for transport systems such as road hauliers, postal services, or courier firms.
☐ A transformation in the state of the customer is the aim of service industries, so that insurance firms aim to make people more secure; building societies lend money for people to improve their standard of living; osteopaths aim to improve the physical well–being of their patients.

Many organizations operate all four types of transformation process. A typical manufacturing firm will not only make goods, but sell and transport them direct to the consumer or to an intermediary such as a wholesaler or retailer, and provide an after–sales service. We tend to think of a restaurants as operating predominantly in the service sector, yet all restaurants have a manufacturing operation that transforms raw material foodstuffs into dishes for consumption. Retailers are not just concerned with ownership change but they are involved in place transformation too.

A good illustration of the inter–related nature of both production systems and the various types of transformation process can be found in the retail chain of Marks and Spencer, whose primary product ranges are clothes and food and drink.

Marks and Spencer, one of the most successful chains in Britain, and with branches in Europe has vigorously pursued a policy of offering high quality products at an acceptable price to a mass market. It relies on a high turnover of goods. An important output is therefore a high level of customer satisfaction, both with the product and the service. Three kinds of feedback are important to this process; the customer's willingness to make return visits to the store; the careful research of customer needs; and the shop policy of accepting returned goods, which may then be repackaged and resold. The pursuit of quality is reflected in store layout and staff selection and training, but most significantly in the choice of supplier.

KEY CONCEPT 6.2

THE CONFLICTING OBJECTIVES OF THE PRODUCTION SYSTEM

Within most production systems there is an inevitable tension between the needs of management to construct an efficient operating system which focuses upon minimizing costs and the needs of customers for goods and services which meet their specifications of design, cost and delivery. Many of the techniques used by management in production design, scheduling and control aim to resolve such potential conflict. In more recent years, the trend has been away from statistical techniques to focus on strategies which seek a greater compatability between production and the other functional activities, especially marketing, and on the creation of more flexible operating systems.

Marks and Spencer expects a high level of quality in the goods it buys to sell on. This has had a remarkable effect on the British textile industry. The policy of the company to buy British has meant that 90% of Marks and Spencer stock is British. It is by far the most important single buyer in the home textile market, taking 20% of the total British output. The demands for quality standards, good design, and reliable delivery have led to improvements in the textile industry itself, and enabled it to increase its competitiveness on a world scale, especially through the introduction of new technology. The relationship with suppliers, not only in clothing but in food and wine, becomes even more involved in that many of the products are sold under the store's own label, yet manufactured by independent producers. This is a good illustration of the fluidity of system boundaries as well as involving Marks and Spencer in the manufacturing process. However its major concern, retailing, is a good illustration of transformations taking place in ownership, place and the state of the consumer.

Conflicting objectives and changing solutions

We have seen that our production system has a number of different objectives. These include production functions.

☐ Of a certain number of items at a certain level of quality.
☐ Within a certain time period.
☐ Within acceptable financial and social costs.
☐ At a price that will ensure sufficient sales and produce an acceptable return on investment.
☐ With the flexibility to adjust to changing demands.

Consumers wish to purchase goods in the quantity and quality they require, receive them at the time they need them, and all at a price they deem reasonable. However, if we select an unframed painting at an art shop, we know that a hand–crafted frame in a special material will cost more than framing it ourselves using a ready–made frame, and that we may have to wait some time for the job to be done by an expert. Many consumers are willing to make trade–offs, to pay more for quality, to wait for made–to–measure items. Many are not, and managers are left with the

Customer satisfaction	V	Efficient utilization of resources
The required quantity of goods and services. Quality of goods and services. Acceptable price. On demand.		Product design. Job and work design. Location. Process planning and control. Scheduling. Stock levels.

Figure 6.2 The conflicting objectives of the production process.

task of balancing a number of potentially conflicting objectives to achieve both customer satisfaction and the efficient utilization of resources. This is illustrated in Figure 6.2.

The main reason for conflict goes back to the inter–related nature of the production system as the following illustration shows. In an attempt to reduce costs, managers have a number of different options. They can cut back on raw materials or staff, which may result in goods of lower quality and a generally poorer service; they can expect the workforce to increase productivity for the same reward; or they can gear up for higher pro- ductivity by ensuring long production runs in the case of manufacturing or reducing the time spent with clients in the case of the service in- dustry.

All these options give rise to potential conflicts. Goods of lower quality may not be acceptable to the consumer, unless the price is cut, thus negating the original cost–cutting exercise. The workers may resist attempts by management to increase the tempo of work. In manufacturing, the introduction of long production runs has a trade–off in the form of reduced flexibility and lack of choice for the consumer.

The production manager needs to balance the opposing forces which are the cause of such conflicts. The development of operational research during World War Two resulted in the post–war emphasis on the 'nume- rate manager', a concept which found a ready application in a range of production management techniques. These included value analysis, devel- opments in work study, linear programming, network analysis, statistical quality control, and the emphasis on specific measures of efficiency such as machine utilization, work in progress, labour utilization and so on. Such techniques are used in the non–manufacturing sector as well, as the concepts of staff–student ratios and optimum class sizes in education will testify.

Many of the techniques mentioned above are primarily concerned with efficiency. Whilst efficiency is important, it can distort the system. In manufacturing, the achievement of long runs may be the most efficient use of materials, machines and labour, but it can frustrate some customers who may require a quick response to their order, and valuable customers may go elsewhere. A doctor faced with a waiting room full of patients may be more efficient by limiting consultation time, but with the attendant danger that a potentially serious problem could be overlooked. Efficiency is often the goal, when greater attention needs to be paid to effectiveness in the form of adaptation and flexibility.

As a result, the application of more complex quantitative techniques can produce a limited focus. In recent years attention has shifted to a greater emphasis on the management of the whole system and its relationship with other systems. The production manager emerges as a mediator, coping with different demands both within the production system itself and between that and other systems. This role is sometimes termed boundary management. We develop these themes in more detail in our discussion of production strategies at the end of the chapter. In the meantime, we look a little more closely at the relationship between production and the other activities of the organization.

The relationship between production and other functional areas

The centrality of the production function and the boundary role of the production manager brings into focus the relationship between the production function and the other functional areas. Examples of such relationships include the following.

Innovation. As we saw in the previous chapter, innovation is at the heart of new product development with obvious implications for the production function. Production capabilities and capacities must be important considerations at the design and development stage. An innovative product design in manufacturing is no use if it cannot be made by the workforce within certain cost parameters. Similarly, a new design for a business studies degree course must take into account the skills of the teachers and the capabilities of the students.

Purchasing. We will deal with the purchasing function in more detail later in this chapter. As the procurer of raw materials and the guardian of the quality of those incoming materials, purchasing has a key role in the production process for manufacturing, and as we saw in the example of Marks and Spencer, for retailing as well. Purchasing also makes an important contribution to overall costing. So central is this function to production that, in many firms, it has been extended to have responsibility for the entire flow of materials throughout the process. This extended function is referred to as materials management, a term we use when discussing purchasing and its associated activities.

Marketing. Information about consumer requirements is essential to those operating the production system. Production managers need to know the total demand for their product and when that demand is required. This will assist in the planning of production operations. Feedback from consumers on the utility of the product can assist both the R&D and production functions in the design and creation of future products. Holiday companies frequently ask clients to complete a questionnaire about every aspect of their holiday, not only as a public relations exercise, but to improve the product and the way it is delivered.

Finance and accounting. The accounting function clearly interfaces with production in the development of production budgets and targets. In return, production information is essential to such decisions as pricing and wage determination. The accounting function will also play a major role in decisions to replace major items of capital equipment.

Personnel. Personnel will assist in the recruitment, selection and training of production staff. Other key activities include industrial relations, the design of payment systems including incentives and the control of the safety, health and welfare of the workforce. Traditionally, industrial relations and wage incentives assume a significant role in manufacturing industry, but the role of staff selection and training are crucial to the success of those service industries with high levels of customer contact.

The key activities of production management

In Figure 6.3 we offer a classification of the main activities of production managers. We draw a distinction between the design of the production system and the operation of that system. In this section we include a review of materials management.

The design of production systems

Product design. The two major decisions in product design concern firstly the function and styling of the product, and secondly the range of products or degree of standardization to be offered. In manufacturing, decisions will also be made on the type of materials that are to be used. Design issues clearly interface with innovation (Chapter 5) and marketing (Chapter 7).

In recent years in manufacturing two systems have developed which focus upon the interface between design and production. These are CAD (computer–aided design) and CAM (computer–aided manufacture). Operating together these are known as CADCAM systems. CAD enables the designer through the use of computer graphics and computer memory to evaluate the consequences of various design alternatives. This has assisted in both the speed and the accuracy of the design stage. A linked CADCAM system has a memory bank of standard designs, and the appropriate machines and tools required for manufacture. In many industries this has assisted greatly in the development of modular production methods. A modular system exists where products are built up by the different combination of a family of standard items. In the car industry, for example, a great number of different models can be offered, yet all are based around different combinations of the same body shells, engines, gear boxes and so on.

Developments in modular systems can simplify the production process and represent a form of standardization. A lunchtime sandwich bar may appear to have a very large range of products, when in fact all are based on different combinations of a limited range of ingredients and all are made using similar production techniques. Many companies see standardization as an important means of cost reduction. A college offering a wide variety

System design
  Product design.
  Forecasting demand.
  Capacity planning.
  Equipment design.
  Work design.
  Location and site.

System operation
  Operations planning.
  Scheduling.
  Quantity control.
  Quality control.
  Technology control.
  Labour control.
  Cost control.

Materials management
  Purchasing.
  Inventory control.

Figure 6.3 The activities of production management.

of evening courses, some of which are poorly subscribed, may decide to rationalize its operations around the most popular courses, reducing both staffing costs and overheads. For the manufacturer, standardization often means a better utilization of resources, such as longer production runs and the opportunity to obtain discounts on the purchasing of raw materials and components in bulk. For the consumer, however, it may mean less choice for the customer which may be acceptable if prices are reduced. One of the advantages of the modular system lies in the attempt to maximize both standardization and choice. An important production decision is the extent of standardization that is both desirable and feasible.

Forecasting demand and capacity planning. These two tasks form the basis of a series of decisions central to the production process, since it is here that the direction for the entire operation is set and resources are acquired and deployed. There is a particular need for market information and accurate predictions of demand. This is obviously much easier where goods are made to order, less so when goods are made to stock. In this case historical data are important, but even this may prove inadequate in a highly volatile market of changing demand and high levels of competition.

Even where demand can be forecast with some accuracy, capacity planning may not be straightforward. It can be especially sensitive to product and process innovation, and will be affected by decisions on the type of technology used, organization size and structure, the extent of subcontracting and policies concerning the intensity of labour, the size of the labour force and the hours of operation. Organizing the capacity to meet demand in some kind of sequence is known as scheduling, which we deal with under operations planning.

Capacity planning is especially difficult in service industries. In most instances, the product on offer cannot be stored when the capacity is not fully utilized, as with airline seats and perishable foods. The concern for unused capacity in the hotel industry has led some hoteliers in popular resorts to overbook rooms. This works well given the predicted number of cancellations, but can lead to holiday–makers not being accommodated in the hotel of their choice and their subsequent dissatisfaction. In some types of industry there are well established peaks and troughs.

A number of strategies are used by service industries to reduce the difficulties imposed by capacity planning. A bus company or an airline will dictate demand and capacity by operating a fixed schedule, and in some cases insisting that passengers buy tickets beforehand. Extra capacity can be laid on in times of known high demand. Some services can operate a delayed delivery system to control demand and plan capacity. A garage will attempt to match the cars it accepts for servicing work with available equipment and labour, and will delay bookings to times when capacity is available. The system can and does break down, through overbooking, staff absenteeism, and jobs taking longer than planned. In such situations the problem may be solved by overtime work, but this increases cost and any delay can impair the service the customer feels he is getting.

In the case of the bus company and the car service there is a certain flexibility in both equipment and manning levels. Such flexibility is not available in all situations. A telephone company must establish a capacity to cope with peak demand, which occurs during office hours. At other times the equipment is idle and represents a net cost to the company. In most countries, telephone companies attempt to smooth out demand through the use of cheaper rates for off–peak usage and frequent advertising campaigns to reinforce this in the public's mind.

There are instances where companies have used demand and capacity as a marketing strategy. Certain products have been known to develop a mystique, simply because they are not available. In the USA the demand for Coors beer was allowed to develop, through advertising and publicity, although there was insufficient capacity. The product developed a rarity value and cult status. When the company subsequently increased its productive capacity, a market had already been created. Some foreign car manufacturers, like BMW and Daimler Benz in Germany, deliberately limit the number of cars they release to Britain, thus keeping their product fairly exclusive and enabling them to maintain high prices.

Equipment design. Decisions here relate to the selection of the type of equipment to be used, how much of it is to be manufactured in–house, how much is to be bought in, and what equipment replacement strategies to adopt. There is a close relationship with product design, capacity planning, the nature and skills of the labour force and accounting procedures.

Key debates in this area concern the extent of automation and computerization, job security and job satisfaction. The choice of equipment will influence how the work is to be designed, which in turn will affect organization structure. We will return to these issues in our discussions of technology, labour and organization structure later in this chapter.

Work design. We are concerned here with two types of decision; the physical layout of the production system, and the design of individual jobs. Many of the issues pertinent to equipment design obtain here also and relate to the arrangement of equipment, work stations and people. The dominant considerations here are economic (meeting demand and keeping within cost constraints), technical (product design and utilizing available equipment), and behavioural (fulfilling the needs of both the consumer and the workforce).

Variations in these economic, technical and behavioural factors often result in different types of production system. We return to this theme when we offer a classification of production systems in the section dealing with organizational aspects of production. Work design is one way management attempts to satisfy those conflicting demands shown in Figure 6.2. The layout of a department store usually involves the grouping of like products to capitalize on staff expertise and meet customer expectations. The layout caters for both demand and buyer behaviour by locating fast–moving goods and those often bought on impulse on the ground floor. With goods such as furniture, the purchase is planned and deliberate and the store can afford to locate the furniture department on the upper floors. In a self–service cafeteria, the flowline of goods will correspond with the order in which people eat their meals.

The minimization of cost is a major management consideration and the technique used is known as work study, comprising method study and work measurement.

Method study is 'the systematic and critical examination of the ways of doing things in order to make improvements' (British Standard 3138). The approach taken is usually highly methodical with a set sequence involving a detailed analysis of the present method, the careful development and testing of new methods, the training of the workforce, the installation and regular testing of the new methods. The technique seeks to find more efficient and effective ways of doing work, and as such, embraces equipment design and ergonomics as well as more subjective, psychological aspects of the person/job relationship.

Work measurement is 'the application of techniques designed to establish the time for a qualified worker to carry out a task at a defined level of performance' (British Standard 3138). The most common technique is time study, in which a trained observer times the job as it is being done, making adjustments for rest allowances and so on. Nowadays, work measurement is greatly assisted by the use of PMTS (predetermined motion time standards). Under this system, the work study engineer has a set of tables which list the times for a variety of motions that form the basis of most jobs. Work measurement can be done by simply piecing together the times of the constituent motions of the job.

Work study is useful in planning and scheduling, cost estimation, the determination of maintenance schedules, manpower planning and employee training, as well as forming the basis for most types of output–related incentive schemes. The technique is applied to both manufacturing and non–manufacturing concerns. The standard method for administering drugs to hospital patients was changed as a result of work study. The old system involved drugs being kept in a locked drugs cupboard, and, for each patient, the nurse had to return to the cupboard, unlock it, and retrieve the appropriate drug. This involved most of the nurse's time in walking to and from the cupboard, and a safety risk if ever the cupboard were left unlocked. A new system was devised which is now standard practice in most hospitals. The drugs are kept in a mobile trolley which can be transported from patient to patient. On a more esoteric level, the change from overarm to underarm pitching in baseball to achieve greater speed and accuracy is attributed to the application of work study by Frederick Winslow Taylor!

Locational decisions. The location of the production system in manufacturing industry is usually based upon a variety of factors including the proximity to raw materials and power supply, to transport systems for supply and distribution, to a labour market possessing the required skills. Other considerations can include the level of local rates and taxes, the availability of government grants and even the relative cost of labour. The final point is very relevant to those multinationals who locate their labour–intensive operations where wages are lower (there is a discussion on multinationals in Chapter 2). One of the prime considerations of location is the attempt to minimize all costs, but less objective factors may operate. In the USA, there has been a shift of manufacturing industry from the North and North East to the South and South West. One of the motives for so doing is the relative lack of union organization in states such as Georgia, Arizona, Alabama, North and South Carolina. Whatever the real or imagined economic benefits of this to corporate executives, union avoidance would appear to be an important consideration in the location decision.

Location is an important consideration in the service industry, especially where customers are expected to travel to receive the service. The location of a hospital on the outskirts of a town may solve the land constraint problems of a central site, but the new site must be easily accessible by patients and visitors, otherwise it is failing in its service function. Similarly, large supermarkets located on the edge of towns must make the effort of travel worthwhile in terms of a wider range of produce at cheaper prices. An important consideration here is usually the availability of ample car parking space. A professional practice such as the patent agency in Case 6.2 may need to balance the advantages of operating from a central London site, especially for client consultation and prestige purposes, against the rising costs. A compromise used by some professional firms is the retention of a limited presence in the centre of the city and a relocation for the majority of the operations on a cheaper site.

The operation of production systems

We deal with two main aspects of operations management, operations planning and operations control.

Operations planning. The aim of operations planning is to ensure that sufficient goods or services are produced to meet demand. A basic consideration in manufacturing is whether goods are made to stock or to order. Ford Motor Company has a policy that all cars are ordered before manufacture. On the other hand Chrysler in the USA made various models which were then sold from stock. The fast–food chain McDonalds produces hamburgers to stock based on carefully prepared demand forecasts. Hamburgers that are not then sold within a certain length of time are discarded. McDonalds claim that this system provides greater operating efficiency, and they still have the flexibility to produce goods to order when stocks are inadequate.

Operations planning overlaps with issues of capacity planning which we discussed earlier. In the service industry problems of manufacturing to stock or order reveal themselves in the provision of standardized or customized items. A hairdresser will offer a standardized service to all customers, such as haircut and wash, and a customized service in the form of styling. Restaurants often attempt to offer the best of both worlds. An 'A la carte' menu offers the consumer flexibility of choice, but within a limited range of dishes. In general terms the greater the choice then the greater the problems for the operations planner. The more dishes the chef must make to order, then the longer the potential delay for the customer and the greater the difficulty in serving a group of customers at the same time.

The problem highlighted above is one of *scheduling*. The aim of scheduling is to balance the costs of production against demands for goods and services; to ensure that demand is met in the most efficient way possible. This, of course, gives rise to the classic dilemma of production management as we saw in Figure 6.2. An important strategic consideration here is load–levelling, to ensure that the work is distributed as evenly as possible throughout the workforce, over the entire year, and making the

CASE 6.1

ORLAKE RECORDS

Orlake Records is a manufacturer of gramophone records in a declining market. Since 1979, the trade delivery of singles in the United Kindgom has fallen from 89.1 million to 67.4 million, and LPs from 74.5 to 52.3 million over the same period. Correspondingly trade delivery of cassettes has risen from 23.5 million in 1979 to 69.6 million in 1986. The compact disc industry, while still in its infancy, has a rate of growth which suggests that is will take over 40% of the LP market by 1990 and new developments are taking place in tape technology. Competition among gramophone manufacturers is high, not only in this country but internationally. In the last six years, around twenty British manufacturers have gone out of business.

The actual manufacture is the following stage from the recording studio. There the final tape is converted to a series of vibrations which cut grooves into a master disc, known as the lacquer master. Orlake takes this master and through an electroplating process, makes its own moulds to form the basis of record production. Several moulds may be required depending on the number of presses to be used, the length of the run and the uncertain working life of each mould. The actual record is made by compression moulding, which presses extruded plastic onto the mould on a specially designed machine. This takes around twenty-two seconds for a 12″ LP and fourteen seconds for a 7″ record.

Record companies may use a number of manufacturers, particularly on high selling items. Orlake manufactures for a range of different companies and as a competitive strategy attempts to meet customer needs at low cost, in as short a time as possible. The variety of the work means that most production runs fall between 1000 and 5000 records, with occasional forays up to runs of 100 000, and some less than 1000. The firm uses two types of presses, fully automatic and manually operated. Whilst Orlake is expanding the automated side of the business, certain products such as 'picture' discs and 'shape' discs can only by produced using manual machines. The nature of the business and Orlake's strategic response means that production planning and scheduling is carried out on a daily basis by the production manager in consultation with sales. Even then, schedules are regularly amended. The average turn around for orders is between two and five days.

Quality control was originally the responsibility of the production supervisor, but pressure of work meant that minor faults were deliberately ignored. It is now a separate function and any conflict with production control is handled by the director. Quality control is particularly important when the master moulds are made and a strict procedure had been set up. At the pressing stage, one finished record in every twenty is checked visually. Ninety per cent of all faults can be spotted visually by a trained operator. In addition, a particular pressing is checked audibly every hour. Before storage, a further one record in forty is checked visually, a process that is repeated after nine hours have elapsed to allow the plastic to cool down. Faults found with the moulds can often be rectified manually. If a fault is discovered in a particular batch, then the whole batch is destroyed.

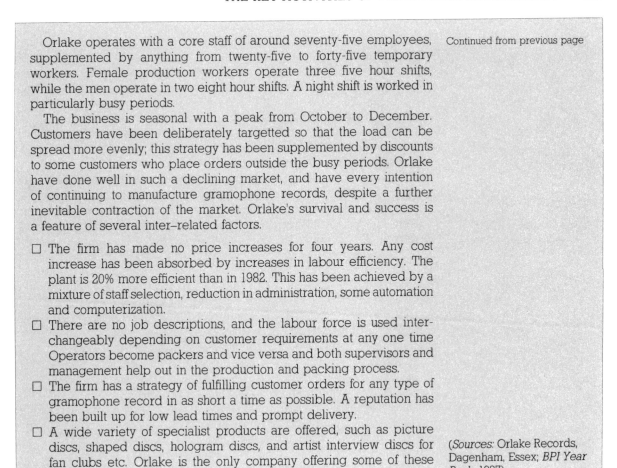

Continued from previous page

Orlake operates with a core staff of around seventy-five employees, supplemented by anything from twenty-five to forty-five temporary workers. Female production workers operate three five hour shifts, while the men operate in two eight hour shifts. A night shift is worked in particularly busy periods.

The business is seasonal with a peak from October to December. Customers have been deliberately targetted so that the load can be spread more evenly; this strategy has been supplemented by discounts to some customers who place orders outside the busy periods. Orlake have done well in such a declining market, and have every intention of continuing to manufacture gramophone records, despite a further inevitable contraction of the market. Orlake's survival and success is a feature of several inter–related factors.

☐ The firm has made no price increases for four years. Any cost increase has been absorbed by increases in labour efficiency. The plant is 20% more efficient than in 1982. This has been achieved by a mixture of staff selection, reduction in administration, some automation and computerization.

☐ There are no job descriptions, and the labour force is used inter-changeably depending on customer requirements at any one time Operators become packers and vice versa and both supervisors and management help out in the production and packing process.

☐ The firm has a strategy of fulfilling customer orders for any type of gramophone record in as short a time as possible. A reputation has been built up for low lead times and prompt delivery.

☐ A wide variety of specialist products are offered, such as picture discs, shaped discs, hologram discs, and artist interview discs for fan clubs etc. Orlake is the only company offering some of these products.

(*Sources*: Orlake Records, Dagenham, Essex; *BPI Year Book*, 1987)

most efficient use of available equipment. A whole series of theories and techniques have been developed to deal with such problems associated with the planning, scheduling and coordination of activities. These include queuing theory, linear programming and the more complex models of operational research. Many of these techniques draw upon mathematical tools, and students seeking further information are advised to consult the quantitative methods text in this series (Slater and Ascroft, 1989).

The problem with all such techniques is that, while they can offer optimal solutions to the problems of production planning and scheduling, they cannot allow for all the constraints operating in a given situation, many of which cannot be measured and many of which are highly subjective. Increased demand for a particular product may, in some cases, only be met by overtime, and the increased labour costs have to be balanced against the extra revenue from the increased sales. In such cases it may be more profitable to refuse the order, unless it comes from a particularly valued customer. Alternative strategies here might include persuading the customer to accept a delay in delivery, or subcontracting the work to another company. In the service industry, customer contact often makes scheduling difficult due to the variations in time demanded by each client. In some banks this kind of problem has been tackled by the introduction of 'automatic teller machines', and a division of labour into those dealing with standard transactions and those dealing with more complex enquiries.

Scheduling decisions can be highly sensitive and illustrate the relationship between the firm and the environment in which it operates; this is especially true of the public sector.

The provision and scheduling of the railways in this country was examined in the 1960s by a committee under the leadership of Lord Beeching. The resulting Beeching Plan meant that several lines were closed and certain towns were left with no railway provision whatsoever. This created widespread political and community opposition. The debate centred around the argument as to whether some public services should continue to operate at a considerable loss or be closed, thus saving the taxpayer money, but depriving some of them of a service they may need. Similar problems face bus companies in planning their routes, especially in less populated rural areas. Planning and scheduling problems are also highly contentious in the health services. Hospitals must schedule operations according to their available resources, which means that only a specific number of non–emergency operations can be budgeted in any one year, resulting in a build–up of waiting lists.

All these illustrations take production planning and scheduling out of the domain of programmed decisions and simplistic techniques, and involve social, political, and ethical considerations.

Operations control. There are various types of control used in any production system. We identify these various forms of control and the mechanisms through which they are achieved in Figure 6.4. As with all forms of control, those managing the system must determine the standards that are to operate. In some types of system such standards may be difficult to measure, for example the quality of education or social work. In other situations there may be conflict concerning the appropriateness of certain standards, for example, between marketing and production about delivery times; between management and unions over levels of productivity.

We can see from the five types of control identified in Figure 6.4 that there is considerable overlap. Labour control has a close relationship to quantity, quality and cost control; productivity is a function of quantity, labour and cost control. A key concern in most organizations today is quality.

We have already noted the tendency of some organizations to focus on the quality of their product and services as a key strategy, and a key factor in the development of a corporate culture. Quality plays a key role in the so–called 'excellent' companies (Peters and Waterman 1982). We refer you to the relevant sections of Chapter 3 and 4 for a more detailed account of these strategic and cultural issues.

In Britain, the government, mindful of the nation's declining position in world trade, has established measures in recognition of the role played by quality in international competition in both the manufacturing and service

1. *Quantity Control.* This is sometimes known as production control and sometimes as progress chasing. It involves ensuring that the throughput of goods and services goes according to the planned schedule.
2. *Quality Control.* This ensures that the quality of the finished product or service meets the standards set in the design stage and also meets with the approval of the customer. In manufacturing it is closely linked with the quality of raw materials and hence the purchasing function. It can be particularly difficult in service industries where standards and expectations can be both subjective and highly variable. In all cases some form of inspection and sampling system have to be planned, although the extent and frequency of inspection will vary according to the type of product and the numbers produced (Case 6.1). In education, quality control is one of the remits of the government inspectorate who visit schools and colleges.
3. *Technology Control.* This refers to the maintenance of plant and equipment. Whilst considerations of maintenance are historically associated with manufacturing industry, the use of computers and various types of office equipment make this an issue in all types of organization. The basic problem is the determination of when a piece of equipment is in need of service. Many firms solve this by instituting a system of planned preventive maintenance. Developments in information technology have meant that, in some cases, visual warning systems can be installed. These operate as a function of the number of times a piece of equipment is switched on, its running time, how intensely it is used and so on. Such systems have been installed in some cars to indicate when a service is due. Some firms prefer to subcontract their maintenance requirements by entering into service agreements with suppliers or by simply renting the equipment as in the case of photocopying machines. In cases such as these, maintenance is generally haphazard and often waits until a breakdown has occurred. At a certain stage in the lifespan of a piece of equipment a decision must be made concerning repair or replacement. In the case of such items as company cars, programmed replacement tends to be the norm.
4. *Labour Control.* Issues at stake here include the extent and style of supervision and the type of incentives used. Interest in more participative forms of management has resulted in more use being made of such techniques as quality circles and profit sharing.
5. *Cost Control.* There is a strong link here with the accounting function and budgeting. Cost control involves the collection and analysis of data on materials, operating, equipment and labour costs and comparisons made with some form of previously determined standard costing.

Figure 6.4 Types and mechanisms of production control.

industries. The Government through the British Standards Institute (BSI) has defined quality assurance as an all–embracing concept involving all stages and all people in the production process. General guidances have been issued under British Standard 4891, urging companies to set quality objectives and establish programmes and procedures to see that such objectives are met. These measures have been strengthened by the estab-lishment of British Standard 5750. The BSI will award this standard only to those companies who are able to show that quality is built into the production system at every stage of the operation, and whose employees display a genuine commitment to quality issues. The government has stated its intention of giving contracts only to those firms who possess British Standard 5750, and the Department of Trade and Industry has published a register listing those companies that have been quality assessed. There are increasing signs that some industries will only buy goods and components from firms that have been quality assessed, and it is predicted that the future purchasing habits of the general consumer will be influenced by British Standard 5750.

With all types of control, someone must decide upon the appropriate form of action when deviations from the standard occur. Various options are available as the following illustrations reveal. In the case of a bottling plant, the decision is fairly straightforward. Empty bottles are washed and then closely inspected prior to being filled; bottles that are cracked or chipped are broken up, bottles that are still dirty are sent through the washing process again. A clothing manufacturer making garments for a quality–conscious retail chain, like Marks and Spencer, has other options. It may be possible to sell elsewhere items which are not acceptable to the original client. Some manufacturers sell slightly imperfect goods to their own staff or to the public as 'seconds'. Such decisions get more complex in businesses such as a restaurant, where overall quality may not be judged until the meal has been eaten, and the only redress is in the form of compensation. Assessments, especially of quality, can be highly subjective and a potential source of conflict between producer and customer.

Materials management

The purchasing function is part of a wider process that has been gaining in recognition and importance over the last few years. This is known as materials management, defined by the Institute of Purchasing and Supply as,

> The concept requiring an organizational structure which unifies into one functional responsibility the systematic planning and control of all materials from identification of the need through to delivery to the consumer. Materials management embraces planning, purchasing, production and inventory control, storage, materials–handling and physical distribution. The objectives of materials management are to optimize performance in meeting agreed customer service requirements at the same time adding to the profitability by minimizing costs and making the best use of available resources.

The importance of materials management is twofold. Firstly, from the perspective of this book, it illustrates, more than most activities, the interaction of the production function with its environment. The price and availability of goods is influenced by various environmental considerations, such as the economics of supply and demand. However, management will operate purchasing strategies in order to control supply and demand and hence the environment. Secondly, materials management can have a significant impact on a firm's costs and hence its profitability. While the 1960s focused on rising labour costs, the oil crisis of 1973, and subsequent rises in the cost of many materials and components, brought the precarious state of raw material supply into sharp relief. Even modest savings on

Materials management has become an important function in manufacturing industry and has superseded the more traditional activities of
purchasing and stock control. It aims to improve organizational effectiveness through the planning, coordination and control of all materials and
in so doing coordinates the activities of purchasing, progress chasing
and stock control. Developments in materials management involve 'Just–
in–Time' methods of production planning influenced significantly by
Japanese management methods.

KEY CONCEPT 6.3

**MATERIALS
MANAGEMENT**

the cost of raw materials and greater care in the management of those
materials as they pass through the organization, can have a greater impact
on profit than increased sales revenue.

The key variables of purchasing are source, quantity, quality, time and
price. We will examine each of these in turn.

Source. Management is faced with a number of decisions concerning the
source of the firm's raw materials and components. The obvious strategy is
one which maximizes the other four variables, obtaining supplies in the
quantity and quality required, when they are needed, and at an acceptable
price. In achieving these aims, managements must decide whether to
produce their owm materials and components or buy them from other
manufacturers; and if the latter, whether to opt for a single supplier or buy
from a number of different suppliers.

The 'make or buy' decision involves consideration of vertical integration,
either through acquiring the raw material supplier or manufacturing your
own components. This will give management greater control over the
reliability of supplies, and may well add a new dimension to the firm as a
supplier to others. There are considerable cost implications to such a
strategy, which are not only financial. Consider the case of a firm that
sets up its own foundry to manufacture its requirements for cast metal products. The foundry has to operate as a profit centre, and since it operates
in an area of declining demand contracts to do work for other firms.
The foundry may be placed in a position of supplying major competitors as
well as having a conflict of priorities over the respective demands of its own
and other organizations. In more general terms we noted in Chapter 4 that
acquisition through vertical integration may not be very successful due to
the different nature of the industries involved.

A firm can build up a good relationship with a single supplier, but there
may be greater security in using a variety of sources, especially where
supplies are unreliable. We have already referred to the series of strikes in
the car components industry in the 1960s which led to the closure of the
major car manufacturers in this country and brought about a change in
purchasing policy resulting in the use of a greater number of suppliers. In
the 1980s, with a less volatile industrial relations climate, there has been
a shift back to firms establishing close relationships with a limited number
of suppliers.

The relationship between supplier and purchaser is often a question of relative power. We discuss this at length in Chapter 4 and you are referred specifically to Figure 4.4. If the purchaser is in a strong position compared to the suppliers then they may have to bid for the contract, enabling the buyer to obtain the most favourable deal. Such bidding and dealing introduce a highly sensitive variable to the purchasing function, so much so that it has been defined as 'a maelstrom of human relations' (Starr, 1972, p 271)

The personal relationships between buyers and sellers are an important ingredient in purchasing. A purchasing manager with a supply problem may well be able to solve it by using his personal relationship with one of the suppliers. Time, effort and expenditure are regularly involved in building up such relationships. There are also cases where personal relationships have resulted in contracts being unfairly secured and even bribery used, as some legal cases over local authority building contracts will testify.

Quantity. The major purchasing decision here is how much to order at any one time. This is a function of cost, storage capacity, and the nature of the production system. The decision can be difficult. For example, a firm operating complex machinery on a continuous process basis may need to stock expensive replacement parts, even though they be needed only infrequently. A decision model has been developed, the 'Economic Order Quantity Model', which establishes a trade–off between the cost of acquisition and the cost of holding stock. Some firms have very precise stock and delivery requirements in an attempt to minimize material costs. This is illustrated by the 'Just–In–Time' method, ascribed to the Japanese and examined in the next section.

The greater the purchasing requirements then the greater the possibility of obtaining discounts. Some highly diverse organizations operate a central purchasing function to maximize such discounts. The needs of several London Boroughs for certain goods is met by a central purchasing function.

Quality. The quality of incoming raw materials and components is a vital ingredient in the quality control function. The purchasing department or the materials manager is usually responsible for the acceptance, sampling and inspection of incoming materials.

Time and price. The timing of a purchase is, like order quantity, a function of the needs of the production system, storage capacity and price. Certain commodities are particularly price sensitive and there can be significant speculation. In the 1970s the price of silver rose dramatically. This was particularly significant for the film developing industry, which used silver as a major ingredient. Some companies refused to buy in a rising market, preferring to wait for what they saw as the inevitable fall. Some of those companies went out of business as their stocks ran out long before prices fell. Some firms, to offset the costs involved in stock-holding, engage in hedging, a process of buying materials and stock at the current price for delivery at some future date. Other purchasing managers get involved with the futures market and options trading, although the speculative nature of some markets increase the risk in decision–making.

In our discussion of purchasing, we have made constant reference to the management of stock, sometimes referred to as inventory management.

Stock is an expensive item and can account for 30% of a firm's total assets. Stock management therefore attempts to balance the needs of the production system against the cost of holding stock. It operates in three main aeas; raw materials and components for product or process; the work in progress; and finished stock. Operating systems such as 'group technology' and materials strategies such as 'Just–In–Time' are attempts to minimize inventory and to hold down costs.

Production and the environment

We began this chapter by challenging the notion that production could be buffered against environmental influences, and we have already seen several illustrations of how a production function interacts with its environment. All the environmental sections of our model relate in some way to the production function. In this section we will explore the more significant aspects of that relationship. We deal first with the interaction of production, the economy and the state with a focus on manufacturing industry. The theme of manufacturing also dominates the examination of production and technology, with an emphasis on new manufacturing techniques based on computerization. We look at the interaction of production and labour and close the section with an examination of production methods in different societies, with a focus on Japan.

Production, the economy and the state

We focus here on manufacturing industry. The importance of this to the national economy has been recognized by successive governments in policies to encourage the growth of the manufacturing sector and in attempts to regenerate flagging industries and firms. We will view the place of manufacturing in the economy and introduce the concept of deindustrialization. This is a term relating to the decline of the manufacturing sector and a much more detailed discussion of the topic can be found in the economics text in this series (Neale and Haslam, 1989).

Deindustrialization. Historically, the manufacturing sector has been the driving force for economic growth, and clear links can be shown between manufacturing output and GDP. Furthermore, changes in capital investment and technology have had a significant impact on productivity and hence manufacturing output and economic growth. A prosperous manufacturing sector means higher incomes for those employed with a subsequent rise in the demand for manufactured goods. The potential that a successful manufacturing sector has for economic growth is much greater than that of other sectors (the *Finneston Report*, 1980, has a more detailed analysis of the contribution of manufacturing to the economy).

It is not just the impact of manufacturing on the GDP that concerns us. A significant proportion (around 30%) of this country's labour force is employed in manufacturing industry, many using skills that are not easily transferred to other sectors. Government policies to support the steel industry and firms like British Leyland in the 1970s were as much related to social and political aspects of unemployment as they were to a concern for economic growth.

After the post–war boom in British manufacturing industry, there was slow down in the 1960s followed by a decline, with the sharpest fall occurring since 1979. Britain's share of world trade in manufactured goods fell from 19.8% in 1955 to 7.9% in 1983, while imported manufactures rose from 8% in 1961 to 31% in 1983 (*Monthly Review of External Trade Statistics*). At a time when changes in technology made possible significant increases in productivity, Britain's annual productivity increases were less than Japan, France, West Germany and Canada and only marginally greater than the USA. During the same period, increases in unit labour costs were significantly higher in Britain than any of those countries (Buffa, 1983).

Deindustrialization has been expressed in terms of employment, productivity and trade. Several attempts have been made to explain the phenomenon. Various scapegoats have been cited, such as poor management, conservative unions, and even the supposed aversion the British traditionally have for manufacturing industry. All these hypotheses are dealt with elsewhere in this book. Other explanations include a lack of investment, an over–extensive and all–consuming public sector, the comparatively high sterling exchange rate, a lack of trade protection by the government and low wage competition from Third World countries. Some of these hypotheses have more credibility than others. Certainly Britain has a lower rate of investment per head of its working population than its major competitors, and the impact of this on innovation was explored in Chapter 5. The true causes of deindustrialization inevitably lie in an interaction of the kinds of factors mentioned. We therefore need to devise a model, not dissimilar to the one on which this book and others in the series is based.

Policies to arrest manufacturing decline have not met with great success. A major factor may be the confused nature of Government policy, which gives tax concessions to manufacturing on one hand, but allows high interest rates to reduce borrowing and hence investment, and a strong sterling rate to lead to a reduction in exports on the other. Before leaving this area we deal briefly with other aspects of state intervention in the production process.

Other forms of state intervention. We identify three other types of state intervention with an impact on the production process.

☐ We saw in Chapter 5 how regulatory laws can affect business operations. We can cite such laws as those relating to the purification of waste water or the emission of toxic waste as by–products of the manufacturing process.

☐ Earlier in this chapter we dealt with government attempts to improve the quality of goods and services by establishing national standards, and encouraging customers to deal only with firms which can operate to those standards.

☐ As part of its regional policy, successive governments have attempted to influence the location of both manufacturing and non–manufacturing industry. This has generally focussed on measures to encourage firms to locate in areas of high unemployment by giving them generous grants and tax allowances.

Production and technology

> Advanced manufacturing technology in the 1980s exhibits some highly distinctive characteristics. The most important is the ability to manufacture a very wide range of component parts and assemblies in a highly flexible fashion. It is this flexibility which distinguishes today's advances from the automation of the 1950s and 1960s ... Companies (and nations?) who do not succeed in implementing this technology stand to lose heavily — perhaps disappearing completely from the manufacturing scene.
>
> (Husband, 1984, p 197)

We saw in the previous section the interaction of manufacturing industry and the economy. There is a widely held view that the recovery of British manufacturing industry in world terms depends largely upon the introduction of advanced engineering methods (Finniston, 1980).

In Chapter 2 we discussed the influence of technology on the labour force and upon the way work is organized. We pick up those themes later in this chapter. In this section we will examine the impact on manufacturing of three major innovations in process technology; numerical control, robotics, and flexible manufacturing systems (FMS).

Numerical control. This is the basic concept underlying automated production systems. It occurs when machinery, tools and equipment come under the control of a digital computer, as in the case of the automatic positioning and direction of a drilling operation on an engine block. Strictly speaking, we should refer to this process as 'computerized numerical control' (CNC). The full extent of CNC can be seen in its application to flexible manufacturing systems. This type of system is an illustration of 'computer–aided manufacture', which we discussed earlier this chapter under the heading of production design. A big advantage of CNC is that it makes possible contour–controlled cutting operations. Such operations previously required the cutting machine to be reset several times.

Robotics. The nearest analogy to an industrial robot is the human arm, to which a variety of tools can be attached to perform a variety of jobs from metal work to painting. The majority of industrial robots operate from a fixed position, with the restricted movements defined by a computer programme.

A study of robotics reveals an inconsistency between the image portrayed in the media and the actual use of industrial robots. Their use and capabilities are less than is normally supposed. Fifty per cent of all industrial robots are to be found in the automobile industry, where their use is generally confined to various types of welding operation and paint spraying (Williams *et al.*, 1987). The greatest number and concentration of industrial robots are found in Japan, where applications also tend to be more varied; for instance the electronics firm, Hitachi, has plans to robotize 60% of its production lines (Thackray, 1983). In this case robotics has been extended to perform the precision tasks of assembling electronic circuit boards.

Robots offer possibilities of continuous operation, improved quality and the liberation of human labour from repetitive, unhealthy and unpleasant tasks as with paint spraying. Very few robots, however, possess tactile or visual capabilities and whilst their potential impact on manufacturing systems will be considerable, for the present, the supposed flexibility they offer a production system has been exaggerated.

> Robots cannot be reprogrammed for new models by pressing a few buttons. That is a myth.
>
> (Williams *et al.*, 1987, p 430)

The main handicap to the more extensive use of robotics in industry is cost, involving not just the cost of the actual robot, but the high costs of developing specific software and machine tools. This problem is heightened in times of economic recession or in cheap labour economies when a plentiful supply of cheap labour may lower the motivation for such an expensive investment.

Flexible manufacturing systems. A flexible manufacturing system (FMS) brings together the various elements of advanced manufacturing engineering to solve the problem of offering consumer choice and a quick response to market changes using a minimum of working capital. Potentially it offers manufacturing industry a solution to the kind of dilemmas outlined in Figure 6.2. An FMS usually embraces the following.

☐ Equipment comprising NC machines, robots, and machine tools.
☐ An automatic transport system for moving tools and workpieces, as well as parts and raw materials.
☐ The whole system is computer–controlled with software for scheduling, tool selection, part selection, fault finding, machine breakdown detection and so on.

In a car plant an FMS would enable a range of different models to be built on the same production line, with the necessary tool changes being automatic, and the required parts being delivered automatically to work stations in the quantity and at the time they were required. A typical FMS would incorporate a multiple tool system, a CNC machine with the capability of performing a number of different machine–tool operations. For example, the drilling of a variety of different–sized holes in a single machine part could be achieved in a single sequence of operations. Prior to such multiple tool systems, such jobs would require a number of different machines, and the consequent moving of workpieces, or time–consuming changeover of machine tools.

The claimed advantages of such a system are many (see for example Piore and Sabel, 1984, and Ebel, 1985). The main ones are identified below.

☐ Higher productivity would be achieved through the better utilization of plant, materials and labour.
☐ A greater number of product variants would be possible in smaller batches offering the consumer greater choice and potential satisfaction.
☐ Reduced set–up times and consequently, shorter manufacturing lead times and a more flexible response to change.
☐ The need for less inventory at all stages of the production process; fewer parts, less work–in–process, and less finished stock.
☐ Improved production and quality control.

A study of eight cases of FMS in Britain revealed that at constant sales level, a fourfold increase in plant investment resulted in higher productivity, a threefold reduction in inventory, and a threefold increase in profit. Further investment in plant together with an increase in sales had an even greater impact on profits (National Economic Development Office, 1985). Whilst this case points the way for a rosy FMS future we must put such optimism in some kind of perspective.

The number of fully integrated FMSs was in 1985 estimated at no more than two hundred worldwide (Ebel, 1985). As with robotics, the main drawback is the high initial cost of setting the system up. A 1986 survey found that 82% of all US, 46% of all European and 42% of all Japanese FMSs had cost over $3 million (United Nations, 1986). This would appear to limit their application to a small number of big firms able to carry such an investment. Where FMSs had been installed in the USA, their use tended to be restricted to products having relatively long runs, which suggests that their potential is not being fully exploited (Jaikumar, 1986).

Despite this potential for variety, the reality for many companies is that the pay back on such substantial investments as CNC machines, industrial robots and FMS is only feasible on long runs. Automation paid off handsomely for Volkswagen because of the high volume production, whereas the relatively low volume of Austin–Rover's output meant that its automation turned out a poor investment (Williams *et al.*, 1987). Furthermore, as we found with robotics, only a limited range of product variety is feasible before costly programming and tooling changes are required. In any case the quest for product variety may well be a marketing myth. The continued manufacture of washing machines to the same basic design and the purchase of second cars and television sets would indicate that the consumer's need for repeat or supplementary purchases is greater than the need for variety.

Innovations in production technology undoubtedly carry the potential for a more effective and efficient production system. We have seen, however, that such enthusiasm must be tempered by the high cost and a recognition of the limitations of the new technology. Investment is no guarantee of business success and a focus on increasing market share may pay better dividends for many companies.

Further complications are caused by the impact of such developments on the labour force. The same technology that has the potential of eliminating the need for people to do noisy, dirty, dangerous work, that can improve working conditions, that offers interesting opportunities for restructuring the organization, also carries the very real threat of job displacement. It is to such issues that we now turn.

Production and labour

The impact of the production system on the labour force and vice versa is such a complex and well documented area that we can only hope to introduce some of the main issues here. These issues include the man–machine interface, training, industrial relations, the quality of working life, payment systems and the problems of introducing change. Some of these

KEY CONCEPT 6.4

**NEW TECHNOLOGY
AND PRODUCTION**

Production systems, especially in manufacturing, have, in more recent times, changed significantly to take advantage of developments in new technology to enhance the effectiveness of the production process. Computers have been used extensively in product design and the operation and control of production systems. Machines that are used in this way are designated CNC machines (computerized numerical control). The concept of CAD/CAM (computer aided design and computer aided manufacture) is one which extends this application as a central feature in the production system as a whole. Robotics represents a specialized form of computer controlled machine offering considerable flexibility to a production system, whilst the greatest flexibility is offered by a totally integrated, computer controlled production system known as FMS (flexible manufacturing system). Whilst computers do play a significant role in modern manufacturing, the extent of their use, especially in the form of FMS is severely limited by their cost.

are dealt with elsewhere in this book and others are considered in greater depth in the organizational behaviour text in this series. We will start here with F.W. Taylor's influence on the organization of production. We will identify some of the problems associated with 'Taylorism', particularly the deskilling hypothesis, and look at 'popular' solutions to those problems, notably job enrichment and autonomous work groups. We then examine the role of payment systems both as an incentive and as a production control device.

Taylorism and deskilling. The organization of labour in the production system is dominated by the work of F.W. Taylor and his treatise on *Scientific Management* (Taylor, 1947). The thoughts attributed to the scientific management school represent an attempt to solve the problems of control due to the growing size and complexity of organisations and the growth of trade unions. The main principle of scientific management draws a distinction between planning and doing, with management, as the planners, controlling every aspect of the work process. This involves the design of tasks and work measurement, the careful selection and training of the workforce, target setting and the design of payment systems. The application and in some cases misapplication of Taylor's ideas resulted in a tendency towards an extensive division of labour, work simplification and tight managerial control. Much of manufacturing industry and many of the larger production systems in non–manufacturing throughout the world exhibit elements of Taylorism, and the ideas of F.W. Taylor were popular not only among American capitalists but with Lenin and Mussolini.

Despite its widespread popularity, the scientific management approach has met with considerable criticism. Taylor's views have been labelled as authoritarian, subjective, unscientific and ultimately unfair. The main thrust of the attack is focussed around the deskilling hypothesis encapsulated in the work of Braverman (1974). The extensive division of labour means that work becomes fragmented, the machine becomes more important than the worker, and control shifts from the skilled worker firmly into the hands of management, whose position is strengthened by their virtual monopoly of knowledge of the work process. Braverman saw scientific management as the essential control of labour in the production process. Deskilling occurs not only in manufacturing industry but in many service industries too, such as large banks and insurance companies. In such establishments work has been fragmented in much the same way as in manufacturing industry, and both the discretion of individual employees and their contact with the public has been reduced by the operation of programmed decisions and standard letters using computer systems.

Criticisms of Taylor's approach tend to focus on managerial control, the reduction of man to the level of a machine, its crude economic approach and even the eccentricity of Taylor himself. More than most management writers, Taylor has been subjected to much hostile criticism which has tended to mask some of the more enlightened aspects of his thinking; his views on training and participation for example. Ultimately the widespread application of scientific management suggests that it offered solutions acceptable to many, even trade unions. Nevertheless attempts have been made to humanize the work environment, as a response to either Taylorism, or his critics, or arising from other motivations. These attempts have focussed on the problems brought about by deskilling.

Solutions to the problems of deskilling. Several theories and techniques have been put forward to counteract the negative impact of deskilling on the individual worker, such as a lack of job satisfaction and alienation. These attempts include human relations management, job rotation, job enlargement, job enrichment, autonomous work groups, participation schemes and the current catch–all for many of these and similar approaches, the 'Quality of Working Life' movement. We will deal with just two of these, job enrichment and autonomous work groups.

Job enrichment owes much to the motivation theories of Herzberg (1968). It focusses on the content of jobs and attempts, by redesigning the work, to give workers more responsibility, more control, a greater sense of achievement and ultimately more satisfaction. Applications tend to be more successful among white collar jobs (where there is more scope for change) and among those who actively seek more responsibility. However successful application in terms of productivity and job satisfaction was found in a series of experiments with several types of employees at ICI in Britain (Paul and Robertson, 1970).

Autonomous work groups have their origins in the notion to socio–technical systems and in particular in the work of the Tavistock Institute in Britain, although the application has tended to be given more scope in Scandinavia (Chapter 1). The approaches vary, although in essence they involve the creation of an autonomous work group which is given responsibility for the completion of a part of the operation. The manager thus freed from labour control operates more as a 'boundary manager' dealing with problems of the immediate environment. We will come back to this notion of the autonomous work group in our discussion of 'group technology' in the next section.

As solutions to the problems of deskilling, both job enrichment and autonomous work groups, like the other approaches mentioned, have been successful in certain situations but tend to operate under severe constraints and naturally have attracted their critics. A recurring theme in this criticism is that both approaches have been introduced to solve management problems of absenteeism, high labour turnover, low productivity and poor profit margins with job satisfaction for the individual as a subsidiary issue. In particular, writers such as Braverman see job enrichment as a reaffirmation of management control. The workforce is offered a palliative but the changes are carefully controlled by management. In most cases radical restructuring has not occurred and scientific management principles still dominate the production system.

Payment systems. An important aspect of the interaction of labour and production is the issue of pay. Pay acts as an incentive for the individual worker to participate in the production process and may also be used by management as a control device. These functions operate side by side. We saw in Figure 6.1 that labour is an input to the production system. The input is brought in and therefore represents a significant cost to the firm, which managements invariably attempt to control. The search for effective means of motivation and control has led to the design of a variety of payment systems.

In manufacturing industry the most common form of payment system is some form of payment by results. This usually operates in the form of a flat rate of pay supplemented by a bonus payment directly related to the output of the individual worker or group of workers. Payment by results takes many forms, but each subscribes to the principles of extra payment for increased output subject to quality, wastage and machine utilization. Such incentive schemes tend to be most value in certain situations typified by the following conditions.

☐ In highly competitive markets, where output or a quick response to customer demands may be vital in establishing a competitive advantage.
☐ Where the workplace is large and some form of impersonal control is needed.
☐ In firms with relatively high labour costs, where some control can be exerted by varying the work flow.
☐ Where workers can control the pace of work either as individuals or members of a group.
☐ Where opportunities for personal involvement with work are lacking and pay is the only motivator.

Many criticisms have been levelled at such methods, nevertheless, their persistence is a measure of their popularity, not just with management but with employees too. Furthermore, some form of payment by results operates in non–manufacturing firms, such as sales commission in retailing. In its crudest form, where payment is only made for work completed (known as piecework) it is the sole form of payment. This is also the case in some professions, such as barrister and dentist.

The importance of pay in controlling and influencing production operations has been recognized by those seeking to change the culture of the organization to gain greater commitment from the workforce. The payment method associated with this is profit–sharing, a system whereby a proportion of pre–tax profits is shared out among the workforce. However, in Britain at least, profit–sharing is not widespread; employees see the relationship between effort and reward to be too remote, and, because of this, management see it as an ineffective control device. In those companies where commitment is a central feature of employment, as in IBM, employees receive an annual bonus based directly on their individual contribution to the organization as judged by management.

Cultural influences and production

In Chapter 2 we examined the role of culture in business and examined the view that industry in general and manufacturing industry in particular was 'alien to the spirit and character of the English people', (quoted in Wiener, 1981, p 113). As a consequence the core process, production, has been especially neglected, and Britain has subsequently lost out in world trade to countries like Germany and Japan. Such views neglect to explain why the British were successful at manufacturing, even in relatively recent phases of its history, such as the 1950s. Instead, we look to other countries' production systems for the secrets of their success. In Germany we are envious of their engineering technology, production planning systems and education and training. However, the greatest amount of attention has been reserved for Japan.

Production systems in Japan

In Chapter 2 we spent some time looking at the phenomenon known as Japanese management. We referred to the increasingly popular view that sees Japanese economic and especially export success in terms of well–planned and executed methods of production management, especially in manufacturing industry. Three aspects of the process are singled out; an attention to detail, the importance of quality control, and a totally integrated production system from the delivery of materials and parts to the distribution of the final product. These are supported by a labour system which places emphasis on total flexibility and is marked by an absence of job descriptions. There are obvious similarities with Orlake records, Case 6.1, which confirms the view offered in Chapter 2 that there is nothing specifically Japanese about Japanese production management. In this section we will view two aspects of the Japanese production system, 'Just–In–Time' and 'Quality circles'.

Just–In–Time. The origins of this system are ascribed to the Toyota car plant, although similar systems operate throughout Japan and are used by Japanese multinationals abroad, as well as spreading to other companies, notably Massey Ferguson, GKN, and Lucas in Britain.

'Just–In–Time' (JIT) aims to obtain the highest volume output at the lowest unit costs. The system is really a method of production control in which precise targets for subassembly are set, based on the demands of final assembly. Because of this JIT is described as a 'pull through' production system. Exact quantities are produced and specific require-ments are placed on materials and parts suppliers, as well as each stage in the production process to deliver just in time for the next stage of operations. Materials intake, work in progress and goods despatch are therefore kept to a minimum.

The claimed advantages for the system are the following.

☐ It smooths out the production flow.
☐ It reduces all types of inventory levels and hence costs.
☐ By preventing production delays it enhances planning and enables the firm to meet its delivery deadlines.
☐ It eliminates time wasted in waiting for components, as well as over–production.

The system has been viewed narrowly as an inventory control device. However, there are significant implications for the entire organization of production. JIT encourages a much closer relationship with suppliers, and those able to meet the demands of the system are often offered high–volume contracts, sometimes as the sole supplier. This is a marked contrast to the kind of strategies used by some firms to guarantee consistent suppliers by using a number of competing components manufacturers. To obtain the maximum flexibility from JIT, it is often introduced with new multi–purpose machinery, enabling the firm to manufacture a wider range of product types in shorter runs. Most significantly, JIT demands cooperation from all stages of the production process and usually requires mechanisms for labour flexibility and teamwork, with implications for the organization structure.

At the Toyota factory, the system is controlled by an information system known as 'Kanban'. This is a system of cards which informs how much is to be produced by each process and the precise quantity each process should withdraw from the previous stage, which may be either another process, a materials store, or even a supplier. In Toyota, the 'Kanban' system is extended to its subcontractors, who must conform to the precise delivery requirements of the parent factory.

Whilst JIT and Kanban can strengthen the ties between company and supplier, as we saw in our earlier discussion, the system can place considerable pressure on subcontractors, who are expected to be at the call of the parent company. The system can only work given the willingness of suppliers to participate. This situation has frustrated some Japanese companies operating in Britain and led to protracted negotiations with British supply companies, some of which find the demands placed upon them too great for the rewards involved.

Quality Circles. Whilst these are attributed to Japan, their pedigree dates back to production committees in First World War Britain and participative management in the USA. Nonetheless it was in Japan where they spread in popularity from their inauguration in 1963. They comprise small groups of employees who work together and who volunteer to meet regularly to solve job–related problems, especially to discuss ways of improving the production process and product quality. They are supervisor–led and have the authority to implement change.

Attempts to introduce them in other countries have met with mixed results (Bradley and Hill, 1983). Those that fail generally do so because of underlying distrust between management and worker and scepticism on the part of management. In Japan they thrive on more cooperative workplace relations, but more particularly, as in Germany, on an underlying ethos that stresses product quality. Toyota sees quality as the responsibility of all workers and has even devised its own name for a system of autonomous defects control, which they term 'autonomation'.

The relative failure of the 'Quality Circle' idea in Britain does not imply a lack of interest in quality. As we have seen from our discussion of organizational culture (Chapter 3) and quality control earlier in this chapter, firms appear to be taking different routes to quality assurance. All the signs indicate that whilst the 'Quality Circle' may be a passing fashion, JIT may well become the norm for manufacturing industry and the pattern of the future. In essence it focusses on the precise planning of production operations and, in so doing, provides guidelines for non–manufacturing as well as manufacturing.

Organizational aspects of production

The centrality of the production function to an organization means that more often than not, the nature of the organization is significantly influenced by the nature of the production process. In this section we will explore the interaction between the production function and the organizational elements of our model. After a brief review of organization size, we will devote this chapter to the inter–related elements of structure, goals and organizational culture.

Production and organization size

The size of the firm, expressed both in terms of numbers employed and capital invested, has a close relationship with the production function. A firm dedicated to mass production is invariably large, both in terms of the number of employees and capital investment. A mass producer of motor cars, such as Ford or General Motors, will employ many thousands of workers at any one of their assembly plants throughout the world, as well as having a substantial investment in flow–line technology. As with most elements of the Business in Context model, the influence is two–way. The sheer size and complexity of the production process in a mass producer of automobiles will influence the size of the workforce and the capital employed. By the same token the size of the firm and its output requirements will determine the precise nature of the production system and in particular the production technology. For example, only the largest of firms with high outputs are able to invest in highly automated production systems at profit.

The relationship persists in other types of business too. The multinational hamburger chain, McDonalds, which specializes in the mass production of a limited range of hamburgers, employs thousands in a variety of outlets throughout the world. Whilst McDonalds's investment in production technology may not be as high as a car manufacturer's, the cost of leasing prime sites in urban areas represents a considerable investment. The production technology employed in an oil refinery requires only a small proportion of labour to that employed in mass production technologies, yet the emphasis on sophisticated process technology means that capital investment is generally much higher. A very large insurance firm will almost certainly use a factory–style flow–line for the processing of the very large numbers of policies it has to handle.

The relationship between size and the production system reveals itself most clearly through the way the production process is organized and its impact upon organization structure.

Production and organization structure

In Chapter 3, we introduced the popular claim that production technology and size have probably a greater influence on organization structure than any other variable. We argued then that the relationship also involved a number of other variables such as strategy, culture and the behaviour of interest groups. Nevertheless, since the production function represents the firm's central activity it would be somewhat surprising if the structure did not reflect both the technology and the strategies associated with producing the goods and services of the organization. There are clear overlaps with our discussion of structure in Chapter 3, and you are advised to refer to the relevant parts of that chapter.

We base our analysis in this section around the classification offered by Joan Woodward, to which we have referred in Chapters 2 and 3. She and her research team studied a large number of manufacturing firms in South East Essex and identified three main types of production technology; unit and small batch, large batch and mass, and process production. The three types accounted for key variations in organization structure. Variations occurred in the number of levels in the hierarchy, the span of control of each manager, the nature of job descriptions, the degree of written communication and the extent of functional specialization (Woodward, 1965). For example, a small batch system is depicted by a more flexible structure than a mass production plant. The most important thing to Woodward was not simply the nature of these variances but that structural design should be matched to the nature of the prevailing technology. Woodward was thus one of the earliest exponents of contingency theory (explained in Chapter 1). For instance a small batch producer could only be successful if it adopted a flexible structure, and that business failure could be attributed to a firm adopting a structure that was inappropriate to its production technology.

We will use a slightly expanded version of Woodward's classification to illustrate the relationship between the production system and organization structure. As we have mentioned, Woodward based her work on manufacturing industry, but the classification may be used to examine structural differences in other types of business as well.

Project production. This is a very specific kind of production system in which the entire production process is committed to the completion of a single task to customer requirements, as in the case of building a ship, fulfilling a major construction contract, developing computer software, or carrying out an extensive management consultancy exercise. The organization structure usually comprises a project team, specifically created for the project in question. In Case 5.4, the Baystate Bank created a project group to introduce automatic teller machines and integrate the work of several banks in the group. Upon completion of the project, the structure is usually disbanded. Many large construction companies use this arrangement within a broader matrix framework (Chapter 3 has a fuller discussion of matrix systems).

Unit and small batch production. Both project and small batch production can be classified as 'jobbing' operations. Whereas most projects are carried out on the customer's own site, small batch production is not. It may, like a project, comprise the production of a single item to customer specification. More often it represents the production of a small number of items. In manufacturing, the organization tends to be focused around a number of processes on general purpose machines, manned by skilled labour. The organization hierarchy tends to assume a somewhat flat shape. Examples of this type of organization would include an engineering company manufacturing precision parts for aeroplane engines, or a high–class restaurant serving a limited number of customers each night.

Large batch and mass production. In manufacturing, the move from small to large batch production usually involves a shift to assembly line methods. In most types of large batch production, equipment is specifically designed around a particular product or range of products, and involves considerable machinery in the movement of goods and materials. At its most extreme as in a car plant, this represents mass production on a grand scale, but most mass market domestic products are made in this way. The typical mass production organization is labour intensive, utilizing semi–skilled labour in repetitive jobs offering little discretion to individual workers. The system is highly bureaucratized with a correspondingly larger number of management levels, inspectors, progress chasers and the like than in small batch production. Firms that come into this category usually have a combination of production types. Components tend to be manufactured in large batches in a scaling up of typical jobbing arrangements, whereas assembly tends to be carried out using a flow–line method.

Similar organization structures can be found in those service organizations catering for mass markets, such as a high street bank, a bus company or a major airline.

Process production. At its most extreme, large batch production represents an almost continuous flow of materials through the process. With such industries as the manufacture of chemicals or the refining of oil, true process production emerges, comprising equipment specifically designed to handle large volumes. In such organizations, the workforce generally operates in small teams dealing with a particular aspect of the process, using cognitive rather than manual skills, and having much more discretion than in assembly line work. Consequently there tends to be less management engaged in quantity and quality control, and in most cases these functions are automated. Such organizations are typified by rather tall hierarchies, but this reflects complex grading systems more often than management control.

The changes that are typified by a shift from jobbing to process operations are summarized in Figure 6.5.

So far we have presented the classification of production systems as

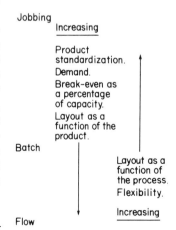

Figure 6.5 Variations in production systems.

A patent agency is a private firm offering a legal service to its clients to enable them to obtain patent protection for their inventions and innovations (Chapter 5 has a fuller discussion of the role of patents). A patent will protect an invention by giving a manufacturer a twenty year monopoly for his product in this country. The patent agent also obtains for his client patents in other countries. In addition most patent agencies also deal with the protection of trademarks, registered designs, and offer advice on other related matters.

The process of obtaining a patent begins by the agent taking instructions from the client. In this case the client may be an individual inventor, a company, the patent department in a firm, or a solicitor acting on behalf of a client. In the case of foreign companies wishing to apply for patents in the United Kingdom, the agent will normally deal with a patent agent from the client's own country. Acting on the instructions from the client, the patent agent prepares a patent application which includes a specification describing the invention. In the case of incoming applications from abroad, the foreign patent agent will normally provide this specification, but it will have to be reviewed in the light of UK practice and, where necessary, translated.

The patent application is then filed with the Patent Office, a government department, whose job is the careful scrutiny of patent applications and the granting of patents if they meet the necessary criteria. The application process is effectively a negotiation process between the Patent Office and the agent. The Patent Office normally initiates each stage of the process and sets a deadline for the agent to reply. Failure to respond in time will result in the entire process being terminated. This system also pertains for each of the countries where patent protection is sought. Success at each stage of the process ends with the granting of a patent.

It can be seen from this that the work of a patent agent involves the continuous meeting of deadlines. It is therefore essential for a patent agency to have appropriate support systems to ensure that individual patent agents are kept aware of approaching deadlines and that the necessary action is taken in time.

When a patent has been granted, renewal fees have to be paid periodically to maintain the patent in force. In most countries such fees are payable annually. A patent agency therefore needs a renewal system so that clients can be asked at each renewal if the fee is to be paid and so that any action can be taken in time. This is a high volume, low income operation which is generally undertaken by clerical staff, usually employing a computer. Some firms subcontract this task to another organization altogether, such as a specialist computer bureau.

comprising four discrete types. In more recent years the search for increased lexibility of operations has resulted in more hybrid forms of organization. The goal of flexibility is uppermost in the development of group technology in manufacturing, and associated developments in the use of autonomous work groups.

Group technology. The idea of group technology emerged from the USSR in the 1950s and was refined in Germany, Britain and the USA. Its aim is to satisfy the consumer demand for flexibility, the management demand for increased efficiency, and the individual worker's need for greater involvement. The first stage in setting up a group technology system is to group the manufacture of all similar components together. These are referred to as 'families' of components. Each component is made from start to finish by a small group of workers operating a range of machines in a flow–line arrangement. Workers are both mobile and flexible, moving from machine to machine according to the logic of the flow of production. A common form of organization is the autonomous work group, referred to in the previous section.

The claimed advantages of such a system are as follows.

☐ Speed, by the reduction of the manufacturing cycle, with less queuing and work in progress.
☐ Increased flexibility.
☐ Reduced operating costs through less work in progress, reduced inventory and less scrap.
☐ Improved control by giving the group responsibility for both production quality and the achievement of output targets.
☐ Improved job satisfaction.

A case quoted frequently in the literature is that of Serck–Audco Valves in Shropshire, where claims were made that an introduction of group technology resulted, over a six year period from 1961, in an increase of output per employee of 50%, a reduction in stock of 44%, a reduced manufacturing time from twelve to four weeks and an overall sales increase, (presumably from improved delivery capability), of 32%. It was estimated that the capital investment involved was recouped four times over by the savings made on stock reduction alone (quoted in Williamson 1972).

Whilst cases such as Serck–Audco offer a glowing reference for the introduction of group technology, as with FMS we must be careful in our attribution of cause and effect in such instances. Dramatic sales increases following the introduction of a new method of production organization may be the cause of other factors such as an increased demand for the product, the closure of a major competitor, a change in product design, or even a new incentive scheme for sales staff. It is often difficult in such cases to isolate the required variables to make an accurate assessment. This frequently leads to controversy over the real impact of changes in production technology and organization.

The use of group technology and autonomous work groups are means of achieving greater flexibility, and the principles are transferable to other kinds of production system in the service sector. However, the systems may not work without the cooperation of both management and the workforce and may in fact be unnecessary in those businesses where flexibility is not a key issue.

Organizational goals and culture

> Manufacturing organizations tend to attract the attention of general managers the way airlines do; one only notices them when they're late, when ticket prices rise, or when there's a crash.
>
> (Hayes and Schmenner, 1978, p 105)

The implication behind this quotation is that management goals are rarely seen in terms of production; financial goals and marketing goals are much more common. We have already indicated elsewhere in this chapter that such a view may be changing. The attempts of many firms to focus on improved quality, often backed by government initiatives such as British Standard 5750, reveal an attempt to shift the culture of the organization around production issues. The Philips factory, manufacturing television sets at Croydon, attempted to reshape the prevailing organizational culture by redrawing the traditional organization chart to show production at the centre and all other functional areas being subsidiary to, and either feeding into or out of production.

The notion of an organization culture based around production is the major theme in Hayes and Wheelwright's 1984 analysis of American manufacturing industry. They support the view that a strong manufacturing base is essential to a healthy economy and that a major handicap is often the attitude of management towards the production function. They see the prevailing culture of the typical American manufacturing firm being dominated by accounting, and in particular the need for a quick return on investment. Managers are highly mobile and have little interest in developing the technical know–how essential for new product development and improving the manufacturing system before they move on to better their careers. Short–term profit is seen as a measure of success, and there is inadequate investment in R&D and plant improvement. Portfolio management through the buying of other companies becomes the substitute for development. Instead of production the emphasis is placed on marketing as the key function to stimulate existing markets through advertising and re–packaged products.

The solution would appear to lie in a greater investment in innovation and, for manufacturing firms, a development of their own machine–tool industry. The development of dedicated machine tools is held to be essential to gain a competitive advantage in the product market. For many firms, this will require a change in the corporate culture which stresses technical competence as its key criterion This is achieved by the selection and development of technically qualified managers, a much greater investment in technical training, and a much greater focus on quality by all employees.

The Hayes and Wheelwright hypothesis draws heavily upon comparisons with Germany and Japan. Whilst the analysis is appealing, their views of both Germany and Japan are subjective and often idealized. Furthermore, we have already seen in the previous chapter that the relationship between innovation and economic growth are speculative. Nevertheless, accounts such as these emphasize the importance of production strategies and it is to these we now turn.

Production strategies

We have already established in this chapter that production is the central function in all organizations. We have also noted that there is often a conflict between the two objectives of operating efficiency and achieving customer satisfaction. We can now restate those objectives in terms of a number of key strategic elements. These are costing and pricing, product quality, dependability, and product flexibility in terms of product range and volume.

These objectives have formed an underlying theme to most of this chapter. They also form the link between production and other functional areas. All the factors are dependent upon product design and development, which we dealt with in Chapter 5, and we shall see in the next chapter how such factors form the basis of marketing strategy. Achieving production objectives would be impossible without the necessary finance and account-ing control mechanisms (Chapter 9), and without recruiting and training a workforce with the necessary skills (Chapter 8).

The specific contribution made by production strategy lies in the following.

☐ Establishing the level of quality for the product or service.
☐ Being responsible for the firm's capital assets and therefore having a major contribution to overall costs.
☐ Establishing sufficient capacity to meet market demand.

An important element of this contribution is the manipulation of the various objectives established at the beginning of this section. Whilst an ultimate aim might be to maximize the twin objectives of operating efficiency and customer satisfaction, we have already noted the difficulties of achieving this in practice. A more practical strategy may be the emphasis of certain characteristics to gain an increased competitive advantage over its rivals, a process we shall illustrate below.

Pricing strategies will be examined more thoroughly in the next chapter. The contribution of the production function to price lies in the cost of developing the product itself, any raw materials costs, and the cost of operating the production system. A firm may see low price as its key marketing strategy. If profit levels are to be maintained then the produc-tion system must be capable of delivering high volumes, and there is a need to keep capital, labour and operating costs as low as possible. As we see in Case 6.3, one of Grundig's major strategies for improving its poor position in the 1980s was a focus on operating costs. There may be an important trade–off here with quality. A restaurant which attempts to reduce costs by buying cheaper raw materials, may find this not to the liking of its customers, and may lose trade and ultimately its reputation.

We saw both in the last chapter and earlier in this one how product quality often gave firms the edge over cheaper versions of the same product, and how some companies build their strategy around this. As we have just seen, this can be a costly strategy not only in terms of raw materials and product presentation, but also in terms of the need to employ skilled, trained staff, the need for establishing good quality control mechanisms, and especially the need to keep improving and updating the product or service. For some firms, like Bang and Olufsen, this can be a successful strategy. For Grundig however, the advantages of a reputation for high quality goods was eliminated by poor control over production operations (Case 6.3).

Dependability refers to the cabability of the firm to deliver its goods or services to the customer's satisfaction, not just in terms of quality and price, but more importantly on time. This can be achieved by carrying large stocks, but this can be costly, as once again illustrated in the Grundig case. A more effective strategy may well involve investing in production systems to ensure effective scheduling, and by paying attention to employee pay and conditions to enhance motivation and reduce absenteeism and labour turnover

The flexibility to alter products and meet volume demands with minimum lead time are often strategies for survival in highly competitive or, in the case of Orlake Records (Case 6.1), declining markets. Flexibility in terms of product type and volume does require a flexible and often multi–skilled labour force, as well as good relations with suppliers. Whilst flexibility can be a distinct advantage, there may be just as great an advantage in going for a high volume in a single product market. This allows the firm to take advantage of the 'experience curve', which can result in a virtuous circle of expansion. An increased market share leads to greater experience in operating the production system resulting in lower costs. When these are passed on in the form of lower prices, the result is even greater market penetration. Such a virtuous circle can be enhanced by investment in production technology to reduce operating costs still further. This kind of strategy, while potentially successful in a expanding market, has severe limitations when the market is declining.

Managements need to decide the most appropriate strategy for their organizations. It is possible for firms operating in the same industry to have significantly different strategies. Texas Instruments has traditionally opted for high volume production, reasonable prices and high market share of calculators and measuring equipment. Hewlett–Packard on the other hand, operating in the same markets, has concentrated on low volume, high quality, innovative products.

Different strategies can even exist within the same organization. The Roux restaurant chain in London operates at the most expensive end of the market in its restaurant 'Le Gavroche', producing highly individual meals at high prices in luxury surroundings. Another of its restaurants, 'Gavvers' serves set meals at a fixed price and aims at value for money. At yet another restaurant, 'Rouxl Brittania', a high volume of pre–prepared vacuum packed meals are cooked for a largely lunchtime clientele from neighbouring offices. These different strategies mix all the elements we have identified above. In the case of the Roux organization there is a link in terms of staff development. The different strategies enable staff to be

Grundig is a German company with its main manufacturing operations in Nürnberg. It is a producer of high quality televisions, video cassette recorders, electronic office equipment and computer controls for CNC machines. It has a reputation for quality and precision which it uses as a marketing theme. It is currently owned by the Grundig family, the Dutch multinational, Philips, and by Swiss banking interests. No one group has overall control, the family still retaining 49% of shares.

The company is the market leader for television sets in Germany. However by 1984 Grundig was operating at an annual loss of DM 290 million. The reasons for the company's decline were several.

☐ In 1983 there were 500 different TV models in stock, some of which had not been made for five years. Stocks of all goods were operating at 28% of sales.
☐ Grundig had invested heavily in the Philips V2000 system of video recording, which proved a marketing failure. As a consequence there is still a large stockholding of such recorders.
☐ The company had suffered badly in the video market at the hands of low-price Japanese competition.
☐ The family control of the company had been highly centralized, traditionally autocratic and somewhat idiosyncratic. Decisions were made that reflected the values of the chairman rather than good business practice in those product markets. Consequently good advice from members of Grundig staff was ignored.

In 1984, faced with these problems and high operating losses, a new chief executive was installed, who came from Philips. The goals of the company under the new regime were to maintain product quality, but to reduce operating costs, to streamline production, and to establish greater control over supplies and stocks. This was achieved through a number of measures.

☐ The model range was reduced quite considerably.
☐ The company invested in a new automated production line for the manufacture of video cassette recorders, to produce high volume output at relatively low operating cost.
☐ The stocks were reduced to 19% of Sales.
☐ Stocks of raw materials and work-in-progress were cut by 14%.
☐ Grundig attempted to rationalize its operations through a joint venture with Blaupunkt. Grundig would make televisions for Blaupunkt who would reciprocate by making car radios for Grundig.
☐ A much greater attention was paid to production planning, cost control and budgeting, as well as a more comprehensive effort to define market sectors.

The new strategies improved turnover per employee by 50%, although the revenue per product was relatively low due to price competition within the industry. The overall impact was measured by the transformation of an operating loss into a profit of DM 50 million by 1986.

(*Source:* A. Fisher, 'The Pain of Recreating a Culture', *Financial Times,* 29 December 1986) trained and developed in less exacting situations before the management has confidence in them operating at the highest level. Most airline companies operate a variety of services on the same route, first class, business class, economy, excursion, stand–by and so on. These are all priced according to the quality of service and the dependability and flexibility offered the customer.

The existence of a number of different pricing strategies for airline seats can be both confusing and annoying, especially when the variability is compounded by a number of market outlets all offering exactly the same product at different prices, which in turn reflect their own costs and profit goals. It is suggested that the most effective production strategy is one where there is a very clear focus. In manufacturing this has been referred to as 'the focused factory' (Skinner, 1974). It refers to a level of consistency both within the production strategy itself and between production and other strategies, thus reinforcing a dominant theme of this chapter and of this book.

Summary

The production function is a transformation process which takes a variety of inputs such as materials and labour, and turns them into goods and services. Viewed in this way the function operates in a variety of industries and settings and is not limited to manufacturing. The main activities of production management involve the design of a system to process inputs and setting up control devices to ensure effective operation. Materials management including purchasing is an important part of the process, especially in manufacturing industry.

A central problem in the management of production systems is the reconciliation of customer satisfaction with the efficient utilization of resources. Traditionally techniques of production management have emphasized efficiency. However there is a growing awareness of other elements, such as the flexibility to respond to changing market demand, and a need to focus on quality.

It is, however, misleading to see production solely in terms of responding to external forces. The function has a central position in nearly all types of organization. In manufacturing, an effective production function has a significant impact on the economy. Concern about deindustrialization has resulted in Britain's regional policy, as well as a growing interest in the way more successful economies view and operate their production systems. The centrality of the function means that it exerts considerable influence on organization structure, although the particular influence of production technology is quite complex.

Changes in technology have particular relevance for production systems, both in terms of product and process innovation. In manufacturing the current debate concerns the likely impact of 'new technology' on both the efficiency and effectiveness of production systems, with the cost of installing such systems as FMS a real constraint. For the labour force, production has considerable influence over employment patterns, wage levels, health and safety, and job satisfaction.

Production strategies are a core element of a firm's overall corporate strategy. The most successful production strategies would appear to be those which display a clear focus and are consistent with the strategies of the other functional areas.

Further reading

Good basic texts are E.S. Buffa, *Modern Production/Operations Management*, 7th ed., (John Wiley, 1983), and R. Wild, Essentials of Production and Operations Management, (Holt, Rinehart and Winston, 1985). The latter offers a perspective on production that is not confined to manufacturing industry, as does J.B. Dilworth, *Production and Operations Management: Manufacturing and Non–manufacturing*, (Random House, 1986). An interesting and personal view looking at strategic, cultural, and comparative issues can be found in R.H. Hayes and S.C. Wheelwright, *Restoring Our Competitive Edge*, (John Wiley, 1984). This book deals with manufacturing industry as does the useful book of readings offered by V. Bignell *et al.* eds. *Manufacturing Systems: Context, Applications and Techniques* (Basil Blackwell, 1985). J. Woodward, *Industrial Organization: Theory and Practice* (OUP, 1965), while dated, offers useful insights into the relationship between production and structure.

Discussion

1. Examine the similarities and differences to be found in the production systems of manufacturing and non–manufacturing organizations. How do the production priorities differ in a firm producing television sets for a mass market from those of a large regional hospital?

2. Design a systems model for a firm like Marks and Spencer, which shows both the types of transformations that are taking place and the other systems with which the firm interacts. What are the key activities and key relationships?

3. What strategies can be employed to solve the conflicting objectives of operating efficiency and customer satisfaction?

4. What types of impact can product design have on the production process?

5. What are the key issues in the design and operation of a production system for a polytechnic or a university? What are the key control issues?

6. Identify the operational aspects that influence scheduling in a restaurant, at an airport, and for a major national daily newspaper. What strategies and techniques would you employ to solve scheduling problems in these three situations?

7. Why is materials management an important aspect of manufacturing industry?

8. What opportunities and threats are posed by the introduction of new technology in the manufacturing process?

9. How do you establish an organization culture which focuses on production? How would you involve the workforce more in the production process?

10. To what extent is the structure of an organization determined by the production system?

11. Examine the production strategies employed by Orlake Records and Grundig in Cases 6.1 and 6.3 respectively. What are the major influences which have shaped those strategies and what other strategies could the management have employed in the same situation? What do the cases tell us about the relationship between production and the other functional areas?

12. What strategies and techniques of production management are used by the patent agency in Case 6.2?

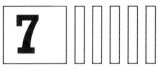

In this chapter we will examine the nature of marketing as it applies to different types of organization. We will attempt to define marketing and chart the development of the marketing concept. The various elements of marketing, research, product, price, promotion, distribution and buyer behaviour will be analysed in turn, as will the key concepts of branding, the product life cycle, and market segmentation. As in our treatment of all functional activities we will use the Business in Context model to look at the environmental, organizational and strategic aspects of marketing. In the two previous chapters we stressed the interface between innovation, production and marketing. This theme will be taken up in this chapter, particularly in the discussion of product development, the relationship of marketing with production technology, the place of marketing in the organization structure, and most significantly when we examine the design of marketing strategies.

Decisions in marketing generally focus on products and services, their prices, their promotion, and the means through which they are distributed. In most advanced industrial societies individuals are faced with a vast choice of such products and services, which can be acquired in a variety of ways, often at a range of prices. Advertising is a pervasive feature of modern life, often so glamorized by the media that the management decision to change its advertising agency is, for a firm like Guinness, a matter of high drama to be played out in the national press. For such reasons marketing, probably more than any other business activity, attracts strong positive and negative feelings. Many members of the public as well as many business studies students associate careers in marketing with the glamour and fictional life-styles of the people portrayed in advertisements. Such a view is misleading, for marketing is much more than advertising and the tasks can involve the much less glamorous work of collecting detailed market information and the problems of getting metal containers made in Mansfield to a customer's factory in Bromsgrove.

It is this high profile nature of marketing that attracts its critics. Marketing is variously accused of creating (among other things), an excessively materialistic society, planned product obsolescence, the high-pressure selling of poor quality products and the excessive political power of the multinational. Borrowing themes from Vance Packard, marketers are seen as 'The Hidden Persuaders' or 'The Waste Makers' or both. The marketers would counter this, listing their credits as the development and supply of products and services demanded by consumers, the provision of essential information for the shopper, and the use of marketing to create public awareness for such socially acceptable goals as improving a nation's health.

Definitions and orientations

Marketing has been variously defined. It is seen as a management activity whereby suitable products are presented to the market in order to make a profit. It is portrayed as an interactive activity, an exchange process in which consumers play an important role, as illustrated by Kotler.

> Marketing is human activity directed at satisfying needs and wants through exchange processes.
>
> (Kotler, 1983, p 6)

Another type of definition elevates marketing from both a management function and an exchange process to a philosophy to guide the entire business operation, as illustrated by Drucker.

> Marketing. . . is not a specialized activity at all. It encompasses the whole business. It is the whole business seen from the point of view of its final result, that is from the customer's point of view. Concern and responsibility for marketing must therefore permeate all areas of the enterprise.
>
> (Drucker, 1968, p 54)

The different definitions of marketing reflect different approaches to the subject. Five such approaches are generally identified.

☐ The *production* orientation assumes that consumers will buy whatever is available, and the emphasis should be on production and distribution. This approach to marketing works best when demand is greater than supply and goods and services are relatively easy to sell.

☐ The *product* orientation assumes that goods and services will sell themselves, usually because of inherent quality and performance characteristics, and that sales promotion is largely unnecessary. This approach also assumes that consumers are generally well informed.

☐ The *selling* orientation assumes that consumers will not buy sufficient goods and services unless they are persuaded to do so by advertising, sales promotion and incentives to the sales force. This approach is often necessary when supply outstrips demand, or in the case of what Kotler (1983) defines as 'unsought' goods, such as encyclopaedias, or with the promotion of political candidates.

☐ The true *marketing* orientation shifts the attention to the consumer. This approach involves the determination of consumer needs and values and the design and supply of goods and services to satisfy them. The assumption here is that the consumer is sovereign.

☐ *Societal marketing* takes the previous orientation a stage further. The attention is still focussed on the consumer's needs, but the assumption here is that those needs are satisfied in such a way as to enhance the well–being of the consumer and society as a whole; goods and services should be socially acceptable, non–harmful and non–polluting.

These five marketing concepts can be seen in operation across a variety of organizations and products. Precision engineering tools tend to sell on the reputation of the product, whilst certain double glazing and kitchen installation firms use aggressive promotion and selling techniques. In some ways the five marketing concepts represent the historical development of marketing. The production concept is well illustrated by the expanding population and market in Victorian Britain, whilst the selling concept coincides with the development of mass production and the depression of the 1920s and 1930s, particularly in the USA. The elevation of the consumer is by contrast a relatively recent phenomenon, although we could argue that successful businesses have always practised a true marketing orientation. Certainly societal marketing can be traced to the greater social awareness of the 1960s and 1970s and the growth of consumer organizations.

If textbooks and professional journals are a reliable guide, then the most popular view of marketing today as held by its practitioners is one which focusses on consumers and the determination and satisfaction of their needs. This view is not without its sceptics. J.K. Galbraith (1972) challenges the consumer–oriented marketing concept, which he calls the 'accepted sequence'. The growth of big business, the complexity of modern technologies and the correspondingly massive investments in product development have disenfranchised the consumer. 'The revised sequence' has taken over in which complex products, beyond the ken of the average consumer, are developed at great cost. The emphasis shifts from the satisfaction to the creation of consumer demand through investment in promotion to safeguard investments in product development.

A discussion which focusses entirely on individual consumers and manufactured products presents a somewhat restricted view of marketing. In the next section we examine the extent to which the marketing is applied in other contexts.

Marketing in different contexts

Marketing as an activity is carried out in a variety of contexts. The most obvious context is of course the sale of manufactured goods to individual consumers as end–users. Marketing also occurs when a firm manufacturing petrol tanks deals with vehicle and lawnmower manufacturers and the like, who use petrol tanks in their products; this is sometimes referred to as industrial or organizational marketing. Equally it is not only manufactured products which may be marketed, but services such as banking and management consultancy. Holiday resorts have always marketed themselves to attract tourists, but in recent years other places, such as Milton Keynes and Telford, have engaged in marketing to attract business development. In addition to the marketing of products and services, some firms actively promote themselves by presenting a corporate image to the public. Marketing is far from being the sole prerogative of profit–making organizations as governments, political parties and charities have discovered. We will deal with each of these aspects of marketing in turn.

Organizational marketing

The concept of industrial marketing can be misleading since it implies the marketing of industrial components for the use in further manufacturing processes as in the case of our petrol tank. Organizational marketing is a more useful term since it can accurately embrace any marketing exchange between two or more organizations. Retail organizations like Marks and Spencer engage in marketing when they buy finished goods from a variety of different sources. In modern times the state has become a very powerful consumer and a very large market in its own right. The state can use this power for social and political ends, by awarding contracts to firms in economically depressed areas or by withdrawing contracts from those firms who do not adhere to government policy on something like wage levels. In general, organizational marketing differs from consumer marketing in a number of ways. Whereas consumers buy goods and services for a variety of reasons which may include less tangible considerations of status, industrial buyers tend to be more concerned with the utility of the product in their own process, as well as its contribution to their costs. Organizational buying is institutionalized and is often carried out by professionals using formalized procedures involving quotations and contracts and often as part of a close on–going relationship between buyer and seller. In the case of a firm such as Marks and Spencer, buyers will specify in detail quality levels, and often how the product must be made. We saw this illustrated in Chapter 2 by the demands made by Japanese manufacturers on their components suppliers.

The marketing of services

It is only recently that many service organizations have fully acknowledged the need to consider marketing in any serious way. The reluctance of the service industry to engage in marketing may be due to the relatively small size of many service operations, the intangible nature of many of their products, and, in the case of the professions, the constraints imposed by their own professional bodies. Significant changes have taken place. The service industry has grown and become fiercely competitive. The major banks facing competition from building societies and other financial institutions have invested heavily in advertising and other kinds of sales promotion. A student opening a bank account for the first time is wooed by a variety of offers such as free overdrafts and gifts. In addition the banks have been careful to target markets such as students, small businesses, and more recently those needing pensions, as well as extending their distribution network by reintroducing Saturday opening and installing automatic cash machines. Airline companies have decided to package their products in a much more tangible way; business travellers are now invited to buy British Airways' 'Club Class' or Cathay Pacific's 'Marco Polo' class and enjoy a number of distinctive product advantages. The lifting of advertising restrictions on the legal profession in Britain has led in some cases to vigorous promotion of price differentials on services such as conveyancing.

The marketing of images

Organizations such as The Post Office, British Petroleum and ICI have spent heavily to convey a specific corporate image, which may well stress efficiency, experience, breadth of operations, company size, social responsibility or all of these characteristics. Theatrical agents have always existed to promote their clients, but the concept of marketing people has been extended to present any celebrity figure who may be 'packaged' to enhance their earning capacity through paid public appearances. The marketing of ideas has also grown in popularity. In 1987 the British government launched a major campaign to inform the population about AIDS, and anti–smoking campaigns by a number of different organizations are now commonplace.

The case of The Post Office represents another broadening of the marketing concept to incorporate the public sector and non profit–making organizations such as charities. Political elections in Britain are now fought out by parties who invest heavily in marketing an image as well as an ideology. The Labour Party, conscious of a need to widen its appeal after three successive election defeats, has targetted the young professional middle classes as future voters and tailored its appeal accordingly. The marketing of political parties presents an interesting combination of the marketing of organizational image, of ideas and of people.

Governments themselves use marketing. Between the financial years 1986–7 and 1987–8 there had been an increase of 90% in government expenditure on marketing of all types and a 287% increase in advertising alone. In all £88 million was spent on press and television advertising. For the 'European Single Market 1992' campaign, the government has allocated £6.7 million for television advertising and almost £4 million for other forms of advertising and promotion. Most government departments have large press and public relations offices; sixty PR staff are employed by the Department of Employment and fifty–three in the Northern Ireland office. (the *Independent*, 12 August 1988, the *Sunday Times*, 4 September 1988.)

The use of marketing by governments raises ethical issues. It invariably supports the particular ideology of the party in power, and may be abused by some individuals to promote their own political careers.

Export marketing

This is often considered as a separate marketing context requiring adaptions of the product, its price and the way it is promoted to account for differences in cultural expectations or constraints imposed by the governments of nation states. Such differences have led many firms to appoint local agents in different countries to market their products or else engage in a joint venture with a local firm. The Danish brewery Carlsberg engages in such joint production ventures throughout the world, either to ease the problems of distribution, to overcome government restrictions on the operation of foreign firms, or both. Not all firms place such a distinction on international marketing. In Case 7.1 Woodville Polymer Engineering refuses to differentiate between home and export marketing as a deliberate strategy.

The elements of marketing

We have already seen that the marketing concept focusses on the consumer and his needs. Marketing strategy is enshrined in the concept of the marketing mix, popularly referred to as the four Ps, comprising product, price, promotion, and place. Consumers constitute an implicit rather than explicit element of the marketing mix, but we shall include them under the heading of buyer behaviour. In addition to these considerations an effective strategy requires information, usually through the process of market research. We are therefore able to identify six key elements of marketing; market research, product, price, promotion, place and buyer behaviour. The six elements will be treated as separate entities although in practice there is considerable overlap. The price of a product, especially when higher than comparable offerings, can be used as a product feature and even a method of promotion stressing the exclusivity of the offering; this in turn depends upon the consumer perceiving and acknowledging a relationship between price and quality. Packaging is a means of protecting the product, an important form of promotion, and a means of facilitating the distribution of the product. The concept of place is concerned with the way the product or service reaches the consumer; in some cases free delivery is presented as a feature of the product to mark it out from competitors. We reinforce these six elements by examining the important concepts of branding, segmentation and the product life cycle in the next section.

Market research

Market research deals with the collection and analysis of information about the other five aspects of marketing. Four types of market research can be distinguished, although there is considerable overlap between them and most firms engage in all types.

☐ Management needs to possess accurate information about its current marketing activities. This will include the number and value of the sales of its current range of products and services, and its market share compared to its competitors. Such information can provide useful feedback on sales variations by region and also by salesman, and may well provide the basis for implementing changes.

☐ Management needs to be aware of developments that are occurring in the market place which might have a direct or indirect bearing upon the

This case looks at changes that occurred in the marketing strategy at Woodville in the mid 1970s and the factors that have influenced the development of the company since that time.

In the mid 1970s, Woodville Polymer Engineering (Woodville Rubbers as it was then known) was a producer of rubber components for the engineering industry, manufacturing such items as rubber seals for the automobile and domestic appliance industry. It was situated in Ross-on-Wye, but had a sister company operating as an autonomous unit in Swadlingcote. Both companies were owned by the American multinational Colt. The parent company's interest was solely financial and Woodville's operating decisions were its own.

The company had a reputation in the industry as being technically competent and as having good customer relations. A major strength was its staff, many of whom had had previous experience in the engineering industry. Despite this apparently comfortable position, the management decided to adopt a more positive marketing strategy to strengthen position as illustrated by the following actions.

☐ The company identified its business as engineering. They had never considered themselves as mere sellers of rubber to the engineering industry, but now they saw their role as making money for their customers. The later change of name identified them more closely with the industry they served.

☐ They set about building an even closer relationship with their customers. Production managers were encouraged to talk to customers about their requirements and in general products were tailored to customer needs. In one of the cases where a customer (Skefko) was advised to modify its proposals to fit an existing Woodville product, the result was a considerable saving for the customer. Customers were encouraged to visit the plant and talk to staff. In general the entire operation was marketing-led and coordinated by sales engineers.

☐ Nine specific industrial markets were targeted. The nine were chosen for their growth potential and that in each market there were five firms or less who controlled 80% of the output. Potential customers were then checked out on financial and product viability. Where possible Woodville's sales engineers were recruited from the industry they served. The industries chosen included domestic appliances, water pump manufacturers, mining and reprographics.

☐ A special target was mass production industries such as the domestic appliance and the motor industry. Woodville was aiming to have 50% of its business in this market, and recognized that a key factor would be the reliability of delivery to establish credibility as a relatively small operator in a large market. In addition, the company was developing work with the Ministry of Defence.

☐ As many of its customers operated internationally, Woodville drew no distinction between home and export orders.

CASE 7.1

WOODVILLE POLYMER ENGINEERING

Continued over page

Continued from previous page

The new philosophy was rewarded by increased profitability and in particular a 600% increase in exports from 1973 to 1976. By 1976 exports accounted for some 40% of business.

The position began to change after 1976. The effects of a worldwide recession began to have an impact in two directions. Firstly, there was a dramatic slowdown in some of Woodville's main markets, especially the motor and domestic products industry. Secondly, the parent company, Colt, found itself considerably overstretched in the American market, used Woodville's financial surpluses to protect other ventures, and consequently reduced investment in Woodville itself.

The result for Woodville was a fall in productivity, sales and profitability. The recession had also affected Woodville's competitors, except that they may have been better placed to keep up with technological developments in the industry. Nevertheless Woodville maintained its position as one of the top ten firms in its industry, perhaps a direct result of its marketing strategy.

By the mid 1980s Colt, intent on rationalization, saw Woodville as an offshore concern in a different business from its core activities. The firm was sold to the British owned Doughty company for around £35 million, and installed as part of the Doughty Polymer Group in 1987. By that time the company's profitability had fallen to around 8%, but this compared favourably with the Doughty Polymer Group's 5% return.

The company continues to pursue its marketing policy, and current growth areas include an extension of the reprographics business to include all kinds of paper-handling equipment and increased work with the MOD. Export business continues to be a major feature and at 50% is still growing.

(*Sources:* Rines, 1976, *Company Information*, 1988)

business. This might include information on new products brought out by other companies, the relative prices of goods in shops, how competitors are promoting their products, or whether changes are taking place in the way consumers buy goods. This second activity is sometimes referred to as market intelligence, for it enables management to build up a picture of the market in whch they operate and chart the significant changes and trends so that strategies may be initiated and changed as appropriate.

☐ Market research involves feasibility testing to assess the market potential of a new product or service; to assess the consumer reaction to pricing policies or price changes; to assess the reaction of consumers to a particular advertisement and so on. When a company like Rowntree–Mackintosh launch a new chocolate bar, the product has invariably been tested on a wide range of people, and their reactions to appearance, taste, price, value for money, and sometimes the method of promotion carefully assessed. An essential element of feasibility research is an analysis of the market itself, especially its size and composition in terms of the age, sex, and occupation.

KEY CONCEPT 7.2

THE MARKETING MIX

The marketing mix generally refers to an overall marketing strategy which involves the manipulation of four key elements. These are decisions concerning the nature of the product and its design; decisions about price; decisions about sales promotion, advertising and customer awareness; and decisions concerning distribution. These four factors are popularly referred to as the 4 P's; product, price, promotion and place. Two important aspects of this are not made explicit. These are market research and buyer behaviour. Decisions about the marketing mix cannot be made without researching the market in all its aspects and that includes a thorough understanding of buyer behaviour.

☐ The fourth type of research is a mixture of the previous three in that it collects information to evaluate a product and the way it is priced, promoted and acquired by the consumer as an ongoing process after the initial launch.

Individual organizations, especially if they are large enough, can do their own market research. However it has developed as a specialist activity over the last twenty–five years or so, and numerous agencies have arisen offering a variety of services. A firm like Audits of Great Britain, for example, operates multinationally and among its many services offered to clients provides regular television viewing figures so enabling firms to target and evaluate television advertising campaigns. Such firms provide their clients with regular market intelligence on market share and trends, tasks often beyond the resources of an individual company. Some market research agencies specialize by product or the type of service offered; some for example have built up reputations for consumer interviewing.

The product

In our discussion of the different contexts of marketing we saw how the term 'product' has a wide connotation and may include manufactured goods, services, people, organizations, places and ideas. A product comprises a number of elements apart from its more obvious features. These can include a brand name, packaging, after–sales service, delivery, warranty and so on. Marketing needs to consider all these aspects of the product. Free delivery or extended guarantees may be seen as essential product characteristics by some consumers.

A product line is the total number of variations of the same basic product, differentiated by quality, cost or extra features. A car manufacturer will make several versions of the same basic model with variations in engine size, type of gearbox, paintwork and so on. The breadth of a product line is closely related to the degree of market segmentation, a concept we introduce in the next section.

A product mix is the total number of different products offered by the firm, sometimes referred to as the product portfolio. The size of a firm's product mix can have a significant impact on its profitability, in that the effect of poor performers may be lessened by the income from better selling items. However, too broad a product mix can cause problems of control. In 1982 Guinness, with a large number of highly diverse activities sold off forty of its subsidiaries to achieve a better control of its product portfolio (Earl, 1984).

Marketing considerations are an important input in the process of developing new products. We saw in Chapter 5 that new product development was not only potentially expensive, but also that the risk of failure was high. Extensive market research is needed concerning such aspects as the utility and acceptability of a new product's design, its target market and the likely acceptable price. An estimate may be made about likely future sales, which when set alongside likely development costs is essential in assessing the business viability of a new project.

We will return to consideration of the product in our discussion of branding, segmentation and the product life cycle.

Price

If marketing strategy were based entirely on the analysis of the neo–classical economists, then price would be the most significant feature of that strategy and would be based on the concept of the price elasticity of demand. A product is price elastic if changes in price influence changes in demand. All things being equal an increase in price will lead to a fall in demand and consequently a fall in revenue and vice versa. All things rarely are equal, and consumers can behave in an unpredictable manner. Many factors influence price and pricing strategy, and operate at the environmental, organizational and strategic levels of our model. We deal with some of those factors under the following headings.

Cost. A business firm wishing to make a profit must use the cost of making a product or providing a service as an important base point in setting its prices. However, the sensitivity of most pricing decisions lies less in the cost of raw materials, labour, and the like than the understanding of those factors which may determine the extent of mark–up on the basic cost price. These include most of the factors identified below. An idea often propounded by neo–classical economists is that cost and therefore price are associated with the economies of scale, and that volume production will lead to price reduction. Whilst this may be true for some products there are many exceptions which challenge both the notion of economies of scale and the necessity of tying price to volume production. We return to these arguments in our discussion of the product life cycle and marketing strategies.

Consumer behaviour. The price of a product may well be related to what a consumer can afford and to what he is prepared to pay. These in turn are related to income levels, the consumer's perceptions of quality and value for money, and the consumer's budget for a particular purchase. In purchasing a new camera for a special holiday or a new word–processor for the office of a small business, the consumer's own target price based on what he wants to pay may be the primary factor. The range of products considered will then be limited to those priced within a range around or below the target price. A manufacturer aiming at a particular target market may be best advised to discover the budgeting behaviour of those consumers before setting the price. One of the main functions of promotional activity is of course to influence the perceptions of the consumer. The brewing industry today in Britain has focussed its attention on the lager market. Many brands are deliberately marketed as highly–priced products offering the consumer 'real' quality. This strategy was successfully pursued by the brewers of 'Stella Artois' to establish their product in a highly competitive market. Such strategies depend heavily on 'brand image' (discussed in the next section), fashion and social influences. The lager market is aimed at the young drinker and the social superiority of drinking a particular brand is stressed.

Economic factors. Price is related to the economy in a number of different ways, all of which have a potential impact on an organization's pricing policy. The affluence of consumers will have an obvious influence on their level of budgeting and regional variations may produce differential demand, especially for certain luxury items. The role of the state in managing the economy may affect both demand and prices. The control of interest rates will influence the extent of consumer credit and hence the size of an individual's budget, as will levels of taxation. During periods of high inflation the government may well introduce measures to control prices. A major influence on price for exporters is the currency exchange rate which fluctuates according to the state of the economy. In early 1985 the pound and the dollar approached parity which made many British goods highly attractive in the USA, giving firms such as Jaguar a significant boost to their profits through increased sales. As the dollar weakened against the pound British exports became less attractive, and for 1987–88 Jaguar cars announced significantly reduced profit figures due in no small part to changes in the exchange rate. As a changing exchange rate brings prices of products more into line with competition from domestic suppliers or other countries' imports, then other criteria than price become more important. The relationship is far from simple, and no matter how attractive the price of imported goods may be, it can be offset by delays in delivery, an inadequate distribution network, or a poor after–sales service.

Competition. Many firms price their products by reference to an existing market, basing their price around that offered by competitors for products of similar features and quality.

Management goals. The price of goods is often related to the extent to which managements wish to optimize profit. We saw in Chapter 2 that management goals rarely conform to simple economic models, and are complicated by considerations of power, politics and personal preference. The desire of a group of managers for a larger market share for their products may result in a low price strategy to build up demand. In some firms price may be deliberately used as a promotion strategy to create an image of product quality in the eyes of the consumer.

Organizational size. The size of an organization may give it market power and the ability to manipulate market prices. This is especially true of oligopolies. The Swiss pharmaceutical firm Hoffman–La Roche controlled by the 1970s around half of the world tranquillizer market, largely through its products Librium and Valium. This brought the firm to the attention of the Monopolies Commission, who, in 1971, accused the company's British subsidiary of exploiting the market against the public interest by charging excessive prices (Stopford *et al.*, 1980). A major supermarket chain such as Sainsbury or Tesco is able, because of its purchasing power and stock turnover, to insist on large price discounts from its suppliers.

We began our discussion of price by challenging the all–important status attributed to the price element in marketing by the neo–classical economists. A much more detailed account of the relationship between price and demand and, in particular, the limitations of the neo–classical approach, may be found in the companion volume, *Economics in a Business Context* (Neale and Haslam, 1989). The role of price in marketing strategy is, as we have have seen, highly complex. Nonetheless it is the only element of marketing strategy that generates income, all other items incurring cost. Pricing policy is therefore a vital strand of strategy, which because of the complexities involved is often difficult for management to judge. We return to such strategic considerations at the end of this chapter.

Promotion

We can identify four types of promotion; advertising, sales promotion, personal selling and publicity. The significant growth of promotion as marketing activity is a function of the growth, complexity and competitiveness of markets and the developments of appropriate technology, as in the newspaper and television industries. It was not until 1896 that newspapers, following the leadership of the *Daily Mail*, recognized the value of advertising revenue to offset rising costs (Cannon, 1986).

All types of promotional activity use psychological theory and communication models of human behaviour, but the nature of the promotion used will depend on a number of factors including the strategy of the organization, the available budget and the type of market. Whilst television advertising may be an appropriate medium for the promotion of consumer goods such as chocolate bars, a specialist magazine may be preferred for promoting expensive camera equipment, and personal selling may be the best way to market industrial goods to other organizations. Some forms of promotion, such as television advertising, are obvious, whilst others, such as shop design, are less so. The Burton Group on taking over Debenhams invested heavily in redesigning the department store interiors to project a new image and attract different market segments.

Promotion like distribution often involves management working together with representatives of other organizations. Advertising for example may involve the marketing manager working closely with an agency as well as representatives of the media. We will return to these aspects when we discuss the organizational aspects of marketing and turn our attention, for the time being, to the various types of promotion.

Advertising. The management of advertising involves four major considerations; the design of the message, the selection of the media, the cost of both production and exposure and the evaluation of its effectiveness.

☐ *The design of the message* reflects the three functions of advertising.

Firstly, it operates to inform the consumer and may be useful in creating initial demand for a product or informing consumers about such things as price changes. Secondly it operates to persuade the consumer to buy the advertiser's product rather than that of a rival. This form of promotion tends to focus on specific features which distinguish a product from its competitors, and by building up a brand image. The third function serves to remind the consumer of the product and encourage repeat purchases. Such promotion is not aimed solely at consumers, but also at wholesalers and retailers to give products shelf space. In general the nature of the message will vary in all these cases. For example, an advertisement which aims to change the buying habits of consumers will often use images with which the potential consumer identifies.

☐ Advertisers have a wide choice of *media*, including national and local newspapers, magazines, cinema, television, radio, and posters. In recent years there has been considerable increase in the use of local independent radio and local newspapers, no doubt reflecting the expansion of both types of media. The selection of appropriate media also involves questions of timing, and an advertising campaign may be carefully scheduled to use various forms of media either concurrently or consecutively to achieve maximum impact.

☐ *The cost of promotion* tends to vary with the media selected. In 1988 a full page advertisement in one edition of The Daily Telegraph could cost around £26 500, whilst the same advertisement in a local paper could cost £2500; and between £14 000 and £26 000 would buy a 30 second television commerical slot in a single television area. The above costs are for exposure only, and do not include the cost of producing the advertisement. Each of those prices may vary considerably with the demand for advertising, the positioning of the advertisement, and the extent to which special deals may be struck between the buyers and sellers of advertising space. The major problem with such expenditure is the degree of waste, since much advertising can be ignored by large sections of the population and the real impact is often difficult to evaluate. We will deal with the problems of evaluation in our discussion of marketing strategy.

Sales promotion. This incorporates a wide variety of different techniques including free samples, money–back coupons, trading stamps, contests and so on. Manufacturers promoting goods through the trade often provide attractive point–of–sale displays or product expertise in the form of a specialist salesperson. Firms such as Dunlopillo, Aristoc and many of the cosmetic manufacturers train and pay their own staff to operate in department stores. Exhibitions and trade fairs are popular ways of promoting goods both to the trade and to industry as a whole. Such forms of sales promotion apply to services as well as manufactured goods. British Rail has introduced several types of fare structure to attract off–peak users, and new restaurants often invite a specially targeted clientele to a launch evening. The case of cheap rail fares illustrates the interaction between sales promotion and pricing strategies.

Sales promotion is sometimes referred to as 'below–the–line' advertising, and is often underestimated in considerations of promotion. It is estimated that sales promotion comprises over 50% of all expenditure on promotion activity, and has achieved a particularly rapid growth since the 1960s. The growth has been attributed to increasing rates of inflation and changes in management thinking. Rising inflation has made the consumer more conscious of special offers, whilst management have apparently grown sceptical of the effectiveness of advertising and believe there to be a much clearer and direct relationship between expenditure on sales promotion and sales figures themselves (Strang, 1976).

Personal selling. This form of promotion is favoured by the sellers of industrial goods recognizing the importance of building up good personal relations between seller and buyer. However, the cost of employing a sales force to maintain regular contact with customers means this can be a most expensive form of promotion. In recent years a much cheaper form of personal selling has developed, especially amongst the manufacturers of double glazing and fitted kitchens by employing part–time workers to contact potential consumers by telephone.

Publicity. This can be an important form of promotion in that the credibility of products or services may be enhanced by linking them with news stories. Many newspapers now have specialist business features or even supplements, and such stories can be an effective way of keeping a firm and its products in the public eye. Some of the larger firms institutionalize this function by employing a specialist public relations department.

An examination of promotion raises many important issues. Advertising in particular has been challenged for developing an overly materialistic society, and the ethics of advertising goods such as cigarettes and alcohol has been questioned by a number of interest groups. The high cost of promotion sets up considerable barriers to the entry of new firms and may operate in favour of big business. Expenditure on promotion may be more effectively directed at product improvements or improving after–sales service. We return to these issues later in the chapter and continue our coverage of marketing elements by looking at the concept of place.

Place

Place refers to the processes by which products and services reach the consumer and involves consideration of marketing channels and physical distribution. A marketing channel represents the flow of goods and services, and may comprise several stages involving intermediaries such as transporters, agents, wholesalers and retailers.

Intermediaries play a number of different roles. They are usually able to distribute goods to customers in a more cost–effective way than the manufacturer is able to do, particularly where goods are mass produced and items are fast moving. For the first six months of 1988 the *Daily Mirror* sold an average of 3.1 million newspapers every day. This would be impossible without a complex and well organized network of transport, wholesalers and retailers to ensure that newspapers are available for readers each morning. In this case the intermediaries break down the number of newspapers into more easily managed batches and are geographically dispersed to ensure an effective delivery. Such wholesalers and retailers handle the other daily newspapers as well, and so facilitate the buying process by offering consumers choice. Manufacturers and consumers are therefore linked in a cost–effective network. The cost of a single newspaper establishing its own network would push up prices to many times their current value.

An intermediary is also an important source of market research and sales promotion, since it stands in closer proximity to customers than the manufacturer. For the same reason intermediaries are often better placed to offer a comprehensive after–sales service. Some intermediaries may offer limited processing facilities such as cutting glass or mixing paint to order. For the manufacturer the intermediary shares some of the risk by buying goods in bulk to sell on (some of which may not sell), and in so doing helps finance the manufacturer's operations.

Those manufacturers seeking greater control over the distribution process have tried to integrate vertically the marketing channel network. Perhaps the clearest example of this is franchising. We see in Case 7.2 how Austin–Rover has tried to impose improved standards of customer service upon its dealer network. However we have already noted in this chapter the power which can be wielded by big supermarket chains over some manufacturers; a case of the marketing channel controlling the manufacturer.

Not all marketing channels involve intermediaries. In the case of industrial goods it is more common for the manufacturer to deal directly with the purchaser, often by building up a relationship between the sales and purchasing departments in the respective organizations. As we saw in the discussion of materials management in Chapter 6, there is a growing tendency for very close relationships to be built up between components suppliers and manufacturers particularly with the introduction of 'Just–In–Time' production methods.

In all cases it is important that the marketing channel makes the goods and services accessible to those who seek them. The importance of accessibility varies with the nature of the product on offer and the needs and wants of consumers. It is important for a fast–food restaurant to be located near centres of population and to be sited so as to encourage casual callers; accessibility becomes less important for the prestigious restaurant rated by food guides, since customers will often be willing to travel several miles. Hospitals too, especially those offering casualty services, need to be located near to and be easily reached by the populations they serve.

Buyer behaviour

An understanding of the needs, wants and behaviour of consumers are vital elements in designing a marketing strategy. Buyer behaviour involves considerations of why people buy and how they arrive at the decision to buy. Several writers have attempted to formulate theories of consumer behaviour so that marketers can predict the outcomes of various strategies (for example Rogers, 1962, Nicosia, 1966, Howard and Sheth, 1969). As yet the predictive validity of such theories and models leaves much to be desired.

The weakness of such theories lies in the very complexity of buyer behaviour. We have seen how changes in the economy can affect consumer perceptions of their own purchasing power. In addition we can identify a number of psychological and sociological influences. These include perception, attitudes, patterns of learning, motivation, personality, social class, peer groups and culture. A knowledge of such factors is an important contribution to marketing strategy and may be used in the development of the marketing mix. Advertisers use these influences in a number of ways; by linking products to certain social groups with whom the consumer identifies, by using 'experts' to extol the virtues of particular brands in an attempt to influence the perceptions and attitudes of the consumer.

Predicting buyer behaviour becomes particularly important with innovations, and is an important ingredient in decisions concerning new product development. Rogers (1962) attempted to differentiate people according to their response to innovative products and identified five types; innovators, early adopters, the early majority, the late majority and laggards. The innovators and early majority comprise an estimated 15% of the population, and are important as opinion leaders in the diffusion of innovations. The implications for the marketer is to establish the characteristics of these groups and focus the marketing communication accordingly. The diffusion of new products is seen as a chain reaction of influence between pioneering consumers and the mass market. Whilst Rogers found that early adopters tended to be younger, more affluent, more cosmopolitan than later adopters, such generalizations, like so many models, have foundered at the sheer complexity of buyer behaviour. For example, a consumer may be an early adopter of the latest in camera technology but particularly conservative where furniture, clothes or holidays are concerned. In this case we would need to identify the opinion leaders for each product group.

Considerations of buyer behaviour often focusses attention on specific target groups. These are referred to as market segments and we deal with the concept of segmentation in the next section. Not all product markets are highly differentiated. A product such as Coca Cola is bought by the widest possible range of consumers.

The complexities of buyer behaviour has led some to conclude that consumer marketing is inherently more complex than is the case with industrial or organizational marketing. Such a perspective ignores the complexities in organizational marketing, which may be different to those in consumer marketing, but are just as real. These complexities include the nature of management values and organizational politics, and those involved in the relationship between the buyers and sellers of industrial goods.

Branding, segmentation and the product life cycle

These concepts deal with issues raised under the various headings of the marketing mix. We deal with them separately here because of their importance.

Branding

Branding is the process through which the product is given a name to distinguish it from the range of other products on offer. The name can be given to a whole range of products, thus identifying them with a certain producer, as with Kelloggs, or be given to individual products even though they originate from the same stable. For example, the washing powder market is dominated by two producers, Lever and Proctor and Gamble, yet each markets a range of washing powers under different brand names; in fact many believe them to be the products of a range of different companies. There may be several reasons why a firm is keen to differentiate a number of brands within the same product range; to appeal to different market segments, or simply to capture those consumers who like to switch brands; to gain more exposure and shelf space in retail outlets; and, in the case of firms such as Proctor and Gamble, as a means of structuring the organization around brands to create healthy internal competition.

Apart from the brand name, a particular logo or mark may be used, and some manufacturers feel it important to create a brand style so that any one of their products from a given range is instantly recognisable. Alfred Sloan insisted to his design teams that all General Motors cars possessed the definitive 'GM look' (Sloan, 1986).

A relatively recent development in branding has been the growth of 'generic' or 'own' brands. These can be found especially in the major retail stores such as Sainsbury's, Safeway and Tesco. A generic is a product that is sold under the brand name of the retailer and applies to all kinds of products. It may in fact be identical to a nationally known brand on the same shelf, but is generally sold at a cheaper price to appeal more to the price–conscious shopper. In some cases generics have acquired a brand image that goes beyond price and value for money to indicate real product quality. Marks and Spencer deliberately promote this image with their own generic name 'St Michael'.

The importance of branding for the marketer lies in the process of creating brand awareness, brand image and ultimately brand loyalty, thereby ensuring repeat purchases of the product. Branding is also useful in helping the consumer search for goods. The hope is that over time the consumer will develop value judgements about certain brands and use these as a basis for discriminating between products. In this way the brand becomes representative of a whole bundle of product attributes, such as quality or value for money, and can be a vital element in the selling of products as symbols (Levy, 1959). In this way certain brands such as Martini are promoted as offering the potential consumer a life–style as well as a product.

The use of brand image and its variability is illustrated in a newspaper article by Terry Coleman (1988) on the selling of cars. The Audi 100 was launched in Britain under the Audi–Volkswagen brand, doubtless stressing the Volkswagen image of reliability. In the USA the same car with a few minor adjustments to the trim became the Audi 5000 and was sold as an Audi–Porsche, capitalizing on the latter's reputation for expensive, fashionable, high performance cars, and appealing to the large American demand for sports cars. Coleman does note that the same car was sold in South Africa mainly as a taxi!

A successful brand image can be a great attribute to a company when launching new products, as they may well acquire the favourable attributes of other products belonging to the same brand. Branding is, however, valuable for all products, new or otherwise, in that it can add value to the product. It is for this reason that many firms protect their brand names by registering them as trademarks. The registration of a trademark enables its owner to use the law to prevent competitors from using the same or similar brand name or mark for the same type of product or service. This also protects the consumer from being deceived and confused about the origin of the goods.

Branding is not without its critics, who claim that it misleads consumers by drawing false distinctions between products and directs investment away from product development and into packaging and promotion to maintain the myth of product differentiation. Branding is further attacked for its encouragement of status consciousness. For many teenagers a simple pair of training shoes will not suffice; they must be the brand favoured by their peer group at that particular time. It is not just the teenage market that is pursued by marketers promoting a particular brand image. Increasingly markets have become highly differentiated and branding can assist in the process of market segmentation. It is to this aspect we now turn.

Segmentation

Segmentation occurs when the market is broken down along a number of different dimensions. Commonly used segments include geographical location, age groups, gender groups, income groups, social classes, and those groups that may be differentiated according to their life style. Kotler defines a market segment as 'consumers who respond in a similar way to a given set of marketing stimuli' (Kotler, 1983, p 40).

Market segmentation and product differention go hand in hand, in that products are designed, developed, promoted and even priced and distributed with a particular market segment in mind. True segmentation occurs when genuinely different products are made for the different market segments. The concept of segmentation is the essence of the marketing concept as identified at the beginning of the chapter; the production of goods and services to meet the specific needs of consumers.

Segmentation is an increasing feature of marketing, as the following illustration of the holiday industry will show. Many package tour holiday companies originally promoted all their holidays in a single brochure, leaving the consumer to select the most appropriate holiday from the entire range offered. Thomson Holidays will be producing around fifteen different brochures for 1989, each aimed at a different market. 'Freestyle' holidays are aimed at the 18–30 group, whilst 'Young at Heart' aim for the older market. The main brochure 'Thomson Summer Sun' caters for the mass market, but the 'A la Carte' holidays aim to capture those groups with a higher disposable income and a different life style. Life style is also an important consideration in the 'Ski', 'Small and Friendly', 'Simply Greece' and 'Lakes and Mountains' holiday offerings. Whilst few companies aim to match Thomson for product differentiation, others do target specific markets, Bales for exclusive long distance holidays and Saga for holidays and cruises aimed at the older age groups.

Not all such product differentiation is motivated solely by the desire to

Segmentation is the process through which the total market is broken down to create distinctive consumer groups. The criteria used to form such groups vary and may include geographical location, social class, occupation, sex, lifestyle, and so on. Once market segments have been identified then products can be developed which focus upon a particular group in an attempt to maximize both the marketing effort and the needs of consumers. Some firms specialize in catering for the needs of a particular segment only, whilst others produce a range of products each aimed at different segments of the same market. In this case, the branding of each product becomes especially important to distinguish it from the others. The process of broadening the segments to which a product might appeal or changing the market segment altogether, is known as repositioning.

KEY CONCEPT 7.3

SEGMENTATION

cater for consumer needs. The growth of the winter holiday market may be related to affluence and changing life styles; it is also related to the hotel owner's and tour operator's desire to utilize capacity all the year round. In some cases winter holidays are aggressively promoted and attractively priced to push up market demand. In this case some segments, such as the retired population, are especially singled out.

So far we have focussed upon consumer goods, but segmentation is a feature of industrial goods as well. Many engineering companies in the components industry have successfully targeted specific groups and tailored their products accordingly. As we saw in Chapter 2, Japanese companies often forge very close relationships with their suppliers, although this is more a case of the segment defining the product rather than the manufacturer targeting a segment.

An important strategic decision in marketing is the determination of the most appropriate segments for the marketing effort. There would appear to be three broad options.

☐ Producing a single product or a small range of products for a single segment or limited range of segments.
☐ Producing many products serving many different market segments.
☐ Producing a single product for an undifferentiated mass market.

The choice will depend on a range of factors, including whether the segment can be accurately identified, whether it is large enough to be profitable, whether it can be served within certain cost constraints, and of course, management goals.

Aiming for a limited market segment can be a highly successful strategy, as shown by such companies as Mothercare and those holiday companies such as Bales and Kuoni, who provide more expensive holidays. Such a strategy can be restricting, and once a certain market size and share have been reached the company may need new products and new markets to continue growing. Mothercare recognized this by extending its market to cater for older children as well as its original market of baby and maternity wear. Kuoni in an attempt to capture a younger market launched a group of holidays using cheaper accomodation. A deliberate attempt to change its market segment was adopted as a survival strategy by the British motorcycle industry in the mid 1970s. Faced with overwhelming competition from Japanese bikes the British industry continually retreated up market, ultimately to be defeated in that segment as well by the Japanese. The British manufacturers went for an inappropriate segmentation strategy and might have been more successful had they invested in the process technology to manufacture reliable, low cost, mass–produced bikes (Earl, 1984). This inter–relationship of marketing, product development and process technology recurs in our discussion of the product life cycle and marketing strategy.

A differentiated product range serving different markets has long since been the strategy followed by the major car producers (Case 7.2). It is a strategy pursued by firms operating in the service industry too; building societies for instance offer a range of investment plans to suit the needs of different groups. Excessive segmentation can pose problems and it has been referred to as 'marketing mania' (Levitt, 1975). The development, production, promotion and administrative costs associated with product differentiation can render excessive segmentation an expensive strategy, particularly where minor product changes result in major process adjustments. Differentiation may be a strategy for survival in a declining market as shown by the Orlake Records case in Chapter 6, but the strategy may not always work. The willingness of the British textile and steel industries to take on any order, whatever its size, led to dramatic cost increases and merely hastened the decline of those industries, when product concentration might have been a more appropriate strategy (Earl, 1984).

An important element of segmentation is positioning. This refers not only to choosing the correct market segment for your product, but also to finding the appropriate niche in that market, to differentiate it from its competitors on such matters as price and quality. Repositioning occurs when the same product is offered to a different group, either to combat falling sales or as a general growth strategy. This was successfully achieved by Guinness, who in the 1970s aimed their promotion at the younger drinker with highly successful results. Manikin cigars attempted the same ploy but were less than successful; the new target market found the cigar too strong for their taste, whilst the original market disliked the new style of promotion.

The product life cycle

The product life cycle assumes that all products have limited lives, during which they pass through a series of stages all of which have implications for sales and profitability. The classic life cycle is depicted by four phases as presented in Figure 7.1.

During the *introduction* phase sales are slow, as both consumers and distributers become aware of the product and decide to adopt it. The costs of development and promotion are high and firms may suffer initial losses.

During the *growth* phase there is a rapid acceptance of the product and a dramatic increase in sales. This is generally sustained by improved dis-

This case is set against the background of a declining British car industry and focusses on a single marketing strategy, 'The Customer Satisfaction Initiative', launched in 1988 by the Austin-Rover company. In order to place the strategy in its true context, some background information is essential.

The background

The Austin Rover Group was formed when the government-controlled British Leyland was broken up into different operating units. By far the largest of these was the volume cars division, producing automobiles for the mass market. This division became known as Austin-Rover, and the company inherited many of the policies and the problems of BL, which in turn had inherited them from its predecessor BLMC (although to avoid confusion the company will be referred to throughout as Austin-Rover). The main problem was the British car industry itself, and in particular Austin-Rover's market share. In 1971 this stood at 40%. By 1984 it had fallen to 18% Up to the mid 1970s the British market had been dominated by Austin-Rover and Ford, but there were two major differences.

Firstly, Austin-Rover concentrated exclusively on the home market; the company had never enjoyed a major presence in Europe and both its dealership and distribution network were poor outside Britain. Ford, by contrast, was a multinational with a strong base in Europe, and in an ideal position to capitalize from the growing internationalism of car production, where different models for different markets were wholly or partly manufactured in a particular country. Secondly, Austin-Rover had the greater share of the private market whilst Ford dominated fleet sales.

The oil price rises of the 1970s affected the car market worldwide and British producers in particular, as the government's deflationary measures led to reductions in demand. In addition the market in which Austin-Rover operated had become more competitive. Ford decided to compete in the small car market for the first time, launching its Fiesta range in 1976, and most significantly, the market share of imported cars had risen from 10% in 1969 to 35% in 1977. The major threat was seen as the Japanese car industry, which quickly gained a reputation for reliable, value-for-money cars. Generally the imports had little effect on the fleet market, where Ford maintained its position. In addition to these market changes, significant organizational changes were happening in Vauxhall and Ford, involving a greater integration with European operations.

The decline of Austin-Rover during this period has been the subject of considerable debate. The trade unions were a popular scapegoat. Poor labour relations were a feature, but other factors were more significant. The company had failed to capitalize upon its successes in the 1960s. There was a lack of investment in developing a viable product range and in modernizing the plant. The company became known for the poor quality of its products and unreliable distribution.

In the 1980s several changes took place at Austin Rover. A new pro-

Continued over page

Continued from previous page duct range was launched backed up by considerable investment in new technology. A significant reorganization occurred involving considerable rationalization of both management and labour. The company began a joint venture with the Japanese firm Honda to produce the Triumph Acclaim and later, the Rover Sterling. New showrooms were opened in Europe and significant inroads were made into the Portuguese market.

The reorganization and investment in new technology improved the company's productivity, but given the size of the British and European car markets and Austin-Rover's market share it was doubtful whether there would be sufficient pay-back in terms of volume sales. Export to Europe was still dogged by a traditional European reluctance to buy British cars and a poor dealership network; in volume terms the Portuguese market is marginal. The new model range received an un-enthusiastic press and the cars were not seen as innovative. Moreover, traditional problems of reliability had not been solved. Warranty costs to Austin Rover were an average £79 per car, compared to £60 at Ford, £30 at Vauxhall, and £10 at Nissan. Most significantly, the British market was shaken up by the re-emergence of Vauxhall as a major producer.

It is against this background that Austin-Rover set about imporving its market share by focusing on the service given to customers.

The customer satisfaction initiative

This was introduced by the company in 1988, emphasizing the relation-ship between the dealerships and their customers. The aim is,

> to ensure the satisfaction of customers' total requirements by creating a process of continuing improvement . . . to be known as an organization that actually cares about its customers, and through its dealers pro-vides a service which is second to none.

Six key initiatives have been identified.

☐ Two types of franchise standards have been set; minimum and en-hanced operating standards. These are applied in four areas; environ-ment and equipment, staff, systems and controls, and marketing. In all over 260 different elements are identified where minimum stan-dards have to be attained. The ultimate aim is for all dealerships to reach enhanced operating standards over a period of time.

☐ Support programmes have been set up by Austin-Rover to assist dealerships in reaching the required standard in all areas of their operation.

☐ Every staff member needs to understand the customer satisfaction initiative. This is achieved by the following means.

　☐ Each garage appointing a 'Customer Care Manager' with overall responsibility for the initiative.

　☐ Holding training workshops for the executives and management in each dealership.

　☐ Organizing launch evenings for each dealership which all em-ployees should attend.

　☐ Organizing training days for all staff on a rota basis.

□ Reinforcing the training by a system of distance learning packages.

□ The company's residential training centre has been relaunched as 'The Marketing Institute' to 'set new standards in dealer training'.

□ Dealers are to be rewarded for excellence and increased effort. Managers will be given targets based not on volume of sales or work, but on a 'Customer Satisfaction Index'. This comprises the performance of staff against the standards, feedback from customers, participation and success in the distance learning programme, and quality sampling by Austin-Rover personnel making anonymous visits and telephone inquiries. Points will be awarded, dealer and individual league tables introduced and top performers will be rewarded by overseas trips. Those dealerships who fail to achieve the minimum standards will have 1% of their dealer margins withheld. Those who achieve enhanced operating standards will gain ½% bonus.

□ As part of an improved marketing effort, targeted direct mailing will be introduced and a new 'lifestyle magazine' launched under the editorship of a well known television personality and journalist.

Continued from previous page

(*Sources:* Marsden *et al.*, 1985; Williams, Williams and Haslam, 1987; Austin Rover Sales and Marketing 'Customer Satisfaction Initiative', 1988.)

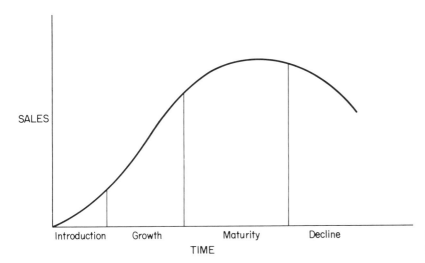

Figure 7.1 The product life cycle.

tribution, product improvements, and even price reductions. There are normally high profits for pioneering firms, but a growing market attracts competitors leading to brand differentiation. Whilst the production learning curve may lead to a reduction in costs, the need to satisfy an expanding market can involve costly investment in new production processes. The end of this phase is marked by a high level of competition, recognized by Wasson (1978) as a separate phase which he termed 'competitive turbulence'.

As it becomes saturated the market reaches *maturity*. Sales and profits are still high but there tends to be considerable investment in maintaining sales. This is achieved through product changes, increased promotional activity and price–cutting. Products are sometimes relaunched at this stage, usually with new features, different packaging and often an attempt to create a new image. Firms seek to maintain brand loyalty at the same time as attempting to broaden the market by repositioning. At this stage the less competitive firms drop from the product market.

The *decline* phase is marked by a falling off in sales, and while some firms do well as others leave the market, survival is often dependent upon successful product diversification.

The product life cycle can be useful as a framework for planning a marketing campaign over time and as an indication that marketing strategies need to be adjusted to match changes in the cycle. There is an implicit assumption in much of the writing that careful marketing policies can do much to slow down the cycle of decline, i.e., the cycle may be manipulated by the marketing mix. An understanding of the life cycles of a range of products may be an important factor in determining the introduction of new products and ensuring that the product mix is well represented at the introductory, growth and maturity stages. A company has significant problems if its entire product range is in the decline phase at the same time.

The utility of the product life cycle has been questioned on several counts. Firstly, it is a gross simplification of the behaviour of markets and seems to ignore changes in the economy, the behaviour of competitors, the actions of governments and even dramatic swings in consumer fashion. Secondly, the cycle is highly variable for different products, in both the length of time it takes to reach the decline stage and the amount of time spent in each phase. The path for any product is extremely difficult to plot and the model is therefore a poor guide to marketing strategy. Thirdly, even if we accept that the model is descriptive of a general process, it may be difficult to assess when a product has reached a particular stage. A temporary rise or fall in sales may be mistaken for a fundamental shift in the cycle, so that action is taken that is inappropriate at that time. Fourthly, the model is criticized for ignoring the production implications of a changing market position.

Each stage of the product life cycle has implications for the design of the product, the volume and variety of production, and the nature of the process. In this way the product life cycle is related to a process life cycle. The introductory stage of the product life cycle is marked by a highly flexible production process. As markets reach their maximum potential the capacity can only be met by relatively inflexible mass production systems. The cost of such systems necessitates a high market demand and long production runs. There is a similarity here with the 'revised sequence' (Galbraith, 1972), discussed earlier in this chapter. In this situation marketing becomes production–led rather than demand–led. However, the relationship between the product and process life cycles has been complicated by the introduction of flexible manufacturing systems (there is a discussion of this in Chapter 6).

The environmental aspects of marketing

Marketing, probably more than any other of the business functions we have dealt with, operates at the interface between the firm and its environment. We will see in this section how marketing activities are not only influenced by environmental factors, but that the management manipulation of the the four Ps represents a deliberate attempt to shape consumer behaviour and hence the market environment within which the firm operates. Marketing strategy is therefore a key element in the corporate strategy of any organization. We will view the relationship of marketing with the environment of the firm by looking in turn at the economy, the role of the state and consumer interest groups, technology, and finally cultural and social factors.

Marketing and the economy

For some, marketing as a subject has emerged as a branch of applied economics, and economic theory is used as the basis for the development of marketing strategies. Marketing activity is influenced by economic factors in a number of different ways as the following illustrations reveal.

We have already seen how marketing is a very important feature in the strategies of those firms operating in the service sector. In this way major economic changes in the shift from manufacturing to service industry have brought about new directions in marketing. The entry of new firms into the market place, especially in the form of overseas competition, may necessitate a change in marketing strategy for existing firms to retain their market share. Changes in supply and demand reflecting changing levels of employment and income call for changes in marketing strategy. Falling demand may call for price reductions, attempts to broaden the market by appealing to new segments or diversifying into new areas of activity. In economically depressed areas attempts by the unemployed to set up shops are often doomed to failure owing to the low levels of demand in that area. Where demand is so low, then little in the way of marketing strategy can change the basic position. Changing rates of inflation together with the level of economic activity will affect savings and the availability of credit. Where price inflation rises at a faster rate than wage inflation, the demand for certain luxury goods may fall. Some firms combat this by offering favourable credit terms to customers in an attempt to boost sales.

These illustrations show how marketing strategy has often reacted to changes in the economy. However, many firms will attempt to manipulate the economy through its marketing activities. In Chapter 5 we examined the link between levels of investment in new product development and economic growth at both the level of the firm and nationally. We have seen that one of the functions of promotional activities is to persuade consumers and hence attempt to manipulate demand. We have noted several times in this book how very large companies, especially those operating multi-nationally, are able to manipulate markets to their advantage through product development, pricing and promotional strategies in such a way as to affect national economies.

Whilst the relationship between marketing and the economy is significant, we saw in our discussion of price elasticity that economic theory has its limitations in our understanding of marketing behaviour, ignoring as it does a range of important cultural, social and psychological influences.

Political and pressure group influences also play a part and it is to these we now turn.

Marketing and the role of the state

The state represents a powerful presence in the market place as a dominant employer, supplier and purchaser. It has been estimated that well over one half of all commercial transactions in Britain involve the state directly (Cannon, 1986). We have already noted the increases in Government advertising expenditure. The state is involved in marketing in a number of different ways.

☐ The state provides information on Government policy.
☐ Advertising is often used to direct the behaviour of individuals as in the case of health education or to encourage the unemployed to take advantage of training schemes.
☐ The pricing and promotional policies of state–controlled industries can be used to direct public expenditure and consumption, as in the case of energy. The potential for the government direction of markets in this way is considerable. In reality, particularly in the example of the energy industry, the actual control is often diluted through the absence of an effective coordinating policy.
☐ The state attempts to regulate the marketing activity of private firms in a number of different ways. Most of these measures are aimed at regulating free competition and protecting individual consumers and the environment.
  ☐ In terms of product development, the British Standards Institute (BSI) has devised technical standards to which products should comply to ensure minimum standards of quality, and to protect both the consumer and the environment against the potentially dangerous product.
  ☐ We have seen in Chapter 5 that the granting of patents gives inventors a monopoly to market their products in return for making their invention public. The aim of such legislation is both to reward and stimulate innovation.
  ☐ Through its law relating to monopolies and mergers the state attempts to define and prevent unfair competition.
  ☐ The abolition of resale price maintenance under The Resale Prices Act 1977 has loosened the control of major manufacturers over the market place and so protected the consumer from unfair business practices.
  ☐ The Trade Descriptions Act 1968–72 tackles the problems of deception in advertising and sales promotion.
  ☐ The Sale of Goods Act 1893 and The Supply of Goods (Implied Terms) Act 1972 set out the contractual rights of consumers on such issues as the return of goods and warranty.
  ☐ Many governments attempt to limit the advertising of certain types of products such as cigarettes and alcohol.
  ☐ Britain's membership of the EEC means that firms are subject to a range of further regulations affecting firms and consumers alike, as

Consumerism has developed as a social movement to inform and assist consumer choice and to act as a pressure group to represent the interests of consumers. These interests are represented to organizations in an attempt to influence product design, price and distribution. Consumer interest groups also act as watchdogs to guard against unsafe products and dishonest producers. That consumers are now more aware and better informed is due largely to the activities of consumer groups and the publicity given to consumer matters over the last twenty or so years.

KEY CONCEPT 7.4

CONSUMERISM

with the pricing of agricultural produce or the description of products when promoting them for the European market.

Those students requiring a detailed account of the legislation pertaining to marketing are advised to consult the law text in this series, *Law in a Business Context*, Cole and Shears, 1989.

The various measures outlined above are reinforced by a state bureaucracy. Many marketing issues are dealt with by The Department for Trade and Industry and government backed offices such as The Office of Fair Trading and The Advertising Standards Authority. As we can see, many of the measures are aimed specifically at consumer protection and some of them are the direct consequence of consumer pressure groups. We now deal with such interest group activity under the heading of consumerism.

Consumerism

The concept of consumerism has developed in the last twenty–five years around four tenets; the right of the consumer to be informed, the right to choose, the right of redress and the right of safety. If we accept that marketing is nothing more than the effective satisfaction of consumer needs and wants, then consumerism would in fact be synonymous with marketing, and the presence of organized consumer groups would be no more than an important source of information and market research. The consumer movement has however developed as a political interest group to represent the rights of consumers, largely because those rights are seen to be threatened by the marketing activity of many firms. It is interesting to see Baker (1976) deal with consumerism as 'marketing under attack'.

The crusades against dangerous products by people such as the American Ralph Nader; the growth and success in Britain of organizations such as the Consumers Association and the Campaign For Real Ale; magazines such as *What Car*; the popularity of consumer programmes on television and radio; all these have both focused the attention of the public on consumer affairs as well as feeding its need for information. Consumer information exists to satisfy a need, but like marketing promotion itself it has created an even greater need. Most national newspapers now give significant editorial space to consumer matters and concern themselves with a range of consumer issues, from testing new cars and bottles of wine, to offering advice on financial matters, to highlighting sharp practice in the business world.

As well as feeding off its own publicity and success, the growth of consumerism is often related to the factors identified below.

☐ The public needs protection against the effects of dangerous products. A series of articles in the trade press and newspapers in the 1970s in the USA focussed the public's attention on the number of accidents involving Ford Pinto cars, all the result of the location of the petrol tank. The pressure was such that Ford withdrew the model.

☐ The public needs protection against the dishonest behaviour of some producers. The growth of fierce competition in the home improvements has resulted in the Office of Fair Trading receiving a number of complaints about such firms misleading the public about the true cost of credit. The Financial Services Act 1987 emerged partly to protect consumers by regulating those firms dealing with such matters as investment, insurance and pensions; several complaints had been received that investment returns were less than promised and costs were much higher than expected. Strict rules now operate for the promotion of investment and pension plans.

☐ The growth of pressure groups like the Campaign For Real Ale is a reaction to the monopoly power wielded by the main producers in a particular industry. The brewing industry was moving towards a market dominance by a handful of producers and the gradual elimination of beer brewed by traditional methods in favour of a product that was more easily stored and transported. The campaign not only brought pressure against the major producers to produce more 'real' ale but was successful, with the aid of considerable media coverage, in creating a much greater public demand for that product.

☐ Consumers themselves are better educated, more affluent and, largely because of the growth of the consumer press, more informed. The result has been increased expectations and demand for products of a higher quality. Whilst this is probably true for all consumers, the growth of consumerism is undoubtedly a middle class phenomenon, closely related to the degree of affluence of particular consumer groups.

As an interest group the consumer movement has been influential in broadening public awareness of consumer matters and bringing about a range of protective legislation. In many cases this has led to improved goods and services and more effective marketing. There are still those who feel that the consumer lobby needs to go much further to protect the rights of consumers, whilst others, particularly in business, may resent the influence of consumer groups on governments, fearing that excessive regulation may stifle innovation.

Marketing and technology

These interact in three different ways. Firstly, we have seen in Chapter 5 the process of product design and development, and its protection through the patent system. We also noted that marketing was an essential vehicle for the information and promotion of new products and processes. Secondly, in our discussion of the product life cycle we identified the clear relationship between process technology and levels of demand. It is no good management using product development, pricing and promotional strategies to increase demand if that demand cannot be met by the existing production system. Thirdly, developments in technology have had significant impact upon the marketing process. Among the most obvious aids to marketing have been the developments that have taken place in mass distribution. A range of developments have taken place in retailing to simplify the process of purchase. The system of 'electronic funds transfer at the point of sale' (EFTPOS), may well, together with the credit card obviate the need for cash. A wide range of goods may now be bought over the telephone using credit cards for payment, and some firms have set up computer databases of suppliers willing to offer such goods to consumers at highly competitive prices. We saw in Case 5.4 how the introduction of automatic teller machines was a key marketing strategy used by a banking group to fight off growing competition.

The role of cultural and social influences in marketing

In our discussion of segmentation we suggested that markets were increasingly segmented and the marketing effort was correspondingly targeted at specific groups. Invariably the basis for such segmentation is social and cultural. Differences within societies and between culturally distinctive groups has resulted in different patterns of product adoption. The popularity of a product among one social group is no guarantee that it will appeal to another, totally different group; for example, devising a marketing campaign to find a mass market for snails may well prove difficult in Britain and the USA! Yet marketing is more than a product of social and cultural factors; managers often use such factors in promotion. Using the aspiration of one group in society to acquire the life style of another group is a common theme in advertising. The growth of the teenage market is both a reflection of changing social values and a deliberate creation by producers actively seeking new business opportunities. As with other aspects of our model the influences are invariably two–way with marketing acting as both a product and a cause of social change. Several social and cultural factors illustrate our point.

Changing demographic patterns relating to age, sex, location and naturally incomes may have a profound effect upon marketing. An ageing population in many Western industrial societies has opened up new marketing opportunities in such industries as tourism, and in general focused the attention of marketers towards a sector they had previously seldom considered. Geographical shifts in population may have a considerable impact upon consumer demand and property prices. Rising property prices in the London and the South East of England have had a knock–on effect on the property market of surrounding areas. This has manifested itself in changes in the types of new property being built, the prices of those and existing dwellings and the way the property is promoted by estate agents. Small terraced housing in areas within commuting distance of London become desirable cottage residences to tempt the buyer with dreams of country living. Such changes also have an impact on the marketing of public transport systems.

Values and attitudes are important influences on the marketing process. Core cultural values such as family life and concern for children are constantly used in advertising, and marketers take care not to transgress such social mores. Reference groups such as experts, peers, social classes, and those groups portraying a desired life style are frequently used in marketing communication as mechanisms of attitude change.

Advertising in particular uses and builds upon social attitudes as the following two examples show. Ford in the USA sells its German–built Lincoln–Mercury Scorpio as 'imported from Germany for select dealers', whilst Austin–Rover's television advertisement to launch the Rover 800 'Fastback' shows the car as a product of British technology being driven by German businessmen. Both promotions are using the widely–held belief that the Germans develop superior technical products. The Americans use this value directly in their advertising. Austin–Rover on the other hand appear to be promoting the superiority of British technology, yet the promotion is based on the credibility of German technical know–how and the use of Germans as 'expert witnesses'.

Such cultural stereotyping has benefited the Germans considerably as exporters of manufactured goods, and they have been especially successful with more technical products such as machine–tools. Japan on the other hand had to overcome damaging negative stereotyping, which saw its exported goods in the 1920s and 1930s as cheap, imitative products (Wilkinson, 1983). The cultural stereotyping extends to the role of marketing itself, and the emphasis placed on different elements of the marketing mix. The Germans are noted for their emphasis on product development and careful targeting, whilst the Americans are noted for their emphasis on promotional activities and selling.

As with all such stereotyping the differences that exist within a country are often greater than those between countries. The last point does however raise the issue of the role of marketing within the overall strategy of the firm and in the next section we explore the organizational relationships of the marketing function.

The organization aspects of marketing

We have already dealt with several organizational issues elsewhere in this chapter. In examining the different orientations to marketing we saw how the marketing goals have developed over time and how much they vary between organizations. Several references have been made to the impact of organizational size on marketing. We have noted that increasing size has led to increasing specialization within the marketing function and how the costs associated with the various marketing activities have acted as barriers to entry, favouring big business in the achievement of market dominance. As we noted in Chapter 3, there is increasing recognition that so–called 'excellent' companies are built around clearly–defined cultures. An important element of such organizational cultures is a close identification with the needs of the customer. In the Austin–Rover case in this chapter, we show how the company has attempted to change its culture and image by involving all personnel in the marketing effort.

In this section we will focus on structural issues pertaining to marketing, dealing firstly with the way the function is organized and secondly with the relationships between the marketing personnel and those representing other functional areas.

The organization of marketing

Marketing was initially viewed as being synonymous with sales. With the growth of the firm and the development of its markets came the problems of organizing the sales force, often achieved by creating sales territories operating under a hierarchy of district and regional managers. The need for improved market research and sales promotion created research and advertising units as sub–divisions of the sales department.

The growth of increasingly complex markets, the emergence of large organizations, and changing attitudes by management towards consumers, all called for corresponding developments in the functional organization of business activities. Marketing emerged as a function in its own right, with the previously dominant sales department as a subsidiary activity. The marketing effort now spawned further specialisms in advertising, sales pro-motion and market research, and some marketing departments also assumed responsibility for new product development. In the larger organizations, marketing management became the coordination of a range of specialist marketing activities.

This functional organization of marketing mirrored functional developments occurring elsewhere in the firm, but some companies were experimenting with other forms of organization structure. As we saw in Chapter 3 in our discussion of structure, divisionalization occurred because some firms such as General Motors found it most appropriate to organize around products or markets. The marketing efforts in many organizations went down the same route.

In the 1920s Proctor and Gamble developed the concept of product management. Under this arrangement the firm is organized around its products and each brand or group of brands has its own manager. Such a structural arrangement may be necessary where product knowledge is highly technical, or where the firm is dealing in totally different product markets. The benefits which may be gained by management from such an arrangement include an increased knowledge of the product market and an ability to respond quickly to changing market demands. A healthy internal competition can be built up, leading to increased sales. Furthermore, product management has often been a good training ground for aspiring senior managers as it interfaces with most aspects of the firm's operation. The customer gains by dealing with people who have real product knowl-edge. Product and brand management can be costly ways of organizing the marketing effort. Specialist activities such as advertising may be un-necessarily duplicated, or else product managers may lack expertise in the more specialized areas of marketing. In firms where every brand has its own manager there may be overstaffing of management at the lower and middle levels, with the ensuing problems of career progression.

An alternative structural arrangement would be to specialize around different markets. The markets may be differentiated geographically, by industry, or even by customer. In consumer marketing some form of geographical specialization is a fairly traditional approach; sales forces have tended towards regional organization for ease of administration and control, and television advertising is invariably regional. It is in the marketing to organizations, with the prospect of high volume, high value orders that specialization by industry or by customer is regarded as a factor in increasing sales. The Xerox Information Systems Group switched from selling by product to selling by industry, and organized its marketing efforts accordingly. The advantages of this approach lie in building up a close relationship with individual customers and gaining insights into their operations (Hanan, 1974). Some firms operating in the computer market, like IBM and Digital, offer a consultancy service to potential customers; this leads to improvements in the customer's own operating systems and potentially more sales for the computer company. Gaining experience of the customers' operating problems and their marketing environment is often invaluable to the process of developing new products. Such a structure would seem most appropriate where the market is becoming increasingly competitive and there are long–term advantages to be gained from building up such close relationships with customers.

As we saw in Chapter 3, organization structures rarely conform to ideal models. Many firms have marketing departments which display elements of all the structural variations identified above. A system of brand manage-ment can be backed up by a centralized research or advertising function. The marketing effort can be organized according to different industrial markets but may be further differentiated according to product. The system is further complicated in that marketing departments frequently use agencies external to the firm. The last twenty–five years have seen the growth of advertising agencies. Some, like Saatchi and Saatchi, have achieved a highly profitable multinational standing and a very high public profile as the creators of the Conservative Party's successful election campaigns. Specialist agencies also operate in market research and sales promotion. The advantages of using agencies lie in their ability to stand back and offer an independent assessment of the firm's marketing activities, to offer specialist expertise which the company may not possess and act as a source of fresh ideas.

Dealing with outside agencies can be a costly exercise and may be a potential source of conflict. In fact, any structural differentiation within the marketing function itself may set up internal conflicts. Brand differentiation and management may create competition but that same competition has the potential for unhealthy conflict. Tensions can exist between marketing management who direct operations and the sales force who must carry them out. Much wider tensions can exist in the relationship between marketing and the other functional areas and it is to this we now turn.

Marketing and the other functions

Turner (1971) writing about the rise of Donald Stokes in the British Leyland hierarchy, identified his influence in changing the orientation of

Issue	Stereotype marketing response	Stereotype production response
Capacity	We never have enough when we need it.	Market forecasts must be more accurate.
Scheduling	We need greater flexibility, faster change times, and a quicker response to changing market demands.	Change is disruptive and should be minimized.
Product line	A varied product line is essential for customer satisfaction.	Variety means short uneconomic runs.
New products	These are essential for the firm's survival.	There are too many minor design changes. Too much change is costly.
Warranty and aftersales	Costs involved in this must be reduced. It is the responsibility of production quality control.	Consumers use products in the wrong way. Much warranty work can be avoided.
Distribution	We never have enough stocks.	Stocks must always be kept at a minimum.
Quality	Customers should be able to get quality products at a reasonable cost.	Quality and low cost are incompatible

Figure 7.2 An illustration of the potential conflicts between the marketing and production functions. (Adapted from B.P. Shapiro, 1977.)

the then Bus and Truck division from production to sales. He paints a picture of Stokes as essentially a salesman who sometimes promised orders the manufacturing departments could not meet. Turner notes that this made him very unpopular with the production managers and set up tensions between them.

The Stokes case is probably fairly typical of the kind of conflict which can occur when two different orientations have to come together. Probably the most comprehensive treatment of the conflict between marketing and manufacturing is offered by Shapiro (1977). He identifies several areas where the priorities of the two departments may differ as illustrated in Figure 7.2, and a similar version of the same problem may be found in Figure 6.2.

Shapiro felt that the need for cooperation was greatest amongst the manufacturers of industrial components and he identifies a number of reasons for such conflict.

☐ The two functions are evaluated according to different criteria. Marketing personnel are rewarded for achieving a high sales turnover and a high market share, whilst the primary orientation of manufacturing is towards the achievement of minimum cost and a smooth operation flow. The marketing staff are encouraged to create change by developing new opportunities whilst the production staff tend to resist it since it increases costs.

☐ It is often difficult for the two types of personnel to cooperate since they operate in different cultures. The marketers often deal with rather vague concepts like customer preferences whilst production staff deal with information that is generally quantifiable. Moreover the orientation of marketing is essentially to customer groups outside the organization, whilst the production orientation is predominantly internal.

Shapiro acknowledges that all such conflict is not necessarily dysfunctional; persuading customers to adopt standardized parts may enable the firm to offer a better service as well as reducing costs. Where conflict is disruptive it may be tackled in a number of different ways. Management might consider different reward criteria; marketing staff could be rewarded for accurate forecasts rather than meeting some artificially contrived quota, and production staff rewarded for meeting delivery times. Conflict may also be avoided by encouraging more interaction and mixed career paths.

Such tensions may be found in many firms, but for others, such as Woodville Polymer Engineering described in Case 7.1, the cooperation and harmony between manufacturing and marketing is the essence of the company's success. In addition, the type of tensions identified by Shapiro are complicated by a range of factors such as the size and history of the firm, the nature of the process technology, and economic changes affecting demand. All these may aggravate or minimize the conflicts. The developments in flexible manufacturing systems identified in Chapter 6 have gone a long way towards easing some of the tensions, although the use of FMS is limited to a small number of firms.

We have concentrated on the relationship between marketing and manufacturing, but similar tensions may occur with other functions; with R&D over product design or with accounting over methods of payment. Nor are such conflicts the sole property of the marketing department. We have already identified the type of conflict that can emerge between the R&D and manufacturing functions and in the next chapter we see the traditional antagonisms that occur between the personnel department and line management. Such conflicts are the inevitable consequence of organizational size and managerial specialization. They may however be minimized by strategies focussing on coordination. We introduced such notions in Chapter 4 and develop them as far as marketing is concerned in the next section.

The strategic aspects of marketing

The process or developing a marketing strategy bears a striking resemblance to the process of developing a firm's corporate strategy, underlining the centrality of marketing to the firm's planning process. Opportunities are analysed, target markets selected, market share objectives are set and the particular marketing mix is developed. The marketing mix is central to the whole process since it identifies and guides the strategic options. Strategic considerations in marketing therefore embrace all of the factors we have discussed in this chapter. We will use the four elements of the mix to examine the various strands of marketing strategy. Finally we examine how these various elements may be combined and stress the integrated nature of marketing and the other functional strategies.

Product strategy

> The historic fate of one growth industry after another has been its suicidal product provincialism.
>
> (Levitt, 1960, p 34)

References have been made to product strategy in our discussion of innovation and production in the previous two chapters, as well as earlier in this chapter. Levitt's quote from his highly influential article 'Marketing Myopia' is a plea to management for a marketing–led product development strategy. Most industries, he feels, restrict themselves by defining their businesses too narrowly, largely because they are product oriented rather than customer oriented. He cites the case of the decline of the US railway business which identified itself too rigidly with railways rather than the transport needs of its customers, and lost ground to the airline and car industries.

Following the market in this way may be desirable but depends upon the firm possessing the appropriate financial resources and skills. A firm's competitive edge may lie in the production of highly specialized goods, and skills and resources may not be easily transferred. In such cases survival may depend upon acquisition or merger.

In general terms a product strategy needs to consider the type and range of products on offer, the style and quality of those products, the use of brand names and packaging, and the nature of the services that are offered with the product, such as warranty and after–sales care. We saw in our discussion of the product life cycle that product market planning needs careful consideration of the production process.

Pricing strategy

We have already discussed the various constituents that determine the price of a product, and singly or together these form the basis of pricing strategy. 'Cost–plus' pricing consists of a standard mark–up after all costs have been taken into consideration. 'Target profit' pricing involves establishing the price in accordance with projected demand using some form of break–even analysis. In this way a book can be priced according to two criteria; the minimum sales required to cover production costs and the required profit margins based on estimated sales figures.

Both the 'cost–plus' and 'target profit' methods are based on the assumptions that prices are related solely to cost and demand. As we saw earlier, this is too simplistic a view. The pricing strategy needs to take account of factors external to the firm, in particular prices charged by the competition and the perceived value of the product by the consumer. In the former case there is a tendency for firms operating in the same product market to adopt a going rate, although, as we shall see later, more aggressive tactics can be pursued by firms breaking into new markets. By contrast to the going rate, pricing goods according to their perceived value can lead to considerable variation. Such a strategy is based on the customer's assumption that 'he is getting what he pays for' and he relates price to quality and hence to the cost of producing the goods or services. However a high price can be used to denote exclusivity and so attract a particular market segment. Of course, management may simply be pricing goods to see what the market will stand, but such a strategy may encourage new entrants with more cheaply priced products.

All these factors come together in the pricing strategies relating to new products. The simplest method may well be to price goods by comparison to the nearest equivalents, roughly in accordance with the going–rate method. However, two general strategies have been identified, skimming and penetration.

Skimming occurs when the initial price is high. This tends to occur where the price elasticity of demand is low and the barriers to entry are high. The product must appeal to a market segment where price is not an important consideration. This will generally be a high income group of market leaders, but it may comprise, for products such as cameras and Hi–Fi equipment, the lower income 'enthusiast'. The price will offset the high development cost for this type of product and so ease the firm's cash–flow. A skimming strategy is usually accompanied by extensive promotional activity particularly in up–market and specialist magazines. Once a reputation and a market have been established there may be a reduction in price to broaden the market, using the original purchasers as important opinion leaders. Price reductions may also be necessary to maintain a market share as competitors arrive on the scene. Several products have been priced in this way. Both the video cassette recorder and the compact disc player entered the market at high prices, with considerable price reductions as the market expanded and the competition increased.

A penetration strategy involves setting a low price to attract a mass market at the outset. Such a strategy is used where demand is price sensitive and where economies of scale can be gained by mass production. Penetration is usually associated with competitive markets. However, the strategy can be used to discourage competition by raising the barriers of entry, since those entering the market must be certain of high sales to offset development costs. Such a strategy has been used by many firms. Texas Instruments dominated the American hand–held calculator market in this way and in 1988 Amstrad attempted to dominate the business market for personal computers by selling at 50% less than its rival, Apricot.

We can see that the pricing decision needs to take account of a range of interconnected factors. Additional complexities can and do exist. The same product may be differentially priced for number of reasons. It may be discounted for bulk purchase or to specific groups such as senior citizens and students. The same cinema seat may be differentially priced for different performances to even out demand, and particularly to attract customers to less popular showings earlier in the week. The price may be a function of the number and type of distribution channels. Imported goods may be more expensive because they pass through more intermediaries, and products are generally more expensive in a prestigious store. Such variations can be confusing and lead to customer complaints, as some airline companies have found. The price of the same seat on the same flight may vary considerably depending upon when and where the ticket has been bought. Tickets bought well in advance and those bought on a standby basis are much cheaper, as are those obtained from discount agencies and 'bucket shops'.

A further complexity is that the pricing strategy generally changes over the life of a product as a function of demand, market share, and changes in the economy. Price cuts may be introduced to regenerate a product nearing the end of its life cycle or to beat off competition, and price rises may be needed to keep pace with inflation.

Promotion strategy

Earlier we identified the three main functions of a promotion strategy; to inform, to persuade, and to remind. We also suggested that effective strategy was dependent upon selecting the most appropriate message and media for the product and target market. Two important decisions remain; how much to spend, and how to gauge whether a campaign has been effective or not.

It is clear to management that a promotion strategy must be affordable, yet setting an appropriate budget is far from easy. In addition to the notion of affordability three common methods are identified by marketing texts (Kotler, 1983, Cannon, 1986). The 'percentage–of–sales' method sets the budget according to the previous years sales figures or is based on sales forecasts. The inherent flaw in such a strategy is that promotion is a function of sales rather than vice–versa; nevertheless such a method is simple and may appeal to the cautious decision–maker. The 'competitive–parity' method pegs promotional expenditure to that of the major competitors in proportion to the market share. The 'objective–and–task' method has probably the most rational appeal in that specific targets are set and the budget apportioned accordingly. Such a method enables the results of the expenditure to be assessed against the objectives.

In most organizations the marketing manager has to operate from a budget allocated as the result of some complex decision–making process involving all managers in all functional areas. Dhalla (1978) accuses many managers of short–sightedness is setting the promotional budget. He feels that promotion should be treated as a capital investment and not, as in most cases, as an operating cost.

Promotion may be evaluated on three levels. The first consideration is that the particular advertisement or sales promotion has been seen and by how many and what type of people. The second consideration is that the public and in particular the target market are aware of the product and its attributes. The final and most important consideration is that the promotion results in the desired action on the part of the target market. In the case of consumer products then the ultimate test lies in the number of sales, whereas a government campaign to reduce drinking and driving will have to be measured by the number of convictions.

The evaluation of a promotion campaign is especially difficult for a two main reasons. Firstly a decision has to be made about the time scale for such an evaluation. Is the impact of an advertisement to be measured over a week, a month, several months or longer? Secondly it may not be possible to isolate the impact of a promotional campaign from the influence of other variables such as changes in the economy, the behaviour of competitors, changes in social behaviour and so on. Accurate evaluation under such conditions may require extensive econometric models or a level of experimentation not feasible in most organizations. Few firms have done as DuPont, and tested advertising expenditure in their paint market by varying the amounts in different parts of the same territory to assess the impact on sales. They discovered that the effect of the heaviest expenditure was weakest in areas where they had a high market share. Perhaps this is a pointer to the diminishing returns of advertising expenditure (case quoted in Buzzell, 1964).

Not all promotion activity has the strategic intention of increasing demand for products as the following case illustrates. In 1987 Burroughs Wellcome had developed a drug that had been successful in trials in slowing down the effect of the AIDS virus for some people. The company was concerned that the launch would be accompanied by media exaggeration and many would be misled into thinking that a cure had been found. The product was launched simultaneously, in open forums at major hotels in several American cities. In each case the launch was linked by television to a panel of medical experts and questions were encouraged. Such a promotion served to limit demand for the drug specifically to those cases who could benefit the most.

Distribution strategy

Distribution strategy is concerned with such issues as the type and number of channels, the location of those channels and how they might be controlled. Stock policy is an important consideration here, and incentives in the form of discounts may be required to persuade intermediaries such as warehouses to hold stock.

As we can see from Austin–Rover in Case 7.2, an effective distribution strategy is essential if a firm wishes to expand in new or existing markets.

An integrated marketing strategy

Integration can occur along three different dimensions; within each component of the mix; between the various elements of the mix; and between marketing and the other functional strategies. We will deal with each in turn.

☐ The various activities and strategies associated with each component of the mix should work together. For example, effective promotion is generally achieved through a campaign in which press and television advertising and sales promotion are carefully coordinated to achieve the maximum impact upon the consumer.

☐ The elements of the mix should work together. Price reductions are often accompanied by a promotion campaign and both need the reinforcement of sufficient stocks and effective distribution in anticipation of increased demand. Improvements in product quality necessitating increases in price need to be sensitively handled in promotion.

☐ The effective integration of marketing with the other functional strategies, especially those of innovation and production, is considered essential to the firm acquiring a competitive advantage. An effective product portfolio should be built around the skills and other resources of the organization. A business school which attempts to offer courses in international business but lacks staff with the necessary expertise may attract a poor reputation and see support for all its courses suffer as a result. Some see this integration of functional strategies as an iterative process, requiring the constant monitoring of markets, products, processes and technology, and the firm working these elements around its chosen field of distinctive competence (Skinner, 1974).

Summary

Marketing involves the understanding of customer needs and behaviour and the researching of markets for the effective development, pricing, promotion, and distribution of goods and services. These activities operate in a number of different consumer and organizational contexts and can incorporate the marketing of people, places, company image, and ideas as well as goods and services.

The product, price, promotion and distribution elements of marketing are known as the marketing mix. There is a growing trend for firms to segment the markets in which they operate calling for variations in the marketing mix for each target market.

Marketing operates at the interface between the organization and its environment, and changes in the economy, state regulation, technology and social trends all call for changes in marketing strategy. Marketing managers use their knowledge of the environment, especially of those social and cultural influences which shape behaviour in an attempt to manipulate demand for their product. In recent years marketing activities have been significantly affected by consumerism and Britain's membership of the EEC.

The development of an effective marketing strategy depends upon an understanding of the workings of the market place, of customer needs and the appropriate mix for the market segment and prevailing environmental conditions. The implementation of that strategy depends upon the integration of marketing with the other functional specialisms.

Further reading

The text which dominates reading lists in business schools is either P. Kotler *Marketing Management: Analysis, Principles and Control* 6th edition (Prentice Hall International, 1988) or P. Kotler, *Principles of Marketing* 3rd edition (Prentice Hall International, 1986). Much of the same information appears in both books. (Please note that in this chapter references are made to the second edition of Kotler's 'Principles' text). Two books aimed more at the British market are M.J. Baker, *Marketing: An Introductory Text* 4th edition (Macmillan, 1985) and the very readable T. Cannon, *Basic Marketing* 2nd edition (Holt, Rinehart and Winston, 1986). All these books deal with most of the issues raised in this chapter. Some excellent illustrations of marketing policy can be found in P.E. Earl, *The Corporate Imagination* (Wheatsheaf, 1984) and his more accessible. *The Economic Imagination* (Wheatsheaf, 1983). An excellent treatment of the marketing/manufacturing interface is offered by R.H. Hayes and S.C. Wheelwright, *Restoring Our Competitive Edge* (John Wiley, 1984).

Discussion

1. Assess Drucker's claim that marketing is not a specialized activity since it encompasses all the activities of the firm.

2. How far and in what industries do the five orientations to marketing operate today?

3. Critically analyse Galbraith's assertion that consumer–oriented marketing has been replaced by the 'revised sequence'.

4. For what reasons do governments engage in marketing? Does this raise any ethical problems?

5. What type of market research information would you need in the following situations; a holiday company offering a new resort location, a manufacturer developing a new motor for domestic appliances, a restaurateur planning a more expensive menu?

6. What factors would you consider to determine the price of the following; a new high performance sports car, a new breakfast cereal, a management consultancy contract?

7. Why does market segmentation occur and what are its drawbacks for management and the consumer?

8. How useful is the product life cycle concept to management?

9. To what extent is a marketing manager able to change the environment in which the firm operates?

10. What are the essential ingredients of an effective marketing strategy?

11. Taking the Woodville and Austin–Rover cases in turn, assess the marketing strategy in the context of the firm's organizational and external environment.

12. Can the criticisms levelled against marketing be balanced by the social benefits it provides?

Personnel 8

Personnel management deals with those management activities that are concerned with an organization's human resources. In this book we identify two broad areas of operation; people–processing and industrial relations. People–processing is concerned with such activities as selection, training, appraisal and payment. Industrial relations is concerned with issues relating to trade unions, negotiation, bargaining and the handling of industrial disputes.

The activities of personnel management illustrate well the workings of the Business in Context model. The growth of the personnel management function as a specialist activity has been influenced by a number of key environmental variables, in particular the intervention of the state through an increasingly complex system of employment laws, the workings of the labour market, the strength of trade unions and the level of economic activity. We will see how personnel strategies have varied in accordance with changes in the economy and the activities of organized labour. In addition to these environmental influences, the role and status of personnel management within the organization has had a significant part to play in the scope and effectiveness of personnel strategies.

In many respects we are viewing the personnel function at an interesting time. The history of personnel management is clearly a history of reaction to constraints both external and internal to the firm. By the late 1980s some senior managers are taking a different approach to personnel management. Strategies relating to selection, training and motivation are being viewed as key strategies in changing the organizational culture of the enterprise, and major employers like Ford are actively seeking such changes with its personnel function playing a leading role.

In this chapter we will deal with these environmental, organizational and strategic issues. Firstly we will make some attempt to identify in more detail the activities of personnel management.

Identifying the personnel function

In this section we will attempt a general definition of personnel before identifying those activities most commonly associated with it. There would seem to be as many definitions of personnel management as there are

---

KEY CONCEPT 8.1

PEOPLE PROCESSING

People processing relates to those activities of personnel management to do with the acquisition, development, motivation and control of individuals at work. It includes the various activities associated with recruitment, selection, training, appraisal, pay administration and welfare.

KEY CONCEPT 8.2

INDUSTRIAL RELATIONS

Industrial relations is concerned with the relations between employers and their representatives and employees and their representatives over such matters as work practices, pay, conditions, job security and forthcoming changes. The relationship involves elements of negotiation and bargaining, which in practice are usually dealt with by management on one hand and trade union representatives on the other. The importance of industrial relations to the general conduct of business is acknowledged by the State in most countries and a corresponding development has taken place in laws covering employer and employee rights and laws governing the conduct of collective bargaining. The conduct of industrial relations is influenced significantly by the general state of the economy and the ideology of the interested parties.

---

books on the subject. This is hardly surprising, as we have already noted that the activities are highly dependent upon the context in which they operate. For example, a discussion of personnel management in Britain would place a much greater emphasis upon industrial relations than it would in the USA, where trade unions play much less of a role, and collective action is much rarer. Despite these variations, a useful starting point is the definition put forward by the Institute of Personnel Management.

> Personnel management is a responsibility of all those who manage people as well as being a description of the work of those who are employed as specialists. It is that part of management which is concerned with people at work and with their relationships within an enterprise. It applies not only to industry and commerce but to all fields of employment. Personnel management aims to achieve both efficiency and justice, neither of which can be pursued successfully without the other. It seems to bring together and develop into an effective organization the men and women who make up an enterprise, enabling each to make his own best contribution to its success, both as an individual and as a member of a working group. It seeks to provide fair terms and conditions of employment and satisfying work for those employed.
>
> (IPM, 1963)

If we ignore its somewhat idealistic stance and an absence of precisely defined tasks and duties, the definition serves the useful purpose of distinguishing between a business function and a departmental presence within an organization. Many students of business conclude mistakenly that all businesses conform to textbook models, relating as they do to fairly large scale organizations differentiated according to specialist departments.

In a recent study by Daniel and Millward (1983) it was estimated that if all firms, including small businesses, were considered, then 75% of companies would have no specialist personnel manager. The personnel function is such organizations is often performed by a manager who deals with personnel matters along with other duties. For example in many professional groupings, like accountants or solicitors, one of the senior partners is usually given responsibility for personnel matters, but this constitutes just one of his or her duties. Some smaller firms may operate the personnel function through a one–person secretary–cum–records department. The absence of a personnel specialist may even be deliberate policy. Hewlett–Packard, the American multinational, did not introduce a personnel department until staffing levels had reached 1200, its founders preferring the personnel function to be the responsibility of all managers (Beer *et al.*, 1985).

In Figure 8.1 we present a detailed list of the various activities associated with personnel management. All firms will have a need for some of these activities, in that management, for example, must conform to the prevailing employment laws and operate some system for paying employees. At some stage all firms have a need for the recruitment and selection of new staff or the reallocation of existing staff. The extent and formalization of these activities depends very much on the size of the labour force, the extent of trade union membership and whether or not the firm has a specialist personnel department, as well as other influences raised in the next two sections.

The activities identified in Figure 8.1 may be performed in a variety of ways. We can identify three broad categories.

☐ They are performed by a personnel specialist or by a general manager with an overall responsibility for personnel matters, or by individual managers themselves. In this case the personnel specialist may operate a system of employee appraisal or each manager may be responsible for recruiting and selecting their own staff.

☐ Personnel specialists operate only in an advisory capacity to other managers. In this case members of a personnel department will advise on the setting up of personnel systems which will be operated by other managers. Examples of this could include the establishment of a job evaluation and grading system of criteria for promotion.

☐ In this case, the personnel specialist will act in conjunction with other managers, as for example in interviewing candidates for a vacancy, or designing and implementing a training programme for a sales department.

As we have seen, in smaller firms, the activities tend to be carried out by all managers and no specialist operates. In larger firms with formalized procedures a mixture of all three methods occurs. A personnel manager may advise the sales manager on the type of person he is seeking to fill a vacancy and assist in the drafting of a job advertisement. A number of candidates may be interviewed by the personnel manager alone and a short–list drawn up for a second interview at which the sales manager will take a leading role.

The following sections will explore the complexities of personnel activi-

Activity	What it involves
Manpower planning and control	The analysis of a company's manpower needs in light of its current manpower resources and the nature of the labour market. Such planning lays the foundation for policies related to recruitment, selection, training, pay and so on.
Recruitment	The first stage usually involves a detailed job analysis followed by the selection of the most appropriate method of recruitment, be it the use of government job centres, using specialist recruitment consultants or placing advertisements in newspapers. Decisions made here aim to attract a field of suitable candidates.
Selection	The use of one or more of a variety of techniques including application forms, interviewing and tests to select the most appropriate person from a field of candidates. The interview tends to be the most favoured method of selection. Decisions are usually made against some general or specific criteria relating to the type of candidate required.
Training and management development	This involves the analysis of the type of training required and the people to be trained, followed by the selection of the most appropriate method. This can range from simple on–the–job instruction to sending people on specific courses. In many firms the training and development of managers is seen as a special case involving long–term planning and consideration for individual career development.
Appraisal	This is a contentious issue in personnel and sometimes resisted by trade unions. It involves the setting up of formal systems to assess the contribution of individuals to the organization. The system is often designed by personnel specialists but administered by all managers.
Pay administration	This is a complex area involving decisions about the rate of pay (often involving negotiation with trade unions), about the way pay is differentially distributed (using some form of job evaluation or individual merit rating), and about the viability of one of a variety of payment schemes such as flat rate payment, payment by results, profit–sharing and so on. Decisions made in this area have broadened to include the number and range of fringe benefits such as pensions, company cars, cheap mortgages and the like.
Job and organizational design	In some cases personnel managers contribute to decisions about how jobs are to be carried out and how the organization is to be structured. This may involve the design and administration of programmes such as job enrichment, organizational development or the quality of working life.

Activity	What it involves
Collective bargaining	Personnel management are invariably involved in the preparation of the employer's case and usually in the negotiations with employee representatives. Once collective agreements have been made, it is usually the job of the personnel manager to apply such agreements and deal with the outcomes.
Grievance and disputes handling	Related to the above, the personnel manager is usually in the front line in dealing with situations arising from individual or collective grievances. In larger firms specific procedures are laid down, but in all cases there is an expectation of the personnel manager to solve disputes as and when they arise.
Legal advice	With developments in employment law (outlined in the next section) many personnel managers are seen as the resident expert in legal matters pertaining to employment and act as a guide to other managers.
Employee communications and counselling	The personnel specialist is often given responsibility for communicating general information to the workforce as well as administering specific programmes for employee participation such as suggestion schemes. Some firms go further and involve the personnel manager in employee advice and counselling.
Personnel information and records	The need for personnel records has increased as firms have grown in size. Such records, kept by the personnel department, are often an important source of information upon which personnel decisions are based.

Figure 8.1 The activities of personnel management.

ties, examining the relationship between personnel and external groups such as government and trade unions, the influence of organizational politics and the contribution of personnel to overall management strategy.

The environmental aspects of personnel

The development of personnel management as a specialist function in organizations owes much to the influence of external events. The growth of markets led to increases in the size of the firm with a corresponding demand for recruitment, training and some centralized payment administration system. The growth of trade unions, especially in Britain, created the need for industrial relations specialists among management. The impact of two world wars created problems for the labour supply and a corresponding attention being paid to training methods and employee consultation. Full employment in the 1960s once again focussed the attention on labour shortages and methods used to tackle them, such as the

Factories Act 1961
Contract of Employment Act 1963, 1972
The Industrial Training Act 1965
Race Relations Act 1968, 1976
Equal Pay Act 1970
Industrial Relations Act 1971
Employment and Training Act 1973
Health and Safety at Work Act 1974.
Trade Union and Labour Relations Act 1974, 1976.
Sex Discrimination Act 1975
Employment Protection (Consolidation) Act 1978
Employment Act 1980
Employment Act 1982
Trade Union Act 1984
Employment Act 1988

Figure 8.2 Major employment law since 1960.

retraining of existing staff and active recruitment from other companies. In the 1970s the focus turned to state intervention and the problems created by new technology. We can see that all five environmental aspects of our model interact in some significant way with the personnel function. We deal with each one in turn.

The role of the state

The state operating through government policies and the legal system has had considerable influence on the personnel function in four areas; legislation, the introduction of specific policies concerned with the supply of labour, which we shall refer to as manpower policies, incomes policies and third–party intervention.

Employment legislation. Employment legislation is concerned with the rights and obligations of employers and employees and the conduct of industrial relations. The growth of employment law in the 1960s and 1970s, and the growing impact of the 1980s laws governing the conduct of industrial relations have had a significant impact on the work of personnel. In Figure 8.2 we show the growth of employment legislation since 1960 by listing the major Acts of Parliament. Students requiring more information on employment law are advised to consult the law text in this series (Cole and Shears, 1989).

Many of the laws have had a direct impact upon the day–to–day work of personnel managers. The Industrial Training Act 1964, with its introduction of the levy–grant system for approved training, resulted in the expansion of training programmes. Recruitment advertisements must be carefully drafted so as not to contravene race and six discrimination legislation. The Arbitration Conciliation and Advisory Service (ACAS) set up by the Employment Protection Act 1975 has had a significant impact on the conduct of industrial relations. Several of the laws have set up a judicial system of Industrial Tribunals as in the case of redundancy and unfair dismissals cases. The preparation of such cases on behalf of the employer is often

In the 1980s significant changes have taken place in the nature of labour law. The coverage of labour law has grown considerably since the 1960s, but there has generally been a marked resistance by both unions and management to attempts by governments to regulate collective bargaining. Since 1980, a marked change has occurred imposing much greater restriction on the union freedom to strike, to control its members through the closed shop and in the way it elects its leadership. The unions regard such laws as an imposition on their freedom and as politically motivated. The Government see the laws as contributing to economic stability, and protecting the freedom of the individual in society.

KEY CONCEPT 8.3

THE CHANGING NATURE OF LABOUR LAW IN BRITAIN

done by a personnel specialist. Despite the growth in the tribunal and the number of cases petitioned, only a small percentage reach the final stages. Most cases are dealt with through a variety of conciliation procedures, sometimes involving ACAS (described later in this section), but almost inevitably involving a personnel manager.

The expansion of employment law has been an important causal factor in the increased number of personnel specialists. For example, the Industrial Training Act of 1964 required firms to pay a government levy which could only be reclaimed upon the satisfactory completion of an approved training programme. In many firms this resulted in the establishment of training departments staffed by specialist training officers.

Some commentators see the expansion of labour law as a vehicle for the increased status of personnel managers (for example Legge, 1978). Managers faced with a complex array of new legal provisions seek expert advice and often turn to the personnel specialist as their source. A recent survey has noted that the industrial relations legislation of the 1980s has given many personnel managers a new lease of life (Millward and Stevens, 1986). However, not all such legislation had had the impact predicted. The industrial Relations Act of 1971 attracted much media attention and was elevated to the status of a political *cause célèbre*. In reality its provisions were dismissed by some management as much as they were by the trade union movement, its measures were largely ignored and its impact lessened long before its repeal in 1974.

The industrial relations aspect of personnel work may well be entering a new era in which legislation plays an ever–increasing role. There is clear indication that this area of personnel management has been politicized as never before. In the main, the Labour Party, with its traditional allegiances to the trade union movement has introduced legislation which has tended to establish and further the rights of individual workers. The Conservative Party on the other hand has been more concerned with establishing laws which control the internal affairs of trade unions and which attempt to regulate collective bargaining. As new laws have been introduced and repealed by successive governments, personnel management has had to respond and amend its policies accordingly. The politicization of personnel management is seen most clearly in the public sector where, for example in the 1980s, Trade Unions in coal mining and the health service have taken stands against government policy on such issues as pit and hospital closures, on pay restraints and attempts to reduce public spending in general. This has clearly placed personnel management in those industries in a political arena where consultation and collective bargaining with trade unions has significant political implications.

The legislation of the 1980s is based on the assumption that trade union power needs to be curbed and that the general public needs to be protected against the damaging effects of strikes and other forms of industrial action. The three Acts, the Employment Acts of 1980 and 1982 and the Trade Union Act of 1984 have affected the conduct of industrial relations by changing the law in the following ways.

- ☐ Trade unions as organizations are now responsible for the actions of their members. If, during a strike, damage is caused to property, then the union may be held responsible. Previously trade unions were immune and only individuals could be sued.
- ☐ A much tighter legal definition of a strike has been drawn up. A strike can only take place if it relates wholly or mainly to industrial matters such as pay and conditions and can only occur between an employee and his or her direct employer. This has effectively ruled out any form of political strike and any form of secondary action, such as a sympathy strike to further the cause of a group of workers at another plant. In addition a strike can only be called following a properly conducted secret ballot.
- ☐ Senior trade union officials must now present themselves for re-election every five years by secret ballot. The government clearly feels that trade union leaders should be more accountable not only to their members, but to the public at large.
- ☐ The concept of accountability has been extended to include new legal restrictions on the closed shop. A ballot must be held by unions wishing to operate a closed shop and support must be obtained from 80% of the membership.

Other provisions of this legislation include restrictions on picketing and the introduction of a compulsory ballot to test union members' support for contributions to a political fund.

The legislation of the 1980s reflects a major shift in the government's attitude towards industrial relations. The initial impact of the legislation was difficult to assess, since few firms sought legal redress during industrial action. Mercury, the communications company, successfully took legal action against the Post Office Engineering Union when they refused to join up the British Telecom network to the Mercury System. Mercury had acquired the right to operate an independent telephone service under the government's liberalization and privatization policy. The union claimed its refusal to work and eventual strike action was to protect jobs at British Telecom. The court ruled that the action was primarily an opposition to government policy and hence political. The new laws have also been used to the benefit of Eddie Shah in extending his newspaper empire in the North West. He took the National Graphical Association to court to prevent it blockading a non–union printing plant. He succeeded in winning his case and gaining significant damages from the union.

Many of the court actions have involved smaller employers who have probably most to lose from a dispute. It was Mercury and not British Telecom who took action against British Telecom's workers. Many larger companies are reluctant to use the Courts for fear of alienating the trade unions. Contrary to the image of industrial relations portrayed in the popular press, management and unions, in most firms, have reasonably good relations, which recourse to the law may damage. Nonetheless the new legislation has significantly changed the nature of collective bargaining and consequently the work of personnel specialists. There has been a marked reduction in the number of disputes in British industry. This could be related to changes in the law. It could also be related to economic conditions which we will discuss later. In some cases it is clear that changes in legislation have been accompanied by deliberate attempts on the part of management to change the employment relations culture of the enterprise. This is part of an attempt to replace traditional adversarial bargaining with a more cooperative approach. This theme reccurs in our discussion of labour matters later in this section and when we discuss personnel strategies towards the end of this chapter.

Manpower policies. There has been an attempt on the part of several governments to achieve a stable balance between supply and demand in the labour market through a series of manpower policies. For twenty years since the end of the Second World War unemployment remained below 2% and the major concern was the development of mechanisms to improve the supply of skilled labour. A government White Paper in 1962 linked the inadequacy of training in British industry to the country's economic problems. The problem was tackled by the Industrial Training Act 1964 referred to earlier. Its impact was immediate with a dramatic increase in levels of training. Training Boards were set up for each industry and several innovations were introduced. The Engineering Industry Training Board radically restructured its apprenticeship scheme to produce trainees with more flexible skills in a shorter time. Skills shortages, however, have persisted to dog British industry.

Despite the continuing skills shortage in some areas the focus shifted to introducing measures to combat the problem of rising unemployment. Such measures have tended to fall into two categories; those aimed at increasing the demand for labour and those attempting to reduce the total supply of labour. Schemes to increase the demand for labour have included wage subsidies, job creation, community enterprise programmes and the youth training scheme while those measures to reduce the labour supply have included early retirement, job release, temporary short–time working and job–splitting.

Various government training programmes have been introduced to tackle both the problems of skills shortages and unemployment. The Youth Training Scheme has been in operation a number of years, whilst in 1987 the Job Training Scheme for long–term unemployed adults was introduced.

Whilst some firms see such schemes as sources of recruitment of cheap labour, more recent government proposals have met with employer opposition which tends to favour a return to the specialist training of apprenticeship–type programmes. The unions are sceptical of all such schemes fearing that they will disrupt traditional patterns of recruitment and dilute skills.

CASE 8.1

**IBM'S PERSONNEL
POLICIES**

IBM is the world's largest and most successful computer manufacturer. It has been established in Britain since 1951 and is a market leader in most of its product ranges. There are no unions at IBM and the company has never experienced a strike or had to lay people off. Paradoxically, many of its current employment and personnel practices were developed during the depression in the USA and many were ahead of their time. The company scrapped payment-by-results methods for its manufacturing employees in 1936, treating all employees as salaried staff and in effect offering them lifetime employment. Around the same time the company introduced job enlargement and flexible working and embarked on a programme of involving all employees in the design of new products. Employee training has always been a major feature of the company

In Britain the company expanded rapidly in the 1960s and was still growing in the 1980s. Only 27% of employees work in manufacturing, the majority operating in marketing and technical services. Pay is high compared to other firms and labour turnover is exceptionally low. A feature that has always intrigued British commentators is the absence of a trade union. The management claim that the employees have no need for a union nor do they want one. This is supported by an ACAS survey in 1977 which discovered that only 4.9% of employees wanted a union and 91% claimed they would refuse to join if a union were introduced.

A trade union would certainly contradict the stated corporate commitment to individualism. Additionally it is claimed that a union is not needed since the company offers terms and conditions far in excess of those usually demanded by trade unions. The key features of the employment practices would seem to be the following.

☐ A fairly sophisticated system of manpower planning, employee recruitment and training.
☐ Lifetime employment for all employees with the expectation that employees will change jobs as and when required.
☐ Single status for all employees in terms of canteens, facilities, and fringe benefits. The only exceptions are overtime payment for manufacturing workers and company cars for some senior management and some sales staff.
☐ Salaries are determined centrally, usually by making a favourable comparison with other firms. The exercise is carried out annually to ensure pay rates keep ahead of those in other companies. Once established, increases are always based on merit and determined through a management-by-objectives type appraisal scheme.
☐ Training is emphasized, with management receiving a average of forty days training a year (forty times the national average). Much of the training focusses upon human resource management.
☐ An opinion survey of all staff is held every two years, to ascertain attitudes towards such factors as working practices, pay and conditions, and personnel practices. The response rates are very high.
☐ Emphasis is placed upon managers sorting out their own problems. A

Continued from previous page

centralized personnel function operates a 'hands off' policy. The company prefers to leave personnel matters to individual managers, especially grievance handling.

☐ Then company operates two formalized communication procedures. A 'Speak Up' system encourages employees to raise business-related problems, whilst an 'Open Door' system allows employees to appeal against decisions taken by their own managers.

IBM would seem to operate a successful employment relations policy that is well-linked by its employees. The company expects a great deal of its employees, but offers them secure jobs at relatively high rates of pay. The policy has been criticized on a number of counts. The company has been accused of being anti-union and ensuring that unions never become established. Whilst the firm operates a philosophy which stresses individuality as part of its commitment to entrepreneurship, individuals are nevertheless expected to conform to IBM norms of behaviour, even to participating in out-of-work company social events and activities. The company has also been accused of operating a recruitment policy which ensures that only those committed to the IBM way will be selected. In general, sceptics have attempted to label IBM as running an oppressive system, which is only possible in the rarified environment of a successful hi-tech company.

However, any firm which has developed such a strong corporate culture leaves itself open to attack by those who see it as too good to be true. The reality is probably that IBM have developed a system which works for itself, which seems to operate in both the interests of the company and its employees. The employment relations policies are probably far more sophisticated than in most unionized companies. The extent to which it offers other companies a model to follow may well be limited by the ability of their management to carry such policies through effectively in non-IBM setting.

(*Sources:* Drucker, 1968, Bassett, 1986.)

Incomes policies. With few exceptions, post–war governments have attempted to control inflation by holding down wages using various types of incomes policy. These have varied from mere exhortations for voluntary restraint as in 1964–6, to statutory controls as in 1966–9. Often such statutory measures include periods of total pay freezes. The Labour government 1974–9 launched its Social Contract which incorporated a series of incomes policies aimed at reducing the level of inflation in return for concessions to the trade union movement. Such conessions included the repeal of the 1971 Industrial Relations Act, the introduction of the Employment Protection Act, improved social security arrangements and by setting up the Bullock Committee, a move towards greater industrial democracy. The Conservative government, which came to power in 1979, formally rejected the use of incomes policies. None the less, policies of holding down wage rises in the public sector could be construed as tantamount to an incomes policy, and have been the basis of several lengthy disputes in the public sector, notably in the health service and education, as with the teachers strikes of 1985.

Incomes policies have rarely been very effective, except where the government is able to exert direct influence on its own public sector. Most incomes policies have collapsed after a few months or have been ignored by major employers. However, the introduction of incomes policies created two important by–products as far as the personnel function was concerned; the growth of productivity bargaining and fringe benefits.

Productivity bargaining developed during the 1960s around the notion that pay rises would only be given in exchange for changes in work practices, which might include increased productivity or a reduction in manning levels. The most famous of such agreements took place at the Esso Refinery at Fawley (Flanders, 1964). The National Board for Prices and Incomes created in 1965 advocated productivity bargaining as a means of achieving economic growth and attempted to encourage its widespread growth. Such changes placed increased emphasis on local agreements and often were a source of much union opposition, in both cases extending the role of personnel.

Productivity bargaining has re–emerged in the 1980s, but outside the framework of incomes policies. The main thrust of current productivity deals is to reduce costs and maintain overseas trade in a competitive situation. In some cases this has meant that trade unions have cooperated closely with management, especially where jobs have been at stake. In 1981, the Sunderland operation of Coles Cranes introduced a highly successful productivity deal with the backing of the trade union. Costs were reduced, exports rejuvenated and wages increased. We must note, however, that the firm was operating in an area of high unemployment and union bargaining power was relatively weak.

The growth of fringe benefits such as company cars, discount purchase facilities, private health care and low–interest personal loans can in part be ascribed to the restrictions imposed by incomes policies. Firms seeking ways of rewarding certain employees and keeping within government guidelines extended their remuneration schemes to include a wide range of such fringe benefits.

Third party intervention. Governments have always been willing to intervene in those industrial disputes they see as damaging to the nation's economy. The government currently funds the Arbitration, Conciliation and Advisory Service (ACAS), set up in 1974 and given statutory rights under the Employment Protection Act 1975. ACAS consists of a full–time Chairman and nine part–time members made up of equal parts of TUC nominees, CBI nominees and academics. It is staffed by civil servants.

It functions include the following.

☐ Bringing the two sides in an industrial dispute together so that agreement may be reached (conciliation).
☐ Bringing the two sides together but making recommendations for an agreement (mediation).
☐ Making a decision on behalf but with agreement of the two sides (arbitration).

□ Carrying out an investigation into a major dispute and making recommendations to guide future action (inquiry).
□ Establishing codes of practice for the conduct of industrial relations.

ACAS is therefore a state mechanism which attempts to influence the conduct of industrial relations without either party recoursing to the use of law.

The role of the economy

We can see from Figure 8.3 that the 1960s and 1970s saw an unprecedented increase in those involved in personnel work. As a rough guide, it is estimated that members of the Institute represent half those involved in personnel.

Whilst we have attributed part of that growth to developments in legislation, there is a clear correlation between personnel management and the state of the economy. In the two decades of full employment prior to the early 1970s considerable emphasis was placed on recruitment, selection, training and payment systems, to overcome labour shortages and assist in the substitution and retention of skilled labour. During the same period the increased bargaining power of the trade union movement, especially at workplace level, resulted in increases in shopfloor collective bargaining and hence an increased workload for the personnel manager.

Traditional activities of personnel management such as recruitment and training are clearly related to full employment economies. The continued growth of personnel throughout the 1970s is harder to reconcile with the economic expansion argument since it was a period of slow–down and considerable economic problems. However, if we see the growth of the personnel function as a reactive process where organizational responses lag behind the real stimulus, then the growth of the 1970s may be seen as response to problems first recognized in the late 1950s and early 1960s. Its impact upon personnel management organization extended well into the 1970s.

Given the hypothesis that economic growth and full employment lead to a thriving and active personnel function, then the reverse hypothesis might also be true; that an economic recession will reduce not only the need for recruitment selection and training, but that the negotiating power of trade unions will be impaired, resulting in a reduction of the extent and frequency of collective bargaining negotiations.

Evidence related to this remains mixed. Some report that personnel managers are weathering the recession better than most other management groups, in that new opportunities to demonstrate competence have been created in the form of redundancy management and achieving lower wage settlements in a generally peaceful industrial relations climate (Guest, 1982). The current climate is even seen as an opportunity for personnel to move away from its traditional role towards a greater concern for the development of managers and high skill personnel (Hunt, 1984). This theme of creating a new approach for personnel is examined more closely when we discuss personnel strategies. Some of the activities of personnel management in a recession are illustrated by Case 8.2.

1959 – 4 308 members
1969 – 10 636 members
1979 – 20 194 members

(from Guest and Horwood, 1982)

Figure 8.3 Membership of the Institute of Personnel Managers.

There are some who take a pessimistic view of the changing role of personnel management. Kingsley Manning quotes the director of a large company,

Ten years ago my department seemed to make all the running; virtually nothing happened without our involvement. But now we have to fight just to get to know what's going on.

(Manning, 1983, p 76)

This reduction in personnel activity has been particularly apparent in the field of industrial relations. There has been a slowing down and reversal of trade union growth. A consequence of this has been a shift in emphasis from shop floor to centralized bargaining reducing the role of personnel management in workplace negotiations. This is not always the case. In Perkins Diesels (Case 8.2) the negotiation of new work practices meant that the emphasis shifted back to the shopfloor. However, in most cases, during a recession the weak bargaining position of the trade unions has resulted in speedier negotiated settlements.

The focus of attention has undoubtedly been the impact of economic recession on the role and function of the personnel management. Given improvements in the British economy and a drop in the level of unemployment by the late 1980s we may speculate on the future direction of personnel activities. Three scenarios may be appropriate.

☐ In some firms, especially more traditional engineering companies, personnel activities have remained much the same. Business has gone on as usual, albeit at a reduced rate. An improvement in the economy will simply mean increased activity in those traditional areas.
☐ More enlightened companies have adapted the traditional activities to the new demands of the 1990s. Ford Motor Company for example has recognized the need for training in computer skills and information technology by setting up 'open–access' learning centres where employees are encouraged to develop new skills. The same company has recognized that falling birth rates will have an impact ultimately on recruiting and has set up special programmes to develop closer links with local schools.
☐ Other companies have used the changed economy to adopt totally new personnel strategies. Some have adopted a more aggressive stance towards trade unions whilst others have taken steps to change the organizational culture towards greater commitment to joint management–worker goals. There are clear influences here from Japanese Management (Chapter 2) and the concept of the 'excellent' company (Chapter 3).

In all these cases economic influences are present with others and must be seen in conjunction with the role of the state, the power of trade unions, management ideology and the organization structure. This reinforces the idea that the elements of our model cannot be viewed in isolation. We shall return to these strategies at the end of the chapter.

The Perkins Engine Group is owned by the Canadian firm, Varity, a company which also controls Massey Ferguson. The company makes diesel engines of all types ranging from seven to 1500 brake horse power. Its main manufacturing operation, Peterborough Engines, is based in the town of the same name and currently employs nearly three quarters of the total workforce. Despite the acquisition of Rolls Royce Diesel Engines in 1984 and Lesley Gardner Diesels in 1986 the overall size of the company has been reduced from over 10 000 in the 1970s to 4900 in 1989. Such a reduction has not been possible without a significant change in personnel strategies and in the work of the personnel function.

In the late 1970s the company appeared to be in a healthy position. The demand for its products was high and the concern was to operate at full capacity. The plant was working seven days a week and the 10 000 employees were working an average of 10% overtime per person. The company was turning out 1000 diesel engine a day with 86% of these for the export market. The company adopted fairly typical personnel and industrial relations strategies for the engineering industry. Payment-by-results was the norm, training tended to focus on an engineering apprenticeship programme, and industrial relations negotiation was highly centralized. The main trade union at Perkins (the AUEW) was strong, with a high membership amongst shop-floor employees. There were a high number of short unofficial disputes that were highly localized. The high demand for the company's product meant that stoppages had to be avoided at all costs. The strategy adopted by the company was for a central personnel department to handle all industrial relations matters, including the negotiation for local disputes in a bid to formalize procedures and take grievances away from their immediate location. As a consequence, local line management were seldom involved in industrial relations and related personnel issues.

In 1980 the demand for diesel engines fell sharply. In response the management opted for the following.

☐ A strict control of all overtime working.
☐ The introduction of some short-time working.
☐ Setting up a series of programmes to introduce changes in working practice that would enhance the competitiveness of the firm.
☐ A mixture of voluntary and compulsory redundancy.

The urgency of change was all the greater because of the company's heavy reliance on export markets and hence competition from diesel engine manufacturers all over the world, who were also competing for a declining market share. The management recognized that such changes could not be made without consultation with the Trade Unions and the workforce, so that communication became the key to the implementation of the strategic changes. The changes were brought about through a variety of methods.

☐ All changes were negotiated with the Trade Union and the AUEW participated fully in the exercise. The union recognized that survival

CASE 8.2

THE PERKINS ENGINE GROUP

Continued over page

Continued from previous page

of the firm was the issue, but found the dilemma of protecting jobs for some whilst sanctioning the redundancy of others difficult to reconcile with traditional trade union practices. The redundancy issue was particularly difficult in that management could not afford to let all those go who wanted to under a generous voluntary scheme. The financial burden would be too high and such programmes might leave the company under–staffed in certain key areas. Compulsory redundancy was therefore inevitable with the subsequent difficult negotiations and disputes.

☐ The union had also to agree to new work practices. These generally involved the broadening of jobs and the introduction of more flexible work methods through the ending of demarcation agreements. Discussion and negotiation on this issue was specific to individual departments and sections, effectively decentralizing industrial relations. Line management became much more involved in personnel matters as the emphasis on the introduction of new work practices was shifted to man-management at the local level.

☐ There was a concern that all employees received a clear picture of the threats facing the company and fear that information could easily be distorted. The director took it upon himself to brief personally all senior management and trade union leaders. Team briefings were held throughout the organization. A company video was produced which examined the current position and explained the need for change. A training school programme was set up which gave sessions on the firm's position and encouraged feedback.

☐ A 'Fair Days Work Charter' was produced which stressed the need for all employees, both staff and hourly paid, to
  ☐ Work for the whole day.
  ☐ Achieve output and quality targets set by management.
  ☐ Suggest ways of improving work methods and equipment.
  ☐ Work cooperatively.

By 1982 employment levels had been reduced to 6000, but it was decided that the strategy had to continue throughout the 1980s despite the acquisition of new plants such as Rolls Royce. Redundancy became an annual exercise with the usual mix of voluntary and compulsory to preserve key skills. Three new strategies emerged.

Firstly, a major reorganization took place. The company was restructured around autonomous strategic business units operating as independent profit centres. Senior management are given considerable responsibility and scope to enhance the competitiveness of their business unit. Entrepreneurship is encouraged and a fair proportion of senior management salary is tied to performance. There are plans to extend this scheme to all employees at some future date.

Secondly, considerable emphasis has been placed on the training of employees to widen their range of skills to enhance flexibility and to increase the general level of skill throughout the organization. The company's programme was considered successful enough for them to win a National Training Award in 1987.

Thirdly, new investments have been made in automation to improve quality and reduce staffing costs. Assistance with modernization has been obtained by the company participating in an EEC funded project for the furtherance of technology transfer by the dissemination of operating experience and best practice.

As a result of the various changes the company has become much leaner, focussing on the employment of skilled, flexible employees.

Continued from previous page

(*Sources:* Jackson, 1983, *Company Information*, 1988)

Personnel management and the labour force

From our brief review of personnel activities in Figure 8.1 we can see that the personnel function interacts with the labour force in two ways. It deals with individuals in the labour market through the activities of manpower planning, recruitment, selection, training and by administering payment and other reward and control systems. Secondly, it deals with the organized labour force through the mechanisms of joint consultation, collective bargaining and conflict management. We have already referred to these two activities in terms of people processing and industrial relations management.

People processing. Operating within a given labour market, the personnel manager will attempt to fulfill the organization's demand for labour. This will be achieved mainly through the processes of recruitment, selection and training, often within the framework of a manpower plan. In some cases the labour market will act as a total constraint to the extent that severe labour shortages in a given area may cause management to rethink its plans. In other cases the labour market operates as a partial constraint, and attempts will be made to entice workers away from existing jobs by offering them attractive pay packages and opportunities for career development. This can cause high levels of mobility among certain groups such as computing specialists in an otherwise depressed labour market. In other cases the firm attempts to change the composition of the labour market, meeting labour shortages by training substitute labour or by attracting certain groups back to work, such as married women with children, by providing working conditions compatible with school hours.

The student relying on textbooks may be forgiven for the assumption that personnel management is an exercise in scientific management. This exercise is a matching process between the labour market and the needs of the organization employing a variety of scientifically–based techniques of selection, training and employee motivation and retention. The student is confronted by a vast literature expounding such theories and offering a variety of such techniques. However, part of this literature has concentrated upon a critique of these same theories, analyses and techniques often labelling them as intuitive and subjective.

Personnel management textbooks see selection in terms of a matching process between the candidate and the job description. The decision to employ or reject a candidate is ultimately the prerogative of line management, but the administration of the process tends to be carried out by personnel specialists applying scientific principles of structured interviewing and psychological testing.

In most cases there will be a job description resulting from a job analysis. The process of creating a job description will generate criteria against which job candidates will be judged. Managers will use such information to build up stereotypes of 'ideal' candidates. However, the job description could well be dated and in any case, the manager is just as likely to establish criteria based upon his or her own prejudices.

The most popular form of selection method is the interview. Management literature abounds with advice for the would–be interviewer, but such advice owes more to general experience and deductive reasoning than it does to empirical research. There is considerable evidence that the interview is a relatively poor selection device and is particular poor in terms of cost effectiveness to the company. However, it is retained because not better method has yet been devised and because it allows management to exercise judgement in the selection process.

If we view other areas of personnel processing we will find much the same story. Attempts by personnel managers to use 'scientific techniques' often adapted from the behavioural sciences have met with mixed results. This is true of a range of techniques incorporating the use of psychological tests, in selection and placement, appraisal schemes, approaches to training and devising methods of payment to increase worker motivation.

The major problems with using such techniques in people processing are reliability and validity. Reliability refers to the extent to which a measure of consistency can be achieved as for example in getting interviewers to behave in a similar fashion and ask candidates similar questions. Validity refers to the extent to which a technique used in personnel has some practical value for the organisation. Does a selection interview actually discriminate between suitable and unsuitable candidates? Will a training programme lead to improved worker performance?

Because of such problems, personnel managers have difficulty in proving that the work they do contributes in a measurable way to the effectiveness of the organization. For example, the results of a management development programme may not be apparent for a number of years, if at all, and many of the managers may have left the organization by that time. The difficulty of personnel proving its worth is a theme developed when we examine the relationship between personnel management and an organization's goals later in this chapter. It is not surprising that many personnel managers feel safer dealing with the day–to–day firefighting of industrial relations problems than devising policies and procedures where the outcome is uncertain. It is to industrial relations that we next turn our attention.

Industrial relations management. We can identify four major activities associated with industrial relations management.

☐ *The recognition of Trade Unions* involves both the recognition of the employee right to organize and the recognition of the union right to represent employees in such matters as wage negotiation. In some industries recognition has been slow. The recognition of the National

Union of Bank Employees by the major clearing banks was only achieved in 1967 after considerable disruption and eventual strike action. In other cases management will positively encourage their employees to join trade unions since they view a healthy union membership as contributing to the stability of workplace relations. This acceptance and encouragement has been a major factor in trade union growth and consequently the development of the personnel function. In recent years there have been new variations on the theme of recognition.

A key approach in companies such as IBM, Hewlett–Packard and Marks and Spencer is the development of employment relations strategies that do not involve trade unions. We return to this theme when we discuss personnel strategies and in Case 8.1. The growth of Japanese firms in Britain and their preference for company unions has led to the establishment of single union agreements being made in companies such as Nissan (Case 2.3) and Sanyo. Under such agreements management will allow only one trade union to represent all employees in the workforce. This has caused considerable consternation in the trade union movement, but agreements have been reached between Nissan and the Amalgamated Union of Engineering Workers (AUEW) and News International and the EETPU as presented in the case in Chapter 1.

☐ *Collective bargaining*, as we can see in Figure 8.1 involves management and unions in the negotiation of wages and conditions. The growth of localized bargaining in the 1950s and 1960s widened both the role of personnel managers and shop stewards as actual negotiators. The activities of personnel management in collective bargaining include research, assisting in policy formulation, negotiation and in general developing a climate to assist the bargaining process by encouraging inter–union cooperation and minimizing areas of avoidable conflict. In addition personnel managers provide information and facilities for shop stewards, in accordance with the Industry Act, 1975 and the Employment Protection Act, 1975.

Both management and unions have resisted the introduction of legally binding contracts as the outcome of collective bargaining. However, the changing climate of single union agreements has been accompanied by an increase in contractual bargaining.

☐ *Disputes and grievance procedure:* the process of collective bargaining inevitably involves a degree of conflict. Many firms operate a disputes procedure to resolve such conflicts. In most cases the formalization and complexity of the disputes procedure is directly related to the size of the firm. A breakdown in negotiation can result in a strike, although the occurrence of these is rare, contrary to popular opinion. Most disputes procedures have provisions for third party intervention, such as the use of ACAS.

Those firms who favour single union agreements, such as Nissan and News International, tend also to favour a new approach to disputes procedure. This new approach usually includes the following.

☐ A 'legally binding contract'.
☐ A 'peace' clause whereby the employees agree not to strike and the

employers agree not to lock workers out for the duration of the contract and while the new contract is renegotiated.
☐ An agreement on pendulum arbitration, whereby the arbitrator must opt for one side or the other.

Such provisions limit the use of the strike weapon to an irrevocable breakdown in the negotiation of a new contract, and a recourse to pendulum arbitration is an attempt to avoid unwanted compromise. Much has been written about such measures, but it is too early to predict whether they will form a new model for industrial relations management.

☐ *Administering procedures relating to employee participation* can involve a sophisticated arrangement of works councils and employee committees, as employed by the John Lewis partnership. For many firms, however, it involves no more than the administration of an employee suggestion scheme.

A survey of personnel management in manufacturing industry and the health service found that those working in personnel regarded industrial relations as their most important activity. In a private sector manufacturing concern, four of the seven most commonly performed tasks involved industrial relations and included

☐ Giving advice to managers on their legal obligations as employers.
☐ Operating discipline, grievance and disputes procedures.
☐ Taking part in negotiations.
☐ Acting as the industrial relations specialist at the workplace.

(Guest and Horwood, 1980)

We have already noted that in the 1980s personnel management has been undergoing shifts in emphasis. This is especially true for industrial relations, although we should be cautious about the speed and extent of that change. There has clearly been a reduction in trade union membership and activity. Industrial relations may have become more of an issue in the public sector, but for the rest, personnel managers may have to seek a new focus for their activities. Variations in approaches of modern personnel managers towards industrial relations will be viewed when we discuss personnel strategies at the end of this chapter.

Personnel management and technology

In chapter 2 we examined the impact of technology and in particular technical change on jobs. We deal with two areas of significance to personnel management; training and industrial relations, although the type of technology and changes in technology have implications for recruitment, selection and payment systems as well.

Technical change invariably results in a mismatch between the needs of the firm and the skills of the workforce. For example, there are more jobs in Scotland in micro–electronics than in coal and iron and steel, and more traditional industrial base. Some firms tackle the mismatch by the use of outside contractors, but longer–term cost–effectiveness will probably lie in developing training programmes. Such training focuses not only on the development of 'high tech' skills but upon general workforce orientation towards using new technology, as in using computer terminals to input data and upon more general management training. The creation of a more flexible workforce has been identified as a training priority for many organizations.

The commonly accepted view of the impact of technical change on industrial relations, doubtless fuelled by media coverage of events at places such as Wapping (Chapter 1) is that it created problems, largely because trade unions resist change. This resistance is inevitably linked to fears over job losses, deskilling and increased management control. It was such issues that concerned the Fleet Street printworkers for several years in their opposition to photocomposition.

However, certain factors may temper this perspective.

☐ The TUC has adopted a stated policy of influencing the direction of new technology to maximize its benefits and minimize its costs.
☐ A recent survey has concluded that the reaction of most workers to technical change has been favourable. It is equated with investment and optimism, and is often seen as a route to better jobs and higher wages (Daniel, 1987).

There is however general agreement that in many companies the level of consultation over technical change issues is low. This was a major cause of the failure of the TUC's attempt to introduce 'New Technology Agreements' in the 1980s and a major cause of problems in general.

The nature of the technology offers some groups of workers more bargaining power than others because they operate and control key technologies. This power has as impact on the negotiating process. A number of disputes in the 1970s in British Leyland were centred on the toolroom, where stoppages involving relatively small numbers of the total workforce caused the entire operation to cease since those who manufacture the tools for a particular industry are central to the entire operation. Mineworkers have traditionally used their position as the providers of an essential fuel supply as strong bargaining weapon. In their disputes of 1972 and 1974 the National Union of Mineworkers used an overtime ban as a tactical weapon to reduce coal stocks in the power stations before calling for an 'all out' strike. The resulting power cuts and their impact on the rest of industry was a significant influence in the collective bargaining process. Not all workers enjoy bargaining power as a result of controlling key technologies. The postal workers in their dispute of 1971 had their case weakened by firms using alternative courier services for mail and by making greater use of alternative technology in the form of the telephone service.

Cultural influences

We have noted the considerable influences exerted by the state and the level of economic activity upon personnel activities. It is therefore not surprising for such a reactive function to be influenced by cultural factors. Differences may be observed between the operation of personnel management in different countries as the following illustrations will show.

In Britain the function clearly reflects the growth of trade union activity and a general preference for localized collective bargaining. In the USA the activities of personnel are shaped by prevailing social attitudes which favour the use of law and tend to be distrustful of trade unions. As a consequence much greater use is made of the law in such matters as the employment contract, equal opportunities and trade union collective bargaining. In addition there is much lower trade union membership than in Britain and therefore much less evidence of traditional industrial relations activity by personnel managers. In fact some companies in the USA have developed personnel strategies which actively discourage trade union organizations and focus on keeping the unions out by offering attractive welfare provisions and pay packages. In West Germany, with its highly centralized system of collective bargaining, industrial relations is not a major concern of the personnel manager. Specialist management functions such as personnel play a much smaller role in Germany than elsewhere, a correspondingly higher status being accorded to line management. There would appear to be little interest in the techniques of personnel management such as the use of job analysis and job descriptions. In major companies in Japan, personnel policies reflect the operation of a dual–labour market bestowing considerable advantages on a privileged group of employees, including lifetime employment and a whole range of company welfare provisions. (The section on Japanese Management in Chapter 2 has a fuller account).

Despite these differences there is some evidence of practices converging. We have already noted the influence of Japanese companies in Britain and the interest in single union, 'no–strike' agreements. Many American companies operating in Britain tend to be non–unionized and the type of strategies employed by firms like Hewlett–Packard and IBM (Cases 3.5 and 8.1) have gained currency amongst personnel practitioners in Britain.

On a different level altogether, similarities would appear to exist. Wherever personnel management is practised it has been traditionally dogged by a low status image. In the following section we will explore reasons for this and in our discussion of personnel strategies suggest why this may be changing.

Organizational aspects of personnel management

In this section we will view the relationship between organization size and personnel activities and focus on the relationship between the personnel function and other management activities in the organization structure. A major theme to emerge in personnel's dealings with management from other functional areas is that of goal conflict. Attempts to resolve such conflict have, of late, focussed upon the creation of a particular organizational culture. We will deal with this aspect at the end of the section.

Personnel management and organization size

The relationship between the growth of the firm and the development of formalization, differentiation and specialization has already been discussed in Chapter 3. The development of personnel management departments in firms during the early part of this century can be clearly attributed to the increasing size of the organization. A control mechanism was needed, particularly in the areas of recruitment and payment systems, giving rise to specialist positions of 'wages officer' and 'labour officer'. Such positions concerned themselves with recruitment, discipline, timekeeping and general administration of the payment system including the control of bonus payments. This growth of the size of firms was also a major factor in the changes in collective bargaining, placing more emphasis on bargaining within individual firms rather than at industry level. We have already noted how this resulted in the creation of industrial relations specialists.

In a recent survey it was found that whereas only 7% of firms employing fewer than fifty people had personnel specialists, the proportion rose to 93% for firms employing over 2000 people (Daniel and Millward, 1983). Furthermore, we can see that the increasing size of the firm also results in the increasing specialization within the personnel function itself. For example at Ford Motor Company the function is split into two main areas. On group deals with day–to–day industrial relations issues whilst the other group deals with such issues as training and management development. Within this broad split further specializations occur.

Personnel management, organization structure and goals

We can identify three problem areas in the operation of personnel management within organizations. These are as follows.

- ☐ Conflict between personnel and other functional managers. (These are sometimes referred to generically as line managers.)
- ☐ The difficulties encountered by personnel managers in proving their worth to the organization either because of the suspicion of line management towards new techniques or because of the way personnel organize their own work.
- ☐ Conflict within personnel management itself between professional and organizational goals.

In general the research has focussed on case studies where problems have been identified in the relationship between personnel and other departments. Little is known about how successful personnel departments operate and how they successfully integrate with other functional areas. This may well give a somewhat stereotyped view of the personnel function and ignore a wide range of situations where personnel managers are happy with their role and are seen to be effective. The various cases should be viewed within the limitation.

The line and staff model has often been used to analyse the personnel function, depicting personnel operating in an advisory capacity only.

> The personnel department here is as it should be, as service to the line. For example, if we want more labour they get it, train it, and arrange for it to be paid. They provide information for negotiating too, but I do the real negotiating (General Works Manager quoted in Legge, 1978, p 51).

Legge sees this relationship between personnel and line management as a basis for conflict in that line have a 'confused, hazy and/or stereotyped perception of the potential nature and scope of a personnel department's activities.' and 'tend to consider that personnel departments are 'out of touch' with the kind of problems and constraints which face them' (Legge, 1978, p 52.) In particular, other managers feel that personnel do not identify as closely as they do with the profit goals of the organization.

In her case studies Legge saw a vicious circle operating, as illustrated in Figure 8.4. Personnel are not involved in planning and decision–making, resulting in human resource problems that are left to personnel to sort out; pressure of time and lack of resources lead to crisis management resulting in line management having a poor perception of the personnel function and hence its non–involvment in decision–making. The circle is reinforced by the failure on the part of some line managers to recognize the need for a specialist role for personnel, since many personnel activities are carried out by all managers, as in the case of selection and training. Attempts to break free of the circle by personnel specialists adopting specialized techniques based on the behavioural sciences are often rebuffed by a suspicious line management. In this way carefully constructed appraisal schemes flounder in the face of line management opposition. As a result, Legge sees many personnel managers 'opt for an easy life' and concentrate on a more acceptable welfare role.

In a study of personnel management in manufacturing and the health service, personnel themselves contributed to the kind of problems Karen Legge outlined. Personnel managers enjoyed crisis management and took on a variety of different activities to boost their credibility in the eyes of the rest of management. This resulted in too broad and too heavy a workload with the consequence of ineffectiveness and incompetence. Personnel management were thus unable to contribute effectively to the goals of the organization as identified by line management (Guest and Horwood, 1980).

The question of effectiveness and personnel proving their worth was also raised by Legge.

Personnel management by definition, is chiefly concerned with the acquisition, maintenance and development of one of the resources (i.e. the human resource) through which the organizational ends are achieved rather than with the ends themselves. They are concerned with means rather than ends and inputs rather than outputs, and in situations where there is difficultly in determining the relationship between the two.

(Legge, 1978, p 60)

The two consequences of this are firstly that the credit for a successful personnel policy is taken to line management who actually perform the policy, but personnel carry the blame for an ineffective policy. Secondly, it is extremely difficult to quantify the outcome of personnel activity or even isolate its effect. As we have already mentioned, the success of a management development programme may be so diffuse and long–term that any financial assessment is impossible.

The following example illustrates the difficulty personnel managers have in proving their value to the organization. A northern bus company concerned about the growing labour turnover among its bus drivers used exit interviews conducted by the personnel manager in an attempt to reduce the number who actually left. The interviews which were conducted whenever

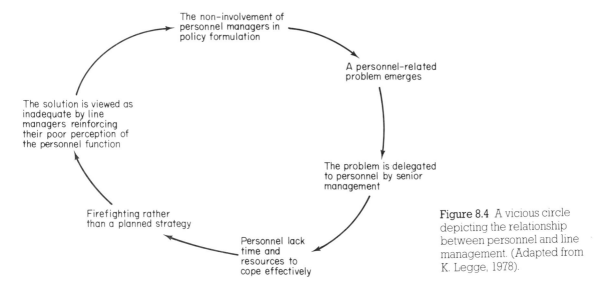

The non-involvement of personnel managers in policy formulation

A personnel-related problem emerges

The solution is viewed as inadequate by line managers reinforcing their poor perception of the personnel function

The problem is delegated to personnel by senior management

Firefighting rather than a planned strategy

Personnel lack time and resources to cope effectively

Figure 8.4 A vicious circle depicting the relationship between personnel and line management. (Adapted from K. Legge, 1978).

a bus diver gave notice of terminating his contract appeared to have very little impact for the first six months, but then the numbers leaving began to fall. Closer examination of this particular situation revealed that during the period when turnover was highest, a bus company in a neighbouring area was recruiting at a higher basic wage, while the time of falling turnover coincided with a downturn in the economy when all job opportunities were much scarcer. In other words, personnel often deal with external forces outside their control.

We can now see that the first two problem areas are linked. The conflict between personnel managers and other managers is a function of personnel's seeming inability to prove their worth.

Our third problem area concerns the potential conflict between organizational and professional goals. Personnel managers are popularly portrayed as a group in the middle, owing allegiance to both the needs of the workforce and the needs of the organization they serve. As we saw from the IPM's definition of personnel management at the beginning of this chapter, there is no conflict in that the good professional is concerned 'to achieve efficiency and justice, neither or which can be achieved without the other'. It is clear that professional high ideals can conflict with the daily pressures of getting the job done. In practice, however, such conflict is rarely felt by personnel practitioners. They generally see themselves as part of the management group and as such subscribe to management goals, even though they do not always operate as line management would like.

The kind of problems identified above can be tackled through the creation of an organization culture which stresses cooperation and consensus. It is to this we now turn.

The role of organization culture

We have seen how personnel managers reflect the culture of a particular enterprise. In general terms the activities of personnel, especially those concerned with recruitment, selection and training, ensure that employees fit the prevailing culture of the firm. This takes on a more fundamental aspect in those firms that have identified a mission and build their organization culture around that mission. We deal with such aspects more fully when we deal with organizational cultures in Chapter 3. In such firms the personnel function assumes a role of major importance.

Certain local authorities have made considerable attempts to change the culture of their organizations in accordance with (usually) a guiding political ideology. The focus is usually on the criteria used in the recruitment and selection of new staff, with a special concern for equal opportunities, as the following job advertisement reveals.

> As part of Lambeth's Equal Opportunities Policy, applications are welcome from people regardless of race, creed, nationality, age, sex, sexual orientation or responsibility for children or dependents.
>
> (from the *Guardian* 20 Nov 1985)

We can see from Case 8.1 that IBM lays great store by selecting the right type of individual, investing heavily in management training and establishing excellent conditions of employment. In cases 2.3 and 3.5 in Nissan and Hewlett–Packard respectively, the importance of selection again emerges. In Hewlett–Packard the culture is sustained by paying attention to management style as in their technique of 'management by wandering around'. In all these cases the senior management see employment relations as a major route to establishing the kind of company they want.

We will examine this and other approaches to personnel strategy more fully in the next section.

Personnel management strategies

In our discussion of the impact of economic factors upon personnel activities we identified three possible scenarios for the future direction of personnel management. We now broaden those out to examine a range of strategic options.

An examination of a variety of companies reveals that specific personnel and industrial relations policies are notable by their absence. From her case studies Legge concludes:

> In company decision–making, the personnel management considerations involved in production, marketing and finance decisions were not so much overruled (although this also occurred . . .) as went by default.
>
> (Legge, 1978, p 37)

She noted that where policy did exist it was fragmented, short term and largely reactive. There are signs that attempts are being made to change this approach. We examine strategies and personnel by looking at manpower planning, industrial relations strategies and some new directions.

Manpower planning represents the basic strategic planning device of personnel management. It enables management to forecast future manpower requirements against current manpower resources and developing strategies to cope with the gap between the two.	KEY CONCEPT 8.4 **MANPOWER PLANNING**

Manpower planning

Traditionally, strategies in personnel management have been based around manpower planning. This process is concerned with matching future manpower requirements with future manpower availability and involves consideration of both the quantity and the quality of the labour force including the analysis of such factors as the age profile of the staff. A variety of techniques have been used from simple demand–supply models to more sophisticated statistical models of the type used by the Civil Service to plan its own manpower requirements. The output of a manpower planning exercise should set the guidelines for personnel strategies in recruitment, selection, training, retirement and so on. The resulting strategies will vary depending on the relationship of the predicted future demand to predicted future supply.

For example, a firm whose demand for labour exceeds the predicted supply may have to consider changes in its payment strategies with a view to attract more recruits or investigate the possibilities of introducing new technology to replace labour. Where the existing labour supply exceeds the predicted future demands then plans may have to be formulated for early retirement, redundancy or perhaps looking to marketing strategies to increase the demand for the firm's goods and services. Even where demand and supply are evenly matched, then a manpower planning exercise may well give management useful insights into the nature of labour utilization and suggest where improvements can be made.

Even a simple manpower planning exercise can produce useful information. Management who study population statistics will be aware of the declining birth rate and the impact this will have on the recruitment of school leavers in the 1990s. Some firms such as the Ford Motor Company in Essex have set up programmes to counteract a shortfall in the future supply of labour by building closer relationships with local schools and by projecting on improved image to the local community. They hope that such exercises will motivate more local school leavers to seek employment with them.

Industrial relations strategies

Earlier in this chapter we presented the view that a key feature of British industrial relations was a localized approach to collective bargaining. Not surprisingly this has resulted in a number of different models of industrial relations management. An attempt to classify these has been made by Alan Fox (1974a) who identifies four different approaches, the traditionalists, the sophisticated paternalists, the sophisticated moderns and the standard moderns.

The *traditionalists* represent management whose predominant view is the opposition to all kinds of trade union groups. Such a strategy can result in direct confrontation as was seen in the much publicized Grunwick dispute of 1976 when the managing director of a film processing plant in Southall denied union recognition to a group to Asian workers. The ensuing dispute had racial was well as industrial relations implications. For some the economic recession of the 1980s has encouraged the traditionalists to emerge from their closets embodied in 'macho–management' stereotypes, with Michael Edwardes (ex of British Leyland) and Ian McGregor (ex of British Steel and the Coal Board) as heroic figures. The extent to which such strategies will dominate is highly questionable and may owe more to media distortion than accurate analysis.

The *sophisticated paternalists* are the Hewlett–Packards and own much to the 'human relations' approach to management. A great deal of time and effort is taken to ensure workforce commitment to overall company objectives. Such companies are typified by fairly sophisticated personnel policies and the acceptance of techniques associated with organizational development and the quality of working life.

The *sophisticated moderns* on the other hand see consultation and negotiation with trade unions as the keystone of their personnel policies. Such firms have well–established procedures for determining pay and conditions and often have mechanisms for employee participation. Most of the major oil companies, local government and the large public (or ex–public) corporations such as British Gas exhibit such strategies. Perkins Diesels (Case 8.2) also see negotiation as an important part of organization change.

The majority of personnel managers however would seem to fit into the fourth of Fox's classifications. The *standard moderns* have no real strategy as such but adopt the standard reactive response to problems. They manage by 'firefighting', and as such fit in well with our illustrations of person nel management when we discussed the influence of organizational structure and goals. Perhaps the largest number of companies fit into this category.

We can see from those models that there is considerable variation in personnel strategy and that the explanation for the variation is a function of a number of key variables. These are the variables that form the basis of our model of business namely, the state, the economy, culture, technology, the labour force, organization size, structure, goals and ownership.

New directions?

In some companies there is evidence that personnel are reacting to changing circumstances. The relative weakness of trade unions has reduced the need for extensive exercises in collective bargaining and conflict management. In some cases, as we pointed out earlier, managements have taken this opportunity to reduce manning levels, increase labour flexibility and generally roll back the influence of trade unions. In declining industries there is reduction in recruitment and training and a focus on redundancy management and early retirement. In growth areas there is an increased concern for recruitment, training, and the retention of a core group of highly skilled labour.

There is speculation that such changes will eventually weaken the position of personnel managers in that full–time workforces will be smaller, many of their traditional activities will have declined, or handled more cost–effectively by using external consultants as and when required.

These directions appear to be pursuing the old theme of personnel reacting to it environment. Throughout this chapter we have suggested the possibility that a changed set of strategies may be emerging. These strategies are more positive and have emerged as the result of a number of influences, including the lessions learned from Japanese companies and the so–called excellent companies and the decline of traditional trade unions. We can identify three models.

☐ We have seen an adaptation of the practices of the Japanese and American multinational companies to fit the British environment. Such strategies would include the kind of single union, no–strike deals identified earlier. As well as being a management strategy this also represents a changed strategy on behalf of trade union organizations. Trade unions may adopt such strategies to survive in an unfavourable climate.

☐ An attempt has been made by some personnel managers to adopt a much more proactive role by focussing more on issues relating to productivity and developing personnel strategies to enhance cost effectiveness. We saw from our discussion of quality assurance in Chapter 6 that employee training and changing employee attitudes are key strategies in achieving improved quality. A good illustration of such policies is presented in Case 8.2.

☐ The vogue strategy for the 1980s is known as 'Human Resource Management'. The emphasis here is upon long term personnel strategies aimed at integrating the personnel function more closely with the other functional areas. The strategy is focussed on the effective utilization of human resources and stresses flexibility of the labour force, commitment to common goals and the establishment of a consensus among all employees. (A good summary of this strategy may be found in Guest, 1987).

This focus on productivity through people, greater employee commitment and involvement, the development of skilled, flexible employees, and a strong corporate culture may indicate that personnel strategies will emerge as the key management strategies as organizations enter the 1990s.

We must be careful however that the well–publicized accounts of practices in some organizations do not mislead us. Certainly changes have taken place, but we should remind ourselves that Japanese style personnel practices have their limitations when applied to a British context. Furthermore, new approaches such as 'human resource management' may offer promises, but also offer some rather vague concepts and tend to be based on some rather questionable assumptions and theories.

The findings of recent detailed empirical surveys would indicate that traditional approaches and traditional personnel activities persist in a larger number of firms (Daniel and Millward, 1983, Millward and Stevens, 1986).

Summary

The role and activities of personnel management have emerged largely as a reaction to some problem or crisis and the development of the function is clearly related to economic growth, the increasing size of organizations, government legislation and policy, the growth of the labour movement and developments in collective bargaining. Expectations of the decline of the personnel function in the face of a receding economy and declining trade union movement have as yet been premature, and opportunities may exist for developing a new role, especially as the economy picks up.

Focus on the activity of personnel management in Britain reveals a preoccupation with industrial relations, whilst an analysis of other types of activity such as selection reveals a largely intuitive and subjective approach behind a scientific management façade.

Traditionally personnel managers have had a low status as a result of their association with a welfare role and the fact that most of their activities can be carried out by all managers.

Such analyses at the level of the organization may well explain a lack of personnel strategy both at the corpoate and operational level beyond basic manpower planning. However, perhaps too much emphasis has been placed upon the role problems of personnel managers, and more evidence is needed of situations in which personnel managers operate effectively. Evidence in the 1980s suggests that whilst traditional activities still predominate in many companies, personnel strategies are displaying new dimensions. These include a greater concern for productivity and cost–effectiveness, and adaptations of the strategies employed by others, especially some Japanese and American companies.

Further reading

The most intelligent treatment of personnel management is provided by K. Legge, *Power, Innovation, and Problem–solving in Personnel Management* (McGraw Hill, 1978), and the same author provides a good analysis of trends in the 1980s in K. Legge, Personnel Management in Recession and Recovery (*Personnel Review* Vol 17, No 2, 1988). A practical approach to the subject is offered by D. Torrington an L. Hall, *Personnel Management: A New Approach* (Prentice Hall International, 1987). A good review of the literature is offered by D. Guest and R. Horwood, *The Role and Effectiveness of Personnel Managers* (LSE, 1980), a study which also provides useful insights into the way personnel organize their priorities and deal with their problems. Recommended reading in industrial relations includes G.S. Bain ed. *Industrial Relations in Great Britain* (Basil Blackwell, 1984) and W.W. Daniel and N. Millward, *Workplace Industrial Relations in Britain* (Heinemann 1983). A reflection of current developments is offered by P. Bassett, *Strike Free* (Macmillan, 1986).

Discussion

1. Is there a case for the elimination of personnel specialists so that the activities of the personnel function can be performed by all managers?

2. Assess the role of the state in the development of personnel management as a specialist activity. In what way have government policies of the 1980s shaped personnel strategies?

3. In what way have changes in the economy influenced what personnel managers do and the way they go about their activities?

4. How significant will industrial relations management be in the 1990s? What changes do you forecast in the key activities?

5. What are the main causes of tension between personnel managers and other management groups? What strategies would you recommend personnel employ to reduce such tensions?

6. What differences are likely to be found in the personnel function and its activities in the public and private sectors?

7. How would you establish a manpower plan for a) a small expanding computer software firm, b) a medium–sized company manufacturing electrical components for the car industry, and c) a university or a polytechnic? What key problems would emerge in each case and what steps would you take to resolve them?

8. What are the key environmental and organizational factors which have shaped the personnel strategies and procedures in IBM and Perkins Diesels (Cases 8.1 and 8.2 respectively)? Can other companies draw lessons from these cases? Are there any reasons why personnel strategies should be non–transferable?

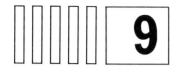

9 Finance and accounting

In this chapter we examine the role played by the finance and accounting function in the operation of a business. We identify three main functions: the raising of funds or financial management; the contribution of accounting to management control and decision–making, often referred to as management accounting; and the function of financial reporting. We show these three elements in Figure 9.1, and deliberately portray them as overlapping activities. For example, a management which decides on a strategy of business expansion into new markets and new process technologies (a decision based on management accounting calculations) will need to present accounting information to a bank or another potential investor (financial reporting) to persuade them to back the expansion with the necessary capital (financial management).

Accounting procedures and processes are very much a product of the organizational and wider environments in which they operate. We will examine the various economic, legal and social influences on the finance and accounting function, and look at variations resulting from the size of the organization, ownership patterns and organization structure. We shall also look at the accounting practices of large multi–divisional companies by examining the procedures for cost allocation and transfer pricing. We end the chapter by giving a broad overview on the contribution of finance and accounting strategies to overall management strategy.

Throughout this chapter it is the intention to present accounting not as a series of technical calculations but as a management function that is influenced significantly by those who prepare and use accounting information. For example, the determination and disclosure of profit levels will be guided by regulations governing accounting practice. It may also be influenced by forthcoming wage negotiations with trade unions and with a view to minimizing liability for tax. Budgets are determined by management to guide future activities in accordance with plans. The process of budget–setting and resource allocation is also, in many organizations, a product of organizational politics, power and influence.

It is not our intention to give an introduction to bookkeeping and various accounting techniques. There are a range of suitable introductory books that students may consult and we recommend some at the end of this chapter. For those seeking a much broader coverage of the finance and accounting issues in organizations, you should refer to the accompanying accounting text in this series by Berry and Jarvis (1989). Many of the issues

Figure 9.1 Finance and accounting activities.

Financial management is that part of the accounting and finance that is concerned with the financing of an organization's activities. Finance is avilable from share issue, bank borrowing, state funding and through internally generated funds. The financing of most private companies occurs mainly through the generation of funds internally, such as the redistribution of profit.

KEY CONCEPT 9.1

FINANCIAL MANAGEMENT

are also dealt with in more depth in the series economics text by Neale and Haslam (1989).

Finance and accounting in business

Accountants form the largest professional group in Britain, and, numerically at least, are much more significant here than elsewhere. A recent survey established the presence of 120 000 qualified accountants in Britain, compared with 20 000 in France, and only 6000 in Japan, and 4000 in West Germany (Handy, 1987). Many of those accountants in Britain operate in business either as finance and accounting specialists or as general managers. Professional accountancy is often regarded as a training route for senior management in this country.

As we shall see later, such statistics reflect a difference in the nature of businesses in the various countries and may even be misleading. For example, the management accounting function exists in many German firms, but is performed by business economists. The variations in the number of accountants in different countries are however thought by some to reflect significant cultural differences in the way businesses operate. It has often been claimed that the traditional accountant's attitude to risk aversion can hold back entrepreneurial decision–making and, as we have seen elsewhere in this book, a preoccupation with short–term accounting calculations and financial returns may have damged the long–term competitiveness of manufacturing industry (in for example Hayes and Wheelwright 1984 and Chapter 5 and 6 of this book).

As stated in our introduction we shall examine the function in terms of the three activities of financial management, management accounting and financial reporting, depicted in Figure 9.1.

Financial management

Financial management is concerned with the raising of capital to finance the organization's operations and with ensuring that the company can generate sufficient revenue to cover the cost of raising this finance. That cost may be in the form of interest rates payable to banks or dividend paid out to shareholders. There is a clear overlap with management accounting in that the funds must be managed by putting them to the most effective use. For example, investments must be carefully appraised. We may identify four sources of finance; shares, bank lending, internal funding, and the state.

Shares. The major source of finance from shares comes in the form of new share issues. Despite the recent publicity given to this through the privatization of such as British Telecom and British Gas, probably less than 10% of all finance comes from share issue (Wilson, 1980). In recent years the creation of the Unlisted Securities Market, whereby firms not large enough to have a full Stock Market listing are able to sell shares, has had significant impact on the financing of small firms. Overall, however, shares still play a minor role in the raising of funds and recent evidence suggests that where new share issues do play a part, the money is spent not on investing in current activities, but to fund acquisitions (Mayer, 1988).

The Stock Market was created to encourage potential investors to finance businesses over which they had no direct control, yet for the majority it is simply a secondary market in which shares are bought and sold by investors, with no funding activity involved. A great deal of stock market activity revolves around the dealings of financial intermediaries. We have discussed their role alongside more general issues relating to the separation of ownership and control in Chapter 3.

Banks. Borrowing from banks is more common than raising finance through share issues, but on the whole British banks are less willing to lend and less willing to take an active role in the management of business activities than their counterparts in other countries. Banks play a much more significant and much more integrated role in France, Japan, and West Germany. In countries such as Germany lending terms are also more favourable to industrial borrowers, both as far as interest rates and the length of the pay–back period is concerned. Not only are British banks somewhat conservative in their lending policies, they are also, when acting as institutional investors, quite likely to sell their shares when things go wrong. Inadvertently, through their activities on the Stock Market, banks may weaken the financial position of a company, which can encourage a takeover bid.

The reluctance of British banks to finance business was argued by the Wilson Report to be a function of the poor performance of British industrial firms, which did not merit investment (Wilson, 1980). There is recent evidence that the banks are conscious of their poor image as far as investment is concerned, and all the major high street banks have engaged in costly advertising and publicity campaigns to attract the business borrower. It would seem, however, that high interest rates are still a major obstacle to bank borrowing.

Internal funding. Many texts play down internal sources of finance, yet all the evidence points to this as the major source of funding for most private companies in Britain, many obtaining as much as 70% of funds this way (Wilson, 1980, Mayer, 1988). The finance will come mainly from the redistribution of profits, although funding can be raised through the sale of assets.

State funding. The State in Britain plays a relatively minor role in the funding of business. Apart from the investment in prestige projects such as Concorde and microchips, the activities of the State in Britain have generally been restricted to supporting declining industries and firms and preventing mass unemployment in economically deprived regions. This would seem to be the logic behind the Government's regional policy and its investment in British Steel and British Leyland. We refer you to Chapters 2 and 5 for a further discussion of such issues.

There are several reasons why management prefer to finance their businesses internally. The major factor is the fear that the involvement of banks and shareholders will weaken their control of the company. This is certainly the case as far as bank borrowing is concerned, but less so for shareholders. However, as we saw in Chapter 3, institutional investors can have considerable influence on management decisions. The shareholding route may be especially resisted by small business owners fearing a diminution of their control over the business. As we suggested above, a major reluctance on the part of British managers to borrow from banks is the relatively high interest rates and the short time usually allowed for paying back.

There are a number of other factors which influence the source of finance. The attitude of management to risk may be an important factor. A cautious manager may wish to limit the extent of bank borrowing at all costs. The extent to which internal funds can be made available depends on the ability of management to satisfy its shareholders through dividend pay–out. There are also significant differences in the funding of activities between large and small firms, a point we shall return to later in the chapter.

Management accounting

Management accounting is the application of accounting techniques to provide management with the information to assist in the processes of planning and control. There is a clear overlap with financial management, in that management accounting is concerned with the use of funds, and with financial reporting, in that management accounting uses the data collected as a basis for its calculations.

In terms of planning, management accounting assists in the formulation of plans for other functional areas. For example, an assessment of future labour costs will assist the process of manpower planning. Predictions of the future cost of raw materials will help in devising appropriate purchasing strategies and, where predicted costs are high, may even stimulate the development of new products using alternative materials. An important contribution to the planning process is the assistance offered by management accounting techniques of investment appraisal in selecting the most appropriate course of action from a range of alternatives. Such techniques are more valuable as environments become increasingly complex.

Management accounting plays a very important role in the wider process of management control. It enables clear parameters to be set in the form of budgets and represents a method by which many problems can be sensed and measured. It is especially useful as a control tool for three reasons. Firstly, the data produced offer management one of the few methods of quantifying the effect of their decisions and of the organization's operations. Secondly, management accounting integrates the information from all the activities of the business and enables management to view operations as a whole. Thirdly, it deals with the control of funds that are essential to an organization's survival.

We deal with five aspects of management accounting; budgeting, cost accounting, investment appraisal, the management of cash flows, and the contribution of the management accountant to management decisions. There is considerable overlap between these categories. For example, the control of assets would inevitably involve budgetary control, and the contribution to general management decisions would include all the other four categories. Management accounting is central to strategic planning, and many of the issues reappear when we discuss strategy at the end of this chapter. For the moment we examine each of the categories in turn.

Budgeting and budgetary control. A budget is a quantitative statement of expectations concerning the allocation of resources and performance. The two aspects of budgeting are the establishment of standards and the setting up of mechanisms to measure and control performance. As a result, budgeting has a central position in the design of most management and accounting information systems.

Budgets are used in many different ways; to allocate funds and supplies, as a means of delegating management authority, as targets to motivate employees, and as a means of control of both spending and performance. For example, the Polytechnic of East London allocates funds to each department designated as a cost centre. The allocation varies according to the size of the department and the nature of its work, so that science and engineering may get a large capital expenditure budget to purchase essential equipment. Budgets are allocated under a number of headings including equipment, office supplies, library purchases, the funding of conferences for staff and so on. Such a mechanism serves two main purposes. Firstly it attempts to ensure that expenditure keeps within clearly defined limits. Secondly it spreads the complex task of managing this expenditure by delegating to department heads.

Budgets are normally based on historic information, usually last year's budget. In a highly bureaucratic organization, resistant to change, this can cause difficulties when the needs of organization members change. For example, many higher education institutions are slowly coming to terms with the fact that business studies courses have expanded rapidly and now provide them with a large proportion of their total student body. In many cases this is not represented in budget allocation which is based on out–of–date information. The problem is intensified in that the developments in business computing have meant that the capital needs of business studies departments, in the form of computer equipment, have also grown dramatically, whilst current allocations favour traditional science and engineering courses.

In all organizations there are often significant difficulties in changing the budget allocations. This is because budgeting is a bargaining process dealing with the allocation of scarce resources and those with most to lose have a vested interest in maintaining the status quo. It is for this reason that increasing attention has been given to the behavioural aspects of budgeting (Hopwood, 1974 is a good example). The bargaining process can be useful in that it can force management to confront long–held assumptions and face up to underlying tensions which affect decision–making. However there is a danger that conflict will be dysfunctional. This is especially true where budgeting in the form of targets is used as a control device, and more so where it forms the basis of the organization's reward system. In this case, and also where scarce resources are at stake, there may be a temptation for managers to distort information to place both them and their departments in the most favourable light.

Budgeting is therefore inseparable from the process of organizational politics and the way the organization is structured. In some cases this process has been acknowledged and attempts have been made to introduce some form of participation in the budget planning process.

Cost accounting. Cost accounting involves the analysis and allocation of costs. In large organizations this can be a complex process involving paper transactions between different units, especially in multi–divisional firms. We return to this aspect when we discuss the influence of organization structure on accounting procedures. The nature of costs varies considerably. Some costs such as rents are relatively fixed, whilst others such as the amount of raw materials used by a manufacturing firm will vary with the intensity of production. Some costs, such as wages, are highly detailed, whilst others such as expenditure on hospitality can be relatively vague.

In recent years traditional cost accounting methods, usually based on historic data, have been challenged, firstly by high rates of inflation in the 1970s and more recently by other changes. In many manufacturing organizations changes are taking place which are challenging the basis of historical costs, and managements are having to devise new methods of costing. These changes include the introduction of new manufacturing technology to reduce the cost of production and a renewed emphasis placed upon improving quality, increasing operating efficiency and reducing the uncertainty of materials and components supply. We have referred to these changes elsewhere in this book.

Investment appraisal. Capital investment involves the commitment of funds now with the expectation of acceptable earnings in the future. Such decisions are made about the purchase or renting of new or additional premises, investment in new equipment, the development of a new pro-duct, or even the acquisition of another business. A careful appraisal of such investments is necessary due to the usually large amount involved and the key impact such investments might have on the future viability of the company. A variety of investment appraisal methods have been devised, including payback, rate of return, net present value (NPV) and yield.

NPV is a popular method since it estimates future returns on investment, but assesses them on current values. Managements are therefore able to make more informed judgements. Despite the popularity and frequency of their use, NPV calculations are not without problems. They are difficult to use for long–term investments without management making some rather big assumptions about such things as the future behaviour of markets and the future costs of raw materials. The more assumptions which have to be made then the less accurate the forecasts are likely to be. A problem associated with this is that strong management commitment to a particular investment project may result in a self–fulfilling NPV calculation. The figures are simply made to work to justify the decision. A study of the coal, steel and car industry in Britain in the 1970s concluded that large investments were justified on the basis of highly dubious input data; investment decisions which were subsequently proved unwise (Williams *et al.*, 1986).

The management of cash–flows. The management of cash flows is concerned with the movement of cash into and out of the organization. This is an important activity since the firm needs to ensure that it has sufficient cash to cover its current expenditure. Many small firms find their severest problems occur with the management of cash flows. A business start–up has a considerable cash outflow to begin with and it may be some time before sufficient revenue is established to cover these initial costs. Several businesses have ceased trading with full order books, simply because they have insufficient incoming cash to pay bank interest charges and so are unable to stay in business and capitalize on their orders.

Cash–flow management can be particularly difficult in times of high inflation, when there is a danger that profits become absorbed by escalating costs. Some firms also experience cash–flow difficulties in expanding economies. In such situations there is a temptation to turn profit, not into cash, but into new investments by budgeting against future profits. Such a situation led Laker Airways to overreach itself by investing in expensive new passenger aircraft at a time when its markets were limited by the restrictive practices of other airlines. The company was forced into liquidation.

A current concern of cash–flow management is the management of stocks. Many manufacturing firms are attempting to reduce their outgoings through a better control of inventory. Strategies employed include the development of close links with a limited number of suppliers and operating such production control methods as 'Just–In–Time' (Chapter 6 has a fuller discussion of such strategies).

General contribution to management decision–making. Any discussion of the various elements of management activity can give the misleading impression that such activities are discrete. In reality the work of the management accountant does not focus on any one of these activities singly, but uses them all in conjunction to assist in the general process of management desion–making on an on–going basis. The accountant would be expected to contribute to most types of management decision, and certainly would have an input in major decisions such as plant closure and decision to make or buy.

Financial reporting

Financial reporting involves the collection and presentation of data for use in financial management and management accounting. The two major forms of financial statement for companies are the balance sheet and the profit and loss account. The broad content of these two statements is

Financial reporting is the presentation of financial information in a form that is useful to interested parties. As well as being a legal requirement of many firms, the publishing of such information is useful in management decision–making, for potential investors, for trade unions and even for a firm's competitors. Since the financial information can be available to such a wide audience, management must decide on the extent of disclosure beyond the minimum required by law.

KEY CONCEPT 9.3

FINANCIAL REPORTING

Assets	Liabilities
Fixed assets	*Capital*
Buildings	Share capital
Plant and equipment	
Transport	
Assets leased to third parties	
Current assets	*Current liabilities*
Stock	Creditors
Debtors	Loans
Bank balance	Overdrafts
Cash	
Investments	

Figure 9.2 The content of a typical balance sheet.

Income	Expenditure
Sales revenue	Raw materials
Income from investments	Wages
	Heating, lighting etc.
	Rent and rates
	Advertising
	Insurance
	Depreciation
	Tax
	Dividend

Figure 9.3 The content of a typical profit and loss account.

presented in Figures 9.2 and 9.3. The balance sheet represents the summary of a firm's financial position at the end of an accounting period. The profit and loss account provides detail of a firm's income and expenditure throughout the accounting period. The form and content of such statements is determined partly by the demands of the Companies Acts 1948–81 and partly by the recommendations of the Statements of Standard Accounting Practice (SSAPs) issued collectively by the various professional accounting bodies in this country.

As we noted above, such information is particularly useful to management in the planning, organizing and controlling of resources. It is not only management who are interested in the financial information of individual businesses; the following also have need of such information.

The *State* requires public companies to be accountable and present their accounting information in a standardized form according to the requirements of the various Companies Acts 1948–81. These state that all public companies must present to Companies House, a balance sheet, a profit and loss account, a directors report, and notes on the accounts where necessary. As we shall see later there is some relaxation of these requirements for smaller businesses, but only relating to the extent of information provided. As well as stipulating the various accounts to be presented the law also determines what must be disclosed. The broad content of a balance sheet and a profit and loss acount is presented in Figures 9.2 and 9.3 respectively.

The State also requires financial information to levy appropriate taxes on businesses. The nature of the tax laws certainly affects how firms report, and most use reporting conventions which minimize their liability for tax.

The accounting information provided by firms under the requirements of the Companies Acts and tax law is used by the State for the purposes of economic planning and forecasting.

Investors need the information to make informed judgements about future investments, as well as needing to protect their existing investments. The accountability of public companies to their investors was the major factor in the development of rules governing disclosure.

Employees may need the information, especially if they are involved in a profit–sharing or share ownership scheme. Published accounts are of course particularly useful to trade unions in planning wage negotiations. In more general terms, a company concerned to involve its employees in the running of the enterprise may see the disclosure of financial information as an important element of the participation process.

Creditors such as banks and suppliers are naturally concerned with the firm's liquidity and need to assess the risk involved in offering credit and of course to safeguard against fraud.

Competitors usually find the financial information paticularly useful as a yardstick against which their own performance may be measured, and may derive useful insights into what other firms are doing.

Consumers will use the information to ascertain the risk of placing expensive or long–term contracts and perhaps to assess the fairness of a company's pricing policy.

The major issue in financial reporting is the extent of disclosure. The wide availability of the accounts of public companies certainly influences their content and the way information is presented. Managements have a fair amount of discretion since the much of the content of accounts is subject to interpretation, such as allowances for depreciation and the valuation of assets. As a result, firms are often accused of manipulating their financial information to minimize tax liability or to present a strong management case in wage negotiation with trade unions. In addition firms are also conscious that financial information will be available to competitors and may wish to hide certain facts from them. We have already seen in our discussion of management accounting that financial information can be presented in such a way as to legitimize certain courses of action in preference to others. All this reinforces the notion that accounting is a behavioural and political rather than a technical exercise.

The environmental aspects of finance and accounting

In the last section we saw that financial reporting was greatly influenced by State regulations concerning the disclosure of information for public accountability and for reasons of collecting taxes. In this section we focus on two further environmental influences on the accounting and finance function; the economy and cultural differences.

In keeping with our Business in Context model, influences are two–way. The finance and accounting practices of firms have an impact upon the environment in which they operate. Economic resources in society are often allocated on the basis of accounting information. The financial statements provided by companies are eagerly awaited by trade unions and the information they provide can form the basis of their arguments in the next round of pay talks. The closure of the Cortonwood colliery in South Yorkshire was based on accounting information provided for the management of the National Coal Board. The impact of such closures on the local community is considerable. The impact in this case precipitated a bitter coal mining strike which lasted over a year. (A discussion of the kind of accounting procedures which resulted in the closure of Cortonwood can be found in Berry, T. *et al.*, 1985. We return to this case later in the chapter.)

The role of the economy

In general, accounting practices will vary according to the nature of the economy in which they operate. For example, in many Third World countries there is little need for sophisticated accounting techniques and systems of basic cash accounting predominate. The raising of finance that we discussed in the previous section is a function of the state of the market and the way this influences profit levels, share prices and bank interest rates. Two specific economic features have held particular interest for accountants; inflation and currency exchange.

The relatively high rates of inflation experienced by the British economy in the 1970s led accountants to rethink the basis for their calculations and made popular the concept of inflation accounting and resulted in a Government report (The Sandilands Committee on Inflation Accounting). A major problem in times of high inflation is that profits can be overstated by basing costs on historic data made largely irrelevant by inflation. In such situations systems of adjusting balance sheets to account for fluctuating prices were developed. Whilst these have less relevance in 1980s Britain, inflation accounting techniques are widely used in such countries as Brazil.

Like inflation, fluctuations in currency exchange rates make historic cost accounting difficult. The effect is particularly significant for those firms reliant on export markets. For example, the Swiss multinationals Nestles and Ciba Geigy have as much as 98% of their business outside Switzerland (Choi and Mueller, 1978).

Cultural differences

Many differences can be observed in the accounting practices of different countries. These differences reflect a variety of factors such as the nature of the legal system, the pattern of ownership and control, the system of taxation, the strength of the accountancy profession, and the general social climate.

In France and West Germany financial reporting systems are highly prescribed by law, yet there tends to be less emphasis on financial reporting in France, largely because the dominance of family ownership, and hence the private nature of many companies. In Britain and the USA reporting requirements are less prescriptive but the information needs of shareholders are much greater, especially in the USA where share ownership is more diffuse. Patterns of ownership are themselves related to the influence of the accounting profession. Public ownership requires accountability and hence accountants play a major role in the auditing of company accounts. Much less auditing is required in France, which may account for their relatively low numbers of accountants. In general, a social climate which encourages openness, social responsibility and consumerism, as in the USA, results in significantly different patterns in the disclosure of financial information than those found in a much more closed society such as Switzerland.

There has been considerable pressure for the standardization of accounting practices across countries. Some harmonization has taken place within the EEC and this was reflected by certain changes in the financial reporting requirements of British firms. The pressure for standardization comes from a variety of quarters. Financial reports prepared in one country are used by financial analysts and investors in another as part of the growing internationalization of capital. Standardization would greatly assist multinational companies to consolidate their accounts, assess potential acquisitions more effectively and even enable them to transfer accounting staff from one country to another more easily. It should not be forgotten that many of the major accounting firms operate multinationally too and harmonization would greatly assist their operations.

The organizational aspects of finance and accounting

The nature of any organization impinges significantly upon accounting procedures. This is inevitably shown when changes occur in ownership or in the goals of the enterprise, bringing about changes in the organizational culture. For example, the takeover of one firm by another may well result in the consolidation of accounts and perhaps a change in the accounting practices. The privatization of a number of companies in Britain in the 1980s has changed the nature of the organization from a service centre to a profit centre, with a corresponding impact upon accounting practices.

In the public sector, significant changes are taking place as well. In Case 4.3 we presented the changes that were occurring in British polytechnics through incorporation in 1989. One major change has been the withdrawal of local authority accounting controls and the subsequent elevation of the management accounting function within polytechnics themselves. Another change affecting all public sector organizations has been the greater emphasis placed on income generation beyond that normally provided. This places an extra burden upon public bodies but may also give them greater flexibility to pursue their own goals.

For the remainder of this section we focus on two organizational issues; the accounting implications of the size of the firm, and the influence of structure on accounting procedures. The two issues are linked, as we shall see when we examine the problems of cost allocation and transfer pricing in large multi–divisional firms.

The accounting requirements of large and small firms

Differences in the size of businesses affects their ability to raise capital, the complexity of their accounting procedures and controls, and the extent of their financial reporting. Differences are therefore to be found in all the three functions of finance and accounting that we identified in Figure 9.1.

Larger firms, not suprisingly, have much more complex accounting procedures and generally employ a number of professional accountants in a specialized functional department. In smaller firms the accounting function is often external to the firm, with a subsequent reliance on the advice of an outsider, who may not have the detailed knowledge of an internal management accountant. Larger firms may have the problems of satisfying large numbers of shareholders, but their very size often gives them an advantage in raising funds from external sources. In any event, large and complex organizations can often finance themselves internally through their ability to switch funds from one unit to another. Small firms have much more problems raising finance and tend to be more concerned with the management of cash–flows.

As with the proposals to harmonize accounting procedures between nation states there is a lobby to standardize practices across all types of firms irrespective of their size. However, the cost of preparing complex financial statements can be daunting for a small business and the benefits of such information much less than for large firms. Paradoxically in the light of its general views on harmonization, the EEC champions different accounting practices for large and small firms. This was reflected in Britain in the 1981 Companies Act which removed the requirement of smaller firms to produce profit and loss accounts and directors' reports, and introduced less onerous requirements for balance sheet information. In reality however, this does not appear to meet the information needs of banks on which small companies are so heavily dependent for finance. To satisfy their lending requirements, banks are insisting on stringent financial control mechanisms in small firms and much more detailed financial reporting than is required be law (Berry A. *et al.*, 1987). As a result, the pressure for standardization may well come from the banking community.

Organization structure, cost allocation and transfer pricing

We have already seen how organization structure and accounting procedures tend to reinforce one another, in that a large organization may delegate responsibility and control costs through the creation of individual budget centres. In very large organizations the organization structure generally matches the finance and accounting responsibilities of the firm. A centralized headquarters will act as an investment centre determining new initiatives, as well as allocating profit targets for each division. In turn the divisions will determine targets for each operating unit and designate each one as a cost centre in control of a budget. There are occasions when mismatches can occur, as in the case of a department manager who has no effective budget, and hence limited powers of operation.

The operation of budgetary control can produce a more efficient and effective management control system. It also carries the potential problem of encouraging functional insularity to the detriment of the firm as a whole. Units can become so preoccupied with achieving their own targets and keeping within their own budgets that they may refuse calls for assistance from other units through the fear that this will erode their own performance levels. In some manufacturing firms this has resulted in a total lack of continuity between departments and between production shifts. This has led some firms to examine team–building techniques developed by social psychologists to enhance greater cooperation.

Such problems increase with the size of the firm and with the necessity for funds to flow across many different units of the same organization. The problems come to a head in large multi–divisional firms where each unit operates as a profit centre and is accountable to top management for the achievement of predetermined profit targets. We examine two aspects of this problem; cost allocation and transfer pricing.

The problems of cost allocation occur when central services such as headquarters administration, research and development, and perhaps maintenance must be paid for by those units in the organization with the responsibility for generating income and profit. A decision needs to be made on the basis of the apportionment of such costs. Some firms vary cost allocation according to the size of the profit centre, as a proportion of their costs, or the extent to which use is made of the central services. The final criteria are often difficult to measure accurately, but any method is open to challenge by those managers who see their profits eroded by costs which lie outside their control. Some managers are resentful that their efforts are diluted by sections of the firm that do not generate income but merely incur costs. In some cases this has resulted in the marginality of service departments such as personnel and R&D. Once again accounting becomes the focus for political debate at the level of the firm.

Transfer pricing is the process through which goods and services produced in one section of the organization are sold internally for use by another. The need for transfer pricing mechanisms is a function of the development of the multi–divisional firm and associated profit centres. An effectively operated transfer pricing mechanism can contribute to the optimum allocation of a firm's resources and to the motivation of divisional managers towards efficient operation and hence to the overall prosperity of the organization.

Such mechanisms occur wherever there is a need in one unit of the organization for the services of another. A form of transfer pricing occurs in higher education as the following illustration reveals.

Polytechnics and universities tend to be organized around specialist subject departments. A department which offers a business studies course may have the need for specialist law inputs which reside outside that department. In many colleges a transfer pricing system has been devised whereby those departments servicing another are allocated points based on the number of hours and students they service. These points with those generated from their own departments form the basis for staffing allocations. A major problem with such a mechanism is that it may encourage departments only to service those areas where they ensure high rates of return.

This is a similar problem to the one we outlined when we discussed organization structure in Chapter 3. A foundry operating as a profit centre in a manufacturing firm may find that the pressure to meet targets conflicts with the demands placed upon it for goods from other units in the same organization. Management may be faced with the dilemma of having to meet internal demand when higher returns may be obtained through meeting the requirements of customers external to the firm. The issue of transfer pricing is particularly pertinent to the operation of multinational firms and it is to this aspect we now turn.

Transfer pricing and the multinationals

A great deal of transfer pricing activity occurs between member organizations of large multinational corporations. It has been estimated that as much as 40% of all business trade is accounted for by dealings between members of the same corporation (Choi and Mueller, 1978). Whilst this can cause the kind of organizational political problems outlined above, there are three main reasons for the extensiveness of such activity. These relate to issues of taxation, competition and issues relating to the need of the multinational to protect itself against social, economic and political changes occurring in the host country. These issues should be viewed in conjunction with the discussion on multinationals in Chapter 2.

☐ *Tax reasons*. Through its activities worldwide a multinational company can move profits from high to low tax areas using the transfer pricing mechanism. Firms operating in high tax areas are charged inflated prices for goods and services produced in low tax areas. Whilst this represents only a paper exchange of funds within the same organization it can result in some firms showing a much greater profit than others. In normal circumstances pressure is brought to bear on poorly performing profit centres. Such problems may be avoided by the use of dual reporting systems; one for external consumption and the other for internal use only.

☐ *Competition reasons*. Some multinationals subsidize member firms through the transfer price mechanism. In order that a new company may develop itself in an established market the other firms could supply goods and services at low prices, buying back the finished products at a high price.

☐ *Protection against change*. A multinational will wish to protect itself against those economic and political changes which threaten its prosperity and ultimate existence. Problems caused by high inflation, currency exchange and devaluation in a particular country can be tackled by charging high prices for goods supplied to the subsidiary in that country, and buying goods back at low prices. By operating in this way the multinational keeps finance 'in the family' and prevents it being siphoned off by individual nation states.

The kind of behaviour outlined above has naturally led some multinationals into direct conflict with the governments of those countries in which they operate. A famous case is that of Hoffman–La Roche, the Swiss pharmaceutical company and the patent holder for Librium and Valium. Through these two products alone, the company has a virtual monopoly of the world tranquillizer market. The British Government in 1971 considered that Hoffman–La Roche was operating against the public interest in this country through its pricing policy on the two tranquillizers in question, and called in the Monopolies Commission to investigate. The Commission found that the parent company in Switzerland, Hoffman–La Roche, was supplying its British subsidiary, Roche Products, with the active ingredients for Librium and Valium at the transfer price of £370 per kilo and £922 per kilo respectively, out of a total manufacturing cost for Librium of £437 per kilo and for Valium of £979 per kilo. The Commission discovered that the raw materials could be purchased in Italy at a cost of £9 per kilo for Librium and £20 per kilo for Valium. The Commission concluded that Hoffman–La Roche were acting against the interests of the public but was hampered in its investigation by the lack of accounting information from the Swiss parent company; a British government body having no jurisdiction in Switzerland, and no access to information produced under totally different rules for financial reporting. The price differences were explained by Hoffman–La Roche in terms of administrative and research costs, and a pricing policy based upon what the market would bear. The company probably gained significant tax advantages by operating in this fashion (Stopford *et al.*, 1980).

Strategic aspects of finance and accounting

The three functions of finance and accounting represent strategies of financing and controlling operations, of distributing resources and power through budget allocation, and of information disclosure. Additionally, financial tools and information are invariably used in the making of strategic decisions in other functional areas, such as the decision to invest in new products or equipment, or to take on extra staff. Financial analyses form the basis of most acquisition attempts and were a primary factor in Nestle's recent bid for Rowntree Mackintosh.

We can therefore see that the finance and accounting function assists management decision–making on a number of key issues that are central to the viability of the firm. These issues include the sources of funds, investment decisions, acceptable levels of debt, the minimization of tax liability and the extent of the pay–out to shareholders.

As with all the functional areas we have discussed in this book there is a growing recognition that the strategies associated with the different activities are linked in some kind of synergistic way. In manufacturing industry, evidence is emerging that cost and quality are not necessarily trade–offs but essential ingredients of the same strategy. A greater attention focussed on improving product quality can also be successful in lowering costs. This can become a virtuous circle in that extra funds are released for further investment in quality improvement.

Throughout this chapter we have been careful to point out the inexact nature of accounting methods. We can summarize the various limitations on the use of accounting information in strategy formulation.

☐ Because of the problems of measuring many aspects of business activities, accounting information can be highly subjective.
☐ Financial statements are summaries. Information is therefore selected and interpreted according to the needs of the compiler and user of financial statements.
☐ As a result of the above, financial information is often used deliberately to achieve political ends such as the justification of an investment decision or a pay claim.
☐ There is an added danger in all this in that many assume the data to be scientific and objective, and use it accordingly.
☐ Because of the bias in accounting to what can effectively be measured, management may place undue emphasis on short–term results and neglect the longer–term implications of strategic decisions, or base too many decisions on historic data which are made redundant by changing circumstances.

A good illustration of the interpretative problems associated with accounting information is offered by the NCB decision to close Cortonwood Colliery as part of its rationalization strategy. A Monopoly and Mergers Commission Report calculated the revenue of the colliery at £44.3 per tonne, whilst its cost were calculated at £50.5 per tonne. On these figures the mine was clearly unprofitable and losing the Coal Board in excess of £1.7 million a year. A study of the accounting methods used by the NCB questioned the basis for many of the costs used, but more significantly suggested that many of the costs such as surface damage and essential services would not be avoided by closing the colliery. If these unavoidable costs are eliminated from the equation as constants, then Cortonwood could be shown to be making a net contribution of £5.45 per tonne of coal mined (Berry T. *et al.*, 1985).

Summary

The finance and accounting function in business comprises financial management, management accounting, and financial reporting.

Financial management is concerned with the funding of the business and ensuring such funds can be met by the organization. The major sources of finance are share issues, bank lending, state finance and internally generated funds, usually through the reinvestment of profit. It is this last source that would appear to be most significant for firms in Britain. Management accounting is concerned with assisting management in planning and control. It involves the preparation and control of budgets, the analysis and allocation of costs, the appraisal of capital investments, the management of cash flows and general contribution to strategic decision–making.

Financial reporting involves the preparation of financial statements such as the balance sheet and profit and loss account, and must take account of the needs of the various groups who are to use this information. A major issue is the extent of disclosure.

The finance and accounting function is greatly influenced by the environment in which it operates. Financial reporting is subject to strict state controls and accounting practices have developed to cope with economic changes such as inflation, and fluctuations in the value of currency. Despite pressures to harmonize accounting practices there are considerable differences between countries reflecting a number of cultural influences.

Accounting practices vary also with the size of the organization, with large and small companies having their own special problems. As organizations increase in size and develop appropriate structures decisions will have to be made on the allocation of costs and transfer pricing. The latter becomes a particularly useful mechanism in the hands of the multinational corporation.

Accounting information forms the basis for most strategic decisions within the organization. Its value should be placed alongside a number of limitations, not least of which are the subjective nature of accounts and the role played by accounting information to justify organizational political decisions.

Further reading

A basic accounting text that is easy to understand is F.P. Langley and G.S. Hardern, *Introduction to Accounting for Business Studies* (Butterworths, 1985). A readable text on management accounting that offers a number of useful examples is J. Sizer, *An Insight into Management Accounting* (Penguin 1989). Organizational issues are well represented by C. Emmanuel and D. Otley, *Accounting for Management Control* (Van Nostrand Reinhold, 1985), whilst a good examination of the behavioural aspect of accounting is presented by A. Hopwood, *Accounting and Human Behaviour* (Accountancy Age Books, 1974).

Discussion

1. What is the value of the professional accountant to business? Why do professional accountants proliferate in Britain?

2. Why is the internal funding of business so popular in this country?

3. What would be the most appropriate methods the following organizations could use to raise revenue to fund new activities; a very small firm

just making a mark in the office supplies market; a polytechnic or university; a multinational car manufacturer?

4. What specific contributions can the management accountant make to strategic decision–making? What limitations can be placed on the value of this contribution?

5. Identify the different needs of the users of accounting information. Can current methods of financial reporting hope to satisfy them all?

6. What are the specific finance and accounting problems and priorities for small as opposed to large companies?

7. What are the advantages and disadvantages to various interested parties associated with cost allocation and transfer pricing activities in multi-divisional firms?

8. Identify the behavioural and political nature of management accounting. What problems does this cause and how might they be minimized?

10 Conclusions

It is difficult to draw conclusions from a textbook such as this without recourse to some rather bland and meaningless predictions about such topics as 'the future of business' or 'new developments in business ideas'. Nevertheless, given that the preceding nine chapters have been spent examining business through the workings of a model, it seems appropriate to highlight some of the themes and issues which have emerged. In identifying these issues we run the risk of attracting the kinds of criticisms we have levelled at the attempts of others. We do however temper our thoughts with a few notes of caution.

Major themes

This book has stressed five major themes.

Businesses operate through a network of complex inter–relationships. To aid our understanding we have simplified the world of business by identifying a number of core business activities and three contexts in which those activities operate; these are the strategic, organizational and environmental contexts. Together, these activities and contexts make up the Business in Context model. The various elements that make up business activities interact with one another as do the various elements which make up the different contexts. In addition, influences go backwards and forwards across the various levels of the model to create the complex patterns of inter–relationship.

The idea that influences operate in several directions is very important to our understanding of business. Businesses are undoubtedly shaped by the various contexts in which they operate. In turn businesses shape the environment in which they operate. The business activities of one firm become part of the competitive environment of another. What we label as the economy is the product of business activity. A firm is said to adopt new technology as if it were a gift from the gods, yet developments in technology are the product of human endeavour and the technology adopted by one firm has its origins in the activities of another.

The various interactions and influences we have described occur in a number of different contexts. We can think too narrowly that the term 'business' only refers to those organizations operating in pursuit of profit. We have stressed throughout this book that business activities occur in all kinds of organization, including schools, hospitals, government offices and charities.

Business decisions are made by people and as such are subject to a range of behavioural influences and political considerations. Whilst a number of 'rational' techniques have emerged to guide decision–making in each of the business activities, it is often the 'non–rational' factors that are most significant. We use the terms rational and non–rational with caution, in that a decision and decision–making method which may appear less than rational to us, may of course be perfectly rational to the decision–maker.

Because of the behavioural and political nature of business activities, it is important to acknowledge the existence of a number of different perspectives on business issues. The development of a new method of manufacture is to the manager an attempt to improve the efficiency of the operation. To the worker it may represent a threat to job satisfaction and job security. To the consumer it may mean a more available and cheaper product, but it may also represent unacceptable changes in product design. This rather crude illustration reinforces the necessity of viewing business issues from the perspectives of all interested parties. Business ideas often fail simply because managers have not considered the possibility that they may not be acceptable to all concerned.

The notion of different perspectives is a strong theme of the entire Business in Context series. Each of the subsequent books in the series examines the workings of the Business in Context model and a range of related business issues from a different perspective, each with a grounding in a different academic discipline.

Major issues

A number of major issues common to all business activities seems to be emerging as we move into the 1990s.

☐ There would appear to be a convergence of all types of organization on a business model we have in the past only associated with profit–oriented firms. Educational establishments, local authorities and hospitals are re–examining their methods of management and control and are seeking various methods of income generation.

☐ A history of business ideas reveals that at various times each of the various activities of business claims the focus of attention. We have been urged to innovate out of the recession, to focus on operating efficiency, to market what the customer requires, and to create a distinctive organization culture around a value system shared by all personnel. There is now a greater realization than ever before of the need to develop an integrated business strategy and that none of the functional activities can exist in isolation.

☐ The basis for such integration is a set of core ideas which reappear constantly in the literature and in discussions about business. A major theme is the importance of learning from the good practices of others, which accounts for the interest throughout the late 1970s and the 1980s on cross–cultural research and especially the dissemination of best practice from those economically successful nations like Japan. The

The issues in context

core ideas themselves include a concern for improved quality and productivity, a rediscovery of the importance of entrepreneurship, and a focus on achieving business results through people.

We must temper our enthusiasm for these new business ideas for a number of reasons.

We have noted throughout this book that the relationships in business between intentions, actions and outcomes are not only difficult to measure but that the complex nature of the business environment makes causal relationships difficult to prove. We saw this in the various attempts to show a link between innovation and economic growth, and again in our analysis of the small firms policy of the British Government.

The history of business ideas is also the history of particular fashions and fads, which have either been short-lived or have persisted only in isolated pockets of resistance. Many firms have embarked upon policies for management-by-objectives, job enrichment, Quality Circles and the like only to discard them them at some later stage. The problem is not always the inadequacy of the technique, but more usually the conservative nature of management and the insufficient attention paid to its introduction and utilization.

Many of the new ideas that have emerged are undoubtedly products of the environmental conditions in operation at a particular moment in time. Thus we can attribute Japanization, 'excellent' companies, the rediscovery of entrepreneurship, consensus industrial relations and the like to a particular economic climate, particular kinds of business operation, the presence (in Britain at any rate) of an ideologically strong Government, and the relative weakness of labour. The extent to which such notions are viable in the same form in different circumstances is open to question.

Some of the business developments have their negative side. We have seen the devastating effects on some communities of the growth of regional unemployment and that the current vogue for part-time workers, YTS trainees and the like has created a secondary labour force which enjoys less security and fewer rights as employees.

There is undoubtedly a tendency for the commentators of any period to regard their time as an age of discontinuity. Our analysis of business reveals much more of a continuity. For many firms, current changes simply pass them by and business goes on much the same as usual apart from the various incremental changes that are bound to occur. An analysis of business over the last forty years reveals several constants, not least of which is the continuing power of the multinational enterprise. Many of the changes that do occur are products of the environment and are just as likely to change again as the environment itself changes. Undoubtedly there are significant changes that will leave their mark, but these changes are themselves new expressions of the very traditional management goal of enhancing the effectiveness of their operation.

References

Abernathy, W.J. and Utterback, J.M. (1978) Patterns of Industrial Innovation Chapter 33 of *Corporate Strategy and Product Innovation* ed. Rothberg, R.R., The Free Press, New York.

Adam, G. (1975), Multinational Corporations and Worldwide Sourcing in *International Firms and Modern Imperialism* ed. Radice, H., Penguin, Harmondsworth.

Ansoff, H.I. (1968) *Corporate Strategy*, Penguin, Harmondsworth.

Ansoff, H.I. and Stewart, J.M. (1967) Strategies for a Technology–based Business. *Harvard Business Review*, **45**, Nov–Dec, pp 71–83.

Armstrong, P., Glyn, A., and Harrison, J. (1984) *Capitalism Since World War Two*, Fontana, London.

Bain, G.S. ed. (1983) *Industrial Relations in Britain*, Basil Blackwell, Oxford.

Bannock, G. (1981) *The Economics of Small Firms: Return from the Wilderness*, Basil Blackwell, Oxford.

Bassett, P. (1986) *Strike Free* Macmillan, London.

Beasley, J.E. (1985) Strategies for Corporate and Business Success — A Survey, OMEGA, **13**, 2, pp 51–58.

Beer, M., Spector, B., Lawrence, P., Quinn Mills, D., and Walton, R. (1985) *Human Resource Management: The General Manager's Perspective, Text and Cases*, The Free Press, New York.

Berle, A.A. and Means, G.C. (1932) *The Modern Corporation and Private Property*, Macmillan, New York.

Berry, A., Citron, D., and Jarvis, R. (1987) *The Information Needs of Bankers Dealing with Large and Small Companies*, Certified Research Report 7, Certified Accountant Publications Ltd, London.

Berry, A. and Jarvis, R. (1989) *Accounting in a Business Context*, Van Nostrand Reinhold, London.

Berry, T., Capps, T., Cooper, D., Hooper, T., and Lowe T. (1985) NCB Accounts — A Mine of Mis–information *Accountancy*, January, pp 10–12.

Bhaskar, K. (1980) *The Future of the World Motor Industry*, Kogan Page, London.

Bignell, V., Dooner, M., Hughes, J., Pym, C., and Stone, S. eds. (1985) *Manufacturing Systems: Context, Applications and Techniques*, Basil Blackwell/Open University, Oxford.

Binks, M., and Jennings, A. (1986) New Firms as a Source of Industrial Regeneration in *Small Firms Growth and Development*, Scott, M. ed., Gower, Aldershot.

Blauner, R. (1964) *Alienation and Freedom*, University of Chicago Press, Chicago.

Bolton, J. (1971) *Small Firms: The Report of the Committee of Inquiry*, HMSO, Cmd 4811, London.

Bradley, K. and Hill, S. (1983) After Japan: The Quality Circle Transplant and Productive Efficiency, *British Journal of Industrial Relations*, **21**, 3, pp 291–311.

Braverman, H. (1974) *Labor and Monopoly Capital*, Monthly Review Press, New York.

Bright, G., Colvin, M., Loveridge, J., Page, R., and Thompson, C. (1983) *Moving Forward: Small Businesses and the Economy*, Conservative Political Centre, London.

Brittan, S. (1983) The Myth of Kondratieff, *Financial Times*, April 7th.

Brossard, M. and Maurice, M. (1976) Is there a Universal Model of Organizational Structure? *International Studies of Management and Organization*, **6**, pp 11–45.

Buffa, E.S. (1983) *Modern Production/Operations Management*, 7th edition, John Wiley and Sons, New York.

Burnham, J. (1941) *The Managerial Revolution*, Day New York.

Burns, T. and Stalker, G.M. (1966) *The Management of Innovation*, Tavistock, London.

Burrell, G. and Morgan, G. (1979) *Sociological Paradigms and Organization Analysis*, Heinemann, London.

Burrows G. (1986) *No–strike Agreements and Pendulum Arbitration*, Institute of Personnel Management, London.

Buzzell, R.D. (1964) *Mathematical Models and Marketing Management*, Harvard University, Boston.

Cannon, T. (1986) *Basic Marketing*, 2nd edition, Holt, Rinehart and Winston, Eastbourne.

Carroll, D.T. (1983) A Disappointing Search for Excellence, *Harvard Business Review*, **61** Nov–Dec, pp 78–88.

Casey, B. (1986) The Dual Apprenticeship System *British Journal of Industrial Relations*, **14**, 1, pp 63–82.

Chandler, A.D. (1962) *Strategy and Structure: Chapters in the History of American Capitalism*, MIT Press Cambridge, Mass.

Chandler, A.D. (1977) *The Visible Hand: The Managerial Revolution in American Business*, Harvard University Press Cambridge, Mass.

Channon, D.F. (1973) *The Strategy and Structure of British Enterprise*, Macmillan, London.

Child, J. (1969) *The Business Enterprise in Modern Industrial Society*, Collier–Macmillan, London.

Child, J. (1972) Organizational Structure, Environment and Performance: The Role of Strategic Choice, *Sociology*, **6**, 1, pp 1–21.

Child, J. (1984) *Organizations: A Guide to Problems and Practice*, 2nd edition, Harper and Row, London.

Child, J. (1984b) New Technology and Developments in Management Organization OMEGA, **12**, 3, pp 211–23.

Child, J. and Kieser, A. (1979) Organization and Managerial Roles in British and West German Companies: An Examination of the Culture Free Thesis, in Lammers, C.J. and Hickson, D.J. eds, *Organizations Alike and Unlike*, Routledge and Kegan Paul, London.

Child, J., Fores, M., Glover, I., and Lawrence, P. (1983) A Price to Pay? Professionalism and Work Organization in Britain and West Germany *Sociology*, **17**, 1, pp 63–77.

Choi, F.D.S. and Mueller, G.G. (1978) *An Introduction to Multinational Accounting*, Prentice Hall Inc., Englewood Cliffs, N.J.

Cole, W. and Shears, P. (1989) *Law in a Business Context*, Van Nostrand Reinhold, London.

Coleman, T. (1988) Travels with my Rover, *Guardian* 13 August.

Collard, R. and Dale, B. (1985) Quality Circles: Why They Break Down and Why They Hold Up, *Personnel Management*, February, pp 28–31.

Crouch, C.J. (1978) The Changing Role of the State in Industrial Relations in Western Europe in Crouch, C.J. and Pizzorno, A. eds, *The Resurgence of Class Conflict in Western Europe Since 1968*, Vol. 1, Macmillan, London.

Crouch, C.J. (1982) *The Politics of Industrial Relations*, Fontana, London.

Curran, J. (1986) *Bolton Fifteen Years On: A Review and Analysis of Small Business Research in Britain 1971–86*, Small Business Trust, London.

Cyert, R.M. and March, J.G. (1963) *A Behavioral Theory of the Firm*, Prentice Hall, Englewood Cliffs, N.J.

Daniel, W.W. (1987) *Workplace Industrial Relations and Technical Change*, Policy Studies Institute, London.

Daniel, W.W. and Millward, N. (1983) *Workplace Industrial Relations in Britain*, Heinemann, London.

Davis, S.M. and Lawrence, P.R. eds (1977) *Matrix*, Addison–Wesley, Reading, Mass.

Dawson, S. (1986) *Analysing Organizations*, Macmillan, London.

Deal, T.E. and Kennedy, A.A. (1982) *Corporate Cultures*, Addison–Wesley Reading, Mass.

Dhalla, N.K. (1978) Assessing the Long–term Value of Advertising, *Harvard Business Review*, **56**, Jan–Feb, pp 87–95.

Dilworth, J.B. (1986) *Production and Operations Management: Manufacturing and Non–manufacturing*, Random House, New York.

Donovan (1968) *Royal Commission on Trade Unions and Employers Associations 1965–68*, HMSO, Cmnd 3623, London.

Dore, R. (1973) *British Factory — Japanese Factory*, University of California Press, Berkeley, Calif.

Drucker, P.F. (1964) *Managing for Results*, Harper and Row, New York.

Drucker, P.F. (1968) *The Practice of Management*, Pan Books, London.

Drucker, P.F. (1985) *Innovation and Entrepreneurship*, Heinemann, London.

van Duijn, J.J. (1983) *The Long Wave in Economic Life*, George Allen and Unwin, London.

Earl, P.E. (1983) *The Economic Imagination: Towards a Behavioural Analysis of Choice*, Wheatsheaf Books, Brighton.

Earl, P.E. (1984) *The Corporate Imagination: How Big Companies Make Mistakes*, Wheatsheaf Books, Brighton.

Ebel, K.H. (1985) Social and Labour Implications of Flexible Manufacturing Systems, *International Labour Review*, **124**, 2, March–April, pp 133–47.

Eilon, S. (1985) Recasting the Die, OMEGA, **13**, 3, pp 135–42.

Emery, E. and Thorsrud, E. (1976) *Democracy at Work*, Nijhoff, Leiden.

Emmanuel, C. and Otley, D. (1985) *Accounting for Management Control*, Van Nostrand Reinhold, Wokingham.

Evans, H. (1983) *Good Times Bad Times*, Weidenfeld and Nicholson, London.

Finniston, M. (1980) *Report of the Committee of Inquiry into the Engineering Profession*, HMSO, London.

Fisher, A. (1986) The Pain of Recreating a Culture, *Financial Times*, 29 December.

Flanders, A. (1964) *The Fawley Productivity Agreements*, Faber and Faber, London.

Fox, A. (1974a) *Beyond Contract: Work, Trust and Power Relations*, Faber and Faber, London.

Fox, A. (1974b) *Man Mismanagement*, Faber and Faber, London.

Foy, N. (1983) The Public Productivity Poser, *Management Today*, July, pp 67–71.

Galbraith, J.K. (1972) *The New Industrial State*, 2nd edition, Penguin, Harmondsworth.

Galbraith, J.R. (1971) Matrix Organization Designs, *Business Horizons*, **14**, pp 29–40.

Galbraith, J.R. and Nathanson, D.A. (1978) *Strategy Implementation: The Role of Structure and Process*, West Publishing Co., St. Paul, Minnesota.

Gamble, A. (1985) *Britain in Decline*, Macmillan, London.

Ganguly, P. and Bannock, G. (1985) *U.K. Small Business Statistics and International Comparisons*, Harper and Row, London.

Glueck, W.F. and Jauch, L. R. (1984) *Business Policy and Strategic Management*, 4th edition, McGraw–Hill, Singapore.

Goldthorpe, J. (1977) Industrial Relations in Great Britain: A Critique of Reformism in Clarke, T. and Clements, L., *Trade Unions Under Capitalism*, Fontana, Glasgow.

Gould, A. and Keeble, D. (1984) New Firms and Rural Industrialization in East Anglia, *Regional Studies*, **18**, 3, pp 189–201.

Granick, D. (1972) *Managerial Comparisons of Four Developed Countries*, MIT Press, Cambridge, Mass.

Grant, W. and Marsh, D. (1977) *The CBI*, Hodder and Stoughton, London.

Greater London Council (1983) *Small Firms and the London Industrial Strategy*, Economic Policy Group Strategy Document No. 4, GLC, London.

Griffin, T. (1984) Technological Change and Craft Control in the Newspaper Industry: An International Comparison, *Cambridge Journal of Economics*, **8**, 1, March, pp 41–61.

Guest, D.E. (1982) Has the Recession Really Hit Personnel Management? *Personnel Management*, October, pp 36–9.

Guest, D.E. (1987) Human Resource Management and Industrial Relations, *Journal of Management Studies*, **24**, 5, pp 503–21.

Guest, D.E. and Horwood, R. (1980) *The Role and Effectiveness of Personnel Management: A Preliminary Report*, The Nancy Seear Fellowship Personnel Management Research Programme: Research Report No. 1, LSE, London.

Hanan, M. (1974) Reorganize Your Company Around its Markets, *Harvard Business Review*, **52**, Nov–Dec, pp 63–74.

Handy, C. (1974) *Understanding Organizations*, Penguin, Harmondsworth.

Handy, C. (1987) *The Making of Managers: A Report of Management Education, Training and Development in the USA, West Germany, France, Japan and the United Kingdom*, MSC, NEDC, and BIM, London.

Harbison, F. and Myers, C.A. (1959) *Management in the Industrial World: An International Analysis*, McGraw–Hill, New York.

Harrison, P. (1981) *Inside the Third World*, 2nd edition, Penguin, Harmondsworth.

Hayek, F.A. (1984) *1980s, Unemployment and the Unions*, Institute for Economic Affairs, London.

Hayes, R.H. and Schmenner, R.W. (1978) How Should You Organize Manufacturing? *Harvard Business Review*, **56**, Jan–Feb, pp 105–18.

Hayes, R.H. and Wheelwright, S.C. (1984) *Restoring Our Competitive Edge: Competing Through Manufacturing*, John Wiley, New York.

Heald, D. (1985) Will Privatization of Public Enterprises Solve the Problems of Control? *Public Administration*, **63**, Spring, pp 7–22.

Herzberg, F. (1968) One More Time: How Do You Motivate Employees? *Harvard Business Review*, **46**, Jan–Feb pp 53–62.

Hetherington, P. (1986) Perfection in the Land of Rising Productivity, *Guardian*, 5 March, p 23.

Hill, T. (1983) *Production/Operations Management*, Prentice Hall International, Hemel Hempstead.

Hofer, C.W. and Schendel, D. (1978) *Strategy Formulation: Analytical Concepts*, West Publishing, St. Paul, Minnesota.

Hofstede, G.H. (1980) *Culture's Consequences: International Differences in Work–Related Values*, Sage, London.

Hofstede, G.H. (1985) The Interaction Between National and Organizational Value Systems, *Journal of Management Studies*, **22**, 4, pp 347–57.

Hofstede, G.H. (1986) The Usefulness of the Organizational Culture Concept, *Journal of Management Studies*, **23**, 3, pp 253–7.

Honour, T.F. and Mainwaring, R.M. (1982) *Business and Sociology*, Croom Helm, London.

Hopwood, A. (1974) *Accounting and Human Behaviour*, Accountancy Age Books, London.

Howard, J.A. and Sheth, J.H. (1969) *The Theory of Buyer Behaviour*, John Wiley, New York.

Hunt, J. (1984) The Shifting Focus of the Personnel Function, *Personnel Management*, February, pp 14–18.

Husband, T.M. (1984) Management and Advanced Manufacturing Technology, OMEGA, **12**, 3, pp 197–201.

Hyman R. (1972) *Disputes Procedure in Action*, Heinemann, London.

Institute of Personnel Management (1963) Statement on Personnel Management and Personnel Policies, *Personnel Management*, March.

Jackson, M.P. (1982) *Trade Unions*, Croom Helm, London.

Jackson, P. (1983) How Perkins Positively Tackled the Recession, *Personnel Management*, November, pp 24–7.

Jaikumar, R. (1986) Post–industrial Manufacturing, *Harvard Business Review*, **64**, Nov–Dec pp 69–76.

Jessop, R. (1980) The Transformation of the State in Post–War Britain in Scase, R., *The State in Western Europe* Croom Helm, London.

Jewkes, J., Sawers, D., and Stillerman, R. (1970) *The Sources of Invention*, W.W. Norton, New York.

Johnson, G. and Scholes, K. (1984) *Exploring Corporate Strategy*, Prentice Hall International, London.

Kamata, S. (1983) *Japan in the Passing Lane*, Allen and Unwin, London.

Kaplinsky, R. (1983) Firm Size and Technical Change in a Dynamic Context, *The Journal of Industrial Economics*, **32**, 1, pp 39–59.

Kennedy, C. (1988) Global Strategies for 3M, *Long Range Planning*, **21**, 1, pp 9–17.

Kondratieff, N.D. (1935) The Long Waves in Economic Life, *Review of Economic Statistics*, **17**, pp 105–15.

Kotler, P. (1986) *Principles of Marketing*, 3rd edition, Prentice Hall International, Englewood Cliffs, N.J.

Kotler, P. (1988) *Marketing Management: Analysis, Planning and Control*, 6th edition, Prentice Hall International, Englewood Cliffs N.J.

Kumar, K. (1978) *Prophecy and Progress*, Penguin, Harmondsworth.

Lane, K.A. (1985) The U.K. Machine Tool Industry, OMEGA, **13**, 4, pp 247–9.

Langley, F.P. and Hardern, G.S. (1985) *Introduction to Accounting for Business Studies*, Butterworths, London.

Lawrence, P. (1980) *Managers and Management in West Germany*, Croom Helm, London.

Lawrence, P.R. and Lorsch, J. (1967) *Organization and Environment*, Harvard University Press, Cambridge, Mass.

Legge, K. (1978) *Power, Innovation and Problem–Solving in Personnel Management*, McGraw Hill, London.

Legge, K. (1988) Personnel Management in Recession and Recovery: A Comparative Analysis of What the Surveys Say, *Personnel Review*, **17**, 2.

Levitt, T. (1960) Marketing Myopia, *Harvard Business Review*, **38**, July–Aug pp 24–47.

Levitt, T. (1975) Marketing Myopia: Retrospective Commentary, *Harvard Business Review*, **53**, Sept–Oct pp 177–81.

Levy, S.J. (1959) Symbols for Sale, *Harvard Business Review*, **37** July–Aug, pp 117–24.

Lindblom, C.E. (1959) The Science of Muddling Through, *Public Administration Review*, **19**, 2, pp 79–88.

McCaskey, M.B. (1982) *The Executive Challenge*, Pitman, London.

McClelland, D.C. (1961) *The Achieving Society*, Van Nostrand, Princeton.

Manning, K. (1983) The Rise and Fall of Personnel, *Management Today*, March, pp 74–7.

Mansfield, E. (1963) Size of Firm, Market Structure and Innovation, *Journal of Political Economy*, **71**, 6, pp 556–76.

Marris, R.L. (1964) *The Economic Theory of Managerial Capitalism*, Macmillan, London.

Marsden, D., Morris, T., Willman, P. and Wood S. The Car Industry: Labour Relations and Industrial Adjustment, Tavistock Publications, London.

Martin, R. (1981) *New Technology and Industrial Relations in Fleet Street*, Clarendon Press, Oxford.

Mayer, C. (1988) New Issues in Corporate Finance, *European Economic Review*, June.

Mensch, G. (1979) *Stalemate in Technology*, Ballinger, Cambridge, Mass.

Miliband, R. (1969) *The State in Capitalist Society*, Quartet, London.

Millward, N. and Stevens, M. (1986) *British Workplace Industrial Relations 1980–84*, Gower, Aldershot.

Minkes, A.L. and Nuttall, C.S. (1985) *Business Behaviour and Management Structure*, Croom Helm, London.

Minkes, A.L. (1987) *The Entrpreneurial Manager*, Penguin, Harmondsworth.

Mintzberg, H. (1973) Strategy Making in 3 Modes, *California Management Review*, **16**, Winter, pp 44–53.

National Economic Development Office (1985) Advanced Manufacturing Technology, NEDO, May.

Neale, A. and Haslam, C. (1989) *Economics in a Business Context*, Van Nostrand Reinhold, London.

Needle, D.J. (1984) The Selection Process in Britain and West Germany: A Cross–Cultural Comparison, Unpublished M.Sc Thesis, London School of Economics.

Nicosia, F.M. (1966) *Consumer Decision Processes: Marketing and Advertising Implications*, Prentice Hall, Englewood Cliffs, N.J.

Northcott, J. and Rogers, P. (1984) *Microelectronics in British Industry: The Pattern of Change*, Policy Studies Institute, London.

Ohmae, K. (1982) *The Mind of the Strategist*, Penguin, Harmondsworth.

Oram, S. (1987) Fleet Street Moves On: A Managerial Perspective, *Industrial Relations Journal*, **18**, 2, pp 84–9.

Parker, R.C. (1982) *The Management of Innovation*, John Wiley and Sons, Chichester.

Pascale, R.T. (1978) Personnel Practices and Employee Attitudes: A Study of Japanese and American Managed Firms in the United States, *Human Relations*, **31**, pp 597–616.

Paul, W. and Robertson, K. (1970) *Job Enrichment and Employee Motivation*, Gower Press, London.

Pavitt, K. (1983) Characteristics of Innovative Activity in British Industry, OMEGA, **11**, 2, pp 113–30.

Peck, M.J. and Goto, A. (1982) Technology and Economic Growth: The Case of Japan in Tushman, M.L. and Moore, W.L. eds, *Readings in the Management of Innovation*, Pitman Books, London

Perrow, C. (1961) The Analysis of Goals in Complex Organizations *American Sociological Review*, **26**, pp 854–66.

Peters, T.J. and Waterman, R.H. (1982) *In Search of Excellence: Lessons from America's Best-Run Companies*, Harper and Row, London.

Pettigrew, A.M. (1973) *The Politics of Organizational Decision–Making*, Tavistock, London.

Pettigrew, A.M. (1979) On Studying Organizational Cultures, *Administrative Science Quarterly*, **24**, pp 570–81.

Piore, M. and Sabel, C. (1984) *The Second Industrial Divide: Possibilities for Prosperity*, Basic Books, New York.

Porter, M.E. (1980) *Competitive Strategy: Techniques for Analysing Industries and Competitors*, Free Press, New York.

Price, R. and Bain, G.S. (1983) Union Growth in Britain: Retrospect and Prospect, *British Journal of Industrial Relations*, **21**, pp 339–55.

Pugh, D.S., Hickson, D.J., and Hinings, C.R. (1969) The Context of Organization Structures, *Administrative Science Quarterly*, **14**, pp 115–26.

Rainnie, A. (1985) Small Firms Big Problems: The Political Economy of Small Businesses, *Capital and Class*, **25**, Spring, pp 140–68.

Ray, C.A. (1986) Corporate Culture: The Last Frontier of Control, *Journal of Management Studies*, **23**, 3, pp 287–97.

Rice, A.K. (1958) *Productivity and Social Organization*, Tavistock, London.

Richards, M.D. (1978) *Organizational Goal Structures*, West Publishing, St. Paul Minnesota.

Rines, M. (1976) Woodville Rubbers 600% Bounce, *Marketing*, September, pp 21–3.

Rogers, E.M. (1962) *Diffusion of Innovations*, Free Press, New York.

Rothwell, R. and Zegveld, W. (1981) *Industrial Innovation and Public Policy*, Frances Pinter, London.

Rumelt, R.P. (1974) *Strategy, Structure and Economic Performance*, Harvard University Press, Cambridge, Mass.

Sandberg, W.R. (1984) Norton Villiers Triumph and the Meriden Cooperative in Glueck, W.F. and Jauch, L.R., *Business Policy and Strategic Management*, McGraw–Hill, Singapore.

Sato, K. and Hoshino, Y. eds (1984) *The Anatomy of Japanese Business*, Croom Helm, London.

Scase, R., ed. (1980) *The State in Western Europe*, Croom Helm, London.

Scase, R. and Goffee, R. (1980) *The Real World of the Small Business Owner*, Croom Helm, London.

Schmookler, J. (1966) *Invention and Economic Growth*, Harvard University Press, Cambridge Mass.

Schumpeter, J.A. (1961) *The Theory of Economic Development*, Oxford University Press, Oxford.

Scott, J.P. (1979) *Corporations, Classes and Capitalism*, Hutchinson, London.

Selznick, P. (1949) *TVA and the Grass Roots*, University of California Press, Berkeley, Calif.

Sethi, S.P., Namiki, N., and Swanson, C. (1984) *The False Promise of the Japanese Miracle*, Pitman, London.

Shapiro, B.P. (1977) Can Marketing and Manufacturing Coexist? *Harvard Business Review*, **55**, Sept–Oct pp 104–14.

Sheehan, A. (1967) Proprietors in the World of Big Business, *Fortune*, 15th June.

Shonfield, A. (1968) A Note of Dissent, *Royal Commission on Trade Unions and Employers Associations*, Report Cmnd 3623, HMSO, London.

Sloan, A.P. (1986) *My Life With General Motors*, Penguin, Harmondsworth.

Simmonds, K. (1986) Marketing as Innovation: The Eigth Paradigm, *Journal of Management Studies*, **23**, 5, pp 479–98.

Sizer, J. (1989) *An Insight into Management Accounting*, Penguin, Harmondsworth.

Skinner, W. (1969) Manufacturing — The Missing Link in Corporate Strategy, *Harvard Business Review*, **47**, May–June, pp 136–45.

Skinner, W. (1974) The Focused Factory, *Harvard Business Review*, **52**, May–June, pp 113–21.

Slater, R. and Ascroft, P. (1989) Quantitative Methods in a Business Context, Van Nostrand Reinhold, London.

Smith, R. (1982) Word Processing Installation, *Employment Gazette*, June, pp 270–2.

Sorge, A. and Warner, M. (1980) Manpower Training, Manufacturing Organization, and Workplace Relations in Britain and West Germany, *British Journal of Industrial Relations*, November, pp 318–33.

Starr, M.K. (1972) *Production Management: Systems and Synthesis*, Prentice Hall Inc., Englewood Cliffs, N.J.

Stewart, H. and Gallagher, C.C. (1985) Business Death and Firm Size in the U.K., *International Small Business Journal*, **4**, 1.

Stopford, J.M., Channon, D.F., and Constable, J. (1980) *Cases in Strategic Management*, John Wiley and Sons, Chichester.

Strang, R.A. (1976) Sales Promotion — Fast Growth, Faulty Management, *Harvard Business Review*, **54**, July–Aug, pp 115–24.

Strinati, D. (1982) *Capitalism, the State and Industrial Relations*, Croom Helm, London.

Taylor, D. (1984) Learning from the Japanese, *Employment Gazette*, **92**, 6, pp 279–85.

Taylor, F.W. (1947) *Scientific Management*, Harper Row, New York.

Thackray, J. (1983) America's Robotic Rising, *Management Today*, Feb, pp 54–7.

Thomas, R.E. (1982) *The Government of Business*, Philip Allan, Oxford.

Tighe, C. (1986) Behind the Lines at Nissan, *Sunday Times*, 13 April p 67.

Torrington, D. and Chapman, J. (1983) *Personnel Management*, 2nd edition, Prentice Hall International, London.

Trade Union Congress (1986) *Report of the 118th Annual TUC Conference*, TUC, London.

Trist, E.L. and Bamforth, K.W. (1951) *Some Social and Psychological Consequences of the Long–Wall Method of Coal–Getting, Human Relations*, **4**, pp 3–38.

Turner, G. (1971) *The Leyland Papers*, Eyre and Spottiswood, London.

United Nations (1986) *Survey on Flexible Manufacturing Systems*, United Nations, New York.

Walton, R.E. (1987) *Innovating to Compete*, Jossey Bass, San Francisco.

Wasson, C.R. (1978) *Dynamic Competitive Strategy and Product Life Cycles*, Austin Press, Austin, Texas.

Wheelwright, S.C. (1981) Japan — Where Operations Really Are Strategic, *Harvard Business Review*, **59**, July–Aug, pp 65–72.

White, M. and Trevor, M. (1983) *Under Japanese Management — The Experience of British Workers*, Heinemann, London.

Wiener, M.J. (1981) *English Culture and the Decline of the Industrial Spirit 1850–1980*, Cambridge University Press, Cambridge.

Wild, R. (1985) *Essentials of Production and Operations Management*, Holt Rinehart and Winston, London.

Wilkinson, B. (1986) *The Shopfloor Politics of New Technology*, Gower, Aldershot.

Wilkinson, E. (1983) *Japan Versus Europe*, Penguin, Harmondsworth.

Williams, K., Haslam, C., Wardlow, A. and Williams, J. (1986) Accounting for Failure in the Nationalised Enterprises — Coal, Steel and Cars Since 1970, *Economy and Society*, **15**, 2, pp 167–219.

Williams, K., Cutler, T., Williams, J. and Haslam C. (1987) The End of Mass Production? *Economy and Society*, **16**, 3, pp 405–39.

Williams, K., Williams, J. and Haslam C. (1987) *The Breakdown of Austin Rover*, Berg, Leamington Spa.

Williams, V., (1984) Employment Implications of New Technology, *Employment Gazette*, **92**, 5, May, pp 210–15.

Williamson, D.T.N. (1972) The Anachronistic Factory, *Proceedings of the Royal Society*, A331, pp 139–60.

Wilson, (1980) *Report of the Committee to Review the Functioning of Financial Institutions*, HMSO, London.

Winkler, J.T. (1977) The Coming Corporatism in Skidelsky, R. ed, *The End of the Keynesian Era*, Macmillan, London.

Woodward, J. (1965) *Industrial Organization: Theory and Practice*, Oxford University Press, London.

Index

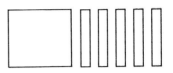